India Exclusion Report 2015

India Exclusion Report 2015

India Exclusion Report 2015
A comprehensive, annually updated analysis on the exclusion of disadvantaged groups in India

ISBN: 978-93-82579-39-7
First Edition: 2016

YODA PRESS
268 A/C Vasant Kunj
New Delhi 110 070
www.yodapress.co.in

Typeset in Minion Pro by Ram Das Lal
Printed at Saurabh Printers Pvt. Ltd.
Published by Arpita Das for YODA PRESS, New Delhi

The *India Exclusion Report 2015* is supported by UNICEF, UNFPA and UN Women. The opinions expressed in the Report do not reflect the views of these organisations.

Contents

Preface

This is the second edition of the India Exclusion Report, for the year 2015. As with the first Report 2013–14, the attempt of this highly collaborative, trans-disciplinary annual enterprise is to bring together experts from many fields—scholars, human rights and development workers, policy makers, and persons from disadvantaged communities—to examine the outcomes of public policy, law, programmes, budgets, institutions and their functioning for all peoples, and specifically for peoples of disadvantage.

The particular questions that these Exclusion Reports ask are: who, if anyone, is excluded—or adversely included—from equitable access to public goods, why and by what processes is such exclusion or adverse inclusion accomplished, and what can be done to change this to a more just and equitable set of outcomes?

This series of Exclusion Reports attempts to be strongly evidence-based and empirical. At the same time, the diverse contributors to these Reports are bound by a kernel of shared normative and political convictions related to ideas of the just state, the just society, equity and solidarity. The Exclusion Reports are guided by specific constructs of the public good, exclusion and the role of the state, on which we elaborate in the introductory chapter.

Structure of the Report

There are five parts to the India Exclusion Report 2015.

1. India Exclusion Report 2015: An Overview

This first part of the report begins with a discussion of the major conceptual elements that form the foundation of the report, particularly the ideas of public goods and exclusion.

It goes on to present an overview of the entire report, and attempts to present a tapestry which brings together some of the major findings of the report, across the various chapters and sections.

2. Public Goods

The second part of the report examines exclusion in relation to equitable access to three public goods. These are (i) urban primary health care; (ii) urban water and sanitation; and (iii) just conditions of work for women. The reason we chose to bring the first two together in the same report, despite the worry of an urban bias to this report, is that water and sanitation are important determinants of health. Therefore, chapters examining the complementary public goods of urban primary health care, and urban water and sanitation would be able to speak to each other.

In the context of each of the public goods interrogated in the current report, we ask the same questions. Why do we believe that this is a public good as defined in the first section? Which individuals or groups, if any, are excluded from equitable access to these public goods? Is this exclusion total, or are the individuals and groups identified included, but on unjust and discriminatory terms?

The next question is: why does this exclusion occur? In particular, since our focus is on the role of the state, what is it in the functioning of the state that contributes to this exclusion? Is it the design or implementation of law, policy and programmes, the allocation of budgets, the functioning of institutions, or a combination of these, that results in the outcome of exclusion from equitable access to these public goods?

We further ask: what are the consequences of this exclusion for the excluded populations? In particular, does exclusion from one public good jeopardise access to other public goods?

The next major questions relate to identifying examples of inclusion in access to public goods. Once again, what is it in the functioning of the state—law, policy, programmes, budgets, institutions—that contributes to this inclusion?

And finally, we seek to suggest recommendations for law, policy, programmes, budgets, and official data collection and dissemination that would contribute to ensuring better, more equitable outcomes of access to the identified vulnerable groups.

3. Budgets and Planning

A fourth portion of the report tries to look at taxation through the prism of exclusion. It subjects to interrogation, from the viewpoint of equity, the magnitude of tax revenue and the manner of its mobilisation, its composition and incidence on different segments of the population, and the integrity of its collection.

4. Disadvantaged Groups

The third part of the report shifts focus from evidence of inclusion and exclusion from equitable access to specified public goods, to highly disadvantaged communities. Here the attempt is to identify in each report particular highly dispossessed and oppressed groups, and to examine their situation in relation to equitable access to a wide range of public goods.

The first set of vulnerable groups identified for this report are single women. Women suffer denials of equitable access to several public goods, but women who are by circumstance or choice single—widowed, divorced, separated, unmarried—face a variety of enhanced disadvantage. The next two chapters comprise groups who are survivors of violence: of communal violence in 2013 in Muzaffarnagar in Uttar Pradesh, and of ethnic violence in the BTAD areas of Assam over an extended period. The Report then looks at adolescents and women drawn into a culturally sanctioned form of sex work, who are called Devadasis. Finally, the Report looks at the conditions of the Jarawa—or as they describe themselves, the Ang—an ancient and, until recently, isolated indigenous group living in India's Andaman Islands.

Contributors

As with the first India Exclusion Report, a very large number of persons contributed to this report as writers, researchers, advisors and reviewers.

The main authors of the chapters in this report are Aditi Rao, Agrima Bhasin, Anamika Lahiri, Chaitanya Mallapur, Coen Kompier, Devaki Nambiar, Geetika Anand, Harsh Mander, Kanchan Gandhi, Kavita Wankhade, Kinjal Sampat, Prachi Salve, Prathibha Ganesan, Radhika Jha, Rajanya Bose, Rajeev Malhotra, Rajiv K. Raman, Rhea John, Saba Sharma, Sajjad Hassan, Sanjay (Xonzoi) Barbora, Saumya Tewari, Shikha Sethia, Smita Premchander, Sridhar Kundu and V. Prameela.

Akram Akhtar, Anushree Deb, Asghar Sharif, Caitlin Mackridge, Dipa Sinha, Emily Davey, Ganapathy Murugan, Girish Motwani, Indranil Mukhopadhyay, Kim Hopper, Kinjal Sampat, Prachi Salve, Radhika Alkazi, Ravi Duggal, Sameer Taware, Samir Acharya, Saumya Premchander, Sejal Dand, Shameem Banu, Shekhar Singh, Sita Mamidipudi, Srirupa Bhattacharya, Swapna Easwar, T. Sundararaman, Uma Shirol and Vishnu MJ contributed to the chapters.

Alia Allana, Ajita Vidyarthi, Amrita Chhachhi, Aparna Chandra, Apoorvanand, Antara Lahiri, Arjun Bedi, Bhrigupathy Singh, Charmaine Ramos, Coen Kompier, Deepta Chopra, Devender Singh, Dipa Sinha, Erhard Berner, Indira Khurana, Jan Breman, Kinjal Sampat, Mrinal Satish, Navsharan Singh, Rachel Kurian, Rajib Dasgupta, Sara Ahmed, Sophie Grig, Subhalakshmi Nandi, Tejinder Sandhu and Yasmin Arif were very generous with their time and counsel, in advising authors and reviewing the chapters.

We are grateful to Amrita Chhachhi, Andrew Fischer, Cesar Rodríguez-Garavito, Des Gasper, Jan Breman, Patrick Heller, and Peter Evans for insights on the conceptual framework of the Report. Special thanks again to Amrita Chhachhi for facilitating a review workshop for the current report at the International Institute of Social Studies at the The Hague and to Amod Shah and Shikha Sethia for agreeing to rapporteur at the event.

A large number of organisations and universities were also part of this collaborative report. These include the Centre for Budget and Governance Accountability, Indian Institute of Human Settlements, IndiaSpend, International Institute of Social Studies at The Hague, Public Health Resource Network, Sampark, the Watson Institute for International and Public Affairs at Brown University, Arth Aastha, Aneka and the Institute of Development Studies, Sussex.

The report was fortunate to have an excellent publisher, Yoda Press, led by Arpita Das, and assisted by Prerna Vijayeni and Sonjuhi Negi. We are grateful to Milanth Gautham for the cover design, and to Sambit Dattachaudhuri and Jasmeet Khanuja for permission to use their photographs.

The overall coordination of the report was carried out with great industry, dedication and patience by Anamika Lahiri and Shikha Sethia. The report would not have been possible without their efforts and leadership. They are assisted by great teamwork from other members of the SR Sankaran unit of the Centre for Equity Studies—Kinjal Sampat, Gitanjali Prasad, Radhika Jha, Rhea John, Ambika Kapoor, Rajanya Bose, Srijit Ghosh, Srirupa Bhattacharya, Sandeep Ranjana, Ankit Sharma and Mohammad Ali Faraz.

Harsh Mander
Director, Centre for Equity Studies

India Exclusion Report 2015

An Overview

Harsh Mander

This is the second edition of the India Exclusion Report, for the year 2015. As with the first Report 2013–14, the attempt of this collaborative, trans-disciplinary annual enterprise is to bring together experts from many fields—scholars, human rights and development workers, policy makers and persons from disadvantaged communities—to examine the outcomes of public policy, law, programmes, budgets and institutions, and their functioning for all peoples, and specifically disadvantaged peoples.

The particular questions that these Exclusion Reports ask are: who, if anyone, is excluded—or adversely included—from equitable access to public goods; why and by what processes are such exclusion and adverse inclusion accomplished; and what can be done to change this to a more just and equitable set of outcomes?

There has been an attempt to ensure that this series of Exclusion Reports is based on strongly empirical evidence. At the same time, the diverse contributors to these Reports are bound by a kernel of shared normative and political convictions related to ideas of the just state, the just society, equity and solidarity. The Exclusion Reports are guided by specific constructs of the public good, exclusion and the role of the state, which we elaborate in the following two sections.

Public Goods and the Role of the State*

The notion of the 'public good' as used in the India Exclusion Reports departs from the neo-classical economist's conception: goods that are by nature such that their consumption by one does not reduce availability nor exclude consumption by others. (In the language of economics, the terms for this attribute are 'non-excludable' and 'non-rivalrous'). Instead, in the tradition of social and political philosophy, the Reports look at public goods as goods, services, attainments, capabilities, functionings and freedoms—individual and collective—that are essential for a human being to live with human dignity.[1] In this sense, the Exclusion Reports do not regard the 'publicness' of the good in question to be intrinsic to the good itself, but something that is determined by the political community at a particular point of

* I am grateful for useful insights and suggestions generously offered by Amrita Chhachhi, Cesar Rodríguez-Garavito, Des Gasper, Jan Breman, Patrick Heller, Peter Evans and participants in workshops on the India Exclusion Report in Brown University in February 2015, and in ISS in The Hague in November 2015. I am grateful also for research support from Gitanjali Prasad and Srijit Ghosh. The responsibility for mistakes of course remains mine alone.

time. Housing, for instance, is considered a public good in many societies, but much less so in India where, for instance, there has been no major and effective programme of urban social housing to date. Likewise, contestations continue over whether healthcare, especially tertiary healthcare, and education, particularly higher education, are indeed public goods.

The idea of what is a public good also alters, sometimes dramatically, over time. Thirty years ago, it would have been hard to predict that there would be such a large social consensus about digital inclusion as a public good as there is today. This building of consensus about what are indeed public goods would require also a prioritising of public goods, because trade-offs can become necessary: the achievement of one public good may require partial sacrifice of another. The public good of a dignified livelihood for street vendors supplying affordable products to lower-income consumers, needs to be balanced against the public good of sidewalks for pedestrians. The earlier India Exclusion Report 2013–14 reflected on the trade-off between security of all in the context of a prevalent fear of terror attacks, and defence of the human rights of a smaller number of persons charged with terror crimes. (The Report argued against a utilitarian premise of the alleged 'greatest good of the greatest number' that would be realised by compromising the access of some persons to established standards of fair trial and legal justice.)

We have stated that the publicness of a good is determined by the political community at any point of time. But we also recognise that in highly unequal and diverse societies that are stratified in complex ways along lines of class, gender, caste, religious and ethnic identities, age, disability, and many others it is problematic to identify anything as *the* political community. Instead it is fitting to recognise that within this 'community', there is highly unequal power. Therefore normative perspectives on what is indeed a public good will differ depending on one's location in the many intersecting schisms of the political community. Recognising this, every chapter on exclusion from public goods in each Report begins with a discussion on what is the public good in question, and why we claim that this is a public good.

It is important to recognise in this context that the question of who is a member of the 'public' is also a matter of considerable contestation. First, does the principle of recognition of equal intrinsic human dignity, which is the starting point of our discussion about the public good, extend only to citizens or to all persons, and to only those presently living or also to unborn future generations? And also once again, it must be recognised that in unequal political communities, formal equal citizenship may be only a thin veneer for a de facto hierarchy of citizenship. The collaborators on this Report share a conviction that the 'public' in the context of public goods must include all persons, regardless of citizenship, and must also include future generations, and not just those living today.

Some critics worry that deriving our definition of public goods from the premise of the equal human dignity of all human beings runs the risk of turning into a tautology because, in this view, equal dignity or the lack of it is a (possible) consequence of state action. We do not agree, because we believe that all human beings intrinsically carry equal human dignity and equal human-ness. State actions, as much as actions of society and markets, may fail to recognise—or even assault—this equal dignity. But this does not change the fact that human beings innately and fundamentally bear within them equal and inviolable dignity.

Finally, it is important to acknowledge that the notion of public goods as used in the India Exclusion Report overlaps in many ways with other 'sibling ideas' like human rights, human development and human security. Gasper makes an interesting comparison between the ideas of human rights, human development and human security, which he suggests form increasingly important, partly interconnected, partly competitive ethical and policy discourses.[2] We could easily add the idea of public goods as conceptualised in this Report to the same family of siblings.

As with the idea of public goods, Gasper suggests that the conception of human rights derives from respect for inherent human dignity and for the common humanity of each and every person. Human rights, he observes, (again like public goods) are a tool for the defence of the weak, enabling connections of this conception of inherent dignity and humanity to the rigour, force and compulsion of law on the one hand, and to policy analysis and action on the other. But he also observes that the human rights language, as used in practice, is not necessarily egalitarian. Historically, rights language has often been associated with defending or claiming privileges, such as the right to property.

The human development approach, led by Mahbub ul Haq and Amartya Sen, succeeded in moving beyond a dominant focus on economic output and economic growth, broadening the range of objectives routinely considered in the development debate and reducing GDP from an end in itself[3] to just one possible means or instrument. This again illuminates the importance of public goods such as health and education. However, Gasper points to serious criticisms from the perspective of equity, because human development did not establish guarantees for individuals, in contrast to the human rights tradition.

The complementary idea of human security, proposed again by Mahbub ul Haq, was not merely for ensuring the physical safety of individuals but equally their ability to secure and hold basic goods.[4] He indicated six areas of security in addition to a conventional concern with security from physical violence: income security, food security, health security, environmental security, community/identity security, and security of political freedoms. This further enriches our understanding of public goods: just as human development ensured the addition of health and education concerns to economic growth, we now understand environmental protection, protection of culture and identity, and political freedom also as public goods. This list will grow and be deepened, we anticipate, in the explorations from one Report to the next.

Exclusion and the Role of the State

The second important construct in the series of India Exclusion Reports is 'exclusion'. In the way we deploy this word, 'exclusion' refers both to complete denials, and to discriminatory and unjust access—or what may be described as adverse inclusion—of individuals and groups to public goods. The Exclusion Reports do not adopt the popular usage of the idea of *social* exclusion. They recognise that exclusions may be caused by the norms, institutions and functioning of society, markets or the state, but the focus of the Report is pointedly and primarily on the role of the state.

The Exclusion Reports focus on the role of the state in preventing, enabling or augmenting exclusion, because we believe that it is the moral duty of a democratic state to prevent or reverse exclusion by social or market forces, and to facilitate and protect equitable access of all persons to all public goods. There is also the practical consideration that in a democratic state, one can hold the state and its institutions legally accountable in ways that one cannot hold society and markets accountable.

It is pertinent to emphasise here that our focus on the role of the state is not built on an a priori assumption that the state must itself provision all public goods. The political and ethical assumption that underlies the Exclusion Reports is instead that the state is responsible for the *outcome* that all persons have equitable access to all public goods. It is against empirical evidence of these outcomes that the Reports attempt to evaluate the role of the state. To accomplish this outcome it may well be concluded that the state needs to provision several public goods. But if indeed empirically it is found that we can achieve the same (or conceivably better) outcomes of equitable access by other state actions, such as regulation, facilitation, provision of incentives and redistribution, rather than direct provision, then we will place those findings before the reader.

A generation ago, there was much greater consensus that education, health care, housing and public transport should be publicly supplied than there is today. The Exclusion Reports attempt to look empirically at outcomes of access to the public good in question in order to determine whether a good should be publicly supplied or not. In the current Report, for instance, a strong case is made for public provisioning of universal and free urban primary health care, but the same case cannot be made as unequivocally for urban drinking water provisioning. That the latter is a public good is indisputable because life itself, let alone a life of dignity, is impossible without it. While it is not clear whether it should be supplied entirely free of charge, ensuring affordable access to all persons through public supply becomes the consensus objective of water policy.

Another reason for according centrality to the state's role in provisioning particular public goods is that the adverse consequences of the denial of certain public goods is higher than those of others. Amartya Sen, during the release of his book *Country of First Boys* in New Delhi on 17 December 2015, pointed out that levels of inequality in India and China are comparable, but the penalties of inequality are much higher in India, because India has not invested enough in health care and education.[5]

This discussion about the role of the state in ensuring public goods is refined by an interesting classification proposed by Flavio Comim.[6] He looks first at what he describes as the Rawls level of public goods: basic or primary goods to be provided or ensured by the state.[7] He believes that the role of the state is not equally central to or definitive of the realisation of other levels of public goods: what he describes as the Amartya Sen level of publicness, or effective access to a range of priority functionings;[8] and even less for what he calls the Martha Nussbaum level,[9] which includes also the culture and attitudes needed to sustain a life with dignity, and thus also matters such as civility, tolerance, non-violence, mutual respect, and solidarity.[10] While this classification of levels of public goods is useful, we believe that the role of the state is critical maybe not for the supply of all of these public goods, but certainly for the facilitation, promotion and defence—moral, legal and political—of the supply of these public goods.

This discussion about exclusion from public goods rests a great deal on the idea of equity, as we are focused on empirical evidence about equitable (not equal) access of various groups and individuals to the identified public good. While equality of outcomes can be empirically determined, the idea of what is equitable is determined by the political community,[11] just as is the idea of the public good, with all the possible ambiguities and contestations admitted to above.

What is more, it is apparent that we are looking at equity not just of opportunity, but also of outcomes. This derives in part from the impossibility of accomplishing true equality of opportunity. After all, for instance, even if we accomplish a situation in which every child has access to a publicly funded common neighbourhood school of high quality, she would still not enjoy opportunity equal to a more privileged child, as she may have non-literate (or no) parents, live in an under-resourced and unsafe slum, lack elementary sanitation, a place to study, and opportunities for exposure and travel, all of which are available to her middle-class classmate in ample measure.

Exclusion is not seen by us in absolute binary terms, namely that one is either included or excluded.

In fact, for all the public goods that we have studied in the India Exclusion Reports 2013–14 and 2015, we have found that there are proportionately small but very significant (and large in absolute terms) populations who are *completely* excluded from each of the public goods we examined, whether it is school education, housing, decent work, legal justice, urban primary health care, urban water and sanitation or gender-just work. These are children who cannot enter school, homeless people, people especially women outside paid work including unpaid and forced work, people denied any access to legal justice, people who go without any kind of health care, and people without any access to safe drinking water or sanitation. It is extremely important to identify these completely excluded groups, whose numbers are proportionately small but whose denials are the most extreme. However, the Exclusion Reports also note that there are much larger groups which are included in their access to these public goods, but that their access is unjust and discriminatory in variety of ways. It is this discriminatory inclusion that we include in our definition of exclusion, regarding exclusion as a spectrum rather than a fixed point. This year, the Exclusion Report also attempts to address a concept known as *adverse inclusion*[12], which describes the situation of previously uncontacted indigenous peoples for whom access to a standardised set of public goods, or conventional inclusion, itself becomes a source of exploitation and alienation.

A final word about the approach attempted by the series of India Exclusion Reports. We hope that the Reports will be judged to be strongly fact-based, deriving their findings and conclusions from impeccable primary and secondary research, and official data sets. But in addition, these Reports are also based on ethical and political ideas of justice and solidarity, of the importance of sharing, of a democratic state accountable for outcomes of equity in the access of all persons to public goods, and of the equal intrinsic dignity, humanness and worth of *every* human being.

Exclusion from Public Goods

The India Exclusion Report 2015 presents an in-depth review of exclusion with respect to three essential public goods: urban health, urban water and sanitation, and access to equal and dignified work for women. The Report also studies the exclusion faced by five especially vulnerable groups: single women, Devadasis, survivors of ethnic conflict, survivors of communal violence, and the Jarawa tribe. These groups are discussed in detail in the different chapters of the Report. The opening chapter tries to put together the main trends and insights from the various themes covered in this Report and use them to offer a detailed analytical overview of the India Exclusion Report 2015. It attempts to accomplish this through an exploration of the following areas: who is excluded from public goods, what are the processes by which this exclusion is accomplished, the consequences of such exclusion, and recommendations to prevent, address and reverse this exclusion.

Who is Excluded from Public Goods?

The current Exclusion Report, like the last one, finds that the persons excluded from or adversely included in the range of public goods studied belong mostly to the same historically disadvantaged groups: women, Dalits, Adivasis, Muslims, persons with disabilities, and persons with age-related vulnerabilities such as children and the aged. The Reports also point to important class-related disadvantages, such as those of occupation and housing. If these disadvantages overlap, such as if one is aged, a woman, Dalit and disabled, homeless and unemployed, the extent of exclusion is also compounded many times over.

Urban Health

The chapter on exclusion from health care as a public good maps multifaceted exclusions of urban poor populations from either any kind of health care services whatsoever, or from services that are affordable, accessible, respectful and appropriate. It highlights vulnerabilities and barriers in accessing health care that are particular to the urban poor. Urban areas are thought to have better health facilities for most people, which in turn is expected to positively shape health outcomes. But for the urban poor, the relative abundance of services in urban areas do not translate into better health care.

The chapter also highlights that people who are excluded from some critical public goods, like housing or just conditions of work, are more likely to be excluded from other public goods as well, such as health care, clean drinking water and sanitation. For this, the chapter on urban health care relies on the methodology used to understand urban poverty developed by a Planning Commission expert group under the chairpersonship of Dr S.R. Hashim. The report, submitted in 2012, indicated three types of vulnerability that typify urban poverty: residential, social and occupational vulnerability.

In identifying the most vulnerable populations from a health perspective, the chapter makes interesting linkages with two other chapters of the Report, namely those related to the denial of access of women to just conditions of work, and the specific vulnerabilities of single women. It speaks of the specific health care denials of single women, separated or widowed women, homeless women and women with mental disabilities, all of whom face harsh and complex forms of vulnerability in the urban context for structural and societal reasons. Some women escape domestic violence only to be forced into homelessness and penury, often supporting children through begging or other hazardous street-based work (including sex work and rag-picking), and remain completely expelled from the support structures of the state. It observes that these homeless women particularly lack access to drinking water, food and sanitation. Among other public goods, primary health care centres—even the few that exist—are mainly facilities only for pregnant women and therefore unable to provide for the other health needs of these women.

The chapter looks at the special health exclusions of other major social groups as well, such as Dalits, Adivasis, the differently abled and homeless children. It observes that Dalits are typically forced to do hard labour for sub-standard amounts without any social security, and many are trapped in occupations such as manual scavenging, which result in high vulnerability to a wide range of health issues, including poisoning, musculo-skeletal disorders, respiratory problems, leptospirosis, skin problems, and so on. Dalit populations also tend to lack access to institutionalised care because of social discrimination.

In the context of Muslims, the chapter once again maps the health consequences of exclusions from several other public goods which are social determinants of health, notably education, housing, and employment opportunities, as well as protection from communal violence. The last of these is examined in detail in a separate chapter in this Exclusion Report.

The chapter goes on to observe that persons with disabilities often have distinct and multiple health care needs relating to their impairments, which compound the general health care needs resulting from poverty and from living in difficult environments such as urban slums. There are major barriers in physical mobility as urban slums leave options such as the wheelchair totally unfeasible, accessible public transport is rare, and even in clinical facilities, patients and carers are often discouraged due to the lack of knowledge of how to navigate facilities to access the services they need. Finally, disabled persons face violence and abuse when seeking all manner of services and entitlements.

The chapter also looks at age-related vulnerabilities. Among children particularly at risk are those living in slums and street-based children, who are deprived of sufficient nutrition, sanitation facilities, drinking water and medical care, and exposed to extreme climatic conditions. Measles, tuberculosis and other vaccine-preventable diseases, scabies, chronic dysentery, and lung, ear, nose and throat infections are common, as are anaemia, malnourishment and simple hunger. Child labour induces orthopaedic ailments, injuries, stunting of gastro-intestinal, endocrine and reproductive system development because of strain and exposure, and greater preponderance of substance abuse as compared to children who are not in labour. Among the aged, the most frequent ailments are cardiovascular illnesses, circulatory diseases and cancers, and their situation is compounded by lack of social and family support often leading to their isolation, even while many elderly individuals require home-based care.

The chapter identifies the urban homeless, including street children, as a population sometimes completely excluded from any kind of health care. First, there is the stigma of homelessness that renders health-seeking unlikely. Many homeless persons simply bide their time with illnesses and injuries. In many cases, homeless persons suffer from multiple morbidities (e.g., injury and mental illness or disability and chronic disease) and rarely do primary health care facilities have the ability to handle these combinations (especially mental illness and disability), so appropriate care is not even available. For ailments like tuberculosis that require the patient to recuperate by resting at home, cared for by caregivers, this becomes impossible if the person has no home or family. Other poorest urban populations frequently report only ad hoc use of painkillers or generic medicines, either suggested by an area pharmacist, neighbour, relative, or employer.

Likewise, the chapter looks at the health consequences for persons denied access to decent work, trapped in low-end jobs—insecure, poorly paid and low-productivity work with unhealthy, unsafe and debilitating work conditions. For example, heavy load workers experience severe spinal and back problems, while waste recyclers report musculo-skeletal disorders, respiratory diseases and chronic fatigue. Rickshaw pullers are exposed to extreme weather conditions and often live on sidewalks to save money on rent; they face high risk of heart ailments because they are unable to rest after pulling; studies have found DNA damage attributable to exposure to air pollutants and physical exertion. Sex workers are far more vulnerable to HIV and other sexually transmitted infections, but also face stigma in accessing health care.

Urban Water and Sanitation

Largely the same disparities persist when we look at access to drinking water and sanitation. While poverty remains the strongest predictor of lack of access to safe drinking water and sanitation facilities, caste also plays a highly significant role: only 57 per cent Dalit and 55 per cent Adivasi households have drinking water within their premises compared to the national (urban) average of 71 per cent. In the sphere of sanitation, a quarter of Dalit and Adivasi populations defaecate in the open, against an overall percentage of 12 per cent. Female-headed households have similarly poor access to a water source within premises, and to exclusive use. However, unlike for caste and gender, the chapter finds no significant differences across religious groups with regard to location and exclusivity of water source, and small differences in access to piped water supply and sanitation.

The chapter on urban access to water and sanitation follows the chapter on health in reporting links between denial of access to one public good and exclusion from others. In particular, it chronicles the health consequences of denial of decent housing—being forced to occupy places such as open drains and the banks of effluent tanks, which have poor infrastructure, lack space and provisions, and thus have problematic access to drinking water and toilets—and of increasing exposure to various forms of pollution. While there are systemic deficiencies in urban water supply that affect all households, slum households are disproportionately affected: only 57 per cent of slum households have access to drinking water within premises compared to the national average of 71 per cent, with access in squatter settlements being even lower than in either notified or non-notified slums. Only two-thirds of slum households have access to a latrine within premises, compared to the national (urban) average of 81 per cent; almost 15 per cent rely on public latrines and 19 per cent resort to open defaecation.

Similar to disparities between economic classes, regional disparities in access to piped public supply of water are also evident—37 per cent of urban households have access to piped water in north-east India, compared to 79 per cent in western India. Likewise, only 12 per cent of households in the East and North east have access to piped sewer systems, even though 72 per cent of households in the Northeast have a latrine for exclusive use. Within a single city too, inadequate access to sanitation in public locations such as schools, informal sector workplaces and public spaces in general, paves the way for exclusion from other public goods, such as education and fair conditions of work. This also creates disproportionate barriers to the participation of already vulnerable populations, such as the homeless and migrant workers, women, children, the elderly and the differently abled. In particular, the access of homeless persons to water and sanitation services is hugely inadequate to ensure their human dignity and health; they are forced to access non-potable water, fetched over long distances, and often including significant costs. They also have to resort to open defaecation, or use paid or unpaid public toilets, which are frequently poorly maintained and afford little safety and privacy, especially for women and children.

Just Conditions of Work for Women

The chapter underlines the distinct nature of disadvantage borne by women workers within and outside the labour market. While women from most income deciles and social categories are typically excluded from just conditions of work to a higher degree than their male counterparts, for instance through pervasive adversities such as lower wages, neglect of needs due to maternity, sexual violence and harassment, and lack of control over land and community resources, exclusion is aggravated for women engaged in certain types of occupations as well as for women burdened by disadvantages of class, caste, religious and ethnic identities, and different abilities.

First, the chapter points to the concentration of women in unpaid work. Based on the NSS 2011–12, approximately 43 per cent of women (42% urban and 48% rural) are engaged only in domestic work, which is time-consuming and physically taxing. While crucial for maintaining the labour force, subsidising business as well as the state,[13] it is not considered as 'productive' in terms of adding economic value and is consequently neglected in policy. Women also perform unpaid work for the market (thus, recognised as an economic activity) as part of family enterprises. Despite effectively working as employees or even as the main producers, they have no legal rights as employees or social security.[14] Social status and poverty intersect to make women from historically marginalised groups especially vulnerable to exploitative labour arrangements, forcing them to provide cheap labour, without agency. With women in conditions akin to bondage, factors such as the confinement of workers engaged in this work in homes or hostels (as seen in the *Sumangali* scheme) and the mediation of the employment relationship through the male head of the household (for instance, in brick kilns and quarries) further serve to render women invisible. The chapter examines specifically the conditions of women engaged in the socially devalued caste-based practice of manual scavenging. Civil society organisations estimate that 95–98 per cent of individuals involved are women;[15] they 'inherit' the work generation after generation and work in extremely unhygienic, hazardous conditions for meagre payments. Despite the fact that it is illegal, the state perpetuates the practice: for instance, the railways and municipal organisations hire individuals from the *Valmiki* community to clean railway tracks, public toilets and sewers. Cases of *panchayats* blocking access to alternate jobs, making threats of violence and evictions, have also been documented.[16] Women selling their sexual labour are especially subject to social stigma, which is strengthened by the non-recognition of sex work as labour and its *de facto* criminalising by the state.[17] Another group of women especially disadvantaged by the nature of their occupation are those in hazardous occupations in sectors such as construction and mining, where they perform extremely strenuous tasks such as head loading, while being remunerated far less than men.[18] For women from vulnerable communities, the combination of low household ownership of assets such as land[19] and lack of marketable skills means that they are pushed into low quality work in the unorganised sector and most adversely affected by economic or job-market fluctuations.[20] The participation of Dalit and Adivasi women in the labour force has always been higher than that of upper caste and Muslim women due to poverty and lower restrictions on mobility, but they remain concentrated in casual wage work. An analysis of NSS data from 2009–10 shows that over 31.5 per cent of Dalit women and 35.5 per cent of tribal women in urban areas were in casual labour, compared to 5.8 per cent of upper caste women. In rural areas as well, the percentage of upper caste women in casual labour was 19.4 per cent, compared to 56.3 per cent for Dalit women and 43.8 per cent for tribal women. Muslim women are concentrated in self-employment, in home-based sub-contracted work with low earnings.[21] Finally, the chapter looks at age-related vulnerabilities in work: elderly women, especially in rural areas, continue to work past their retirement age. NSSO data shows that participation rates for rural elderly women have fluctuated at around 20 per cent between 1983 and 2011–12.[22] In addition, the fact that a majority of elderly women have not completed primary education implies that they are engaged in low-end, unskilled work, with elderly women more downwardly classified as compared to men.[23]

Vulnerable Groups

Continuing its investigation into who is excluded, the third segment of the Report with its detailed portraits of five especially vulnerable groups goes further in describing who is most intensely excluded from a range of public goods.

The first of these is single women, understood as a wide, porous and heterogenous category including widows, divorced, 'abandoned' or separated women, and unmarried women (by choice or circumstance) above the age of 35. The chapter observes how society is profoundly troubled by single women, women who survive independent of male control, support and patronage, outside their socially normalised role as 'mere instruments of the ends of others—reproducers, caregivers, sexual outlets, agents of a family's general prosperity'.[24] Singleness for women in India is a socially and culturally constructed category, and like in all of South Asia, here too the cultural anxieties, neglect, oppression, cruelties, exclusions and violence of an overarching patriarchy towards these women has historically been dramatic. A great deal of these socially embedded exclusions continue into the present day, reflected also in state action, and in the design and implementation of law and policy.

Another intensely vulnerable group of girls and women portrayed in this Report are the Devadasis, victims of the continuing practice of girls being dedicated to a goddess before reaching puberty, and being forced into sex from the time they start menstruating. The chapter notes that Devadasis represent a most vulnerable and exploited group in society, and also usually belong to specific castes among the Scheduled Castes, particularly Madars, Madigas and Valmikis. The chapter is categorical that Devadasis are victims of the worst forms of child labour, as they are subjected to forced sex, rape and other violent atrocities from early adolescence. While all sex with minors is statutory rape, the Devadasi practice is identified in the Report as caste-sanctioned rape, made socially acceptable by terming it local culture.

Two chapters of the Report underline the daunting barriers in accessing public goods that are erected by conflict, and examines in particular mass violence targeted at people because of their religious or ethnic identity. The chapter on communal violence describes conditions faced by survivors of mass communal violence in Muzaffarnagar and Shamli districts in Western Uttar Pradesh in September 2013, which led to the death of 52 persons, and the displacement of around 50,000 persons, mostly Muslims from poorer backgrounds from up to 74 villages. The second chapter focuses on a particular region within western Assam where political violence has resulted in the death and displacement of several thousand persons of different ethnic groups since the early 1990s. The areas in question constitute the Bodo Territorial Areas Districts (BTAD).

The last group profiled in this Report is a Particularly Vulnerable Tribal Group from the Andaman Islands—the Jarawa, or as they describe themselves, the Ang. Numbering just 380 according to Census 2011, their very survival is threatened due to their active contact with the outside world over the last 25 years—and their situation is characteristic of, and holds lessons for, the situation of other uncontacted or recently contacted indigenous peoples, both in India and elsewhere.

How is this Exclusion Accomplished?

Urban Health

In investigating the ways in which exclusion is accomplished, the focus of the Report, for reasons explained in the opening section, is mainly on the role of the state. In the context of health care, the Report points to the inadequate dispensation of schemes, services and programmes within larger exclusionary urban policies and programmes in general. It focuses on constraints starting from the first point of interface with the system, the Primary Health Centre (PHC), where everything from immunisation to first aid, screening for a range of diseases and even deliveries should be carried out at no cost if health care is indeed a public good. But the chapter points to evidence of many barriers: rarely are PHCs located at manageable distances from where the excluded live; they are open only during work hours so that seeking care at a PHC (or a tertiary public hospital, for that matter) usually requires taking a day off from work, thus losing that day's wages; long waiting hours; and expenses of referrals and diagnostics. In addition, PHCs are widely seen as a location only for the receipt of family planning and pregnancy-related care, to the exclusion of screening and wellness programmes for non-communicable diseases, injury, violence and substance abuse prevention, occupational health and risk-related problems, seasonal health promotion in relation to communicable diseases, group-specific outreach and care, etc.

The chapter points to institutional bias towards various vulnerable groups. Disrespectful behaviour by service-providers is a major barrier to seeking care. It quotes a study in Delhi, for instance, which shows that three-fourths of the patients using public health facilities belong to lower castes or socially disenfranchised groups, and nearly 60 per cent of the patients asserted that health care staff are not polite and respectful. Excluded groups such as transgenders and persons living with HIV/AIDS have to face extraordinary humiliation in public health systems.

The chapter underlines that privatisation over the past three decades has also meant the near-complete exit of the wealthy from the public sector and a kind of growing stigmatisation of the public sector itself (which as the afore-cited study suggests, may have caste and class correlations). The resulting institutional bias towards privatisation is in fact another driver of exclusion in urban India: many processes of exclusion are reinforced because of the overall monetisation and tertiarisation of health. On the other hand, the chapter notes that the private sector is itself notorious for eschewing any responsibility towards the poor, even when legally required to show it.

Urban Water and Sanitation

In the context of drinking water and sanitation, the Report points to many barriers—legal, design, technical and political. Exclusion is caused first by legal regulatory regimes: some regulatory acts explicitly prohibit provisioning to properties, households or settlements located on land without clear legal title, and these are in most cases residences of the urban poor and other vulnerable groups. The other significant regulatory gaps exist for treatment of faecal sludge, and waste management. For instance, various Municipalities Acts, echoing the 74th Constitutional Amendment, do not explicitly mandate the treatment of waste water, or even regular cleaning and desludging of on-site installations. Regulatory frameworks are also missing for private players like private water supply tanker operators, and desludging truck operators.

The chapter also describes flaws in programme design and budgetary constraints that act as barriers for the poor to access water and sanitation. There is neither legal requirement nor political will for universalisation in the assured supply (not necessarily free of charge) of these public goods. The focus instead is on large infrastructure projects and servicing the needs of well-off sections of the city. Public provisioning in urban areas has usually been limited to constructing and expanding piped water supply networks, construction of water treatment plants, and to a lesser extent, expansion of sewerage networks and construction of sewage or waste water treatment plants. Private provisioning of infrastructure becomes unaffordable for poor households, who therefore remain substantially excluded. At the same time, neglect of faecal sludge management puts at risk a large section of the society, mainly the urban poor, which is dependent on on-site sanitation. The lack of public facilities like well-equipped homeless shelters, public stand-posts or public toilets, or high costs associated with these facilities, makes access restrictive for the homeless.

The chapter also notes that urban local bodies—which are perhaps most accessible to urban citizens—are the weakest and most disempowered, severely impacting capacity and accountability for service delivery. With the exception of the few larger municipal corporations, they are typically under-funded and under-staffed, and hence dependent on grants from the central and state governments, which are also uncertain, inadequate, and rarely focused on supplying the needs of these most vulnerable groups. Urban local bodies as well as water and sanitation utilities have historically been unresponsive to citizen and customer demands and grievances, especially of the urban poor. Water and sanitation service delivery institutions have traditionally been technology-focused and engineer-driven, with little flexibility to accommodate needs of constituencies that are not 'legal'.

There are also barriers of design and standards. Sanitation facilities in public places are grossly inadequate, but there are no norms to address these deficits. While Town Planning rules specify norms for the provision of water supply and sanitation in institutional facilities, these are seldom enforced or the norms updated. There are also technical challenges in slum settlements often located in environmentally sensitive or vulnerable locations, for instance, near river-beds or other flood-prone areas, and it is difficult to provide solutions in these settlements. Dense slum settlements pose another set of locational and design challenges: to find land for constructing toilets, and provide for periodic cleaning. Water pipes that zig-zag through many Indian slums, installed at low elevations to catch meagre and intermittent supply, also run the risk of their water mixing with the dirty water flowing in adjacent drains.

Just Conditions of Work for Women

In analysing the barriers that prevent women from accessing just conditions of work, the chapter notes that these stem most of all from the hegemonic social and cultural contexts of patriarchy, in which normative beliefs that privilege men over women result in their oppression in work and denial of the ownership of land and capital. The gendered household division of labour, supported by gender ideologies, places the primary responsibility for unpaid work in the 'private realm' on women, leading to unequal bargaining powers in the household. Care work in the labour market is also shaped by this hierarchy and devalued. Ideology also sets norms for the participation of men and women in paid work: concerns about status, for instance, may restrict participation in work outside the home for upper caste women.[25] In certain communities, ploughing is considered taboo for women.[26] These ideologies are carried and reproduced by the market and state.

The macro-economic context of neo-liberal globalisation has created a permissive framework in which women and girls are often preferred as workers because they can be paid less, denied more basic rights in the conditions of work, and denied opportunities to organise. In India, a high growth of around 8 per cent per annum between 2003–4 and 2011–12 did not create commensurate employment but instead turned out to be 'jobless growth'. Rural employment has been more affected than urban employment, with the number of workers in rural areas actually showing a decline in absolute numbers (a reduction of 35 million) and urban employment growing by only 2.5 per cent annual compound rate between 2004-5 and 2011-12.[27] Although there is an increase in non-farm employment, this has not been in high productivity and regular manufacturing jobs but mainly in the low productivity construction sector. Almost two-thirds of new non-farm jobs in rural areas were for casual daily wage workers, with no addition in regular employment.[28] Much of the decline in employment has been because of decline in female employment.

The chapter notes that when women are 'pushed' into the labour market because of economic distress, they are often employed in precarious, informal and low-paid activities. When a crisis triggers women's withdrawal from paid employment, they return to dependent positions within the household with less autonomy and less access to incomes of their own.

One of the factors that has played a role in reducing the demand for women's work in agriculture has been the growing mechanisation in this sector. Further, due to environmental degradation and particularly decline in access to forests and common property resources, there has been a fall in many of the rural activities earlier performed by women, such as collection of minor forest produce. On the other hand, the increased time that now has to be spent on activities such as collecting fuel and water (because of declining availability and inadequate social services to provide these) has led to women spending more time on these unpaid activities at the cost of their ability to participate in the labour market. The effects of macro-economic policies on social hierarchies can become particularly pronounced in times of crisis, which can intensify stigma, stereotypes and violence. The macro-economic framework within which policies are implemented either enlarges or constrains their scope to advance substantive equality for women.

The chapter also finds the state wanting both in the design of its policies for the rights of women workers as well as in the institutional bias that plays out in the implementation of these laws and policies. A majority of women workers in the unorganised sector fall outside the ambit of labour laws. The Factories Act, for instance, excludes home-based workers, sub-contracting and self-employed women by defining the factory in terms of the number of people employed.[29] Key laws—the Factories Act, the Equal Remuneration Act and the Industrial Disputes Act—further exclude women through a systematic neglect or devaluation of concerns crucial for women to continue in paid work. The Factories Act makes women workers responsible for child care including washing, changing their clothes and feeding, and stipulates that crèches are mandatory only in factories with 30 or more women workers.[30] The Equal Remuneration Act mandates equal remuneration for men and women specifically for performing work of a 'similar nature'. These provisions restrict the employment of women, encourage under-reporting and the process that renders them invisible, and do not represent them adequately (or at all) in workers' collective forums, such as for grievance redressal and collective bargaining. The Sexual Harassment (Prevention, Prohibition and Redressal) Act 2013, which is directed specifically at women, is also paradoxically insensitive; for instance, the provision punishing 'false or malicious complaint' reflects the stereotyping of women as 'potential liars' who could 'misuse' the laws. The law lays down 'conciliation' as the first response to a complaint. Women are therefore discouraged from filing complaints. The chapter also notes how institutional bias in implementing laws have contributed to the official condoning of child and adolescent labour in factories, as well as culturally sanctioned exploitative practices like that of Devadasi dedication.

Vulnerable Groups

The chapter on single women traces the contexts and societal perceptions regarding different categories of 'singleness', the particular contexts of the women and the social position they are thereby accorded. It observes that they have been traditionally excluded from the consideration of lawmakers and administrators, since marriage is considered to be the fundamental marker of social respect and 'protection' for women. The state thus absolves itself of the responsibility of providing for single women.

While widows have received some attention in public policy since the days of formal planning in India, other single women have scarcely found a mention in social policy until recently. Even when mentioned, single women are largely constructed as 'vulnerable' or as 'women in distress', depriving them of their agency and imagining them as passive recipients of state and societal charity. Shelter homes, short-stay homes and schemes for the rehabilitation of destitute women were some of the measures usually proposed for single women. Recent recognition of widows' economic vulnerability has led to pension schemes for them, but the amounts are typically small, and other categories of single women are excluded.

Devadasis are almost invariably asset-less, with little or no farmlands, little or no education and skills, and very low incomes. This arises in part because the practice is mostly conducted among the poorest and most vulnerable populations, out of a belief that the health of children, the family's financial status, or simply the transmission of family property (in the absence of male progeny) can be ensured by the dedication of the child. However, since the girl frequently remains illiterate and faces social stigma when looking for work, she is then forced to support her household through sex work, supplemented with manual labour. The practice of long-term patronage that was traditionally the source of financial support for Devadasis is unreliable, insufficient, and frequently accompanied by verbal, physical and sexual abuse. Children of Devadasis have no proof of paternity, and face discrimination and restricted education and work opportunities.

The report rejects narratives that tacitly justify this as a traditional practice of choice. The reality is that behind the ritual dedication lies the economic and social subjugation of those already made vulnerable by caste, class and gender, and this subjugation is normalised as part of the social structure.

The report notes that while the Devadasi practice is spread over many other states, only three states—Andhra Pradesh, Karnataka and Maharashtra—have enacted legislation to prohibit and outlaw it, and to identify and rehabilitate Devadasis. However, even in these states very few cases are registered, and there are virtually no prosecutions and penalties imposed on perpetrators under the laws. They are unable to access alternate livelihoods, or state livelihood and social protection schemes, to a large extent because the practice being declared illegal has made its survivors invisible in the eyes of the state.

Based on participatory research conducted from January 2014 to when the chapter was written, the author delineates how communities surviving the violence in Muzaffarnagar have been denied equal citizenship due in part to institutional bias—including equal treatment in terms of protection from violence, reparation, resettlement, access to legal justice and a number of other basic entitlements. In the aftermath of this predominantly rural riot, even seven months after the violence an overwhelming majority of affected families remained displaced, living in makeshift camps in deplorable conditions (due to which many children died during the winter months). There were no schools in camps, and it was difficult to admit children to nearby schools because of the indifference of the local bureaucracy to their needs. Most displaced children in higher classes were unable to sit for their classes IX and X examinations, in particular girls, and only strong pressure by civil society groups prompted school and college administrations to integrate them.

Examining the processes of exclusion of ethnic communities affected by recurring cycles of mass violence since the 1990s in the BTAD region of Assam, the authors describe the conflicts in histories, narratives, and the political vocabulary surrounding territorial belonging that have underlain the conflict. In particular, there have been a succession of violent clashes since the 1990s between the indigenous Bodo people, and two sets of settlers: one, descendants of tea garden labourers brought in as indentured labour by the colonial rulers from among the tribes of Central India from the mid-nineteenth century onwards, and the other, Bengalis, many of them Muslim, who have migrated mainly for settled agriculture since the early twentieth century from parts of what is now Bangladesh. The chapter maps the continuous exclusion of each of these communities from security, relief and rehabilitation. It also describes in particular the exclusions faced by children in these conflict-battered communities, reflected in disrupted schooling, poor conditions of health and nutrition, and the lack of inter-community bonding. The authors describe the exclusions of these groups from land and livelihoods, and argue that the struggle for land and resources lies at the heart of conflict in the BTAD.

And finally, the report describes the challenge of addressing the issues of a community like the Jarawa in an Exclusion Report, because for them what we conventionally describe as 'inclusion'—access to certain public goods and involvement in mainstream society—is actually what some scholars describe as 'adverse inclusion'.[31] With the Ang themselves, their exposure to disease, sexual exploitation and economic exploitation by contact with poachers and settlers within and around the reserve, indicate the impact that contact can have. While the optimal balance between contact and isolation is perhaps one that no government has yet established, the government has so far used the logic of numbers to keep the Andaman Trunk Road, which bisects and disrupts the Jarawa Reserve, open despite clear Supreme Court directions for its closure. This, even while research shows that it is mostly used by tourists and supply trucks (which could both be diverted to sea routes) rather than by the residents of settlements along the road, whose rights the administration claims to be defending.[32] At the same time, the Forest Rights Act 2006, a law that operationalises the rights of forest-dwellers over the territory they occupy, has not been notified in the Islands, in effect denying the Ang people ownership rights over their land.

Exclusion by Budgets

One of the big stories this report carries has been to look at India's taxation system and its performance from the perspective of exclusion. It is based on the premise that a well-designed, high tax-GDP ratio could support State capacity to secure social protection, and especially entitlements for the poor and the vulnerable, and help create more equitable outcomes in society. Similarly, a progressive tax system, in which taxes levied take into account the ability of an individual to pay, is a potent redistributive tool facilitating a more inclusive and equitable development process.

However, the chapter on taxation highlights that in India, in contrast to some other emerging economies, the tax-GDP ratio is not adequately favourable to create the required fiscal space for augmenting the supply and quality of public goods and essential social services (primarily on account of the narrow tax base and weaknesses in tax administration). Moreover, the tax system is not progressive enough, particularly at the state level, to address equity and inclusion in the development process. It maintains that the Indian government (both centre and states together) is mobilising less revenue, both tax and non-tax, than many comparable countries. This in turn limits the public expenditure for provision of to public goods, as well as the process of strengthening social and physical infrastructure capacity for India's rapid development.

Further, the report points out that the lower tax revenue mobilisation in India is not because its tax rates are low. Rates of taxation on personal incomes and corporate bodies in India are comparable to many developing and developed countries. It marshals evidence to suggest widespread under-reporting of incomes in India, as a result of which only a small proportion of people who ought to pay income tax actually do so, and others who do file tax returns pay less than they should. The chapter also argues that the indiscriminate use of tax concessions to industry has compromised the resource mobilisation efforts of the government and created the scope for exercising patronage and corruption. Tax exemptions and concessions also violate the principle of equity in taxation, because they favour the well-off who are in a better position to negotiate with the government.

On the other hand, the report argues that a high reliance on indirect taxes disproportionately penalises the poor. Indirect taxes do not differentiate between a poor and a non-poor family—they are included in the prices of goods and services and the end consumer bears the burden of the tax. These tax burdens could have serious consequences for the consumption expenditure and standard of living of poor households.

The report looks at exclusion by budgets from the perspective of public expenditures across chapters, in particular India's chronic underfunding of health and other social services. Only around 1.2 per cent of the country's GDP is public spending on health, far lower than other BRICS countries and even Sri Lanka and Bangladesh in South Asia. Across the chapters in the public goods section of the Report, similar chronic underfunding of public services is observed. In many places across the report we argue that while underfunding of public services has a negative impact on all citizens it has a disproportionately strong negative impact on weaker sections of society and compounds their vulnerabilities.

After the new central government came to power in 2014, it cut government budgets on health by a further 20 per cent (INR 20,431.4 crore in 2014–15). Even within that expenditure, the report presents evidence that while the proportion of revenue expenditure on urban health and family planning services across states was 1.47 times that of rural health and family planning services, more funds have not resulted in greater use of the public sector or better outcomes distributed across urban populations. It notes that in 1992–3, the private health sector accounted for 2.5 per cent of GDP, which more than doubled to 5.6 per cent of the GDP by 2004–5. In the same period, public health spending increased marginally, from 0.74 to 0.92 per cent of GDP.

Consequences of Exclusion

Urban Health

The consequences of exclusions from health care, water and sanitation are, first, higher ill-health burdens among the urban poor. Slums are underserviced with drinking water supply, sanitation and both solid and liquid waste management, contributing to major risk factors for communicable diseases. Malaria, dengue, typhoid, diarrhoea and acute respiratory infections are therefore frequently reported among the urban poor populations. Nearly 50 per cent of urban child mortality is the result of poor sanitation and lack of access to clean drinking water in urban slums. Poor sanitation and unsafe drinking water cause intestinal worm infections, which lead to malnutrition, anaemia and retarded growth among children. Diseases resulting from poor sanitation and unsafe drinking water often lead to children dropping out of school.

If open defaecation is the only option available, women go to defaecate early in the morning and then wait until nightfall, leading to several health issues such as urinary tract infections. Infections due to inadequate water and sanitation are responsible for 15 per cent of maternal deaths, and girls and women face additional problems during menstruation. Lack of access to safe water and sanitation facilities can directly (e.g., trachoma) and indirectly increase the risk of certain kinds of disability. While travelling to fetch water or to defaecate, women and girls are also exposed to the danger of rape, assault and molestation.

Unsafe occupations of the urban poor also generate some unique health burdens, such as injuries to ragpickers due to syringes, broken glass, metals and so on being present in garbage, and from stray dogs; high prevalence of sexually transmitted infections among sex workers; and respiratory and other health issues due to toxic exposure among informal industrial workers.

Such high health burdens combined with multiple exclusions from health care create grim health and economic outcomes for urban poor households. Many simply don't seek health care at all, and choose to wait out their ailments, sometimes resulting in death or permanent disability. The high reliance on profit-centred private hospitals and tertiary-care public hospitals are also a financial burden: For the poorest fifth of urban dwellers, on average the cost to treat a single ailment in a single person is the same as over 10 months of household expenditure; costs are this high or even higher for those who use the private sector more. Data from the 61st Round of the National Sample Survey shows an increase in urban poverty by as much as 2.9 per cent if out-of-pocket health expenditure is accounted for.[33]

Urban Water and Sanitation

The cumulative impact of the denial of access

to water and sanitation is to hold generations to ransom, not ensuring them basic services and a modicum of public health for the foreseeable future. The report observes the huge annual economic losses due to inadequate water and sanitation in India. This was estimated at 2.4 trillion rupees, equivalent to as much as 6.4 per cent of India's GDP in 2006. 72 per cent of this total impact was health-related economic impact, whereas access time and water-related impacts made up the other two main losses. In low-income households that do not have access to piped water, there is also loss of productivity and livelihoods due to time spent in fetching water, or in waiting in queues at community toilets. This burdens women more, as women play a major role in the management and handling of water at the household level.

And finally, the report points to several environmental impacts of the current urban and sanitation situation. The lack of sufficient public supply has resulted in severe groundwater pollution in urban areas. Grave failures in safe collection and treatment of waste water have resulted in widespread pollution of surface and groundwater. These in turn have serious public health impacts that affect everybody, but particularly vulnerable groups who may not be able to afford medical treatment, and are located in the most degraded sites.

Just Conditions of Work for Women

The non-recognition and devaluation of women's care work renders women at a further disadvantage when they enter the remunerated workforce. It also subjects them to double burdens of exclusion, unfairly and disproportionately burdened in both care work and remunerated work. Informal employment, with lower likelihood of stability, earnings and legal protection accounts for a relatively larger share of female than male employment.

Within employment, women's earnings are lower than men's, in part due to the segregation of women into jobs that are deemed of low value and therefore eligible for lower wages, for instance in construction work where they are largely involved in unskilled positions. This 'vertical segregation' manifests also in the health and rural education sectors where care roles are overwhelmingly carried out by women. Unpaid care work also limits time available for paid work. Studies show that most women report primarily doing unpaid work out of compulsion, due to the unavailability of other family members, social and religious constraints or the inability to afford hired help. Additionally, in an unequal labour market, where returns to labour are much lower for women, working on agricultural or non-agricultural subsistence activities represents a rational choice for women as it helps increase household income. Women spend between 8-10 hours more on work compared to men from the same households. Time for rest and leisure is therefore limited; women's leisure time is more likely to be fragmented and secondary, and often conducted simultaneously with other activities, such as cooking.

Vulnerable Groups

Consequences of exclusion are most severe among the intensely vulnerable groups profiled in the report. Typically, single women face even higher exclusions from a wide range of public goods than married women because, as previously discussed, both social norms as well as public policy and law are constructed around the idea of the hetero-normative family. Widows continue to face the most severe forms of social stigma and discrimination from the family and the wider community. The ideal of the chaste and subservient widow still dominates cultural consciousness, denying a life of dignity to widows. In particular, their claims to land and property are silenced by torture, violence and murder in the name of 'witch-hunting'. Women who are alone despite their spouses being alive are similarly discriminated against, and face severe exploitation—physical, sexual and economic.

Never-married women are frequently seen as sexually available, socially unequal, or both.

Among Devadasis, the report notes intense exclusion from public goods like education and health. In its survey in three states, it found 78 per cent women were non-literate, and as few as six per cent had completed high school. It also finds them with a high incidence of sexually transmitted diseases, cardiovascular disease, tuberculosis, alcohol and tobacco abuse, and mental illness. As they grow older, they have no access to social security of any kind and survive mainly by hard manual labour.

The chapter on communal violence maps the loss of homes and lack of shelter, sexual violence, dropping out from school and college, the breakdown of livelihoods, and the shattering of social relations that follows a riot. Sexual violence had an especially marginalising effect on women; the continuing fear led to severe restrictions on the women's movement outside their homes. Concerns about 'family honour' and fear of further violence resulted in a large number of under-age girls among survivor families, especially those in relief camps, being married off, ironically with the state government fuelling the push with cash incentives for such weddings.

Fear and insecurity affected schooling, with a large incidence of drop-outs. Many joined the ranks of child labour, helping their families in brick kilns or other odd jobs in towns. The months-long gap in schooling due to displacement, loss of books and uniform, and insecurity and uncertainty weighing heavy on victim families, meant that schooling was severely compromised. The drop-out rate was highest among girls. The breaking of bonds of shelter and livelihood have resulted in the pauperisation of survivors: those who were mobile shop owners, cloth merchants, artisans and other artisanal classes were reduced to taking up unskilled work in agricultural fields, brick kilns and the odd daily wage to make ends meet. For women who were engaged in agricultural work before the violence, even these options have been closed off due to security and dignity concerns. Finally, the violence left a permanent divide between communities: a significant degree of social intercourse and trust between the communities has been destroyed, with a prevailing sense of betrayal. This is manifested in the separation of populations on religious lines and the homogenisation of habitations, resulting in greater polarisation.

The chapter on the survivors of ethnic violence in Assam observes that after each major incident of ethnic violence, people were driven into relief camps, either due to loss of property, or due to fear. The government set up and provisioned the relief camps, and paid compensation. However, after this, the government considered its duty done, and stopped both assisting in rehabilitation, as well as tracking what happened to people when they left the camps. Effectively, this meant that the government assumed people were returning home, and that things had returned to normal. In reality, however, many people are afraid to or unable to return to their homes, and either continue to live unofficially in camps (which are not recognised), or in camp-like situations on the edges of their own, or other, villages. They continue to face numerous denials of many basic public goods including security, sometimes for prolonged periods, and in some camps, for generations. The term 'encroachers' is used as a reference to Bengali Muslims and also perpetuates the discrimination and exclusion faced by the community.

Regarding the Jarawa, the report underlines the dominant impact of the refusal of the local administration to close the Andaman Trunk Road, despite clear instructions from the Supreme Court to do so many years earlier. The road forces the Jarawas into a degree and kind of unequal interaction with the outside world that they never agreed to and find difficult to cope with. The road opens up possibilities for incursions into the reserve all along its length, particularly from the numerous small settlements—mostly illegal—that have come up there, and from tourists and poachers who subject them to many forms of sexual and economic exploitation. Contact and curiosity have led at least some Jarawas to experiment with, and develop a taste for, outsider food, clothing and commodities (including intoxicants) which involves them in highly exploitative, and sometimes dangerous, exchanges and interactions with outsiders.

Pathways to Inclusion

The report attempts to identify good practices that promote the access of otherwise excluded communities to public goods, especially those which are public-led or at least substantially public-funded.

Urban Health

The chapter on urban public health mentions free primary health services in clean facilities (in Pimpri Chinchwad), timely surveillance, disease prevention and outbreak response (in Chennai, Kolkata and Madurai) and a strong community outreach component (in Raipur). The Chennai Municipal Corporation has established a Primary Health Centre exclusively for Senior Citizens, which provides easy and affordable access to medicines and health facilities for common medical issues experienced by the vulnerable elderly population. The Pune Municipal Corporation has collaborated with the SWaCH (Solid Waste Collection and Handling) Cooperative by cost-effectively managing a majority of the city's solid wastes, combined with reversing the problem of exclusion of waste pickers from urban health resources. This is accomplished primarily by making this population visible but also reducing the institutional bias that these individuals normally face by making them partners of the corporation. It also describes some purely non-government initiatives, such as the Sadbhavna Trust working with Bhopal gas survivors in homeless recovery shelters by Aman Biradari in Delhi, and places of safety and treatment for homeless mentally ill women established by the Banyan in Chennai. Although these are non-governmental initiatives, the authors believe that they carry the potential for large-scale replication by public systems for inclusion of vulnerable urban populations into health care.

Among its many detailed recommendations for promoting inclusion in urban public health care, derived from the Technical Resource Group of the Urban Health Mission, the report calls for creating primary health institutions that are physically, economically and socially accessible to urban poor populations. At the base is a nursing station-cum-health sub-centre that should provide all primary health care that does not require the presence of doctors—preventive and promotional health activities, health literacy activities, health and nutrition counselling, vaccinations, antenatal care, regular supplies of drugs, follow-up tests and counselling, and regular free medication for all common urban ailments. The majority of urban primary health centres must be established within or near settlements where the urban poor and other marginalised groups reside, with special Primary Health Centres for the completely excluded, i.e., homeless populations and street children.

In order to address factors that produce exclusion, there should be no requirements of identity proof or documents for those seeking health services. All forms should ask for mother's name only, instead of father's or husband's name, which can discourage or stigmatise children of single women or sex workers. Similarly, as is increasingly the practice, the option to register with one's transgender identity should also be permitted. Urban primary health centres must fix their operating hours in consideration of the working populations that they serve: typically 3 to 9 pm daily, with the exception of centres in red-light areas which could operate in the morning hours. All these services should be entirely free of cost for all individuals. On a rotational basis, special clinics for the aged and differently abled could be introduced in existing facilities, supported by local youth volunteers. Providers of health services, particularly urban primary health centres, should have a formalised help desk and counseling centre run by trained, medical social workers. Such social workers should serve as the first point of contact for survivors of violence, children without adult guardianship, as well as for old and disabled persons.

Urban Water and Sanitation

The report regards many principles incorporated into the National Urban Sanitation Policy (2008)—which aims to achieve open defaecation-free cities with all urban households having access to safe and hygienic sanitation facilities—as progressive and carrying the potential to promote greater inclusion. These include the focus on universal coverage and on 100 per cent treatment of waste, along with the delinking of service delivery from tenure security. The Service Level Benchmarking initiative for environmental services—water, waste water, solid waste and drainage—launched in 2008, is one of the first attempts at the national level to collect data for an expanded set of indicators. In the sanitation sector, benchmarks include coverage of toilets, sewerage network services, collection efficiency, quality of sewage treatment, etc.

In the Parivartan programme in Ahmedabad begun in 1996, the participating slums were provided an assurance by the Corporation that they would not be evicted for the next 10 years. Even though it was not legally binding, it helped facilitate community participation for the upgradation of physical infrastructure (water supply, sanitation, drainage, roads) with significant funds arranged by the Corporation. Starting in 2000, the Bangalore Water Supply and Sewerage Board (BWSSB) started considering the urban poor as potential customers. For this, the requirement of formal tenure documents for new connections was replaced with simple occupancy proof (to address concerns of land tenure), connection fees were reduced and tariff structure for domestic water was revised to introduce lower minimum monthly charge (to address concerns of affordability), and shared connections were offered as an alternative.

The purpose of these examples of inclusion is to demonstrate that, given the required resolve and imagination, public institutions and programmes, or at least public-supported programmes, can secure much higher inclusion in access to important public goods.

The focus of public programmes needs to be on improvements that will benefit all and not a select few. As in Bengaluru and Ahmedabad, provision of services needs to be delinked from tenure security or land ownership, and made affordable and reliable for all. Greater inclusion can also be accomplished by increasing investment in low capital-intensive systems that address the needs of more people, disincentivising excess demand and wastage, and strengthening water and sanitation services in public spaces, which are used especially by homeless and floating populations. While universal access does not necessarily mean provisioning of services for free, services can be kept affordable by setting lifeline water tariffs for the urban poor, along with the provision of de-sludging services. In order to increase accountability and effectiveness in service provision, the report recommends the strengthening of urban local bodies and de-concentration of municipal functions relating to water and sanitation. Mandating 100 per cent treatment of septage and waste water will also go a long way in checking pollution of potable and ground water, with suitable regulations, enforcement, and public investments. Improving collection and disposal functions is crucial to obviate the need for degrading forms of work like manual scavenging.

Just Conditions of Work for Women

Whereas the report recognises that just conditions of work for women would require the battling and dismantling of patriarchy as well as of the neo-liberal framework of the globally dominant economic model, its recommendations focus on the role of the state, or national and state governments, to ensure justice to women as workers. It calls for the state to first recognise and measure unpaid care work, and to accord it the value that is due to it. It also calls for the state to share women's burdens of care work, such as by establishing crèches and day-care centres for children and the aged, and supporting professional home-based care of the ailing aged.

It further recommends the extensive review and reform of labour laws with a much clearer recognition of the fact that women constitute about half the workforce. They should be permitted to undertake night work under safe conditions of work and transport. Work outsourced as home-based work should also entail the same responsibilities for safety, health, minimum wages, social security and overtime payments as for factory-based work.

It also calls for the ban on child labour to extend to adolescent children until they have attained their required education levels, and the recognition that culturally sanctioned practices such as caste-based sex work are actually forced labour in unacceptable conditions. It seeks a much stronger enforcement mechanism for laws that ensure justice and safety of women in work, such as those against sexual harassment in the workplace, against forced and bonded work and child labour, for equal remuneration and conditions in the workplace, the comprehensive decriminalisation of sex work voluntarily undertaken by consenting adults, even as sex work by children and trafficking are more effectively halted, and bringing an end to undignified and illegal tasks such as manual scavenging.

We call for a much stronger framework of social protection, which is individual-based, and therefore accessible to women workers. We call for a strengthening of the legal safeguards underlying the MGNREGA to ensure that it is actually demand-driven, and that women are able to secure work for at least 100 days a year and receive timely wage payments. And finally, beyond the chosen scope of this chapter (we propose to devote a chapter in the next India Exclusion Report to this), we also recommend stronger rights of inheritance for women, and promoting their ownership of land and capital.

Vulnerable Groups

Among the many recommendations for greater inclusion of single women is the recognition of women as de facto heads of households (as in the National Food Security Act), strengthening rights to property ownership and inheritance for women, and amending unjust aspects of personal laws that deal with marriage, divorce, maintenance and inheritance. Legislative amendments are also proposed to ensure the right to maintenance and property for those who may be legally disqualified by virtue of not having a 'valid' marriage in law. Again, because single women and their dependents are often excluded from, or suffer humiliation while accessing, government programmes, the report again recommends that the requirement to provide husband's or father's name should be replaced by being required to specify only the mother's name. It also proposes supporting efforts to organise and collectivise single women, institutionalising practices of gender budgeting, as well as filling gaps in data on gender-based exclusion through further research.

For Devadasis, apart from seeking strengthened enforcement of the many laws that should protect minor girls from 'dedication' and sex-work—including those related to trafficking and child labour—the report also makes important preventive recommendations. These include that all girls from the community and Devadasis' girl children get free and compulsory quality education, with priority in admissions and scholarships. Girl children at risk of dedication should be separated from their families, and be entitled to an extended safety stay in residential homes, rather than the conventional 'rescue homes' which are stigmatised and often custodial in nature. Instead, in residential hostels they can have access to inclusive education as well. Girls above 14 years should be imparted training in life skills and vocational skills to increase their employment opportunities. For Devadasis with no or unproductive land, the government could include providing fertile land with irrigation facilities and credit among the measures for their welfare. In addition to land, the government needs to provide grants for income-generating activities and enterprise promotion support—all of which must be based on credible data gathered from up-to-date, comprehensive surveys of Devadasis.

For survivors of communal violence, recommendations include strengthening the rule of law, and ensuring that the accused are prosecuted and justice is delivered. Related to this is also the demand for ensuring security of life and property, both in relief camps and villages. Legal action must also include countering the politics of hate and polarisation, through prosecution of those who make hate speeches and taking action against irresponsible media reporting. Relief, compensation and rehabilitation are areas that require significant focus in Muzaffarnagar, as well as for survivors of violence everywhere. There is an urgent need for a national policy on compensation, so that it becomes a right that survivors are entitled to automatically, rather than the system of awarding compensation which is usually an outcome of political negotiations between the government and survivors; and to work towards establishing uniformity among the types and quantum of compensation across states and groups affected. Efforts to create opportunities for dialogue between communities would also be helpful in the months ahead.

Recommendations for survivors of ethnic violence are similar in the sense that a more comprehensive policy regarding relief is sought. To ensure a comprehensive rehabilitation process, it is recommended that the state provide comprehensive support to those affected, which includes discussions on peace-building and long-term solutions that address persistent violence in the BTAD. A national policy on internally displaced persons should be formed, whether resulting from conflict, disaster, land acquisition or other factors, as proposed in the draft of the Communal and Targeted Violence Bill prepared by the National Advisory Council.[3] A strong case has also been made for police reform, with the recognition that an excessive reliance on the military undermines security and trust among communities. Acknowledging the effects on children, the report recommends the creation of spaces where children from different communities can interact with each other and bridge the gap. A support group to help children cope with the anxieties that emerge from living in conflict would also be a significant contribution.

In the context of the Jarawas, the report acknowledges that there are very few examples anywhere in the world of isolated indigenous communities with rich self-contained cultures and livelihood patterns being integrated with outside economies and cultures in ways that are genuinely voluntary, humane, just, non-exploitative and egalitarian. On the contrary, most such contacts have typically been of 'adverse inclusion', resulting in intense dispossession, sexual and economic exploitation, alarming health and nutrition declines as well as precarious survival. Some of these trends and dangers are already visible with the Jarawas, although they have voluntarily engaged with the outside world for only a quarter-century. Recognising these dangers, but also that contact with the outside world is now irreversible, the report makes detailed recommendations to protect the Ang from 'adverse inclusion', which include early and strict compliance with Supreme Court orders to close the Andaman Trunk Road, creation of sea routes as an alternative for other populations to use, stronger policing of the forests and waters of the reserve area against poachers and tourists, and ensuring that the community rights of the Ang to their forest reserve are legally recognised and codified so that they are not reduced in the future. Above all, the report underlines the imperative to treat the tribe as equals, possessing the agency and wisdom to decide their best interests.

Concluding Words

The picture that emerges from the report is in many ways grim and troubling, one that affirms that there continue to be significant populations that are consistently and often extremely deprived of access to public goods that are essential for a human life with dignity. Those who suffer these exclusions tend to be from communities that are historically disadvantaged by gender, caste, class, religion, disability and age. It underlines many structural barriers—of persisting patriarchy, macro-economic policy, the unjust design of laws and policies and their implementation—that create formidable barriers for women even today to access just conditions of work. Single women, those in caste-based occupations like the Devadasis, people who survive violence targeting their religion and ethnicity, and members of isolated tribes are vulnerable groups whose conditions this report especially tries to highlight. In urban contexts, the Report also identifies homeless persons and those living in slums, as well as those in unsafe, underpaid and often humiliating occupations, such as casual daily wage work, rickshaw-pulling, waste-picking, sex work, domestic work and street vending among those who are most disadvantaged.

The report recognises many sources of this exclusion, such as patriarchy, caste discrimination, communal prejudice and profiling, but also the functioning of neo-liberal market capitalism. However, its primary focus, for reasons elaborated in the opening sections of the report, is on the role of the state. The diagnosis for exclusion is therefore located in the institutional bias of state institutions, in the faulty design of laws, policies and programmes, and bias, inefficiency and corruption in the implementation of these laws, policies and programmes. It looks carefully at budgetary exclusions: not just at low budgetary allocations for provisioning of these public goods, but also at exclusions in taxation. An extremely important section of the report examines questions of whether we tax enough, and whether we tax the right people, in order to enable the state to ensure equitable access of all to public goods.

However, the report also finds examples in every case of public-led inclusion, confirming that if state policies are designed suitably and sensitively to ensure inclusion of vulnerable populations, it is eminently possible to do so. These examples light small lamps of hope, and lessons need to be learnt from them for large-scale replication. In all its chapters, the Report also offers detailed recommendations for policy-makers to consider, to enhance inclusion in public policy, law and programmes.

It is fitting at the end of this second India Exclusion Report to recall the wise and compassionate counsel to the nation by Babasaheb Bhimrao Ambedkar at the moment when the people of India adopted the Constitution they gave unto themselves. He said:

On the 26th of January 1950, we are going to enter into a life of contradictions. In politics we will have equality and in social and economic life we will have inequality. In politics we will be recognising the principle of one man[35] *one vote and one vote one value. In our social and economic life, we shall, by reason of our social and economic structure, continue to deny the principle of one man one value. How long shall we continue to live this life of contradictions? How long shall we continue to deny equality in our social and economic life?*

The stories in this India Exclusion Report, and the last, are a sobering reminder that India continues to live the life of contradictions that Ambedkar spoke of so presciently six and a half decades ago. We persist in denying that last woman her equal value, her equal dignity. Indeed how long will we continue to do so?

Endnotes

1. For a more detailed discussion of the public goods concept, see Introduction, *India Exclusion Report 2013–14,* New Delhi: Books for Change, pp. 2-5.
2. Des Gasper (2007), 'What is the capability approach?: Its core, rationale, partners and dangers', *The Journal of Socio-Economics* 36.3 (2007), pp. 335–359.
3. Joseph E. Stiglitz, Amartya Sen, and Jean-Paul Fitoussi (2010), *Mismeasuring our lives: Why GDP doesn't add up*, New York: The New Press.
4. Mahbub ul Haq (1994), *New Imperatives of Human Security*, New Delhi: Rajiv Gandhi Institute for Contemporary Studies.
5. Talk delivered by author in New Delhi, 17 December 2015.
6. Flavio Comim, Mozaffar Qizilbash and Sabina Alkire (eds) (2008), *The Capability Approach: Concepts, Measures and Applications*, Cambridge: Cambridge University Press.
7. John Rawls, *A Theory of Justice*, Massachusetts: Belknap, p. 5.
8. Amartya Sen (1999), 'Global Justice: Beyond International Equity', in Inge Kaul, Marc Stern and Isabelle Grunberg (eds), *Global Public Goods*, New York: UNDP.
9. Martha C. Nussbaum (2013), *Political Emotions*, Harvard: Harvard University Press.
10. Comim proceeds to test for the strength of publicness in the BRICS for all three levels, and concludes, on the basis of the data he draws on, that India (like South Africa) is very far below Brazil, Russia and, most significantly as a relevant comparison, China.
11. Martin Bronfenbrenner (1973), 'Equality and Equity', *The ANNALS of the American Academy of Political and Social Science* 409:1, pp. 9–23.
12. Dev Nathan and Virginius Xaxa (2012), 'Introduction and Overview' in Dev Nathan and Virginius Xaxa (eds), *Social Exclusion and Adverse Inclusion: Development and Deprivation of Adivasis in India*, New York: Oxford University Press, pp. 1–19.
13. I. Hirway and R. Antonopoulous (2010), *Unpaid Work and the Economy, London:* Palgrave Macmillan, pp. 7–9.
14. Padmini Swaminathan (2009), 'Outside the Realm of Protective Labour Legislation: Saga of Unpaid Labour in India', *Economic and Political Weekly* Vol. 44: 44, pp. 80–87.
15. See: Rashtriya Garima Abhiyan (RGA), National Campaign on Dalit Human Rights (NCDHR) and the International Dalit Solidarity Network (IDSN) (2014), *Violations of the Right to Water and Sanitation*, p. 4. Available at: 'http://idsn.org/wp-content/uploads/2015/12/Joint-Submission-SR-on-water-and-Sanitation-RGA-NCDHR-and-IDSN.pdf; Jan Sahas Social Development Society (2014), *Socio Economic Status of Women Manual Scavengers* [Baseline Study Report -2014], pp 9. Available at: http://in.one.un.org/img/uploads/Socio_Economic_Status_of_Women_Manual_Scavengers_Report.pdf.
16. Human Rights Watch (2014), 'Cleaning Human Waste: 'Manual Scavenging', Caste and Discrimination in India'. Available at: https://www.hrw.org/report/2014/08/25/cleaning-human-waste/manual-scavenging-caste-and-discrimination-india
17. R. Shukla (2013), 'A Walk Through the Labyrinths of Sex Work Law' in L. Murthy and M. S. Seshu (eds), *The Business of Sex*, pp. 212–42.
18. See for instance: S. Madhok (2005), *Report on the Status of Women Workers in the Construction Industry,* New Delhi: National Commission for Women.

    Available at: http://ncw.nic.in/pdfreports/women%20workers%20in%20construction%20industry.pdf
19. NSSO (2012), *Employment and Unemployment among Social Groups in India*; C. Kompier, A. Prasad, S. Hassan, S. Premchander, S. Katiyar, D. Saheb, D. Verma, N. Saigal, R. Chaudhary and S. Taware (2014), 'Labour markets: Exclusion from Decent Work' in *India Exclusion Report* 2013–14, New Delhi: Books for Change, p. 116.
20. N. Neetha (2013), 'Inequalities Reinforced? Social Groups, Gender and Employment'. *CWDS Occasional Paper*, p. 54.

21. See for instance: Government of India (2006), *Social, Economic and Educational Status of the Muslim Community of India*. New Delhi: GOI, pp. 95–96
22. A. Bheemeshwar Reddy (2014), 'Labour Force Participation of Elderly in India', (Conference paper presented at Population Association of America: 2014 Annual Meeting Program) Available at: http://paa2014.princeton.edu/papers/141609
23. Ibid.
24. Martha Nussbaum (2000), 'Women's Capabilities and Social Justice', *Journal of Human Development* 1:2, pp. 219-247.
25. For instance, see: Mukesh Eswaran, Bharat Ramaswami, and Wilima Wadhwa (2013). 'Status, Caste, and the Time Allocation of Women in Rural India', *Economic Development and Cultural Change* 61:2, pp. 311–33.
26. Case study of women from tribal communities in Dahod, Gujarat, provided for this chapter by Anandi.
27. Jayati Ghosh and C.P. Chandrasekhar (2014), 'Growth, Employment Patterns and Inequality in Asia: A Case Study of India' (No. 486985). International Labour Organization, p. 19. Available at: http://www.ilo.org/wcmsp5/groups/public/---asia/---ro-bangkok/documents/publication/wcms_334063.pdf
28. Ibid.
29. State governments have the power to declare a manufacturing unit as not meeting the above criteria also as a 'factory'.
30. Section 48 deals with crèches.
31. Nathan and Xaxa, 'Introduction', pp. 1–19.
32. Richa Dhanchu (2003), 'Traffic on the Andaman Trunk Road', in Annexures, *The Jarawa Tribal Reserve Dossier*, Paris: UNESCO.
33. I. Gupta (2009), 'Out of Pocket Expenditures and Poverty: Estimates from NSS 61st Round'. Paper presented for consideration of the Expert Group on Poverty, Planning Commission. Delhi: Institute of Economic Growth. Available at:http://planningcommission.gov.in/reports/genrep/indrani.pdf.
34. Prevention of Communal and Targeted Violence (Access to Justice and Reparations) Bill, 2011 Available at:http://www.prsindia.org/uploads/media/draft/NAC%20Draft%20Communal%20Violence%20Bill%202011.pdf.
35. In our understanding, Ambedkar clearly uses the term 'one man' to refer to an individual, irrespective of gender, whose intrinsic value is to be respected.

Part I – Public Goods

'Who cares?'

Urban Health Care and Exclusion

Devaki Nambiar, Prathibha Ganesan and Adita Rao[*]

Girish Motwani, Radhika Alkazi, Ganapathy Murugan, T Sundararaman and Dipa Sinha[**]

In 2015, Delhi experienced possibly the worst dengue outbreak the national capital had seen in the last 20 years—the official count reaching 14,889 cases, and 32 official deaths (44 unofficial) as of November 2015.[1] The heartbreaking deaths of young children in Delhi—and in one case, the double suicide of parents refusing to survive their neglected seven-year-old—trained the spotlight on the gross deficiencies of the health system: the shortage of beds, doctors, blood banks, and medicines in both the public and private sectors.[2] In response, the state government sprung into action, launching a 24-hour helpline to provide all relevant information about dengue and awareness campaigns through TV and radio advertisements.[3] The standard control measure of fumigation,belated and controversial,[4] was redoubled.[5] A number of beds were made available for treatment across hospitals[6] and limits set on prices for various tests.[7] News reports dubbed dengue the great leveller, an 'equal opportunity' infection that did not spare Delhi's better-off.[8]

Such a claim is hard to substantiate. For the 32 official dengue deaths in Delhi from August through October of 2015, there were close to 500 deaths of homeless persons in just August and September.[9] Although it is not clear what proportion of these are attributable to dengue, many likely are, seeing as a large number of homeless persons interact with garbage on a daily basis (either for a living or to subsist) and have no choice but to sleep near stagnant pools of water, both risk factors for infection. Dengue is far from being a leveller for this population, for whom the deadliest month was June of 2015, when the toll crossed 3,500 in the capital city, according to a study published earlier in 2015.[10] As a pavement dweller from Eastern Delhi, Chajju Ram, conveyed to a reporter this fall: 'At a time when the city is facing a dengue crisis, we are still living under the open sky. But who cares?'[11]

This question, about caring, is the heart of the matter in this chapter.

What is Urban Health Care?

As the dengue example amply demonstrates, there is a lack of both care and caring when it comes to health in Indian cities. Health, a state of well-being, is the embodiment of myriad factors: food and nutrition, water and sanitation, education, employment and social security, shaped by societal

* Lead authors

** Contributing authors

*** This chapter was reviewed by Bhrigupathy Singh, Ravi Duggal, Harsh Mander, Rajib Dasgupta, Indranil, Mukhopadhyay, Erhard Berner and Kinjal Sampat

determinants. Conversely, as made plain in the People's Health Charter of 2000, 'Inequality, poverty, exploitation, violence and injustice are at the root of ill-health and the deaths of poor and marginalised people.'[12] Health is critically shaped also by health care, defined as 'a) appropriate infrastructure in the form of primary health centres with attendant basic facilities; b) skilled human resources like medical professionals and other health care and paramedical staff rendering required range of services; c) medicines and supplies which are basic and essential; d) emergency medical care; e) patient information, redressal and f) monitoring and professional accountability.'[13] Health care involves the provision of services—promotive, preventive,curative and rehabilitative—that may be delivered at the individual level (e.g., treatment for a disease) or to populations (e.g., screening for an illness) in communities, through specialised health facilities and other outlets (like pharmacies) and involve a complex mix of providers that may operate in the public and/or private sectors, for profit and not-for-profit, are formally accredited or informal, professional or non-professional, allopathic or from other systems and praxes of medicine, remunerated or voluntary.[14]

Health care, where we place our emphasis in this chapter, is necessary but not adequate for the health of populations. Yet, it is a critical starting point for the achievement of health equity,[15] which as per WHO is defined as 'the absence of avoidable or remediable differences among populations or groups defined socially, economically, demographically, or geographically; thus, health inequities involve more than inequality—whether in health determinants or outcomes, or in access to the resources needed to improve and maintain health—but also a failure to avoid or overcome such inequality that infringes human rights norms or is otherwise unfair.'[16]As Beauchamp (1976) indicates,

> The critical barrier to dramatic reductions in death and disability is a social ethic that unfairly protects the most numerous or the most powerful from the burdens of prevention…This is the issue of justice…Under social justice all persons are entitled equally to key ends such as health protection or minimum standards of income. Further, unless collective burdens are accepted, powerful forces of environment, heredity or social structure will preclude a fair distribution of these ends. While many forces influenced the development of public health, the historic dream of public health that preventable death and disability ought to be minimized is a dream of social justice.'[17,18]

Thirty-two years later, the WHO Commission on Social Determinants of Health put it quite simply: 'social injustice is killing people on a grand scale.'[19] Health and health care are therefore a matter of redressing and averting the very embodiment of injustice.

Urban health care

According to the latest 2011 Indian Census, an urban area is defined as either all places with a municipality, corporation, cantonment board or notified town area committee, etc. or all other places which satisfied the following criteria: (i) a minimum population of 5,000; (ii) at least 75 per cent of the male main working population engaged in non-agricultural pursuits; and (iii) a density of population of at least 400 persons per sq km (these are just moderate deviations from prior definitions employed up till 1991).[20]

For the purposes of this chapter, urban health care is defined as affordable, accountable, appropriate health services of assured quality (promotive, preventive, curative and rehabilitative)—including all the infrastructure, human resources, supplies and diagnostics, provisions for emergencies, patient information/ redressal, and monitoring and accountability—for all populations living in areas defined by the 2011 Census as urban. There is a strong legal and moral precedent for health care as a human right that the Indian state has the duty to respect, protect and fulfil. [21,22,23,24]

Why is urban health care a public good?

Health care, while it can be purchased on the market, can be argued in many ways to constitute a non-excludable and non-rivalrous public good. Take for example tuberculosis. No doubt those who can afford and access care have earlier chances of being diagnosed and treated, which in turn reduces the risk of everyone in the population getting this disease. The mechanism here is herd immunity, defined as an immunological benefit accruing to those who are not direct beneficiaries of a service.[25]

Many global health challenges and their solutions have the properties of global public goods. Aspects of health care as a global public good can be categorised into three broad areas: knowledge and technologies; policy and regulation; and health systems.[26] First, knowledge and technologies, particularly for vaccines and pharmaceuticals, may be commodified as private goods, but need to be clubbed with public infrastructure to ensure access. Second, policy and regulatory regimes in health (e.g., monitoring quality of care in facilities) are also public goods that apply to large populations. Health systems themselves are public goods that need to function effectively in order to ensure the wellness of populations.

Given its epidemiological dimensions mentioned earlier, health care is more accurately defined as a merit good.* A merit good is one whose consumption benefits us individually and the society as a whole, even as individuals and groups in society may not avail of health services of their own accord.[27] The state, then, in its paternalistic role, has the responsibility of paying for such goods. A typical example of this in the health sector is vaccination. While all may not want to get vaccination, the societal benefits of vaccination are such that most governments, including India's, offer them for free.

Another argument, building on a critique of the notion of 'goods', includes health along with protection, food, shelter, and basic resources that are seen together as 'commons', or that which we all share as human beings.[28] The view taken here is that exclusion from health is not an issue of the poor; rather, it is an issue demanding the solidarity and participation of all. As the Fourth Global Health Watch says,

> As neoliberalism has focussed exclusively on competition and flexibility, it has destroyed social relations and communities. This means that not only do individuals have to be protected, but so do societies. This collective dimension is particularly important when poverty is seen not as an individual problem of poor people, but rather as a social relationship. It can never be eradicated if the whole of society is not involved. This demands solidarity and the participation of all.[29]

The role of the state

Governance of population health in urban areas necessarily must fall within the purview of the state, both in the acute sense of providing emergency or ongoing care during ill-health and in the sense of creating an enabling environment for well-being. The arguments for this are many—legal, moral, and economic.

The Directive Principles of State Policy of the Indian Constitution explicitly state that the government is responsible for the determinants of citizens' health, including health care.[30,31] Following the 73rd and 74th Constitutional Amendment Acts

* We are grateful to Dr Indranil Mukkhopadhyay for pointing this out.

Box A. Public Health Services in India: A Historical Snapshot*

Independent India's first planning exercise was prefigured around health. Led by Sir Joseph Bhore, the Health Survey and Development Committee (1943) sought to expand the narrow, urban, elite-centric scope of health service delivery to the scale of an independent nation. In the years following, countries across the world set about establishing or expanding health systems using principles of welfare and the broad-based WHO definition of health.[32] In India, at a systems level, growing emphasis on family planning and population control in the late 1960s began to deflect attention away from health, particularly among the vulnerable, while international donor aid for vertical, technology-driven disease control programmes further compartmentalised health into packages and pockets of care.

[33]Internationally, however, the 1960s and 1970s were a watershed in the understanding of the limits to modern biomedical care and its approach. The landmark 1978 Alma Ata Declaration's definition of health was reinforced by subsequent high-level policy processes in Europe,[34,35] and most recently in the WHO Commission on Social Determinants of Health in 2008.[36] In practice, however, various interests were setting a course away from this vision even as the ink was drying on the Alma Ata Declaration; the world seems to have only moved farther and farther away from this public vision of health.[37]

The years following Alma Ata saw a debt repayment crisis, and concern moved from the provision of public services in individual countries to salvaging the international banking system (dominated by First World countries). This move was reinforced by Structural Adjustment Policies introduced the world over, and in India in the early 1990s. The terms of these policies included sharp cuts in public spending on education and health, removal of subsidies and lifting of price controls on food products (thus impacting nutrition) among others.[38] Acquiescing to these terms, India reduced its allocation to health services by 20 per cent between 1992 and 1993.[39] The groundwork laid at this time—part of the neoliberal Washington Consensus promoted the world over, has mostly endured: support for the private sector has shot up in the health sector in India; underfunding in the public sector such that it can no longer afford, adequately purchase or provide care—shifting this burden to the citizen, and the creation of a division between efficiency and equity (in a fiscal situation where the public sector would be guaranteed to under-perform).[40]

The 1990s onwards marked a significant shift in the role played by the state in terms of its responsibilities to its citizens, and its positionality vis-à-vis the private sector, even in the design of ostensibly 'pro-poor' welfare. The mere fact of introducing reforms in 'mission' and 'scheme' mode (i.e., time-bound and therefore ever tenuous), introducing 'architectural corrections' to the system using ad hoc modes such as contracted labour, targeted programming, as well as demand-side and performance-based incentives are indicative of this shift. Such approaches are necessarily precarious in terms of financing. At the same time, there has been encouragement of Indian Foreign Direct Investment—Indian corporate hospitals franchising care across a host of other countries, thereby adding to their revenue, the amount of their capital and by extension, influence.[41] As Bisht and colleagues have pointed out, the shift has occurred among these corporations from service delivery to medical education, consultancy, clinical research and other areas, allowing them wider and growing influence on the health sector in India overall.[42] While public expenditure on health has stagnated since 2011, the private health care industry has burgeoned at a 15 per cent compounded annual growth rate—more than double that of all other services.[43]

* *We are grateful for inputs from Dr Ganapathy Murugan here.*

of 1992, Article 243G of the Eleventh Schedule and Article 243W of the Twelfth Schedule provides for municipalities to be endowed, by states, with powers to promote public health.[44,45] They have the mandate, therefore, to establish or maintain dispensaries, expand services, abate dangerous trades and practices, supply water, administer vaccinations, and dispose of waste, harmful substances, and control outbreaks.[46] A tall list of legislations concerned largely with regulation also place the state squarely in the role of steward of the health care system (these range from the Drugs and Cosmetics Act of 1940 to the Clinical Establishments Act of 2010).

Emphasising the public nature of health, whether we choose to call it a merit good or otherwise, is very important. It could be that for most commodities and services, the market forces of supply and demand would act simultaneously to bring some degree of control unless there is a clear monopoly. In health care, given the high degrees of information asymmetry, even where there is no monopoly, providers can price services on the principle of 'whatever the market can bear'. This is referred to, by Beauchamp, as market-justice wherein 'while society does prohibit individuals from causing direct harm to others, and has in many instances regulated clear public health hazards, the norm of market justice is still dominant and the primary duty to avert disease and injury still rests with the individual.'[47]

With increasing (uneven) urbanisation, urban poverty is becoming starkly visible. The peculiar features of urban areas have yet to be comprehensively considered in the design of urban programmes and schemes. It is more common for programmes to be replications of rural schemes. There is thus a situation where on the one hand, the urban is the site of growing populations of the vulnerable and also of dwindling provision of public services for all, including the excluded.

In India, the emphasis, that too, scant, of public provisioning by the state has been in rural areas, combined with a massive retreat from public provisioning of care in urban areas. This is further shaped by a most dramatic underfunding of health since the period of Economic Liberalisation from 1991 onwards, whereupon allocations to health were reduced drastically, and incentives for privatisation of health service provisioning were ratcheted up.[48] This paradoxical tendency of the state to eschew responsibility for providing health, and deregulate private provisioning has had results that are literally embodied in the ill health of urban populations.

Exclusions from Urban Health Care

Exclusion from public goods is dynamic and operates across multiple levels in the public and private spheres.[49,50] The relative position of an individual or group often narrows down to whether or not the person or persons are marginalised as a result of social, economic, political and community-level factors, which as Oommen argues, 'could be partial or complete'.[51] The partially excluded are recognised by the state, and benefit from policies and reform measures, while the totally excluded are invisible to, criminalised or otherwise denigrated by the state. While we recognise all these forms of exclusion to be deeply intertwined, our emphasis here is on exclusion where state intervention is desirable. In either case, the meaning and experience of social exclusion is necessarily relative,[52] and painfully more pronounced in urban areas: the most affluent neighbourhoods look over the most blighted; enclaves of prosperity, commerce and creativity abut ghettoes of poverty, exclusion and ostracism.

The most common and recalcitrant feature of urban exclusion in the context of health, is poverty. While agricultural labour is the primary occupation for a majority of the rural poor, the urban poor tend towards another extreme—falling into a breathtakingly wide range of economic activities, often multiple, and mostly informal in nature.[53,54] This both reflects and perpetuates an altogether different set of conditions, capacities, and destinies for the urban poor, which the Planning Commission sought to understand in 2010. It constituted an expert group under the chairmanship of Prof S.R. Hashim to develop a methodology to understand urban poverty. The Hashim Committee Report, submitted in 2012, indicated three types of vulnerability that typify urban poverty: residential, social and occupational vulnerability.[55] Between 2013–14, this framework was used to understand the depth of exclusion by the Technical Resource Group (TRG)* supporting the newly launched National Urban Health Mission (NUHM), to understand urban vulnerability in relation to health. Notwithstanding its possible limitations, we apply this framework in our analysis.

Residential vulnerability arises in the absence of adequate shelter; this includes the lack of housing, precarious and illegal housing. The Hashim Committee report states,

> Swelling populations, fragile and insecure incomes and a legal and regulatory regime that is extremely hostile to the urban poor, combine to exclude poor people from safer, higher value sites in the city. Instead, they are crowded in precarious or illegal locations, such as open drains, low-lying areas, the banks of effluent tanks, the vicinity of garbage dumps, open pavements and streets....[56]

Urban centres exhibit distinct forms of settlements based on income and social categories. The urban poor settle mostly in slums or unplanned colonies that often go unrecognised by urban administration, posing a threat of eviction. These areas are typically located near waste dumps or treatment plants, having poor infrastructure, lacking space and provisions, thus having problematic access to drinking water and toilets, and increasing exposure to various forms of pollution. The National Sample Survey Office (NSSO) in its report on Key Indicators of Slums in India (2012) reports the poor conditions of living in urban slums.[57] In this survey, over a third of slum settlements had no electricity, while close to a third had no access to tap water, latrine facilities, drainage facilities, or garbage disposal arrangements. Only 23.9 per cent of the slums benefitted from any slum benefit scheme (such as the Jawaharlal Nehru National Urban Renewal Mission, Rajiv Gandhi AwasYojana, etc.). At the all-India level, out of an estimated total of 33,510 slums, 59 per cent were non-notified, accounting for almost 3.25 million slum households not officially recognised as slums by the government.[58]

In a highly cash-strained environment, some people have to live on pavements and streets to be able to save money for remittances.[59] Homelessness renders them more vulnerable to injuries, which often go untreated: a study in Delhi found that untreated injuries have resulted in lifelong disabilities, jeopardising the ability to work, further perpetuating homelessness.[60]

Social vulnerability is a result of exclusion of several groups on the basis of ascriptive or biological identities, impinging upon their livelihood, food and dignified living. Some of the socially vulnerable groups identified by the Hashim Committee are women, seniors without care, people with disabilities, the homeless, people living with leprosy, mental illness and AIDS, scheduled castes and tribes, children without adult care, street and working children, and children of destitute and stigmatised parents.[61] Generally speaking, urban women are more independent than their counterparts in rural areas; however, the extent of vulnerability they face

* Mr. Harsh Mander served as Chairperson of the Technical Resource Group of the National Urban Health Mission and Member of the Expert Group to Recommend the Detailed Methodology for Identification of Families Living Below the Poverty Line in Urban Areas (Hashim Committee).

varies with respect to other intersections of identity. This is to say, realities vary drastically, whether one is talking about elderly women, working women, slum dwellers, homeless women, women heading households, or single women.

Being socially vulnerable can serve as a deterrent to care. In Madurai, leprosy patients do not access public services fearing stigmatisation. This is all the more problematic for people with disabilities because their physical or mental restrictions are compounded by secondary health concerns. For example, children with cerebral palsy are at high risk of osteoporosis and fractures due to lack of medication, immobility and poor nutrition. Similarly, individuals with mental illnesses also have various co-morbidities with developmental disabilities.

Occupational vulnerability, stated by the Hashim Committee, comes about due to the 'fact that the large majority of the urban poor are trapped in low end jobs—insecure, low paid, low productivity with debilitating work conditions—mainly in the informal sector.'[62] Third party interventions in the job market based on commissions, lack of social protection at work, seasonal casual employment (like fishing) and so forth are major reasons for vulnerability. Some of the occupations falling under this category are noted to include 'daily wage workers, construction labour, petty traders, hawkers, street children, sex-workers, rikshaw puller[s], domestic workers, etc.'[63] Occupational vulnerability also arises due to health impacts and related illnesses from working in hazardous and exploitative work conditions, as was reported by almost all vulnerable groups during the work of the TRG of the NUHM. For example, heavy load workers experience severe spinal and back problems, while waste recyclers reported musculo-skeletal disorders, respiratory diseases and chronic fatigue. Vulnerabilities of work further stem from its seasonal nature. For example, the fisher folk community has a lean period when fishing is not allowed (3–4 months a year) at which point this community completely depends on state aid, which may or may not be offered in measure commensurate to need.

All these variations and combinations of vulnerabilities were studied at length in the work of the Techncial Resource Group of the National Urban Health Mission, convened by the Ministry of Health and Family Welfare of the Government of India. The NUHM-TRG carried out an extensive field-based policy recommendation appraisal of 31 Indian cities and towns and with over 40 different categories of the vulnerable, undertaken in 2013 by researchers, health officials and activists. It showed the stark and recalcitrant patterns affecting life and access to public services among the urban vulnerable, whose ailing health is the very embodiment of exclusion—at personal, community, institutional, and societal levels. We draw extensively on this experience for the India Exclusion Report placing emphasis on specific vulnerable groups that are being examined. These include women, Dalits, Adivasis, religious minorities (particularly Muslims), persons with disabilities, class-based disadvantaged groups (informal sector workers, migrants), and age-related disadvantaged groups (children and the aged). These populations face residential, social and occupational vulnerability in various combinations.

Women face vulnerability at an altogether different and more pronounced dimension in urban centres, placing them in the lowest stratum of society (economically and socially). All women work, whether in the home or outside it, performing both paid and unpaid labour. Their vulnerability stems from a lack of recognition of their work, under-payment, inequity in intra-household resource distribution, and the lack of power to claim equal resources in the family. In certain situations relating to health, vulnerability for women can be more pronounced in urban areas than in rural: sample survey data from 2014 show that while INR 40 more are spent, on average, for the treatment of rural females suffering from an ailment as compared to rural males, the relationship is inverse in urban areas: at least INR 100 more are spent on average per ailing male as compared to an ailing female.[64]

The unequal nature of patriarchy comes into play also for women who are not in a typical family setting.[65] For example, single women, separated or widowed women, homeless women and women with mental disabilities, all face harsh and complex forms of vulnerability in the urban context for structural and societal reasons. Some women are trapped in spiralling vulnerability: escaping domestic violence, some may be cast into homelessness and penury, often supporting children through begging or other hazardous street-based work (including sex work, manual labour),[66] completely absent from the support structures of the state.[67] In Chennai, at a focus group discussion with nearly twenty homeless mentally ill women, all concurred that 'shelter from violence—verbal, physical, sexual—was the main recourse sought.' Estranged from families, these women lacked access to water, food, sanitation and saw no relevance of primary health care centres which in their experience were facilities only for pregnant women.[68]

Dalits: An important determinant of socio-economic inequities in spheres of well-being, is caste.[69] Landlessness leading to perpetual poverty and food insecurity motivates distress migration to cities, concentrating Dalits in slum areas. The 2011 slum Census reveals that 32 per cent of the slum population in Tamil Nadu and 39 per cent in Punjab is comprised of Dalits.[70] Nationwide, between 2001 and 2011, there has been a 37 per cent increase in the Dalit population within slums.[71] Three sets of challenges have been identified: 1) Dalit children face higher levels of mortality and malnutrition as compared to non-Dalits; 2) across age groups, Dalits suffer due to the low quality of health care they receive ; and 3) Dalits are forced to do hard labour for sub-standard amounts without any social security.[72] Typical occupations such as manual scavenging introduce vulnerability to an astonishing range of health issues, including poisoning, musculo-skeletal disorders, respiratory problems, leptospirosis, skin problems, etc.[73] Dalit populations tend to lack access to institutionalised care, suggested by the higher preponderance of home deliveries among Dalit families.[74]

Adivasis typically live in rural areas; their presence in urban areas is therefore usually because of desperation, often time-bound and cause-specific. For instance, the Narikkuravar community in Tamil Nadu comes to Madurai during the festival season to sell beads and ornaments near ThiruppuramKuntram Temple. Other tribal communities that migrate to the cities include those that are in search of casual labour, sometimes found in the most dangerous of occupations: Adivasi migrant workers in Gujarat routinely brave toxic exposure and death from Silicosis in the state's quartz crushing industry.[75] An ethnographic study found that 'whether for work on construction sites or stone quarries, for brick-making or digging cable trenches, the seasonal flow of Bhil casual labourers from upland villages has contributed directly to the physical expansion of the industrial growth poles in Gujarat such as Surat, Baroda and Ahmedabad.'[76] Officers in the labour department hold such migrants in contempt, thinking that the problems of Adivasis 'are of their own making, whose lack of care for their own welfare, ignorance and "bad habits" are embedded in their culture…they will not care to use (health) services...just go here and there.'[77]

Muslim minorities: Research suggests that both the resilience and the marginalisation of urban Muslims is not uniform across the country.[78] Analysis of the 2005–06 National Family Health Survey suggests that the reason that Muslims have a lower under-5 mortality rate as compared to Hindus (a feature earlier attributable to their greater urbanisation), is associated with maternal height, diet and son preference.[79] Yet, it is not consistently the case that greater access or uptake of resources is what accounts for this advantage.[80] Further, Muslim advantage is least visible in the East and Northeast, where matriarchal societies prevail and the uptake of services is better overall in society (e.g., Assam and West Bengal).[81] Muslims have also been 'blamed' for the laggardly progress in eradicating polio in the country, accounting for about 16 per cent of the population and close to three-fourths of the cases. In a detailed study in Aligarh city, the vulnerability of Muslims to polio has been found to be the result of structural violence meted out as segregation following the Partition of India and Pakistan, differential development of Muslim areas, and lacunae of trust in the government apparatus, following several incidents involving the use of force.[82]

Other research suggests various cases and forms of deliberate marginalisation of Muslims from the social determinants of health, notably in the reach and provisions of the educational system,[83] housing,[84] and employment opportunities, as well as vulnerability to communal violence.[85,86] In recent years, a growing and occupationally expanding middle class of Muslims in urban India (from meat export, leather, Unani medicine to agribusiness, IT, pharmaceuticals and real estate) does not necessarily possess 'the capacity, or even the will, to contribute to the alleviation of their poorer coreligionists.'[87]

Persons with disabilities: In India, those living with loco-motor, blindness, low vision, hearing impairment, mental retardation, mental illness, leprosy cured, cerebral palsy, autism and multiple disabilities are legally acknowledged as persons with disabilities. An increasing trend of moving to urban areas among the population of people with disabilities in India (see Box B) has come to light in the comparison of Census data from 2001 and 2011. The percentage of persons with disability relative to the total population has increased from 2.13 to 2.21 respectively. The decadal growth percentage is significantly higher in urban areas (48.2 per cent) compared to rural areas (13.7 per cent).[88]

The largest groups of children and adults with disabilities lie in the category of loco-motor disability (20.3 per cent), followed by hearing impairment (18.9 per cent), and vision impairment (18.8 per cent). Children and persons with multiple disabilities constitute 7.8 per cent of the community. Further, though speech impairment is not an acknowledged disability as per the law, both the Census and the District Information System for Education (DISE) collect data on this impairment, which is the next largest group (7.5 per cent).[89]

The 2011 Census made a distinction between children and persons with mental retardation (5.6 per cent) and persons living with mental illness (2.7 per cent):[90] mental health issues are among India's most challenging.[91] Studies have also shown the higher burden even for caregivers of children with intellectual disabilities.[92]Although there are no studies, experience and discussions with families of children with disabilities living in the urban slums of Delhi suggest that they come seeking rehabilitation and access to education in urban areas, but as migrants, difficulties in establishing identity, barriers of language and navigating the city with a disability are added challenges. Even with a number of provisions existing for populations with disabilities including District and Regional Rehabilitation Centres, Institutes, Infromation Centres, and a National Policy all of which emphasise community-based rehabilitation, social exclusion is itself a major challenge faced by the persons with disabilities.[93]

Class-based disadvantage in occupational/ residential categories: The urban poor (the poor identified even with the crudest of stratifiers, such as income quintile) face a significant disadvantage compared to the average urban-dweller: Agarwal found that under-5 mortality (at 73 deaths per 1,000 live births) was almost double that in the poorest urban quintiles as compared to the remaining urban population (of 42 deaths per 1,000 live births).[94] In fact, data from the National Family Health Survey (2005–6) shows higher infant mortality, lower childhood vaccination, and comparable levels of anaemia among females when comparing the urban poor to the rural average.[95]

Box B. Spotlight on Disability and Exclusion

Apart from general healthcare needs resulting from poverty, living in difficult circumstances such as urban slums, children and persons with disabilities often have significant and multiple health care needs related to their impairments. Nearly 7 per cent of persons with disabilities belong to vulnerable social groups in the country. Census figures suggest that as of 2011, 2.45 per cent of the India's population with disabilities belongs to the Scheduled Castes while 2.05 per cent belongs to the Scheduled Tribes.[96]

Urban areas are thought to have better facilities for most people, which in turn shapes health outcomes.

Parents of children with disabilities tend to seek information and rehabilitation of their child's condition at urban health facilities, but as is commonly assumed, the relative abundance of services in urban areas do not translate into better health care. For one, children and persons with disabilities face huge barriers in physical mobility as urban slums leave options such as the wheelchair totally unusable. Added to this, transport options in urban areas are inadequately accessible, leaving many children and persons with disabilities vulnerable in seeking adequate healthcare. Access may not always be assured even in clinical facilities, apart from which, patients and their carersare often pushed out due to the lack of knowledge in how to navigate and access their needs in facilities. Finally, disabled children and persons face vulnerability to violence and abuse when seeking all manner of services and entitlements. A 2014 study in Bangalore echoes many of these experiences, finding that communication barriers, lack of resources and back-up services hamper physicians while parents are challenged by financial constraints, stigma and beliefs related to disability.[97]

Many women and girls with disabilities experience 'double discrimination', i.e., additional barriers in accessing health care services, particularly pertaining to reproductive health, or experiencing good health. Men with disabilities are also expected to experience additional barriers to good health.At present, Indian policies and programming have not begun moving away from impairment-based thinking to a more holistic and culturally competent understanding of disability.

Overlapping with the aforementioned categories of women, Dalits, Adivasis, Muslim minorities, the disabled, and those with class disadvantage are occupational and residential categories that policy documents have defined as being uniquely vulnerable in the urban context.[98] We discuss these briefly.

Construction workers: The construction industry accounts for nearly 44 per cent of urban unorganised workers, comprising more unskilled thanskilled labour.[99] Most construction workers are migrant labourers who move to different locations frequently. Construction workers form the floating labour force and are disadvantaged with respect to housing and often end up in rough shelters devoid of amenities like water, sanitation and electricity. Since the agricultural sector is declining and is unable to absorb the labour, tribal and other marginalised rural labourers turn to booming construction sites in large cities and towns.[100] A Self Employed Women's Association study on women workers in the construction industry of Gujarat notes that the problems shared by construction workers include lack of job security, accidents, lack of insurance coverage and loss of pay during periods of disability.[101] Alcohol abuse is rampant and 'construction workers are exposed to multiple physical, chemical and biological agents, which make them vulnerable to various health problems that include injuries, respiratory problems, dermatitis, musculoskeletal disorders and gastrointestinal diseases. The work is hard physical labour, often under difficult conditions like adverse weather conditions and the nature of work, hours of work, low pay, and poor living conditions with lack of basic amenities and separation from family, lack of job security and lack of access to occupational health services make the situation worse.'[102] Moreover, the lack of supportive social networks among workers causes dependence on contractors, at whose hands they may additionally faceexploitation.[103] A Labour Bureau studyfound that employers violate a range of laws, including employing children and manipulating attendance to abjure fines, penalties and other obligations.[104]

Rickshaw pullers mainly come from poor socio-economic backgrounds, and have relatively lower educational attainment.[105] A small study in Delhi found that about 45 per cent of rickshaw pullers interviewed were illiterate, and another 40 per cent had gone no further than the 8th standard—a trend that likely holds across urban settings (although this population is relatively understudied).[106] Apart from extractive and exploitative relationships with rickshaw owners, the working hours for these workers are long, subjecting them to exposures to extreme weather conditions (heat in the summer and cold in the winter),[107] exacerbated by a common preference among indebted rickshaw pullers to live on sidewalks to save money on rent. Risks of developing heart ailments is reportedly high among rickshaw pullers as their heart rate does not reach a resting level following the 10 minutes of recovery period after pulling.[108] Studies have in fact also found DNA damage attributable to exposure to air pollutants and physical exertion by rickshaw pullers, a phenomenon only likely to exacerbate as pollution levels surge higher in Indian cities.[109] The TRG team in Agra learned of a range of morbidities, including malnutrition, drug abuse, and intense musculo-skeletal strain. Most rickshaw pullers avoided visiting health care facilities unless it is an emergency to avoid costs of both time and money. Their continuous mobility during the day keeps them away from primary health care facilities; instead, as we learned in Delhi, rickshaw pullers rely on rickshaw owners for their care, typically only in cases of accidents and injuries. Chronic health issues are therefore typically ignored, unless they interfere with labour.

Sex workers: It is estimated that India has close to 2 million sex workers, a large proportion of whom operate in urban areas. Sex workers in urban areas are usually dependent on intermediaries like pimps and 'madams', which compounds the stigmatisation of sex workers in society at large.[110] Violence against female sex workers by intimate partners or others in the workplace has also been reported.[111] A recent pan-India survey of sex workers found that they negotiate a range of other occupations in addition to sex work, often staying in this profession because of its liquidity relative to other informal work options, which are fairly narrow given that most in the profession have low levels of education.[112] In terms of health, research has focused on the sexual risks faced by sex workers: a meta-analysis has found that the odds of a woman of reproductive age who is a sex worker having HIV is 54.27 times that of any other woman in the same category not engaging in sex work.[113] Furthermore, studies demonstrate that access to basic health care (including in areas that the workers themselves prioritise: access to contraception, protection from violence and care for sexually transmitted diseases) is a major problem for sex workers because facilities are either lacking around red-light areas or under-equipped by way of drugs and facilities.[114] In addition, stigma serves as a major barrier for the effective dissemination of community interventions for the empowerment of sex workers.[115]

Children face many forms of exclusion in urban settings. A child's vulnerability is often due to factors that hinder the normal growth and functioning of a child. This is further compounded by factors like homelessness, illegal status, disabilities, lack of social protection, and risk behaviours.[116] Some of the most vulnerable children include those in urban slums, those whose parents are migrant workers and street children. In a focus-group discussion conducted with homeless women with children in New Delhi, we learned that when carers/parents themselves are frequently ill, this affects their ability to provide and care for their children. We have found that children in urban areas face a variety of risks detrimental to their health; in almost all cases, they are socially vulnerable (so that is a given), but in some instances, also subject to additional residential and occupational vulnerabilities, which we outline briefly.

Slum children: According to the Ministry of Housing and Urban Poverty Alleviation, about 7.6 million children within the 0–6 year age group live in slums, representing roughly one in 10 children in Indian cities with slums.[117] A recent figure revises the number to over 8 million, residing in some 49,000 slums across the country.[118] The prevalence of underweight among under-5 children reported in urban slums in India is reportedly 52 per cent to 68 per cent, with Delhi peaking at 82 per cent.[119] A recent report finds that among children under the age of 10, urban children are 20 per cent more likely to be unwell as compared to their rural counterparts.[120] Slum children are heavily affected by the physical and social environment which in turn leads to school dropout and low educational status,[121] and a host of adverse nutritional, reproductive and mental health conditions.[122,123,124]

Street children: There are nearly 71 million street children in India. [125] It is estimated that 72 per cent of the street children are aged 6 to 12 years and 13 per cent are below 6 years of age, with typically boys outnumbering girls.[126] These children live in varying forms of precarity; UNICEF has categorised street children into three broad categories based on the place of living and their association with their families: 1) Street-living children (those who sleep in streets without their families); 2) Street-working children (those who work on the streets during day and return home at night); and 3) Children from street families (those who live with their families on the street).[127] Most children residing on the streets of Delhi according to a recent study were from Dalit backgrounds.[128] Whether with or without families, most street children engage in self-employment activities like rag picking, begging, and street vending. Some of them are also employed in hotels as porters, for example. These children are deprived of sufficient nutrition, sanitation facilities, drinking water and medical care, and are exposed to extreme climatic conditions. Outbreaks of measles, tuberculosis and other vaccine-preventable diseases are frequent. Street children are deprived of basic needs such as shelter, nutrition, medical care, education, recreation, and immunisation, and they have no access to water, bathing facilities or toilets (most of the time, these have to be paid for). Scabies, chronic dysentery, lung, ear, nose and throat infections are common, as are anemia and malnourishment.[129] In our primary fieldwork, we noted many instances of children suffering and dying from illnesses like pneumonia, diarrhoea, and simple hunger. Another scourge faced by street children, among the most visible, is the alarming rise in substance abuse: according to a 2013 report, one in three street children reported the use of inhalants and cannabis, while two out of three reported alcohol use of almost two weeks, and four out of five reported using tobacco (almost daily).[130]

Children from street families: One of the impacts of the rural-to-urban migration is that children accompany the adult migrants, thereby uprooting them from their hometowns. These children also engage in various small-scale employment activities like brickmaking, stone crushing, building construction, and rag picking. These children live in makeshift homes and under dangerous and hazardous conditions like lack of sanitation, water supply, and poor nutrition, all of which lead to a range of morbidities.[131] Common ailments that these children face are fever, dysentery and skin diseases. According to a 2012 Aide et Action study in Odisha on children of migrant workers, 'since the family is temporarily uprooted from their habitation and social fabrics, they often get isolated from accessing government entitlements, social security, social assistance and government supported livelihood and poverty alleviation programmes. The family[,] including the child[,] become invisible at the destination due to lack of attention and support from the government department to include them into various government entitlements and citizenship right[s].'[132]

Child labourers: India is home to the largest number of child labourers in the world. According to the 2011 Census, there were nearly 44 million child workers in India.[133] Another study reports that as many as 12.6 million children are engaged in hazardous occupations.[134] Disaggregated data for urban child workers are unavailable, although some reference is made to occupations such as construction, work in factories, the service sector. Poverty and lack of social security are the main causes of child labour. A range of health sequelae are associated with child labour including orthopaedic ailments, injuries, stunting of gastro-intestinal, endocrinal and reproductive system development because of strain and exposure, and greater preponderance of substance abuse as compared to children who are not in labour.[135] More broadly, this kind of work robs children of their right to survival and development, education, leisure and play, and adequate standard of living, opportunity for developing personality, talents, mental and physical abilities, and protection from abuse and neglect.[136] Child line India quotes a study stating that 'Child labour is highest among Scheduled Tribe, Muslims, Scheduled Caste and other Backward Class children. The persistence of child labour is due to the inefficiency of the law, administrative system and because it benefits employers who can reduce general wage levels.'[137]

The elderly: Approximately 8 per cent of India's population, according to the 2011 Census, comprises the elderly, i.e., those aged 60 and above. This figure is projected to reach 158.7 million in 2025,[138] surpassing thereafter, the population of children below 14 years by 2050.[139] The most frequent ailments among the elderly are cardiovascular illnesses, circulatory diseases, and cancers.[140] A key physical barrier for accessing health services is that many elderly individuals require home-based care, a need arising from illness-related confinement following advancing age.[141] In both urban and rural areas, the confinement of the elderly population at home is very high. The lack of social and family support often leads to isolation of the elderly. Further, the chronicity and disabling nature of morbidities also causes economic shocks, resulting in financial dependency, loss of autonomy, in turn reducing social contact and often increasing isolation and loneliness.[142] There are various other vulnerable populations in urban areas (such as those living with chronic illness, affected by emergencies, survivors of violence), and micro categories of these populations that have unique burdens of ill-health (such as the elderly destitute or the disabled living in slums) whose life stories are humbling and whose health needs are poorly understood. As part of the TRG process, we began to understand these dimensions of exclusion and while we cannot explore these groups in further detail here, we do underscore the importance of using an intersectional lens to understand exclusion, and indeed, to respond to it.

Processes of exclusion in urban health

Drawing upon Naila Kabeer's work on social exclusion of women, a typology of exclusion emerges that sees exclusion as a dynamic process involving 1) social closure—the constraining of access to resources and opportunities; and 2) unruly practices, where there are big gaps between laws de jure and de facto; and 3) mobilisation of institutional bias, whereby a predominant set of values, beliefs, rituals and institutional procedures benefit or privilege certain groups over others.[143] With respect to the state, Mander has developed a somewhat analogous typology whereby the state 1) invisibilises the vulnerable, or, 2) when it sees them, seeks to custodialise or otherwise impede their freedoms, and 3) in various ways, it stigmatises, illegalises, and criminalises them.[144] What we see through these processes is the amplification of vulnerability: the vulnerable may—due to various aspects of their actual and assumed identities—be subject to these processes in various combinations.[145] We explain how, below:

Unruly practices can be seen in the inadequate dispensation of schemes, services and programmes. Of course this is seen within urban policies and programmes in general (for more on exclusion in terms of Budgets, see Box C). In almost all of the 30 cities we visited, we learned that access to health care was constrained starting from the first point of interface with the system, the Primary Health Centre (PHC). The PHC is a 'point-of-first-contact' facility, where everything from immunisation to first aid, screening for a range of diseases and even deliveries should be carried out at no cost. Rarely are PHCs located at manageable distances from where the excluded live. Access is further constrained by the limited hours that PHCs are open and the long waiting hours that seeking care entails. In cities like Bhubhaneshwar, Delhi, and Kochi, seeking care at a PHC (or anywhere for that matter) usually requires taking a day off from work, thus losing that day's wages and trying to reach facilities in good time to obtain an appointment with a professional. In Muzaffarpur, we were told that many of the conditions and cases are referred to other facilities, which are a long distance away, and that a host of additional diagnostics may be prescribed, which then incur additional expenses and time. In general, PHCs are seen as a location only for the receipt of pregnancy-related care. Administrators across cities expressed the strong need for a broader range of services to be provided in urban health facilities at the primary level, including screening and wellness programmes for non-communicable diseases, injury, violence and substance abuse prevention, as well as needs specific to the urban context (e.g., occupational health and risk-related, seasonal health promotion in relation to communicable diseases, group-specific outreach and care, etc.).

We learned from the slumdwellers in Chennai that no services related to screening or treatment of diabetes or hypertension were available at the PHCs near their living areas, conditions that were now outpacing infections and other communicable diseases. Slumdwellers would instead have to spend INR 100 on travel to a tertiary care hospital. Most, from Dhamtari to Gangtok have resigned themselves to the fact that there will be out-of-pocket expenses involved in seeking care—that this is simply a feature of the system, and further that not only care, but also respect from health professionals, must be bought.

It has not been a surprise, therefore, that residentially vulnerable areas have been sites of major epidemics. As Dasgupta (2012) points out,

> The DDA set up 27 resettlement colonies for relocating slum populations from different parts of the city during the Emergency in 1975-77. These resettlement colonies were among the most-affected settlements in the 1988 epidemic, which was a landmark in the contemporary phase of the history of cholera in Delhi. The immediate cause of the epidemic is generally considered to be a breakdown in service provision during the transitional phase as these colonies were being handed over from the DDA to the Municipal Corporation of Delhi. However, there were several intrinsic deficiencies in the resettlement colonies that have not only rendered them vulnerable to the epidemic, but have meant that they remain endemic areas for cholera till date.[146]

The usually fragmented, often hostile and typically lonely experience of health-seeking among the excluded almost demands the advocacy and support of a good samaritan, someone who will root and care for you. The onus of even this, in many cases, is put on the vulnerable themselves. In Thrissur, we learned from elderly day labourers that the onus of finding such a samaritan is not on the system, but on them, individually. In fact, government hospitals do not admit any patients without caregivers!

Institutional bias is evident for a number of vulnerable groups. Batliwala argues that 'the key feature of social exclusion processes is the "othering" and "bordering" of certain individuals and groups. This is achieved not through physical or structural barriers alone but through ideological constructions that justify this exclusion by defining who fits in the social mainstream and who doesn't.'[147] Women often bear the brunt of bias in the form of discrimination during delivery. A 2007 study found that as many as one in four women getting care at public institutions had 'some level of negative experience of care from nurse-midwives, with 10 per cent reporting that they felt their care was hurried or neglectful and an additional 15 per cent reporting that they were shouted at or slapped during labour.'[148] Similar experiences were reported by women going to private hospitals, albeit in smaller proportions. Across sectors, we found that women have been held at ransom; in Patna, we learned of cases where bribes were demanded for deliveries in facilities (which then issue certifications of institutional delivery, on the basis of which the government offers incentives) and for birth certificates, on pain of refusal of care.

Excluded groups including transgenders—hijras and kothis—have to face extraordinary humiliation, often regardless of the health issue or complaint they are facing. At a focus group in Pune, we were told harrowing stories of physical isolation and confinement of in-patients who were transgenders and that they felt as though they were treated like dogs. Flat denial of care is faced by those with physical disability, even in large metros like Delhi. Members of the Sikhaligad community in Pune told us how providers put on gloves even before seeing them,which they see as discrimination based on untouchability.

Another major challenge in seeking care at government services, for people living with stigmatised conditions like HIV/AIDS, is the lack of privacy, and insensitive way in which they are treated. As a construction worker in a Delhi slum remarked,

> It is all right for the hoardings to be screaming about AIDS...you only know what happens when it happens to you. I got myself tested and they told me that I had AIDS. Only my wife knows...how can we tell other people...In the public hospitals you go to the AIDS clinic, and everybody will know you have AIDS. Sooner or later somebody will see you there...and then it is all over...and these people in these clinics...how they treat you...like diseased dogs in the street...like you a [sic.] criminal...so I prefer to go to the private doctor....[149]

A quantitative study of 100 patients of public hospitals conducted in Delhi found,

> social discrimination appears to be institutionalized within the public health facilities. Three fourth of the patients using public health facilities belong to lower castes or socially disenfranchised groups. Nearly 60 per cent of the patients asserted that the health care staff is not polite and respectful, which is partly the result of social discrimination based on caste, class and economic status. Among the workers or service providers, the survey shows that the same class and caste form the majority of the lower end workers such as ward ayahs, ward boys, safai karamcharis (cleaners), and so on, while the upper castes dominate the higher end. This caste break up is directly related to the level of exploitation as lower classes of workers are subjected to more discriminatory practices.[150]

Thus, there appears to be a cycle of discrimination that is meted out not just to patients, but to workers in the health system as well.

It is important to note that many of these

processes of exclusion are reinforced because of the overall monetisation and tertiarisation of health. Middle- and upper-class and caste denizens of urban areas, earlier received state attention;[151,152] now, in its waning, they simply buy their way out of these experiences and vulnerabilities. They have social networks comprising upper class and caste doctors, they live in health-promoting environments, and their work and living arrangements afford them the time and possibility of improving their health. The wealthy in urban areas are thus more visible to the system, always eligible, able to purchase as consumers their wellness and care, and also command respect and support when required. All of this over the past three decades has also meant the steady and near complete exit of the wealthy from the public sector and a kind of growing stigmatisation of the public sector itself (which as the afore-cited study suggests, may have caste and class antecedents). The resulting institutional bias towards privatisation is in fact another driver of exclusion in urban India. In Delhi, for example, even though the number of beds in the public sector is higher than in the private,[153,154] the latter is favoured over the former. In Kochi, a private construction company had made an arrangement with a private hospital to issue health insurance cards to migrant labourers directly recruited by the firm to work on their sites (their peers recruited by contractors could not avail of this system, nor had any access to the private hospital). While the efforts of the firm were to a degree commendable, the fragmentation of coverage, particularly in a situation where risks will not be similarly fragmented, is of concern. Had there been demonstrably greater, universal access for all migrants to public services, the company would have that as recourse for its labourers, but they hadn't yet thought of this as a possibility.

The private sector is itself notorious for eschewing any responsibility towards the poor, even when required. In another example, Krishnan points out,

> The Indraprastha Apollo Hospital was famously given fifteen acres of land in Delhi's SaritaVihar for a grand total of Rs 1, in exchange for the hospital providing a generous amount of free care to poorer patients—but the conditions of the lease, it turned out, were subsequently repeatedly violated.[155]

Encouragingly, following a High Court order, the Delhi government has recently taken to regulating and monitoring the extent to which private hospitals are fulfilling such obligations.[156,157]In Mumbai, by contrast, a highly dubious practice of a private corporate hospital—an 'Elite Forum for Doctors' offering them rewards for number of hospital admissions—was heavily remonstrated against by the Maharashtra Medical Council, following which the Brihanmumbai Municipal Corporation indicated that it had no municipal rule under which any action against the hospital could be taken.[158] Given this kind of a regulatory lacunum, regardless of how they fare, however, private hospitals in urban areas, continue to enjoy heavily subsidised land, infrastructure, water and electricity and tax rebates, even as they continue to ignore the most vulnerable or worse, exploit them for private gain.

Consequences of Exclusion

Consequences for health

The manifestations of marginalisation and exclusion are literally embodied in the illhealth of the urban poor. As we have earlier indicated, the urban poor and slum dwellers have poorer health outcomes than urban non-poor and non-slum dwellers, respectively.

India's health transition is typified by a double burden of communicable and non-communicable diseases; urban areas are also experiencing this trend in a more pronounced fashion. Latest data (gathered between January and June of 2014) from

Box C. Budgetary Exclusion*

India has a larger context of chronic underfunding of health and social services), such that only around 1.2 per cent of the country's GDP is spent on health, far lower than any other BRICS countries, and even neighbours like Sri Lanka and Bangladesh.[159] In 2014, after the new government came into power, it slashed the government budget on health, cutting spending by 20 per cent (INR 20,431.4 crore in 2014–15).[160] Prospects for the public health sector in general, thereafter, have been less than bright.

Our analysis of 2011–12 data from National Health Accounts suggests that the proportion of revenue expenditure on urban health and family planning services across all states was 1.47 times that of rural health and family planning services. Even having 50 per cent more funds appear not to have translated into relatively greater use of the public sector or better outcomes distributed across populations living in urban areas. Recent data suggests that while on average, as high as 52.5 per cent of hospitalisations for childbirth in urban areas are in private hospitals, this is skewed among wealthier denizens of the city.[161] Indeed, as against 80.4% of delivery hospitalisations among the richest quintile occurring in the private sector, the proportion among the poorest quintiles is 31.9 per cent.[162]

The shifts in the public sector pale in comparison with the sheer quantum of subsidy given to the private sector in health. The 1950 Public Charitable Trust Act has paved the way for corporatisation of medical care. The use of this Act increased manifold post neo-liberalisation in the 1990s in India, facilitated by other engines of growth in the private sector, such that setting up a hospital became a mechanism for profit-generation, even profiteering.[163] First was the growth of India's pharmaceutical industry which took on a globalised character. Second, the private sector close to doubled the number of medical colleges in the country. Finally, a trend towards the creation of elite hospitals that sought to market themselves as medical tourism destinations. What was given short shrift in the bargain was the corresponding requirement of the Public Charitable Trust Act for hospitals to provide 20 per cent of the beds at free and concessional rates to the needy. There has never been a solid monitoring mechanism for this, and the actual implementation of this provision is likely miniscule. Unsurprisingly, it is found that in 1992–93, the private health sector accounted for 2.5 per cent of the GDP whereas in 2004–5 it was 5.6% of the GDP, at a time when public health spending increased marginally from 0.74 per cent to 0.92 per cent of GDP.[164]

the National Sample Survey Office demonstrate that while 89 of every 1,000 of Indians in rural areas reported an ailment in the last 15 days, the number was higher (118 out of every 1,000 Indians) in urban areas.[165] Not only is this figure lower in rural areas than urban, the urban/rural difference appears to have grown over time. In urban areas, the gender gap is also significant, with as many as 135 out of 1,000 urban women reporting a recent ailment, against 101 for every 1,000 urban males. As can be expected, morbidity is concentrated among older age-groups,with ailments among the 60 and older age group being far higher among urban females as compared to urban males (inverse of the relationship seen in rural areas).[166]

Broadly, the health issues of the urban excluded can be classified into communicable, non-communicable and occupational illnesses. Communicable diseases are spread through

* We are grateful for the inputs and review of Dr Indranil Mukhopadhyay and Dr Ravi Duggal here.

pathogens and vectors that thrive in the unsanitary conditions that often plague these populations. Slums being underserviced by the municipal administration—with adequate drinking water supply, sanitation, and both solid and liquid waste management—serves as a major aggregate risk factor for the transmission of communicable diseases. Malaria, dengue and typhoid, for example, are therefore frequently reported among the urban poor populations. According to the TRG,

> in urban India, the infant mortality rate is higher by 1.8 times in slum as compared to non-slum areas. Diarrhoea deaths account for 28 per centof all mortality, while acute respiratory infections account for 22 per cent. Nearly 50 per cent of urban child mortality is the result of poor sanitation and lack of access to clean drinking water in urban slums.[167]

Non-communicable diseases are also common among the urban poor. Various behaviours, like alcohol and substance abuse, dietary habits, and physical inactivity, all increase the proximal risk factors for NCDs. While analysing the risk factors for NCDs among the urban poor population in Haryana,[168] it was found that the urban poor are particularly vulnerablebecause offactors like high alcoholism among the male population and unbalanced dietary intake. These have been substantiated by the focus group discussions during the TRG process as many vulnerable communities were found to suffer from various types of NCDs.

Apart from the more common health burdens among the urban poor, the TRG team observed some unique health burdens specific to vulnerable communities. These include injuries to rag pickers due to syringes, broken glass, metals, etc. in the garbage, stray dogs, specific occupational health burdens like spondylitis for head-load workers, high prevalence of sexually transmitted infections among sex workers, respiratory and other health issues due to toxic exposures among informal industrial labourers, and stomachaches among child labourers due to hunger. It was also noted in our focus group discussions that consequences varied over the course of the year: in an FGD with homeless elderly women in Delhi, we learned that during the monsoon, the area where the homeless shelter is located is flooded up to three feet. When asked how they manage during these periods, the response was, 'Road hai, zindabad!' (Long live the road!).

Consequences for health-seeking

As detailed at length in our prior work, exclusion from urban health services has dire consequences for the marginalised. Indeed the larger issue with urban health is that the health system in the public sector is not preoccupied with health more broadly. Instead, there is a focus on maternal health and family planning, while the private sector is preoccupied with illness management.

The central consequence of this is that health—sexual, reproductive, occupational, adolescent, elderly, cardiac, mental, environmental, etc.—is not a priority or a preoccupation of urban dwellers. Across cities that we visited, we found that health is simply ignored by the excluded for reasons ranging from economic (loss of a work day) and social (stigma, lack of essential documents) to institutional (lack of facilities or imperfect timings for consultation).

This neglect perpetuates a complex of intercalating and negatively reinforcing tendencies and techniques of managing illness: care will not be sought, sought in an ad-hoc fashion from inappropriate sources, too late, and/or in the private sector at massive costs.[169,170,171]

Among those suffering from an ailment in urban areas, it is found that although on average the tendency to not seek care is going down in India, the poorest fifth are more than doubly likely not to seek care as compared to the wealthiest fifth;

women are slightly more likely to have an untreated ailment.[172] For populations like the homeless, there is the onerous broader context of stigma that any kind of health seeking is unlikely. Many homeless persons we met in Delhi and Chennai were simply biding their time with illnesses and injuries. As we learned in Delhi, health is not even a priority for elderly homeless women who are desperately seeking pensions and dignified shelter. In many cases, homeless persons suffer from multiple morbidities (e.g., injury and mental illnesses or disability and chronic disease) and rarely do primary health care facilities have the ability to handle these combinations (especially mental illness and disability), so appropriate care is not even available. From what we learned of this situation even in the relatively better-performing cities like Chennai, receipt of care appears to be a matter of coincidence. In fact,we observed an almost complete dependence on charitable clinics, religious institutions, and donated foods and drugs. Further, prolonged homelessness itself is both a cause and consequence of ill health, perpetuating each other in a vicious chiasmus.

For those whom we spoke to in other cities, the preference was to self-medicate, involving the development of lay typologies of 'small' and 'big' illnesses. 'Small' illnesses typically involve the ad hoc administration of painkillers or generic medicines either suggested by an area pharmacist, neighbour, relative, or employer. Once the symptoms of a 'small' disease end, medication taking also ceases, again, based on a rudimentary logic of wellness that may have no linkage to true, clinical well-being (i.e.,'I feel better, so I can stop taking this antibiotic.') Only in the case of children do slum dwellers visit the doctor for smaller ailments as the parents think that children's ailments are important and only a practitioner can best help in overcoming them. For most other health concerns, especially those experienced by adults and the aged, providers were only visited for what were seen as long, drawn-out illnesses that interfere with work. This is borne out by a longer, more systematic ethnographic study in a Delhi slum, which examined 92 illness trajectories, the first resource was to a neighbourhood *daktar* who may not have the right qualifications [as opposed to a *bada daktar* (big doctor], who would cost something around INR 35 per visit, as opposed to at least double at private or government facilities.[173]

For larger ailments, or events like a delivery, injury, or other emergency, clinics and hospitals have to be relied on. For the poor, the government is the first port of call, but as a woman living in Jahangirpuri slum in Delhi made plain, 'sarkari aspatalon mein garib ki koi sunvai nahin.' ('Nobody hears/receives a poor person in a government hospital.') While there is obviously no caveat, the situation with which public sector health professionals must contend is palpably difficult; public providers are expected to deliver high quality care with the most unpredictable and inadequate of allocations, to gargantuan patient loads, all the while negotiating the temptations of the private pharmaceutical sector (by way of perks for referral, prescribing certain medicines and tests, and more). As appallingly revealed in a recent book by those in the profession, doctors are now more often businesspersons than health professionals, operating for private gain even from within the public sector.[174] Public maternity homes in the capital are so overcrowded that turned-away patients rely on non-registered private sector clinics, understandably of lower quality.[175] Transgenders must hesitatingly rely on non-registered practitioners in most cities for sex re-assignment surgery, knowing full well the serious health risks they must incur (Chennai is a noteworthy exception).[176] A recent study in Lucknow found that at least one in three parents of a poor urban neonate suffering from persistent diarrhoea sought care from a spiritual/informal provider.[177] Another provider that many excluded groups rely upon is the neighbourhood pharmacist. Ethnographic research in Mumbai has found that informal providers and pharmacists alike are part of a complex 'unfree' market,[178] which is associated with practices of 'counter-pushing', self-medication and other practices that introduce, rather than reduce, risks to the population.[179]

Private hospitals and clinics dot the urban landscape, and are a major source of health-seeking, particularly in cases of emergency among the vulnerable. In urban areas, the proportion of in-patient care sought in the private sector has grown from 56.9 per cent in 1995–6 to 68 per cent in 2014, over a 10 per cent increase.[180] As can be imagined, the reliance on the private sector is skewed in wealthier income groups (as they can afford it), and yet, in 2014, private hospitals account for 52 per cent of hospitalised cases among the poorest urban quintiles in India, and 56.5 per cent among the second poorest.[181] There are a number of challenges related to seeking care in the private sector, including the ratcheting-up of costs for simple procedures and diagnostics, and the administration of unnecessary procedures to make money (rent-seeking). Most of these add morbidity and the toll on households by way of cost, time, and emotional anguish.

Sometimes, these patterns of harmful health-seeking run in sequence. In the case of a female resident of a Beggar Home in Mumbai, we heard a harrowing story of her experience in her hometown of Mathura. Given an injection from an un-credentialled doctor for a minor ailment, severe heartburn propelled her to spend INR 2,000 to travel to Agra and seek care. She is not even clear what was wrong with her (or if she is fully recovered) even though the private hospital charged her INR 1,30,000 for tests and treatment combined.

Finally, for the poor, many of whom in fact are or began as medical refugees in cities, for the express reason of addressing health needs, well-meaning schemes for financial risk protection offer no succour. For example, Delhi's Arogya Kosh requires three years of residency in the Union Territory to qualify for up to Rs 5 lakhs of financial assistance for treatment addressing kidney and liver ailments. In other cases, even with government support for treatments, the poor are billed for consumables and diagnostics.[182] Such costs are recurrent by their very nature and further dwindle their economic resources.

Additional consequences

The poor, just like any other urbanite, are willing to pay for care. The unit cost of services in a private facility can be as high as INR 2,213 per outpatient visit, while in a district hospital, the figure is INR 94, which can be the same amount as a day's wages for an informal urban worker. In private facilities, having to pay consultation fees means that not only is the income for the day lost (as one has to visit and wait in a facility inordinately), one also has to pay money to just be seen. This is just the beginning: the likely scenario that follows is that tests are required, and a follow-up visit, for which the quickest way is to pay out of pocket. The poor, furthermore, have less expendable income to spare even for such purposes: it is found that the monthly per capita expenditure of the poorest urban decile in 2009–10 was merely a tenth of that expended by the richest decile.[183] Multiple studies have concluded that in poor households compared to rich households, a far greater share of income is spent on health (even if in absolute terms this is less expenditure) given higher morbidity levels.[184] Significant spending is on outpatient procedures, which notably, are not covered by any pro-poor schemes. A 2011 study found that in urban areas, the poorest income quintiles were spending 70.3 per centand 73 per centof their total out-of-pocket expenditure on outpatient expenses and drugs, respectively,4–10 per centhigher than all other income quintiles.[185]

India therefore has the ignominious distinction of being a nation where out-of-pocket expenditures for health area cause of poverty. Data from the 61st Round of the National Sample Survey shows an increase in urban poverty by as much as 2.9 per cent if out-of-pocket health expenditure is accounted for.[186] States such as Uttar Pradesh, Chhattisgarh, Kerala, Maharashtra and West Bengal have been shown to have high out-of-pocket health expenditures and demonstrate significant increases in urban poverty attributable to this.[187]

According to the 71st round of the National Sample Survey, the average total medical expenditure[188] per single ailment is much higher—i.e., INR 741 for males and INR 629 for females in urban areas, as compared to INR 549 and INR 589 respectively in rural areas.[189] Moreover, this survey found that expenditure in private hospitals as compared to public is much higher in urban areas (three times the expense in private than public hospitals for males and almost double for females) as compared to rural areas (1.9 times the expense in private than public hospitals for males and 1.6 times for females). All this results in a greater proportion of expenditure, on average, per person in urban areas as compared to rural (INR 639 as compared to INR 509). For the poorest fifth of urban dwellers, on average the cost to treat a single ailment in a single person is the same as over 10 months of household expenditure; costs are this high or even higher for those who use the private sector more. This trend has lasted at least a decade: analysis of the NSS 61st Round (2004–5) found that Dalit (SC), Adivasi (ST), and Other Backward Class (OBC households) were more likely to incur catastrophic out-of-pocket health expenditure than general-category households in urban areas (the margins were 27.8 per cent ($p<0.001$), 8.6 per cent ($p=0.06$), and 11.9 per cent ($p<0.001$) more, respectively.[190] Finally, urban household expenditure on non-communicable diseases (like cancer, diabetes, and heart disease), is higher compared to rural, by a greater margin among India's poorest income quintiles as compared to the richest quintile.[191]

Practices of Inclusion

Drawing from the TRG process and subsequent fieldwork in various cities, we have compiled the following examples of practices of inclusion that offer particular lessons in redress or prevention of exclusion from urban health. This was triangulated with visits to organisations in Chennai, Mumbai, Pune, Bhopal and Delhi to highlight inclusion in health care.

We would like to note at the outset, that strong public health systems, providing free services in clean facilities (as in Pimpri Chinchwad), timely surveillance, disease prevention and outbreak response (as seen in Chennai, Kolkata, and Madurai), and a strong community outreach component (as seen in Raipur) can go a long way to protecting the health of the excluded. Highlighted below are some examples 'practices of inclusion' that we feel could be quite feasibly scaled up or expanded. Rather than lay out the entire gamut of their work, we have chosen to emphasise only the practices that address the processes of exclusion (invisibilisation/social closure, unruly practices, or institutional bias/discrimination). Our list of practices is not exhaustive and even the practices that are discussed may have their own flaws. Ultimately, we hope to encourage all stakeholders in the urban health sector to derive positive lessons from the work that is discussed below.

In Chennai, the Municipal Corporation has established primary and secondary health care facilities in an attempt to reduce existing inequalities and address two considerably excluded populations. The Shri Balaiah Memorial-Urban Primary Health Centre, exclusively for senior citizens, provides easy and affordable access to medicines and health facilities for common medical issues experienced by the vulnerable elderly population (see Figure 1).[192] The PHC, if scaled up and functional to its full extent, has great potential to deal with the physical and psychological health of the elderly. Similarly, an increasing number of standalone diagnostic facilities, such as the Valluvarkottam Diagnostic Lab in Chennai, under a public-private partnership between the municipal corporation and a private foundation, offer key diagnostics (x-ray, ECG, and ultrasound) at subsidised rates, blood and urine tests at one-third the market price, and dialysis free of cost.[193] Providing such diagnostic capacities referred from primary and secondary facilities improves the access and efficiency of the system and reduces out-of-pocket expenditures. Similar gradation of rates was seen for tests in PHCs in Bardhaman where discounts were also provided to those Below the Poverty Line who didn't have cards.

In Mumbai, the SNEHA (Society for Nutrition, Education, and Health Action) life cycle approach focuses on public health problems of urban slum populations—maternal and newborn health; child health and nutrition; sexual and reproductive health; and prevention of violence against women and children.[194] Working closely with the Brihan Mumbai Municipal Corporation and other government and private stakeholders, SNEHA has created referral networks of government hospitals to manage over 21,000 high-risk pregnancies, trained and improved the relevant skills of 3,000 staff at municipal hospitals, and connected slum-dwelling mothers and their families to professional health services for the various phases of pregnancy. SNEHA has addressed more than 4,000 cases of domestic violence, trained 4,500 police officers and cadets in Mumbai to deal with cases of domestic violence, and trained more than 2,100 public hospital staff to better identify patients who may be victims of domestic violence.[195] In partnership with University College London, SNEHA has developed a vulnerability scorecard to identify the most vulnerable amongst the informal settlements in the Mumbai area. This is a model for vulnerability mapping that has been adapted by the central government as well. The SNEHA model essentially couples projects to prevent negative health outcomes in mothers and their children, with educational programmes to help eliminate the cycle of ill health faced by several

Figure 1. Shri Baliah Memorial Urban Primary Health Centre for Senior Citizens, Rottler Street, Chennai. Photo Credit: Prathibha Ganesan.

of the most vulnerable populations within urban slums. Moreover, their work allows the urban slum dwellers to be more visible to the system, addressing issues of discrimination and institutional bias that the population usually experiences.

A self-governing cooperative in Pune of just under 3,000 waste pickers called the Kagad Kach Patra Kashtakari Panchayat (KKPKP), has created the SWaCH Coop (Solid Waste Collection and Handling), a unique model of addressing public health, while simultaneously ensuring the overall welfare of those in hazardous occupations. Following a law that required waste management instead of dumping, the Pune Municipal Corporation has facilitated door-to-door collection of waste in collaboration with KKPKP.[196] Now, waste pickers no longer have to sort waste (nor do their children), saving time and adding efficiency to waste management, and also saving the Corporation crores of rupees. Additionally, SWaCH/KKPKP members have been issued identity cards which assures them access to health services, checkups and diagnostics at discounted rates. They are also given protective equipment that helps avoid occupational hazards. The SWaCH model essentially brings together waste pickers in the city of Pune for the good of the collective itself, and cost-effectively manages a majority of the city's solid wastes. Membership also has powerful downstream effects on the overall livelihoods of card-holding waste pickers who are members. As such, the SWaCH Coop and KKPKP have both made significant progress in reversing the problem of exclusion of waste pickers from urban health resources, primarily by making this population visible but also by reducing the extent of institutional bias that these individuals normally face.

The Sambhavna Trust Clinic in Bhopal, located just metres away from the previously standing infamous Union Carbide factory, targets individuals who were either affected by the Union Carbide gas tragedy in 1984 or are currently suffering due to the ground water contamination in Bhopal. Through all of its activities, the Sambhavana Trust Clinic maintains an electronic medical record system. The clinic has found this system to be extremely useful in light of the fact that the medical care being provided to victims of either the gas tragedy or ground water contamination is not entirely evidence-based. Keeping the electronic records therefore enables Sambhavna to collect several data, which are then continuously analysed to better understand what approach for the care of these patients works best. By not relying only on individuals' ability to provide documentation certifying that they were affected by the gas disaster in 1984, Sambhavana has created a sense of inclusion to urban health resources for an estimated 50,000 people who otherwise may not have received the care that they needed in municipal hospitals (most of these 50,000) individuals are those affected by ground water contamination).[197] Through its research and political activism, Sambhavana has also secured greater recognition of its target population at municipal hospitals in Bhopal and has reduced the extent of the discrimination faced by these individuals (see Figure 2).

In the National Capital Region, the Aman Biradari Delhi Homeless Male Recovery Shelter, looks to provide shelter and access to facilities, to at least a proportion of the homeless population. With grave ailments like TB or even orthopaedic injuries, even if homeless persons can access public hospitals, they are discharged and advised to go home to rest and be cared for by their families. But if they have no homes and/or families, they simply are forced to forgo care, and in cases like TB risk eventual death, and in simple orthopaedic injuries, to risk permament disability. The shelter 'recruits' homeless men from across Delhi, to their shelter facilities, and helps them access public hospitals, providing necessary post-hospital care, creating a sense of inclusion for this largely ignored population. These individuals, who largely experience discrimination in medical institutions, due to the lack of relevant documentation, are advocated for, and stewarded through the process

Figure 2. Behind the Sambhavna Trust Clinic's main building is a small plantation and area where staff members produce and use plants to manufacture the ayurvedic medicines that the clinic uses. Pictured here is Lalita, who is busy putting together packets of a powder that Sambhavna prescribes to patients suffering from constipation. The powder was manufactured at Sambhavna from the same plants that it grows. Photo Credit: Girish Motwani

of getting identified by the system and receiving appropriate access to resources. Medical attention is provided by a doctor between 4 and 6 pm daily, and staff undertake outreach between 7 and 11am every day. There is no requirement of producing documentation, given that a large proportion of users of these services are migrants, and may not posess any. At intake, however, there is extensive documentation of the conditions and socio-economic profiles of men linked to the shelter to help the organisation better understand the types of populations it is catering to. Additionally, the shelter is linked to various TB speciality hospitals, such as Rajan Babu TB Hospital and Lok Nayak Jai Prakash Hospital, which help diagnose patients and thereafter provide medication, nutrition and sensitisation to the disease. In addition to serving as a recovery shelter while individuals undergo treatment (usually lasting atleast 6 months), as per the Revised National TB Control Programme, DOTS providers also visit the shelter twice a week to administer medication and carry out general checkups. Since the service began, over a period of 18 months (August 2013–February 2015), 18 TB patients residing at the Delhi Health Recovery Shelter have completely recovered from the disease. Within the population that the Delhi Health Recovery Shelter serves, several of the individuals fall into other categories of vulnerability as well: for example, disabled, mentally ill, and substance users. As such, by targeting issues of invisibility and institutional bias, the organisation tackles the problem of exclusion, making a portion of the male homeless population of Delhi visible to the government, and creates inclusion for individuals whomay be experiencing multiple levels of marginalisation.

The Adaikalam Transit Care Centre for women, a branch of the pioneering non-governmental organisation, The Banyan, serves as the largest shelter in India for homeless individuals with mental illnesses. Its multi-disciplinary team offers various social and clinical care interventions.[198] The Banyan provides services to those in need without any government identification; it works with the government to provide such indentification, which is necessary for them to have access to most government entitlements. Since its inception in 1993, more than 2,000 women have utilised Adaikalam (see Figure 3) and 1,275 women have been re-integrated with their families. Mentally ill, homeless people experience a strong institutional bias, therefore the organisation works to connect its clients to government entitlements, creating inclusion and alleviating bias and unruly practices faced by them.

It is noteworthy that the majority of organisations documented above are addressing exclusion by either making a given subgroup of individuals more visible to the government system and/or reducing the institutional bias faced by said subgroup. Most of the activities do not seem to tackle exclusion caused by unruly practices. To reiterate, unruly practices refer to the gaps in law (i.e., what is on paper) and reality (i.e., what is actually happening)—it is a problematic phenomenon when institutions are not doing what they are supposed to be doing. Generally speaking, exclusion is a problem particularly because either there is no way for certain subgroups of individuals to be appropriately recognised by the

Figure 3. The Transit Care Centre (TCC), Adaikalam, of The Banyan offers its clients and residents facilities for several activities. Pictured here is a workshop for clients to practise art and create various crafts. Photo Credit: Girish Motwani.

state or because existing institutions are practising some discrimination against these subgroups. The most important priority for organisations and the Indian government should be to accept that certain definable groups are being excluded from accessing urban health resources and that more policies to reverse the problem of exclusion ought to be designed, implemented, and enforced.

Recommendations

The previous sections have attempted to describe the comprehensive and multifaceted exclusion of urban poor populations from either any kind of health-care services, or from services that are affordable, accessible, respectful and appropriate. This situation is unacceptable by any yardstick of basic equity, and calls for both the building and the sensitive restructuring of urban public health services.

The recommendations listed here are derived and reproduced from the TRG Report, validated and refined further by the fieldwork conducted to document both the overall state of exclusion from urban health resources and the practices of inclusion that currently exist, as well as as drawn from a recent publication by our partners in the TRG process.[199] We suggest an overall architecture for urban health care provision that is attuned to and directly addresses exclusion.

1. Map vulnerability, infrastructure, and access

Since exclusion has its roots in the invisibility of certain groups of vulnerable individuals, action ought to be taken to make these groups visible to the urban health system. It is only after these groups are made visible to the system that we can expect formal, systematic action to be taken. Therefore, it is recommended that cities make the effort to spatially and socially map various elements that would help locate and understand (1) where the socially vulnerable groups exist, (2) what facilities or health infrastructure are available, and (3) what the location of vulnerable groups, their exclusion, and available health facilities mean for issues of access to urban health resources. This effort would yield a map with three layers that should be updated at least once yearly.

The first priority should be to accurately locate the most marginalised groups. This can be done by mapping determinants of vulnerability (e.g., water and housing supply, and sewerage), and locations that concentrate the vulnerable (e.g., slums, resettlement colonies, clusters of homeless people, red-light areas, labour zones, wholesale markets, railway and bus stations). The determinants and locations could include linking information on categories and numbers of vulnerable persons.

Second, the map should indicate the location of existing institutions and organisations—public, private, and governmental—that deliver urban health services ('infrastructure mapping'). This includes, for example, outreach services, primary, secondary, and tertiary health services, inter alia CGHS, state government primary health units, community and district hospitals, medical colleges, ESIC hospitals and clinics, and ICDS centres.

Third, a more focused effort must be given to 'access mapping'. That is, the maps should depict clearly the relationships between the location of the vulnerable groups and health infrastructure, including the differently abled and elderly.

The final map would be the result of the superimposition of the three 'layers'—of vulnerability, infrastructure, and access—it could be used to make decisions about where to expand or improve services, where the risk of outbreaks and morbidity is high, and over time, how improvements are impacting health.

2. Organise services at the community level

The first institutional need for inclusion is to create primary health institutions that are physically, economically and socially accessible to urban poor populations. At the base of this health institutional structure proposed by the TRG is a facility that can be called a nursing station or a nursing station cum health sub-centre, comprising two female health workers, one male health worker, and five Accredited Social Health Activists (ASHAs)per 10,000 population. This exceeds the current NUHM Framework which provides for a single female health worker and five ASHAs per 10,000–12,000 population. The nursing stations must be located near the area of the population they wish to serve, and also at major transit points (like railway and bus stations) to provide drop-in centre care for the highly vulnerable.

More specifically speaking, nursing stations should provide all primary health care that does not require the presence of doctors—preventive and promotional health activities, health literacy activities, health and nutrition counselling, vaccinations, antenatal care, regular supplies of drugs, follow-up tests and counselling, and regular free medication for common urban ailments (for tuberculosis, mental health issues, leprosy, hypertension, diabetes, epilepsy, asthma, etc.) Nursing stations could also be equipped with the capacity to provide counselling services for substance abuse, disability, geriatric, palliative, and domiciliary care. Finally, to make the nursing station most accessible to the people it is serving, it would have to consult directly with them to determine its timings for mornings, afternoons, and evenings.

3. Establish primary health centres near poor and other marginalised populations

The majority of urban primary health centres must be deliberately established within or near (no greater than 0.5 kilometres away) settlements where the urban poor and other marginalised groups reside. This includes urban slums (notified and non-notified); slum-like habitations; other areas with either a lack of piped water supply, underground sewarage and drainage, and extreme overcrowding; urban villages; landfills; red light areas; factory worker and scavenger colonies; leprosy colonies; construction workers' camps; and impoverished inner-city areas. If and only if land cannot be found within these areas in any given city should urban primary health centres be constructed at a maximum distance of 0.5 kilometres from the area.

Beyond this, a small number of Primary Health Centres could be located in middle-class areas, wherever possible, where the poor (e.g., domestic workers) tend to work. Another 5 per cent of the budgets should be allocated to the creation of Special Primary Health Centres for the completely excluded, i.e., homeless populations and street children.

Of all urban primary health centres, between 5–10 per cent should also have special services like mobile clinics (providing services similar to those found in nursing stations) and recovery shelters for homeless adults, street children, and temporary and circular migrants.

4. Ensure inclusion through specific measures

(i) No documents: Individuals seeking care are often denied health services because of their inability to produce documents certifying their identity. Therefore, 'no requirements of any identity proof' is a key institutional arrangement recommended for NUHM. For the purposes of tackling exclusion it would be more effective to design, implement, and enforce a policy that eliminates the requirement of identification proof for those seeking health services. Moreover, it would be even more beneficial, from the perspective of reducing exclusion, if it is never required for an individual seeking urban primary health care to produce proof of address or citizenship or for s/he to have a caregiver.[200]

(ii) Mother's name: For intake/registration, all forms under the UHM should ask for mother's name only, instead of father's or husband's name, which can discourage or stigmatise children of single women or sex workers. Similarly, as is increasingly the practice, the option to register with one's transgender identity should also be permitted.

(iii) Changed timings: Urban primary health centres have been found to provide health services to patients during times where either they are at work or are busy with other activities in the day. The patients normally have to sacrifice a day's payment to avail the appropriate health services from the health centres. Thus, the operating hours of the urban primary health centres itself excludes populations—for example, domestic workers, self-employed individuals, and sex workers. Therefore urban primary health centres must decide their operating hours in consideration of the populations that they are serving. This typically means 3 to 9 pm daily would be a good time, with the exception of UPHCs in red-light areas which could operate in the morning hours.

(iv) Cashless services: The imposition of user fees for primary and curative care services at public/government hospitals, essential medicines, and diagnostics creates enormous barriers of access for individuals who are financially marginalised. The TRG suggests that all these services should be entirely free of cost for all individuals. Linked to this is compliance with legal directives to provide free beds in private hospitals to economically weaker sections.

(v) Special clinics: On a rotating basis, special clinics for the aged and differently abled could be introduced in existing facilities, that mobilise local youth volunteers and are specifically geared towards handling co-morbid conditions that these two populations often have. Creative allocation of space could also be considered in medical colleges' out-patient departments, which could serve as poly-clinic OPDs referred from Primary Health Centres.

(vi) Help desk: Providers of health services, particularly the urban primary health centres, should have a formalised help desk and counselling centre that is run by trained, professional medical social workers. These individuals would be responsible for advising and supporting patients, offer advice about preventive behaviours and promotional health such as the use and consumption of clean water, sanitation, breastfeeding newborns, child-rearing practices, and occupational health. Much like the professionals working at SNEHA Mumbai, such medical social workers should serve as the first point of contact for survivors of violence, children without adult guardianship, as well as for old and disabled persons.

5. Improve efficiency: make the continuum of care seamless and of standard, high quality

Moving beyond reproductive and child care, Primary Health Centres should be sites where vertical disease control programmes are integrated and linked to preventive and promotive services provided by the National Health Mission. This includes basic diagnostics; for more complicated tests, the Centre could serve as a sample collection site.

There is a need to make referral processes—from primary to secondary and tertiary care—

more systematic, and therefore, more efficient. To facilitate referrals, for example, a system of colour-coded cards can be used. Patients needing immediate secondary or tertiary care can be given green cards from personnel at the urban primary health care facility, which would help them receive 'fast track' services through help desk staff at secondary and tertiary centres, receive quick access to the medications they need regularly, without having to make them wait in long queues.

In line with ensuring the continuity, efficiency, and quality of urban health care services, standard treatment protocols ought to be developed and followed carefully for the most common urban health ailments. It follows that the medications necessary for these standard treatment protocols be clearly listed, purchased by providers of urban health services, and sufficiently stocked up at relevant urban health centres. If services at all levels and between all levels are delivered with greater efficiency and with greater attention to standardised protocols, addressing exclusion from urban health resources becomes more manageable.

6. Integrate urban health services: towards a multi-disciplinary approach to service delivery

ICDS centres, which have been directed by Supreme Court to fully serve all slum populations, should be linked with the ASHAs, Multi-Purpose Workers, and the urban primary health centres to be able to provide slum dwellers and other such marginalised individuals with multidisciplinary services, focusing on, for example, (1) the nutrition and health of infants, young children, and expectant and nursing mothers (much like the work that SNEHA Mumbai is engaged in) and (2) the implementation of all national programmes such as those for tuberculosis, leprosy, mental health, and blindness prevention.

Urban primary health centres should also be equipped with referral linkages to supportive health care facilities. For example, primary health centres can be linked with designated public poly-clinics or specialised diagnostic clinics, free residential and outpatient drug deaddiction centres, free residential mental health care recovery centres[201] nutrition rehabiliatation centres, homeless recovery shelters[202] and palliative care centres.

7. Encourage community participation and transparency

Every urban primary health centre should have its own Jan Arogya Samiti (JAS), which is an empowered local health committee consisting of a local elected ward member, representatives from each of the occupational groups present in the health centre's catchment area, and chairpersons or representatives of the area's Mahila Arogya Samitis (MAS; existing committees of neighbourhood women who routinely meet and contribute towards promoting health in their communities). No more than one-fourth of the members of each JAS should be males; a minimum of one-fourth of the members of each JAS should be under 30 years of age; and a minimum of one-fourth of the members of each JAS should be above 60 years of age. Such a distribution ensures that the concerns of different, vulnerable age groups are voiced and addressed appropriately at the level of each urban primary health centre. The health centre's social worker should serve as an observer and help perform the secretariat function in the JAS. JAS should be made responsible for conducting annual audits of the social services that the urban primary health centres offer. These audits should be reported publicly and to the City and State Urban Health Missions, directing them to take corrective measures as and when necessary.

All JASs should have, at the very least, the following responsibilities: optimising the use of existing health services and suggesting ways of improving them and addressing the social determinants of health (this is absolutely essential for community ownership of a given medical initiative); developing a community health plan after a careful assessment of the socio-economic profile (i.e., also the social determinants of health) of a given urban primary health centre's catchment area; conducting yearly social audits; working closely with the MAS and the ASHAs in a given area to recruit community health volunteers and peer educators, who, among other things, would be importantly responsible for improving the health literacy in the vicinity of the urban primary health centre.

8. Improve governance structures for convergence

Municipal health officers should be made responsible for continually monitoring the provision of public services that have a strong bearing on urban health. This includes disease surveillance, vector control, food safety, regulation of slaughterhouses, monitoring of air pollution, biomedical waste, rabies control, as well as linkages to schemes of other departments (Women and Child, Education/ School Health, Social Welfare, Urban Development, Food and Civil Supplies, Roads and Transport). As such, the health officers should be made in charge of implementing an improved surveillance system in their respective cities. City health centres should have a system through which they could report to municipal health offices about disease patterns, especially those linked to environmental causes like water contamination and overcrowding. This system would better enable a city to, for example, trace the source of a hepatitis or dengue outbreak to vector breeding and correlate increases in the incidence of asthma and acute exacerbation of chronic respiratory illnesses to air pollution, rabies and dog bite incidences to stray dog control, or road accidents to the lack of road safety measures. Appropriate corrective measures can be taken to prevent further health consequences if a powerful reporting and monitoring system is designed and implemented. For example, municipal health offices can respond to an outbreak of dengue with increased efforts towards vector control.

As is evident here, there is a lot to be said and as we found, a lot indeed that can be done about exclusion from urban health care in India. Ultimately, as was said repeatedly during the TRG session, if we can at least all face the correct direction, we can hope to have an answer to Chajju Ram's question, 'who cares?'

Endnotes

1. NDTV. Another Dengue Death in Delhi, Toll Touches 43. NDTV. 6 November 2015. http://www.ndtv.com/india-news/1-more-succumbs-to-dengue-toll-touches-43-1240951 (accessed 7 November 2015).
2. B.S. Perappadan, 'Fogging is ineffective in controlling dengue, says CSE'. The Hindu. 21 October 2015. http://www.thehindu.com/todays-paper/tp-national/tp-otherstates/fogging-is-ineffective-in-controlling-dengue-says-cse/article7785985.ece. (accessed 9 November 2015).
3. The Asian Age (2015), 'Fogging effective method to fight dengue: Centre'. 23 October http://www.asianage.com/node/433145 (accessed 4 November 2015).
4. The Indian Express (2015), 'With 10,683 cases in Delhi, 2015 dengue outbreak worst in last 20 years'. 13 October http://indianexpress.com/article/cities/delhi/with-10683-cases-in-delhi-2015-dengue-outbreak-worst-in-last-20-years/ (accessed 4 November 2015).
5. The Asian Age (2015), 'Fogging effective method to fight dengue: Centre'.
6. B.P. Shajan (2015), 'Hospitals to face action for denying treatments'. The Hindu. 16 September http://www.thehindu.com/news/national/other-states/

hospitals-to-face-action-for-denying-treatment/article7656828.ece (accessed 11 November 2015).

7. D.N. Jha (2015), 'Kejriwal government caps test cost at Rs 600, labs protest'. The Times of India. 17 September http://timesofindia.indiatimes.com/city/delhi/Kejriwal-government-caps-test-cost-at-Rs-600-labs-protest/articleshow/48992944.cms (accessed 11 November 2015).

8. A. Kelkar-Khambete (2015), 'How dengue has breached India's class barriers'. Business Standard. 9 October. http://www.business-standard.com/article/specials/how-dengue-has-breached-india-s-class-barriers-115100900196_1.html (accessed 11 November 2015).

9. A. Singh (2015), 'Dengue fears haunt capital's homeless'. The Statesman. 17 September http://www.thestatesman.com/mobi/news/delhi/dengue-fears-haunt-capital-s-homeless/90652.html (accessed 11 November 2015).

10. The Times of India (2015), '33,000 homeless people died on Delhi streets since 2004: Government report'. 18 October http://timesofindia.indiatimes.com/india/33000-homeless-people-died-on-Delhi-streets-since-2004-Government-report/articleshow/49442688.cms (accessed 11 November 2015).

11. Singh (2015), ' Dengue fears haunt capital's homeless'

12. People's Health Movement (2000), 'People's Charter for Health. Dhaka: People's Health Assembly'.

13. S.V. Joga Rao (2005), 'Fundamental Right to Health and Health Care' in L.V. Gangolli, R. Duggal, A. Shukla (eds) Review of Health Care in India, Mumbai: Centre for Enquiry into Health and Allied Themes (CEHAT), pp. 279–94.

14. G. Bloom, H. Standing and R. Lloyd (2008), 'Markets, Information Asymmetry and Health Care: Towards new social contracts'. Social Science & Medicine, 66(10): 2076–87.

15. B.S. Levy and V.W. Sidel (2013), 'The Nature of Social Injustice and Its Impact on Public Health' in B.S. Levy and V.W. Sidel (eds), Social Injustice and Public Health, 2nd edition. New York: Oxford University Press.

16. World Health Organisation. 'Trade, Foreign Policy, Diplomacy and Health Equity: WHO' http://www.who.int/trade/glossary/story024/en/ (accessed 11 November 2014).

17. D.E. Beauchamp (1976), 'Public Health as Social Justice' in D.E. Beauchamp and B. Steinbock (eds), New Ethic for the Public's Health, New York: Oxford University Press, Pp. 101–9.

18. Beauchamp (1976, pp. 102–3) contrasts social justice with market justice, in which 'people are entitled only to those valued ends such as status, income, happiness, etc., that they have acquired by fair rules of entitlement, e.g, by their own individual efforts, actions or abilities. Market-justice emphasizes individual responsibility, minimal collective action and freedom from collective obligations except to respect other persons' fundamental rights.'

19. World Health Organisation Commission on Social Determinants of Health (2008), 'Closing the Gap in a Generation: Health Equity through Action on the Social Determinants of Health. Final Report of the Commission on Social Determinants of Health'. Geneva: World Health Organisation

20. Registrar General of India (2011), 'Provisional Population Totals: Urban Agglomerations and Cities'. http://censusindia.gov.in/2011-prov-results/paper2/data_files/India2/1.%20Data%20Highlight.pdf (accessed 2 April 2015)

21. People's Health Movement (2000), 'People's Charter for Health Dhaka: People's Health Assembly

22. Joga Rao (2005), 'Fundamental Right to Health and Health Care'

23. S.B. Shah(1999), 'Illuminating the Possible in the Developing World: Guaranteeting the Human Right to Health in India'. Vanderbilt Journal of Law, 32:435.

24. The right to health is guaranteed in the International Covenant on Economic, Social and Cultural rights, although details on actual state obligations are not given here or in other international treaties. In India, public interest litigation has been the avenue through which the Indian Supreme Court has allowed citizens to seek protection of their constitutional human rights, using its prerogative to interpret the fundamental right to life to include the right to have good health (Shah, 1999). The Court has thus directed states to provide citizens with basic health services and social conditions essential for the enjoyment of health. The Indian legal system is among the few in the world to have subjected social rights to this type of judicial scrutiny and litigative recourse.

25. L. Gordis (2014), *Epidemiology*, 5th edition, Canada: Elsevier, p. 27

26. D. Woodward and R.D. Smith, 'What may be a GPG in Health? Global Public Goods and Health: Concepts and Issues'. (ND). http://www.who.int/trade/distance_learning/gpgh/gpgh1/en/index10.html. (accessed 2 April 2015)

27. R.A. Musgrave (1957), 'A Multiple Theory of Budget Determination'. FinanzArchiv, New Series 25(1): 33–43.

28. People's Health Movement, Medact, Medico International, Third World Network, Health Action International, AsociacionLatinomaricana de Medicina Social and Zed Books (2014), 'Social Protection: Reimagining Development'. Global Health Watch 4: An Alternative World Health Report. Cape Town/London/Frankfurt/Penang/Amsterdam/Mexico City: People's Health Movement; Medact; Medico International; Third World Network; Health Action International; AsociacionLatinomaricana de Medicina Social; Zed Books;

29. Ibid, p. 186

30. R. Rao and P.R. Panchmukhi, 'Health and the Indian Constitution'. Centre for Multidisciplinary development research monograph seried No.7. (ND). http://cmdr.ac.in/editor_v51/assets/Mono-7.pdf (accessed 30 April 2015).

31. S.B. Ghosh (1954), 'Some Theoretical Implications of Welfare State in India'. Indian Journal of Political Science 15(4): 327–38.

32. L.A. Morenas (2010). 'Planning the City of Djinns: Exorcizing the Ghosts in Delhi's Post-Colonial Development Machine.' Unpublished Doctoral Dissertation. Troy, New York: Rensselaer Polytechnic Institute.

33. D. Banerji (2001), 'The Political Economy of Health and Development'

34. WHO (1986), 'Ottawa Charter for Health Promotion: An International Conference on Health Promotion, The Move Towards a New Public Health.' 17–21 November, Ottawa, Geneva, Canada

35. Department of Health and Social Security (1980), 'Inequalities in Health: Report of a Research Working Group', London: DHSS

36. World Health Organisation Commission on Social Determinants of Health (2008), 'Closing the Gap in a Generation: Health Equity through Action on the Social Determinants of Health.' Final Report of the Commission on Social Determinants of Health

37. A. Sengupta (2012), 'Creating, Reclaiming, Defending: Non-Commercialised Alternatives in the Health Sector in Asia' in D.A. Mcdonal and G. Ruiters (eds), *Alternatives to Privatisation: Public Options for Essential Services in the Global South*, New Delhi: LeftWord

38. K. Sen (2001), 'Health Reforms and Developing Countries – A Critique' in Qadeer, Sen , Nayar (eds), *Public Health and the Poverty of Reforms*, New Delhi: Thousand Oaks/Sage, pp. 137–53.

39. D. Banerji (2001), 'The Political Economy of Health and Development'

40. A. Irwin and E. Scali (2007), 'Action on the Social Determinants of Health: A Historical Perspective'. Global Public Health 2(3): 235–56.

41. Ibid.

42. R. Bisht, E. Pitchforth and S.F. Murray (2012), 'Understanding India, Globalization and Health Systems: AMapping of Research in the Social Sciences'. Globalisation of Health 8: 32.

43. T. Sundararaman and V. Muraleedharan (2015). 'Falling Sick, Paying the Price: NSS 71st Round on Morbidity and Costs of Health Care'. Economic and Political Weekly L(33): 17–20.

44. The Constitution (Seventy Third Amendment) Act of 1992, India. c 2015 http://www.tnrd.gov.in/constitutionalprovision.html#1 (accessed 12 November 2015)

45. The Constitution (Seventy Fourth Amendment) Act of 1992, India. c 2015 http://www.tnrd.gov.in/constitutionalprovision.html#4 (accessed 12 November 2015)

46. B.S. Levy and V.W. Sidel (2013), 'The Nature of Social Injustice and its Impact on Public Health'

47. D.E. Beauchamp (1976), 'Public Health as Social Justice', p. 103

48. D.Banerjee (2001), 'The Political Economy of Health and Development' in I. Qadeer, K. Sen and K.R. Nayar (eds), Public Health and the Poverty of Reforms, New Delhi: Thousand Oaks/Sage, pp. 37–62

49. B. Sivakumar (2013), 'Dalits form 32% of Slum Dwellers in Tamil Nadu'. The Times of India. 2 October http://timesofindia.indiatimes.com/india/Dalits-form-32-of-Tamil-Nadu-slum-dwellers/articleshow/23377468.cms (accessed on 2 August 2015).

50. J. Mathieson, J. Popay, E. Enoch, S. Escorel, M. Hernandez, H. Johnston and L. Rispel (2008), 'Social Exclusion: Meaning, Measurement and Experience and Links to Health Inequalities. A Review of Literature'. WHO Social Exclusion Knowledge Network Background Paper 1.

51. T.K. Oommen (2009), 'Social Exclusion and the Strategy of Empowerment' in H. Bhattacharya, P. Sarkar andAngshuman Kar (eds), *The Politics of Social Exclusion in India: Democracy at the Crossroads*, Routledge

52. In urban areas, complete and partial exclusion can be determined by the relative position of the community or individual in the society with respect to other factors. For example, while gendered forms of exclusion are very common in society, the impact of the gendered discrimination is different for, say,

an educated housewife and a poor, uneducated women working in an informal setting. The impact of exclusion is worsened in the case that the woman is homeless and mentally ill. While educated women experience partial exclusion, uneducated, poor women experience complete exclusion. Likewise, communities and individuals in urban areas experience social exclusion to differing extents and of differing natures.

53. A. Chakrabarti and A. Thakur (2010), 'The Making and Unmaking of the (In)formal Sector'. Critical Sociology 36(3): 415–35.
54. (Chakrabarty and Thakur, 2010) There is a problematic homogenisation of the informal sector in our current understanding of it, relative to the (hegemonic) logic of the formal sector, that both stigmatises the informal sector and charts a linear course favouring formalisation as the only required societal transition (ignoring other possibilities including better social protection for those in the informal sector, etc.).
55. Planning Commission (2012), 'Report of the Expert Group to Recommend the Detailed Methodology for Identification of FamiliesLiving below Poverty Line in the Urban Areas', p. 25 http://planningcommission.nic.in/reports/genrep/rep_hasim1701.pdf (accessed on 6 May 2015).
56. Ibid, p. 27
57. National Sample Survey Office, Ministry of Statistics and Programme Implementation (2013), 'Key indicators of slums in India', New Delhi: Ministry of Statistics and Programme Implementation
58. Ibid.
59. K.C. Sivaramakrishnan, A. Kundu and B.N. Singh (2005), *Handbook of Urbanization in India*, New Delhi: Oxford University Press
60. V. Prasad (2011) 'A Study to Understand the Barriers and Facilitating Factors for Accessing Health Care amongst Adult Street Dwellers in New Delhi, India'. Unpublished Dissertation. University of the Western Cape.
61. Planning Commission (2012), 'Report of the Expert Group to Recommend the Detailed Methodology for Identification of Families Living Below Poverty Line in the Urban Areas', p. 28
62. Ibid, p. 30
63. Ibid.
64. National Sample Survey Office, Ministry of Statistics and Programme Implementation (2015), 'Key Indicators of Social Consumption in India | Health'. National Sample Survey 71st Round (January-June 2014). New Delhi: Ministry of Statistics and Programme Implementation P 10.
65. J. Beall (1996), 'Participation in the City: Where do Women Fit In?' in C. Sweetman (ed.), *Women and Urban Settlement. Oxfam: Oxford*, pp. 9–16. http://citeseerx.ist.psu.edu/viewdoc/download?doi= 10.1.1.309.5830&rep=rep1&type=pdf#page=18(accessed 6 May 2015).
66. H. Mander and S. Jacob (2010), 'Homeless Deaths on the Streets', New Delhi: Centre for Equity Studies; http://centreforequitystudies.org/wp-content/uploads/2012/08/Homeless-deaths-on-the-streets.pdf. (accessed on 15 May 2015).
67. S. Choudhary, A. Joseph and I.P. Singh (2011), 'Homeless Women and Violence'. http://www.hic-sarp.org/documents/Homeless_Women_and_Violence_Shivani_Amita_Indu.pdf (accessed 15 May 2015).
68. Planning Commission (2012), 'Report of the Expert Group to Recommend the Detailed Methodology for Identification of Families Living Below Poverty Line in the Urban Areas', pp. 25
69. R. Baru, A. Acharya, S. Acharya, A.K.S. Kumar and K. Nagaraj (2010), 'Inequities in Access to Health Services in India: Caste, Class and Region'. Economic and Political Weekly XLV(38): 49–58.
70. Sivakumar. 'Dalits form 32% of Slum Dwellers in Tamil Nadu'.
71. Ibid.
72. S.J. Chander (2009), 'Defending the Health of the Marginalised'. http://www.sochara.org/sites/default/files/Defending%20the%20marginalised_0.pdf. (accessed 1 August 2015).
73. Rashtriya Garima Abhiyan. 'Manual Scavengers and their Health'. (ND). http://www.mfcindia.org/main/bgpapers/bgpapers2013/am/bgpap2013h.pdf. (accessed 1 August 2015).
74. K. Navneetham and A. Dharmalingam (2000), 'Utilization of Maternal Health Care Services in South India'. http://mobile.opendocs.ids.ac.uk/opendocs/bitstream/handle/123456789/3018/wp307.pdf?sequence=1. (accessed on 1 August 2015).
75. A. Baviskar (2008), 'Contract Killings: Silicosis among Adivasi Migrant Workers'. Economic and Political Weekly 43(25): 8–10
76. D. Mosse, S. Gupta and V. Shah (2005), 'On the Margins in the City: Adivasi Seasonal Labour Migration in Western India'. Economic and Political Weekly, 40(28): pp. 3025–38.
77. Ibid, p. 3030

78. L. Gayer and C. Jaffrelot (eds) (2005), *Muslims in Indian Cities: Trajectories of Marginalisation*, New Delhi: Harper Collins

79. P.M. Kulkarni, Himanshu (2012), 'Regional Dimensions of Inequalities', in Z. Hasan and M. Hasan (eds), *India Social Development Report: Minorities at the Margins*, New Delhi: Oxford University Press/ Council for Social Development,pp. 102–17.

80. S. Bhalotra, C. Valente and A. van Soest (2005), 'The Puzzle of Muslim Advantage in Child Survival in India'. Journal of Health Economics 29: 191–204

81. Sivaramakrishnan, Kundu and Singh (2005), *Handbook of Urbanization in India.*

82. R.S. Hussain, S.T. McGarvey, L.M. Fruzzetti and S. Helleringer (2015), 'Partition and Poliomyelitis: An Investigation of the Polio Disparity Affecting Muslims during India's Eradicaion Program'. PLoS One 10(3): e0115628.

83. A. Meha and R. Hasan (2006), 'Under-representation of Disadvantaged Classes in College'. Economic and Political Weekly XLI(35): 3791–96

84. S. Thorat, A. Banerjee, V.K. Mishra and F. Rizvi (2015), 'Urban Rental Housing Market: Caste and Religion Matters in Access'. Economic and Political Weekly L(26–27): 47–53

85. Gayer and Jaffrelot (eds) (2005), *Muslims in Indian Cities: Trajectories of Marginalisation*

86. N. Kirmani (2008), 'History, Memory and Localised Constructions of Insecurity' Economic and Political Weekly XLIII(10): 57–64

87. Gayer and Jaffrelot (eds) (2005), *Muslims in Indian Cities: Trajectories of Marginalisation*, p. 312

88. Census of India (2011), 'Disabled Population by type of disability, age and sec-C-20 Table'. http://www.censusindia.gov.in/2011census/C-series/c-20.html, Tables C-20, C-20 SC, C-20 ST (accessed on 20 July 2015).

89. Ibid.

90. Ibid.

91. K.S. Ganesh, A. Das and J.S. Shashi (2008), 'Epidemiology of Disability in a Rural Community of Karnataka'. Indian Journal of Public Health, 52:125–29.

92. A.P.C. Suresh, T.E. Benjamin, J.E. Crasta, M.T.J. Alwinesh, G. Kanniappan and S.M. Padankatti (2014). 'Comparison of Burden among Primary Care-givers of Children with Autism and Intellectual Disability Against Children with Intellectual Disability Only in a Hospital Population in India'. Indian Journal of Pediatry 81(S2): S179–S182.

93. S.G. Kumar, G. Roy and S.S. Kar (2012), 'Disability and Rehabilitation Services in India: Issues and Challenges'. Journal of Family Medicine and Primary Care, Jan–Jun; 1(1): 69–73.

94. S. Agarwal (2011), 'The State of UrbanHealth in India: Comparing the PoorestQuartile to the Rest of the Urban Population in Selected States and Cities'. Environment and Urbanisation 23(1): 13–28.

95. Urban Health Division, Ministry of Health and Family Welfare, Government of India (2008), 'National Urban Health Mission (2008-2012): Meeting the Health Challenges of Urban Populations especially the Urban Poor (With Special Focus on Urban Slums)'. Draft for Circulation. Pp. 31-32 http://www.uhrc.in/downloads/Reports/NUHM-Draft.pdf (accessed on 20 July 2015).

96. Census of India (2011), 'Disabled population by type of disability, age and sex - C20 Table'

97. C.E. George, G. Norman, T.E. Benjamin and D. Mukherjee (2014), 'Barriers to Early Diagnosis, Intervention and Social Integration of Children with Developmental Disabilities: A Qualitative Study from Rural Villages and a Poor Urban Settlement of Bangalore, South India.' Disability, CBR and Inclusive Development, 25(4): 61–83

98. Planning Commission, 'Report of the Expert Group to Recommend the Detailed Methodology for Identification of Families Living Below PovertyLine in the UrbanAreas'. p.25

99. B. Jayakrishnan, B. Thomas, B. Rao and B. George (2013), 'Occupational Health Problems of Construction Workers in India'. International Journal of Medicine and Public Health 3(4): 225–29.

100. Editorial (2008), 'State Apathy towards Construction Workers'. Economic and Political Weekly 43(21): 5.

101. Self Employed Women's Association (2008), 'Labouring Brick by Brick: A Study of Construction Workers'. http://www.sewaresearch.org/pdf/researches/labouring_brick_by_brick.pdf (accessed on 8 June 2015).

102. Ibid, p. 228

103. D. Fernandez and G.D.B. Paul (2011), 'Social Networks of Migrant Construction Workers in Goa'. Indian Journal of Industrial Relations 47(1):65–77.

104. Editorial (1979), 'Plight of Construction Worker'. Economic and Political Weekly 14(39): 1630–31.

105. Gurnam Singh Virk (2013), 'Workers in Informal Economy: A Sociological Study of Rickshaw Pullers in Patiala'. Dissertation submitted to Punjab University, Chandigarh.

106. T. Kurosaki, Y. Sawada, A. Banerji and S.N. Mishra (2007), 'Rural-Urban Migration and Urban Poverty: Socio-Economic Profiles of Rickshaw Pullers and Owner-Contractors in North East Delhi'. Discussion Paper Series. 205. https://hermes-ir.lib.hit-u.ac.jp/rs/bitstream/10086/13600/1/D06-205.pdf (accessed 8 June 2015).

107. Ibid.

108. S. Begum and B. Sen (2004), 'Unsustainable Livelihoods, Health Shocks and Urban Chronic Poverty: Rickshaw Pullers as a Case Study'. CPRC Working Paper.

109. A.K. Pandey, M. Bajpayee, D. Parmar, S.K. Rastogi, N Mathur, P.K. Seth and A. Dhawan (2005), 'DNA Damage in Lymphocytes of Indian Rickshaw Pullers as Measured by the Alkaline Comet Assay'. Environmental and Molecular Mutagenesis 47(1): 25–30.

110. F. Cornish (2006), 'Challenging the Stigma of Sex Work in India: Material Context and Symbolic Change'. Journal of Community and Applied Social Psychology 16(6): 462–71.

111. T.S.H. Beattie, P. Bhattacharjee, B.M. Ramesh, V. Gurnani, J. Anthony, S. Isac, H.L. Mohan, A. Ramakrishnan, T. Wheeler, J. Bradley, J.F. Blanchard and S. Moses (2010), 'Violence Against Female Sex Workers in Karnataka State, South India: Impact on Health and Reductions in Violence Following an Intervention Programme'. BMC Public Health 10: 476. http://www.biomedcentral.com/1471-2458/10/476.

112. R. Sahni and V.K. Shankar (2011), 'The First Pan-India Survey of Sex Workers: A Summary of Preliminary Findings'. Paulo Longo Research Initiative. Sangli: Centre for Advocacy on Stigma and Marginalisation/ Sampada Gramin Mahila Sanstha. http://www.sangram.org/resources/Pan_India_Survey_of_Sex_workers.pdf (accessed 8 August 2015).

113. S. Baral, C. Beyrer, K. Muessig, T. Poteat, A.L. Wirtz, M.R. Decker, S.G. Sherman and D. Kerrigan (2010), 'Burden of HIV Among Female Sex Workers in Low-income and Middle-income Countries: A Systematic Review and Meta-analysis'. The Lancet Infectious Diseases 12: 538–49.

114. G. Gangoli (1999), 'Unmet Needs: Sex Workers and Health Care'. Indian Journal of Medical Ethics 7(3). http://www.issuesinmedicalethics.org/index.php/ijme/article/view/1489/3242 (accessed 15 June 2015).

115. F. Cornish (2006), 'Challenging the Stigma of Sex Work in India: Material Context and Symbolic Change'

116. Childline (2015), 'Vulnerable Children'. http://www.childlineindia.org.in/vulnerable-children.htm. (accessed on 15 May 2015).

117. V. Deshpande (2011), 'Every Eighth Urban Child in India Lives in Slums: Report'. The Hindu. 15 October. http://www.thehindu.com/news/national/every-eighth-urban-child-in-india-lives-in-slum-report/article2541052.ece(accessed on 15 May 2015).

118. Price Water House Coopers and Save the Children (2015), 'Forgotten Voices: The World of Urban Children in India' http://www.pwc.in/assets/pdfs/publications/urban-child/urban-child-india-report.pdf. (accessed 20 May 2015).

119. S. Ghosh and D. Shah (2004), 'Nutritional Problems in Urban Slum Children'. Indian Pediatrics 41: 682–96.

120. P. Salve and S. Tewari (2015), 'Shut Out: India's Poor, Urban Children'. India Spend. 25 July. http://www.indiaspend.com/cover-story/shut-out-indias-poor-urban-children-part-i-72517 (accessed on 28 July 2015).

121. N. Juneja (2001), 'Primary Education for all in the city of Mumbai, India: Challenge set by local actors'. Indian Institute of Educational Planning, UNESCO. http://datatopics.worldbank.org/hnp/files/edstats/INDpub01.pdf (accessed 15 May 2015).

122. National Commission for Protection of Child Rights (2013), Assessment of Pattern, Profile and Correlates of SubstanceUse among Children in India. New Delhi: National Commission for Protection of Child Rights. http://www.ncpcr.gov.in/view_file.php?fid=17 (accsesed 14 October 2015).

123. Ministry of Labour and Employment (2011), State Wise Details of Working Children in the AgeGroup of 5-14 Years as per Census 2001 and Census 2011. http://labour.gov.in/upload/uploadfiles/files/Divisions/childlabour/Census-2001%262011.pdf (accessed 15 May 2015).

124. K. Srivastava (2011), 'Child labour issues and challenges'. Indian Psychiatry Journal. Jan–Jun; 20(1): 1–3.

125. N.K. Behura and R.P. Mohanty (2005), *Urbanisation, Street Children and their Problems*, New Delhi: Discovery Publishing House.

126. A. Chatterjee (1992), 'India: The Forgotten Children of the Cities.' Italy: UNICEFhttp://www.unicef-irc.org/publications/pdf/is_india.pdf. (accessed 1 August 2015).

127. Childline India. 'Street Children'. (ND). http://www.childlineindia.org.in/street-children-india.htm. (accessed 1 August 2015).

128. Save the Children (2011), 'Surviving the Streets: A Census of Street Children in Delhi by the Institute of

Human Development and Save the Children'. http://resourcecentre.savethechildren.se/sites/default/files/documents/5332.pdf. (accessed 2 August 2015).

129. N. Reddy (1992), 'Street Children of Bangalore: A Situational Analysis'. Noida: National Labour Institute.

130. National Commission for Protection of Child Rights (2013), 'Assessment of Pattern, Profile and Correlates of SubstanceUse among Children in India'.

131. Aide et Action (2012), 'Access to Education, Nutrition and Protection of Children of Migrant Workers'. http://www.aea-southasia.org/uploads/unicef_study.pdf (accessed 15 May 2015).

132. Ibid, p. 42

133. Ministry of Labour and Employment (2011), 'State Wise Details of Working Children in the Age Group of 5–14 Years as per Census 2001 and Census 2011'.

134. K. Srivastava (2011), 'Child labour issues and challenges'.

135. K. Goel, S. Ahmad, R. Bansal, P. Parashar, B. Pant B and G. Goel (2012), 'The Social and Occupational Problems of ChildLabour: A Challenge the World is Facing'. Indian Journal of Community Health 24(1): 53–57.

136. V V Giri National Labour Institute. 'Magnitude of Child Labour in India: An Analysis of Official Socurces of Data (Draft)'. (ND). http://www.vvgnli.org/sites/default/files/publication_files/Magnitude_of_Child_Labour_in_India_An_Analysis_of_Official_Sources_of_Data_Draft_0.pdf. (accessed on 27 May 2015).

137. Childline (2015), 'Child Labour in 'India'.

138. United Nations Department of Economic and Social Affairs, Population Division (2008 Revision), 'World Population Prospects'. http://esa.un.org/unpp/index.asp?panel=2. (accessed 26 May 2015).

139. S. Raju (2000), 'Ageing in India: An overview', in M. Desai and S.Raju (eds), *Gerontological Social Work in India: Some Issues and Perspectives*, New Delhi: BR Publishing; as quoted in S. Dey, D. Nambiar, J.K. Lakshmi, K. Sheikh, K.S. Reddy (2012), 'Health of the Elderly in India: Challenges of Access and Affordability.' http://www.ncbi.nlm.nih.gov/books/NBK92618/ (accessed 27 May 2015).

140. S. Dey, D. Nambiar , J.K. Lakshmi, K. Sheikh, K.S. Reddy (2012), 'Health of the Elderly in India: Challenges of Access and Affordability', in J.P. Smith and M. Majumdar (eds) *Needs to Meet the Challenges of Aging in Asia*, Washington (DC): National Academics Press (US) http://www.ncbi.nlm.nih.gov/books/NBK92618/ (accessed 27 May 2015).

141. Public Health Resource Network (2010), 'Lesson Three: Urban Health – Policies, Programmes, and Delivery Structures'. Book 16: Issues in Urban Health. New Delhi: Public Health Resource Network, pp. 36–78.

142. S.I. Rajan and S. Aliyar(2011), 'Population Aging in India' in S.I. Rajan, C. Risseeuw and M. Perera (eds), *Institutional Provisions and Care for the Aged: Perspectives from Asia and Europe*, London: Anthem Press.

143. Naila Kabeer (2000), 'Social Exclusion, Poverty and Discrimination: Towards an Analytical Framework', IDS Bulltein, 31:4

144. H. Mander, 'The State, Marginalised People and Justice'. Unpublished Presentation. (ND).

145. Steering Committee on Urbanisation, Planning Commission (2011), 'Report of the Working Group on Urban Poverty, Slums and Serivc [sic.] Delivery System'. New Delhi: Government of India http://planningcommission.nic.in/aboutus/committee/wrkgrp12/hud/wg_Final_Urb_Pvt.pdf (accessed 3 August 2015).

146. R. Dasgupta (2012), *Urbanising Cholera: The Social Determinants of Its Re-Emergence*, Hyderabad: Orient Blackswan, p. 266

147. Srilatha Batliwala (2011), 'Unpacking Social Exclusion: A Primer for Marginalised Women', CREA, pp. 17-37 http://www.countmeinconference.org/downloads/background_papers.pdf

148. L.A. Hulton, Z. Matthews and R.W. Stones (2007), 'Applying a Framework for Assessing the Quality of Maternal Health Services in Urban India'. Social Science & Medicine 64:2083–95.

149. N. Barua and C.S. Pandav(2011), 'The Allure of the Private Practitioner: Is this the only Alternative for the Urban Poor in India?' Indian Journal of Public Health 55(2): 107–14.

150. Hospital Employees Union, Jobs with Justice and Society for Labour and Development (2007), 'India's Health Care in a Globalised World: Health Care Workers' and Patients' Views of Delhi's Public Health Services'. New Delhi: Society for Labour and Development, p. V.

151. R. Priya (1993), 'Town Planning, Public Health and Urban Poor: Some Explorations from Delhi'. Economic and Political Weekly 28(17):824–34.

152. Public Health Resource Network (2010). 'Lesson Three: Urban Health – Policies, Programmes, and Delivery Structures', pp. 36–78.

153. R. Kaul (2015), 'Five Remedies to Save Delhi's Hospitals'. Hindustan Times. 11 July. http://cjr7.com/five-remedies-to-save-delhis-hospitals/. (accessed 11 July 2015).

154. This ratio is perhaps somewhat exaggerated as the public sector includes beds provided by the Railways, Army, and the Employees State Insurance Scheme. These facilities are not be accessible to all populations. However, it can conversely be argued that while these facilities restrict access based on eligibility criteria, private facilities restrict it on purely financial grounds, i.e., the ability to pay. Further, public facilities are also known to specifically cater to the poorest populations.
155. V. Krishnan (2015), 'Private Practice'. The Caravan. 1 Feb http://www.caravanmagazine.in/reportage/naresh-trehan-medanta-private-practice?page=0,10#sthash.pSnmTAkA.dpuf (accessed 14 February 2015), p. 4
156. P. Kaushika (2015), 'Govt Cracks Down, Will Monitor EWS Admissions in Private Hospitals. The Indian Express. 19 March. http://indianexpress.com/article/cities/delhi/govt-cracks-down-will-monitor-ews-admissions-in-private-hospitals/(accessed 3 Aug 2015).
157. B.S. Perappadan (2015), '30% Beds for EWS Patients Lie Vacant'. The Hindu. 5 August. http://www.thehindu.com/news/national/other-states/30-beds-for-ews-patients-lie-vacant/article7500824.ece (accessed 5 August 2015).
158. M. Kanchan (2015), 'Business of Hospitals'. Economic and Political Weekly L(30): 25–27.
159. High Level Expert Group on Universal Health Coverage (2011), 'Report of the High Level Expert Group on Univeral Health Coverage'. New Delhi: Public Health Foundation of India.
160. Editorial (2014).'Facing Health Crises, India Slashes Healthcare'. India Spend. 25 December. http://www.indiaspend.com/cover-story/facing-health-crises-india-slashes-health care-57629(accessed 3 August 2015).
161. National Sample Survey Office, Ministry of Statistics and Programme Implementation (2015), 'Key Indicators of Social Consumption in India | Health'
162. Ibid.
163. R. Duggal (2006), 'Health Tourism or Reengineered Brain Drain'. Health Action 19(3).
164. Ibid.
165. National Sample Survey Office, Ministry of Statistics and Programme Implementation (2015), 'Key Indicators of Social Consumption in India | Health'
166. Ibid.
167. Planning Commission (2012), 'Report of the Expert Group to Recommend the Detailed Methodology for Identification of Families Living Below Poverty Line in the Urban Areas'. p. 28
168. K. Anand, B. Shah, K. Yadav, R. Singh, P. Mathur, E. Paul and S.K. Kapoor (2007), 'Are the Urban Poor Vulnerable to Non-communicable Diseases? A Survey of Risk Factors for Non-communicable Diseases in Urban Slums of Faridabad'. National Medical Journal of India 20(3):115–20.
169. M.K. Ranson (2002), 'Reduction of Catastrophic Health Care Expenditures by a Community-based Health Insurance Scheme in Gujarat, India: Current Experiences and Challenges'. Bull World Health Organ 80(8): 613–21.
170. K.D. Ramaiah, H. Guyatt, K. Ramu, P. Vanamail, S.P. Pani and P.K. Das (1999), 'Treatment Costs and Loss of Work Time to Individuals with Chronic Lymphatic Filariasis in Rural Communities in South India'. Tropical Medicine & International Health 4(1): 19–25.
171. J.F. Levesque, S. Haddad, D. Narayana and P. Fournier (2007), 'Affording What's Free and Paying for Choice: Comparing the Cost of Public and Private Hospitalisations in Urban Kerala'. International Journal of Health Planningand Management22: 159–74.

    Sivaramakrishnan, Kunduand Singh (2005), Handbook of Urbanization in India.
172. National Sample Survey Office, Ministry of Statistics and Programme Implementation (2015), 'Key Indicators of Social Consumption in India | Health'
173. N. Barua and C.S. Pandav (2011), 'The Allure of the Private Practitioner: Is this the only Alternative for the Urban Poor in India?'
174. A. Gadre and A. Shukla (2015), *Voices of Conscience from the Medical Profession*, New Delhi: Oxfam/CEHAT.
175. Ibid.
176. V. Chakrapani, Y. Singh, A. Aher, S. Shaikh, S. Mehta and J. Robertson (2013), 'Issue Brief: Transforming Identity – Access to Gender Transition Services for Male-to-Female Transgender People in India'. http://www.allianceindia.org/wp-content/uploads/2014/07/2014_AllianceIndia_Transforming-Identity-Access-to-Gender-Transition-Services-for-Male-to-Female-Transgender-People-in-India.pdf. (accessed 21 July 2015).
177. S. Awasthi, N.M. Srivastava and S. Pant (2008). 'Symptom-specific Care-seeking Behavior for Sick Neonates among Urban Poor in Lucknow, Northern India'. Journal of Perinatology, 28: S69–S75; doi:10.1038/jp.2008.169.
178. A. George and A. Iyer (2013), 'Unfree Markets: Socially Embedded Informal Health Providers in Northern Karnataka, India'. Social Science and Medicine 96:297–304.

179. V.R. Kamat and M. Nichter (1998), 'Pharmacies, self-medication and pharmaceutical marketing in Bombay, India'. Social Science and Medicine 47(6):779–94.

180. Urban Health Division, Ministry of Health and Family Welfare, Government of India (2008) 'National Urban Health Mission (2008-2012): Meeting the Health Challenges of Urban Populations especially the Urban Poor (With Special Focus on Urban Slums)'

181. Ibid.

182. K.D. Ramaiah, H. Guyatt, K. Ramu, P. Vanamail, S.P. Pani and P.K. Das (1999), 'Treatment Costs and Loss of Work Time to Individuals with Chronic Lymphatic Filariasis in Rural Communities in South India'

183. Sivaramakrishnan Kunduand Singh (2005), *Handbook of Urbanization in India.*

184. K.D. Ramaiah, H. Guyatt, K. Ramu, P. Vanamail, S.P. Pani and P.K. Das (1999), 'Treatment Costs and Loss of Work Time to Individuals with Chronic Lymphatic Filariasis in Rural Communities in South India'

185. S. Selvaraj and A.K. Karan (2012), 'Why Publicly-Financed Health Insurance Schemes are Ineffectivein Providing Financial Risk Protection'. Economic and Political Weekly XLVII(2): 60–68.

186. I. Gupta (2009), 'Out of Pocket Expenditures and Poverty: Estimates form NSS 61st Round'. Paper presented for consideration of the Expert Group on Poverty, Planning Commission. Delhi: Institute of Economic Growth. http://planningcommission.gov.in/reports/genrep/indrani.pdf (accessed 12 June 2015).

187. Ibid.

188. This applied to the average total medical expenditure for non-hospitalised treatment per ailing person suffering from only one ailment at various levels of care.

189. National Sample Survey Office, Ministry of Statistics and Programme Implementation (2015), 'Key Indicators of Social Consumption in India | Health'

190. R. Pal (2012), 'Measuring Incidence of Catastrophic Out-of-pocket Expenditure: With Application to India'. International Journal of Health Care Finance and Economics 12: 63–85.

191. M.M. Engelgau, A. Karan and A. Mahal (2012), 'The Economic Impact of Non-communicable Diseases on Households in India'. Globalisation and Health 8:9.

192. The Hindu (2009), '2 Health Centres Coming Up Soon for Senior Citizens'. 2 October. http://www.thehindu.com/todays-paper/tp-national/tp-tamilnadu/2-health-centres-coming-up-soon-for-senior-citizens/article153267.ece (accessed 2 March 2015).

193. R. Sujatha (2010), 'Corporation Health Centres to get Semi-auto Analysers'. The Hindu. 8 August. http://www.thehindu.com/news/cities/chennai/corporation-health-centres-to-get-semiauto-analysers/article558181.ece (accessed 17 March 2015).

194. Society for Nutrition, Education and Health Action. Organisation Brief. Mumbai: SNEHA. (ND). http://www.snehamumbai.org/

195. Society for Nutrition, Education and Health Action. SNEHA: About Us. http://www.snehamumbai.org/about-us/about-sneha-mumbai-ngo.aspx (accessed 5 August 2015).

196. SWaCH. What is Swach? http://www.swachcoop.com/about-swachpune.html (accessed 7 August 2015).

197. The Bhopal Medical Appeal. Sambhavna Clinic. http://bhopal.org/about-us/sambhavna-clinic/ (accessed 7 August 2015).

198. The Banyan Projects – Adaikalam. http://www.thebanyan.org/html/adaikalam.html (accessed 7 August 2015).

199. R. Gopinath, K. Richter, K. Srivastava and G. Plotkin (2015). 'USAID/India Health of the Urban Poor Program Final Evaluation Report (AID 386 TO 15 00002/ AID 486 1 14 00001)'. New Delhi: USAID.

200. An urban homeless recovery shelter in the Yamuna Pushta area of New Delhi, The Banyan in Chennai, and the SWaCH Cooperative in Pune are all examples of organisations that are facilitating the identification acquisition process for their patients and residents, clients, and members. Certainly other organisations functioning in the urban health sector, though they themselves might not be requiring identification for individuals to access their services, should similarly facilitate the identification acquisition process.

201. The Banyan has shared living accommodation available for its clients whohave been duly treated at The Banyan but still need some level of long-term care.

202. The Aman Biradari programme has a functional model of linkages between health care facilities and their recovery shelter, which is an important, and often only recourse for those who cannot continue or complete treatment specifically because of their vulnerability.

Tracing Exclusions in Urban Water Supply and Sanitation

Geetika Anand, Kavita Wankhade and Rajiv K. Raman[*]

Anushree Deb and Vishnu MJ[**]

Nearly 70 years since Independence, a large proportion of urban Indians, particularly the poor and vulnerable groups, are deprived of adequate public provisioning in water supply and sanitation. The discourse of 'urban' is increasingly being captured through the rhetoric of 'Smart Cities', even as urban residents are yet to receive basic services. Albeit late, sanitation has now occupied centre-stage in India's policy framework through the current government's flagship: Swacch Bharat Mission.

This chapter seeks to understand the nature of exclusion from water and sanitation services in India, and proposes a way forward to address these exclusions. The initial section of the chapter argues that it is necessary to expand the definition of water and sanitation as a public good if desired health outcomes are to be achieved. The essay argues that while the abysmal level of provisioning in urban areas means that most of urban India represents some or other form of exclusion, certain vulnerable groups, for instance, urban poor, Dalits and women, face a higher extent of exclusion. These differential exclusions are even more evident if the expanded definition of water and sanitation as a public good is taken into account. Further, these vulnerable groups are hit harder because they are unable to afford alternate, feasible means of self-provisioning, and also cannot afford the consequent health care costs.

1. Water and Sanitation as a Public Good

Water and sanitation are the basis for life, and secure health and dignity for societies. The consequences of inadequate water and sanitation are increasingly being documented and there is consensus about their critical role not only for healthy individuals and families, but also for securing public health for communities.

Lack of access to adequate water and safe sanitation can lead to adverse health outcomes, particularly diarrhoeal diseases, which remain the second-largest cause of under-five mortality globally. Research has also highlighted the role of inadequate sanitation, in stunting, an indicator of malnourishment.[3] Apart from health, there are several other impacts of inadequate access to water and sanitation like a disproportionate burden of water collection being shouldered by women, drop-out of adolescent girls from schools, and so on. Exclusion from water and sanitation adversely affects the safety and dignity of women and girls in cities much more than it does for men. Globally,

---

* Lead authors

** Contributing authors

*** This chapter has been reviewed by Sara Ahmed, Indira Khurana and Erhard Berner.

adverse outcomes of lack of adequate water and sanitation have meant that water and sanitation is considered a public good, and the right to water and sanitation is constitutive of many other rights, especially Right to Health, and Right to Life.

Given the public good nature of water and sanitation, it is the obligation of the state to provide these services. The state is responsible for progressively providing access to water and sanitation, ensuring substantive equality, and ensuring that discrimination does not take place.[4]

1.1 Expanding the definition

It is important not to stop at the acknowledgement of water as a human right, but to interrogate more fully what exactly constitutes the right to water and sanitation, and what it would take to secure health

BOX 1: The Global Evolution of Water and Sanitation as a Human Right

Globally, the evolution of the right to water can be traced back to the 1970s. At the United Nation Mar del Plata Water Conference in Argentina, the right to water to 'all peoples, whatever their stage of development and their social and economic conditions' was declared.[5] This conference also resulted in declaring the period of 1980–1990 as the International Decade for Water Supply and Sanitation, during which governments committed to increase access to water and sanitation services. In 1999, the United Nations passed a resolution for 'Right to Development' which included the 'right to clean water'.[6]

The International Covenant on Economic, Social and Cultural Rights, 1966 (ICESCR), ratified by 157 states, does not explicitly recognise the right to water.[7] However, the United Nations Committee on Economic, Social and Cultural Rights issued a General Comment No. 15 in 2002, which recognises the right to water.[8] While the Comments are not legally binding, they often play a substantial role in the interpretation of the Covenant (COHRE). Comment 15 implicitly recognises water, both in Article 11 (adequate standard of living) and Article 12 (mental and physical health).[9] In addition, the Right to Water was explicitly recognised in legally binding international treaties like the Convention on the Elimination of All Forms of Discrimination Against Women, 1979 and the Convention on the Rights of the Child, 1989 and the Convention on the Rights of Persons with Disabilities, adopted in 2006 (UN General Assembly, 1979, 1989, 2006). India is a signatory to all of these covenants and therefore bound to implement them.

In 2010, a UN Resolution formally recognised the right to water and sanitation, and acknowledged that clean drinking water and sanitation are essential to the realisation of all human rights. Following the UN General Assembly resolution, a resolution was passed by the UN Human Rights Council (UNHRC) affirming that the rights to water and sanitation are part of existing international law and confirming that these rights are legally binding upon States. The UNHRC states clearly that 'states have the primary responsibility to ensure the full realization of all human rights, and that the delegation of the delivery of safe drinking water and/or sanitation services to a third party does not exempt the State from its human rights obligations'.[10]

In 2014, another resolution was passed by UNHRC which reaffirmed the right to water and sanitation, and also considerably expanded the definitions and obligations.[11] The resolution referred to three reports of the UN Rapporteur on Water and Sanitation.[12] Together, these documents form the building blocks for a framework for the right to water and sanitation internationally.

and dignity for human beings. Globally, there has been a gradual expansion of the understanding of water and sanitation as a human right (Box 1).

The UN reports in Box 1 indicate an expanded framework for the right to water and sanitation. The 2014 UN Resolution expresses concerns that the current official figures underestimate the number of people without access to adequate water and sanitation since they do not take into account certain dimensions like quality of drinking water, affordability of services and safe treatment of excreta.[13]

Based on the various UN Reports mentioned above, the following dimensions can be taken together to constitute the right to water and sanitation:

Water

- **Access:** Access to water sources should be convenient and without physical or cultural barriers. Access must be ensured in a sustainable manner.
- **Sufficiency:** People need to have access to a quantity of water sufficient for all personal and domestic needs, including water required for hygiene.
- **Quality of potable water:** People have the right to drinking water of safe quality standards.
- **Reliable and regular supply:** Water supply must be sufficiently reliable to allow for the collection of amounts sufficient to realise all personal and domestic needs over the day.
- **Affordability:** People have the right to access adequate quantity of water of acceptable quality, at affordable prices.

Sanitation

- **Access to services:** Sanitation facilities must be available within or in the immediate vicinity of each household as well as in schools, workplaces, health care settings and public places. Access must be ensured in a sustainable manner.
- **Safety of sanitation facilities:** Human, animal and insect contact with human excreta must be effectively prevented. Regular maintenance and cleaning of toilets is critical too.
- **Safe disposal after treatment:** Depending on the technology, fully functional sewers and treatment plants and regular de-sludging or emptying are necessary for on-site or local systems. Sludge and sewage must be safely disposed of to avoid negative impacts on human health, water quality and the environment.
- **Acceptability:** Sanitation facilities, in particular, must be culturally acceptable. This will, for instance, often require privacy as well as separate and appropriate facilities for men, women, children and the differently abled.

It is vital to highlight the importance of paying attention to the full cycle of sanitation: from adequate access at household level to safe collection and treatment. If the full sanitation cycle is not addressed, then the necessary health outcomes will not be achieved.

It is crucial to appreciate that the above dimensions need to be considered together for securing public health outcomes. If good quality water is available at some distance, adequate water will not be consumed for various purposes and hence health outcomes will be adversely affected. If every household has a toilet, but all the faecal matter and waste water is not safely collected, treated and disposed, the community or the city will not be able to enjoy healthy lives.

These dimensions can be further interpreted and broken into indicator sets and benchmarks.

Minimum quantity is, for instance, defined as 'lifeline', i.e., enough for physical survival while quality standards would refer to acceptable physical, chemical and biological characteristics, and so on.

The above-mentioned dimensions that need to form a part of the expanded definitions, however, are not commonly included. The Millennium Development Goals (MDGs), which were the most significant global commitment until recently, had a target to 'halve the number of people without access to improved water and sanitation'. But it measures progress along limited parameters[14], falling considerably short of the above definitions. As part of the recently formulated Sustainable Development Goals (SDGs), Goal 6 aims to 'Ensure access to water and sanitation for all'. The targets under Goal 6 take at least some of the above dimensions into account: safe and affordable water for all, adequate sanitation and hygiene for all, with special attention to women, girls and vulnerable populations, and halving the proportion of untreated waste water.

Right to Water and Sanitation in India

In India, the right to water and sanitation is not explicitly stated in the Constitution of India but jurisprudence shows that existing provisions have been interpreted to mean that it is a duty of the State to provide access to water and sanitation. The Supreme Court has ruled that both water and sanitation are part of the Constitutional Right to Life (Article 21). The Court has stated that 'the right to access to clean drinking water is fundamental to life and there is a duty on the state under Article 21 to provide clean drinking water to its citizens' (A.P. Pollution Control Board II v. Prof. M.V. Naidu and Others, 1999).

While the Central and various state governments have refrained from legally and explicitly committing to the right to water and sanitation, various elements of the expanded definitions find a place in different government documents, most notably the National Water Policy (2012) and the National Urban Sanitation Policy (2008). In addition, initiatives like the Service Level Benchmarks (SLBs), developed by the MoUD, have set benchmarks that take into account at least some dimensions, for instance, sufficiency, treatment facilities for sanitation, etc. These initiatives are discussed later in the chapter.

Indicators for Inclusion in Urban Water Supply and Sanitation in India

Based on the definitions above, it is possible to derive an indicator set to measure exclusions. Table 1 presents the above dimensions, and possible indicator sets for Indian cities, and assesses availability of data (Census, NSSO, SLBs, etc.) for each. Data are available only for a few indicators, posing problems of measuring change. This also necessitates exclusive dependence on case studies to measure exclusions along certain indicators.

2. Understanding the Nature of Exclusion in Urban Water Supply and Sanitation

This section illustrates the extent of exclusion from public services in urban India. To begin with, the overall exclusion from water and sanitation services faced by all sections of society is explored, and then the exclusion faced by specific vulnerable groups is assessed. Further, the differential exclusions can be divided into two broad categories: inter-household disparity (differences across households divided by wealth quintiles, caste or religion), and intra-household disparity (differences among households because of differences in ability, gender or age).[15]

2.1 Water supply and sanitation in urban india: deficits and exclusions

There are several deficits in public provisioning in urban India, hence all sections of the urban

Table 1: List of Indicators for Understanding Nature of Exclusion from Right to Water and Sanitation

No.	Dimension	Rationale for Dimension	Possible Indicator Set (based on available datasets)	Data Source(s)	Remarks
	Water Supply				
1	Accessibility	This is the most basic dimension for exclusion, and most commonly used both in India and internationally.	1. Location of primary source of water 2. Access levels to primary source of water (exclusive v. shared used) 3. Time taken to access water (if from outside premises)	Census/ NSS NSS NSS	Most public datasets measure this variable.
2	Sufficiency	Provisioning of drinking water is not adequate. Availability of sufficient water is required for hygiene.	1. Quantity of water supplied 2. Households' perception of sufficiency of water for drinking and other purposes	SLB NSS	Available for only select cities. The data are for per capita water supplied from ULB/ parastatal. Given that there are distribution losses, it is difficult to estimate the quantity of water that households receive. Only a few micro-studies available. Self-Reporting of Perception (not very reliable)

Table 1: List of Indicators for Understanding Nature of Exclusion from Right to Water and Sanitation

No.	Dimension	Rationale for Dimension	Possible Indicator Set (based on available datasets)	Data Source(s)	Remarks
3	Quality	Good quality potable water is necessary to ensure prevention of water-borne and faecal oral diseases.	1. Quality of water supplied (Various indicators like turbidity, absence of pathogens, etc.) 2. Primary source of drinking water (Availability of treated piped water supply) 3. Households' perception of quality of water	Census/ NSS NSS SLB	Water quality data (determined by various physical tests) are available for only select cities. Most of these tests are conducted from the supply side, and not at the household level. Proxy indicator of quality.
4	Regularity		1. Duration of water supplied 2. Frequency of supply of water	SLB NSS	Available for only select cities.
5	Affordability	Affordability is critical to ensure access.	1. Average amount paid per month 2. Cost of purchasing water (per litre)	NSS	Information on tariffs levied by cities is available. But most households depend on alternate sources of water, for which only a few micro-studies are available.
Sanitation					
7	Accessibility		1. Type and location of sanitation facility 2. Access levels to sanitation facility (exclusive v. shared)	Census/ NSS NSS	Available for only select cities; expressed in percentage, which is not very clear.

Table 1: List of Indicators for Understanding Nature of Exclusion from Right to Water and Sanitation

No.	Dimension	Rationale for Dimension	Possible Indicator Set (based on available datasets)	Data Source(s)	Remarks
8	Safety of Sanitation Facilities	Mere elimination of open defaecation will not necessarily ensure health benefits. The deficits along the entire sanitation chain need to be addressed to enjoy the benefits of sanitation.	1. Type of household arrangement for sanitation (Connection to sewerage network/ septic tank/ improved pits/ etc.)	Census/ NSS	This information indicates the percentage of households with safe sanitation. However, no data exists whether these systems have been constructed to required standards.
			2. Safe disposal of Sludge		No information exists.
			3. Treatment capacity	CPCB	Available only for select locations in the city. There is monitoring at neighbourhood/ward level.
			4. Surface and ground water quality	CPCB	
9	Acceptability	This is necessary to ensure that the constructed sanitation facilities are actually used.	No information collected		

Source: Compiled by authors; (Census of India, 2011; CPCB, 2013a, 2013b; MoUD, 2011; NSSO, 2013).

Notes:

Census: The census operations are carried out every 10 years; the most recent dataset being of 2011. The census covers every household in urban and rural areas of the country. The housing tables in the census give details of services and amenities at the household level, including water and sanitation.

National Sample Survey: NSS on drinking water, sanitation, hygiene and housing conditions is carried out every five years, the most recent dataset being of 2012 (69th round). This is a sample survey and does not cover the entire population; household multipliers are mentioned to enable extrapolation of the sample data.

Service Level Benchmarking: After MoUD introduced service level benchmarks for environmental services in 2008, self-reported utilities data from sample cities are compiled on various benchmarks, the most recent dataset being of 2010-11, which reports data on 1,493 cities.

population face some degree of exclusion. This section presents the overall deficits in urban India for water and sanitation, i.e., for the whole population, before turning to vulnerable groups in the next section.

Water Supply

As highlighted in Table 2, only 62 per cent households had treated tap water as their primary source of drinking water, a proxy indicator for public supply; thus more than one-third of the households do not have access to any form of public supply.[16] [17]

Table 2: Primary Source of Drinking Water for Urban India	
	Census 2011
Tap water	71%
Treated	62%
Not treated	9%
Hand pump/tube well	21%
Well	6%
Surface water sources	1%
Bottled water	Not available
Other sources	2%
Source: Census of India (2011)	

The two-thirds of households with access to public services also do not necessarily have the requisite standard of services. Amongst these, about 80 per cent households have treated water within their premises, an indicator of easy accessibility. More importantly, most households are provided with an insufficient quantity of water: the average per capita supply of 73 lpcd (in 1,493 cities) is far below the desired benchmark of 135 lpcd.[18] Average duration of supply is around three hours against the benchmark of 24 hours.[19] According to NSSO (2013), almost a quarter of households are not supplied water daily.

Lack of adequate publicly supplied water leads to dependence on multiple sources of water by most households. Nearly 23 per cent of households also had a supplementary source of drinking water, indicating insufficiency or unreliability of the primary source of drinking water.[20] There are case studies to illustrate that the percentage of households depending on multiple sources of water might be higher, at least in some cities.

Further, nearly a quarter (estimates ranging from 18 million to 23 million) of households do not have access to water supply within their premises, and only slightly more than half the households have access to a water source for exclusive use. [21] On an average, more than half an hour (31 minutes) is spent to fetch water from outside (including waiting time).[22]

The biggest threat posed by dependence on multiple water sources is the possibility of getting water that is contaminated. However, very few studies examine this issue. The few studies that exist do not examine water quality at the household level; however, there is sufficient newspaper reportage to provide evidence of water contamination (see Box 2). While there is a possibility of piped water supply

BOX 2

A survey done by Pratham Education Foundation, Montreal University and Harvard Centre for Population and Development Studies in a New Delhi slum found that 42 per cent (284 of 685) of household drinking water samples were contaminated with coliform bacteria.[24]

also being contaminated, piped water systems remain the safest way of ensuring that good quality water is supplied.[23]

Thus, the nature of exclusion from public water supply is multi-faceted, ranging from no access to public supply to inadequate supply due to irregular timings, distance between water source and household, etc. While adequate and robust data is not available for all parameters, it would be safe to say that a substantially large proportion of the population suffers from one or other kind of exclusion. There are substantial coping costs associated with these exclusions, discussed later in the chapter.

Sanitation

There are several deficits along the entire sanitation chain. At the household level, nearly 10 million (13 per cent) households do not have access to any sanitation facilities, and hence they resort to open defaecation. Another 6 per cent depend on public or community latrines, and 4 per cent have access only to unimproved latrines.[25]

A high percentage of households (27 per cent) depend on some form of shared facilities, including public toilets, community toilets and shared facilities among multiple households.[26] Shared facilities present their own set of problems: long waiting time, lack of cleanliness, fixed timings and payment, etc.[27]

While individual household toilets remain the most desirable form of sanitation, community toilets are an acceptable solution where concerns like insecure tenure or space constraints make individual toilets difficult and/or impossible. It is necessary to differentiate between public and community toilets. Public toilets are aimed mostly at a floating population, located in public spaces, and are expensive for regular use as payment is usually on pay-per-use basis. Community toilets have captive user groups, and are available for use usually with a monthly pass or at reduced rates, and are hence affordable. However, community toilets

Table 2: Household Arrangements for Sanitation in Urban India

Type of Sanitation Facility		Percentage of Households
Flush/ Pour Flush Connected to	Piped sewer system	32.7%
	Septic tank	38.2%
	Other system	1.7%
Pit Latrine	With slab/VIP	6.4%
	Without slab/open pit	0.7%
Night Soil	Disposed into open drain	1.2%
	Removed by human	0.3%
	Serviced by animal	0.2%
Others		NA
Public Latrine		6.0%
Open Defaecation/ No Latrine		12.6%

Source: Census of India (2011)

are few in number, and available only in a limited number of cities.

The lack of adequate household sanitation facilities constitutes only one form of deficit in the entire sanitation cycle; there are large deficits in safe collection, conveyance, treatment and disposal. As illustrated in Table 2, only one-third of the urban population is connected to networked sewerage systems (mostly in large metropolitan cities, and in rich and middle class colonies), while a much larger proportion of the households depend on on-site systems, primarily septic tanks and pit latrines.

The predominant form of public provisioning in the sanitation chain comprises networked sewerage systems, and centralised sewage treatment plants (STPs) and need to be taken as a proxy indicator of waste water safely treated.[28] For Class I and Class II cities, the treatment capacity is as low as 30 per cent, and the total utilised capacity is only 22 per cent.[29] There are negligible treatment facilities in smaller towns and cities.

While a majority of the population is dependent on on-site sanitation systems, there are hardly any systems and procedures in place for safe cleaning and regular de-sludging of these on-site systems. The most prevalent method of cleaning on-site systems is manual in many places (even if this is banned); increasingly vacuum truck (public and private) are being deployed in some states. Even if the sludge from pit latrines and septic tanks is safely collected, it is mostly dumped untreated in nearby open sites or waterbodies.[30] [31] [32]

Another set of concerns regarding on-site sanitation systems are inappropriate design, poor workmanship and construction. Inappropriate design and construction practices (e.g., not maintaining adequate distance between pit latrines and sources of drinking water, letting effluent from septic tanks flow directly into open drains) can lead to environmental pollution, and contaminate the water often used for household consumption without any treatment.

Similar to water supply, there are multiple exclusions from safe sanitation in urban India. While the absence of sanitation facilities forces some households to resort to open defaecation, absence of safe conveyance and treatment facilities exposes the entire urban population to health risks through various contamination pathways.

2.2 Differential access across groups

The previous section illustrates that a large proportion of households are excluded from public access to water and sanitation in some form. This section focuses on specific vulnerable groups, and examines how these are more excluded than others. Figure 1 and the Annex summarise the key differences in access to water supply and sanitation across different types of groups in urban India based on caste, class, region, religion, gender and type of settlement as compared to the national (urban) average.

Water Supply

While examining exclusions for various groups along all indicators, the starkest differences are observed across economic classes. Taking the example of access to public supply (treated tap water) for drinking purposes, almost 73 per cent of households in Quintile 5 have access while the number drops to 57 per cent in Quintile 1. Again, only 56 per cent Quintile 1 households have drinking water sources within premises as compared to almost 93 per cent Quintile 5 households. With regard to exclusivity of water source, more than two-thirds of Quintile 5 households have a water source for their exclusive use; the percentage drops to 33 per cent in case of Quintile 1.[33] [34]

In case of slum households, while the overall reported access to treated tap water (65 per cent) is marginally higher than the national (urban) average of 62 per cent; the locus of exclusion lies in the location of the source of drinking water. Only 57 per cent slum households have access to drinking water within premises as compared to the national average of 71 per cent.[35] Within different types of slums also, squatter settlements have least access as compared to notified and non-notified slums. At 35 per cent, the exclusive use is also lower among slum households as compared to the national average (47 per cent).[36]

Exclusion along caste lines is also variably observed in water supply. In terms of access to treated tap water, slight differences are observed compared to the national average; the differences start becoming stark when one compares the location and exclusivity of water source. Only 57 per cent SC and 55 per cent ST households have drinking water within premises as compared to the national (urban) average of 71 per cent. Exclusive use is also lower among SC/ST; 35 per cent SC and 39 per cent ST households have a water source for exclusive use.[37,38]

As with the variations across caste groups, female-headed households have similar access to public sources; however, the availability of a water source within the premises and its exclusivity are lower as compared to the national average and male-headed households.[39 40]

Contrary to exclusion based on caste and gender, no significant differences are observed across religious groups with regard to location and exclusivity of water source. However, differences are observed with regard to access to piped water supply. Almost 70 per cent Hindu households have piped water supply as compared to 64 per cent Muslim households; among other minority religions, 72 per cent have piped water supply.[41]

Similar to disparities based on economic classes, regional disparities are observed along all indicators.[42] Only 41 per cent and 37 per cent of urban households in eastern and north east India have access to public supply of water, while as much as 79 per cent of households in western India have access to public supply.[43] Only 60 per cent of households in eastern India have drinking water source within premises as compared to almost 86 per cent among households in the western region.[44] Only around 35 per cent eastern and southern households have water source for exclusive use as compared to 55 per cent and 62 per cent in the North and the West respectively.[45]

Sanitation

Similar to water supply, deficits for sanitation are higher for certain vulnerable groups. Differences are most visible across the economic classes. Dependence on on-site systems increases with decreasing incomes; only 13 per cent quintile 1 households are connected to piped sewer as compared to 57 per cent quintile 5 households. While 98 per cent Quintile 5 households have latrines within premises, the access is restricted to 63 per cent Quintile 1 households. Availability of latrines for a single household's use also decreases among lower income groups; while 80 per cent Quintile 5 households have latrines for household's exclusive use, the percentage reduces to half (40 per cent) in case of Quintile 1.[46]

Slum households have poorer sanitation facilities; only a quarter are connected to piped sewer and another 37 per cent have improved on-site systems. Only two-thirds of slum households have access to a latrine within premises as compared to the national (urban) average of 81 per cent; almost 15 per cent rely on public latrines and 19 per cent resort to open defaecation.[47] Compared to the national average (64 per cent), a lower proportion of slum households have latrines for their exclusive use (38 per cent).[48]

While the overall percentage for households resorting to open defaecation is 12 per cent, the rates are higher for SC (24 per cent) and ST (26 per cent) households. The proportion of households dependent on public toilets for SC (8 per cent) and ST (10 per cent) is also higher as compared to the overall average of 6 per cent.[49] Access to exclusive use of latrines is lower: for SC (43 per cent) and ST (56 per cent) households, as compared to the overall figure of 64 per cent.[50]

Female-headed households have lower access to sanitation facilities. Almost 65 per cent male- headed households have toilets for their exclusive use as compared to 57 per cent female-headed households. Almost 78 per cent female-headed households have latrines within premises as compared to 82 per cent male-headed households; at 14 per cent, open daefecation is also slightly higher among female-headed households as compared to male-headed ones (12 per cent).[51]

No significant differences are observed across religious groups.[52]

Regional disparities are also observed: open

Economic Classes

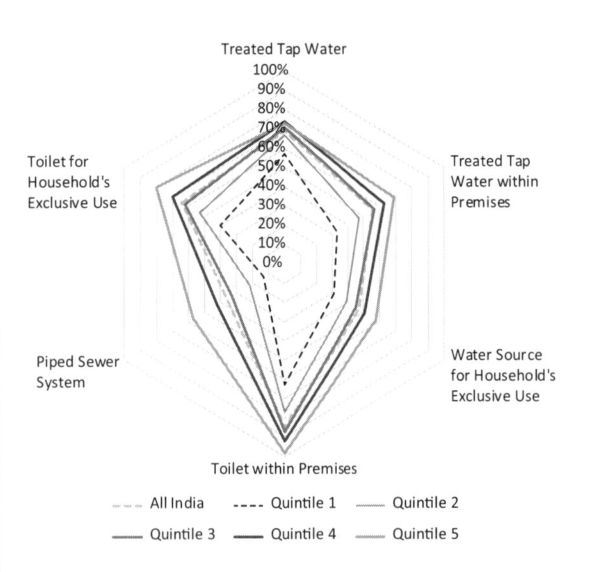

Settlement Type

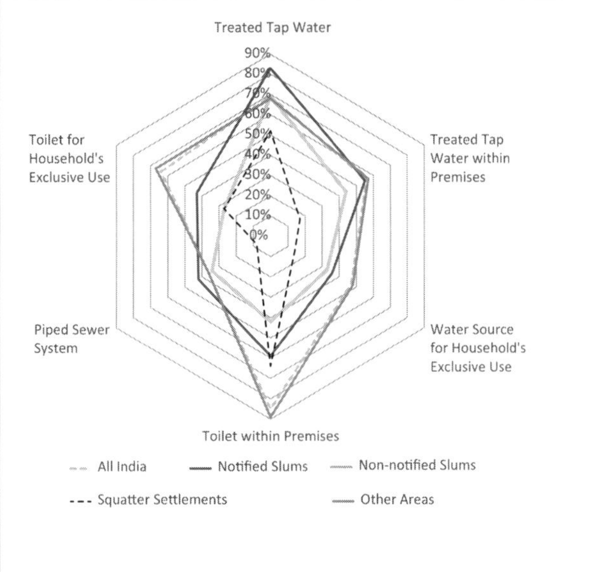

Region

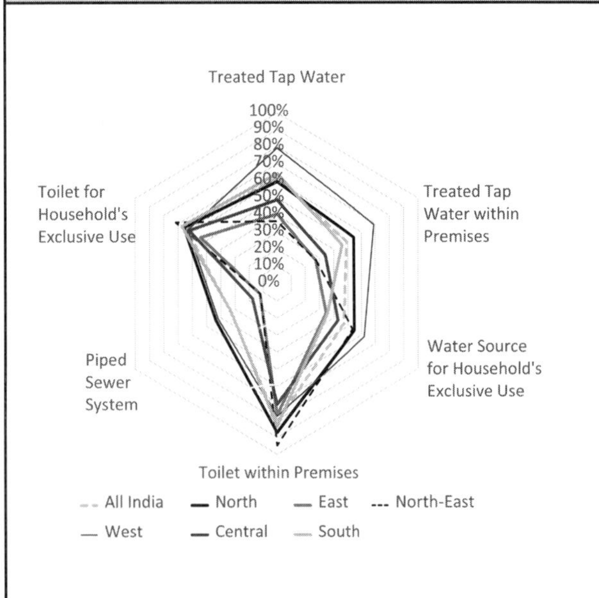

Religion

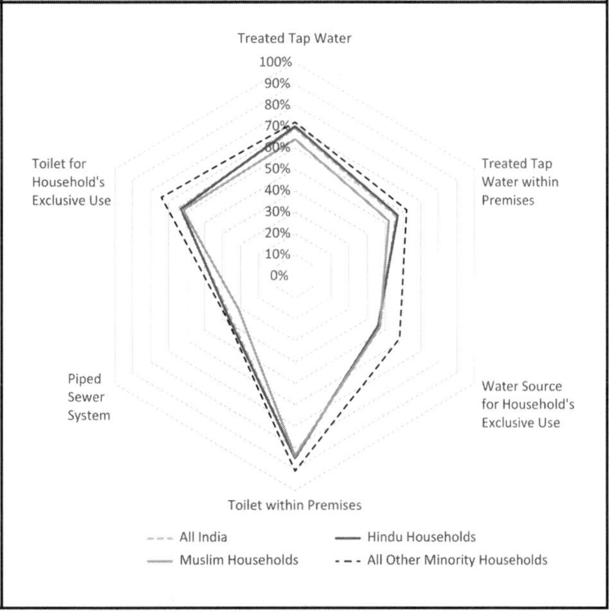

Social Classes	Gender
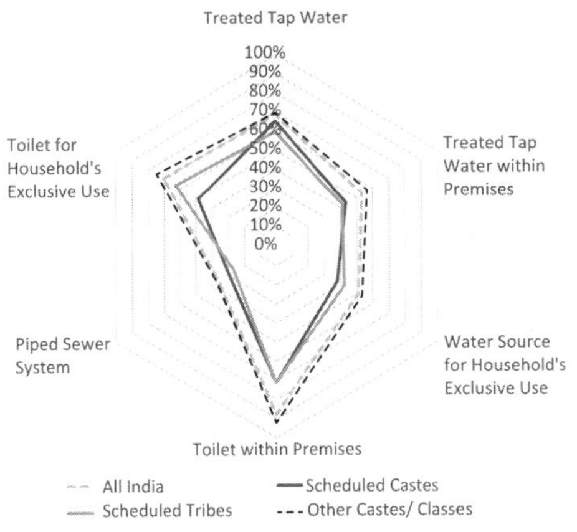	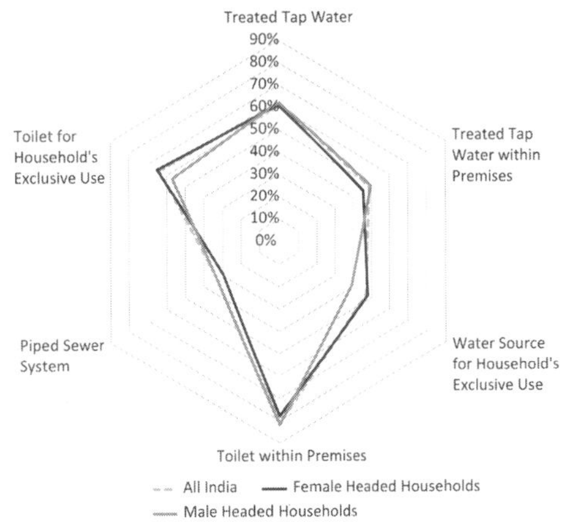

Sources: Economic Classes; Settlement Type; Religion: NSSO, 2013.
Region; Social Classes; Gender: Census 2011; NSSO, 2013.

defaecation in eastern and central parts of the country are as high as 20 and 25 per cent respectively.[53] Only 54 per cent households in eastern India have latrines for exclusive use; at 72 per cent, the figure is highest in the Northeast.[54] Access to piped sewers is as low as 12 per cent in the East and the Northeast; North and the West have better coverage at around 42 per cent.[55]

Intersectionality: Exclusions within sub-groups

While the above analysis has been carried out for discrete categories, the above categories often overlap. In urban areas, Scheduled Castes constitute 12.6 per cent of the population. However, it is interesting to note that according to the Slum Census 2011, 20 per cent of all slum residents in urban areas are SC, indicating a higher percentage of SC in the slums. It is estimated that deprivations (with respect to service delivery and quality of service) occur more for women within any category.

2.3 Access to water and sanitation facilities at schools, workplaces and public spaces

While the household is the primary site of exclusion for water and sanitation, there are other critical sites of exclusion: schools, workplaces, health care facilities and public spaces.

Nationally, the percentage of primary and upper primary schools having drinking water facility has increased from 83.1 per cent in 2005–6 to 95.3 per cent in 2013–14.[64,65] The percentage of primary and upper primary schools with separate girls' toilets stands at 84.6 per cent (showing a substantial increase from 37.4 per cent in 2005–6). However, the progress has not been uniform across the country. States with relatively lower percentage of schools with drinking water facilities include Arunachal Pradesh (76 per cent) and Andhra Pradesh (89 per cent). States with relatively lower percentage of girls' toilets include Jammu & Kashmir (51 per cent), Odisha (62 per cent), Andhra Pradesh (67 per cent), Bihar (67 per cent) and West Bengal (73 per cent).[66]

It is important to note that the mere provision of facilities like taps and toilets is not sufficient. While DISE does not report the usage of facilities, ASER 2014 revealed that boys' toilets in almost 29 per cent schools were not usable, and in 12.9 per cent schools, the girls' toilets were locked while in

Box 2: Urban Homeless—A Case of Absolute Deprivation

The Census of India defines homeless people as those not living in census houses, that is, a structure with a roof. According to the Census of India 2011, there are 2.6 lakh homeless households in urban India with a total population of 9.4 lakh persons. However, these numbers are likely to be an under-estimation due to restrictive definitions and difficulty in enumeration.[56] Ironically, there is little data available about the homeless population, since the standard unit of inquiry for water and sanitation is a dwelling unit.

A study by carried out in Delhi and Bangalore divides the homeless population into three categories following the definition put forward by the Supreme Court Commissioners (2012): rough sleepers (sleeping on pavements and in parks, railway stations, etc.); those living in shelters; and those living in self-made temporary structures in public spaces.[57] Everyday experiences, including coping mechanisms, of accessing water and sanitation for each of these categories are slightly different.

Except for a few homeless persons who live in well-equipped and well-managed shelters, access to water and sanitation services among the homeless is hugely inadequate to ensure their human dignity and health.[58] They have access mostly to poor quality, often non-potable water, fetched over long distances, and often including significant costs. The homeless often have to resort to open defaecation, or have access to paid or unpaid public toilets, which are often poorly maintained and afford little safety and privacy, particularly for women and children.[59]

In one of the rare studies on homeless populations carried out by CES in four cities (Delhi, Chennai, Patna and Madurai) across 340 respondents, it was found that nearly 45 per cent of respondents had to access public toilets on payment, and almost 25 per cent resorted to open defaecation. 67 per cent of the respondents accessed drinking water, often not potable and erratic in supply, for free from roadside taps. 13 per cent bought water from tankers, and 12 per cent got it from shops where the cost of a small plastic pitcher of water was around Rs 5.[60]

The lack of water and sanitation services for homeless populations is embedded in wider processes of exclusion and marginalisation, and the denial of basic social entitlements and rights.[61] Homeless populations lack safe shelter, with which the provision of services is closely associated. A majority of the homeless population do not possess documents like ration cards and voter cards, de facto proof of being a citizen in India, because of unavailability of permanent addresses on their part. These documents have, over time, become prerequisites to access services or any other state benefits.[62] Lack of public taps and their unreliability force homeless persons to buy water. Outsourcing of sanitation blocks for operations and maintenance also means that there is a cost attached to using these facilities, even when the court orders say otherwise.[63]

12.6 per cent they were unusable.[67] ASER 2014 also reported that although 86.1 per cent of the schools visited had drinking water facilities, in 10.5 per cent of schools there was no availability of water.[68]

In a study conducted by Jagori in resettlement colonies of Delhi (2011), girls complained that there were no toilets in their schools. It was reported that teachers had access to toilets but students could not use them. There were only two toilets intended to cater to almost 1,000 girls.

Access to water and sanitation is a critical issue for India's large informal workforce as well; however very few studies on the topic exist.[69] Informal workers usually rely on public or community toilets in localities next to their place of work, which poses larger problems for the female workforce. A study on working women in Bangalore showed that less than half of the respondents had a toilet at their workplace, despite the existence of several pieces of legislation on the matter.[70] Workers in the construction sector were found to be most disadvantaged, having little to no sanitation facilities at work and hence being reliant on public and community toilets. Discriminatory practices exist even among urban, upper class households, with the domestic help in such households facing the brunt of such practices.[71] Domestic help in these households often use separate toilets built away from their place of work. Lack of adequate recognition and separate legislation for domestic workers further worsens their situation.

Public spaces in India generally lack safe water and sanitation facilities. While bottled water has been accepted as an alternative for drinking water in most public spaces, there is no such alternative to a toilet facility. Public toilets in urban India, where they do exist, have mostly been built by urban local bodies or other state agencies. Reviews have shown that these toilets usually suffer from a lack of maintenance and management, and may not even have adequate water supply.[72] Consequently, vulnerable sections of society such as women, children, the elderly and the disabled find it difficult to access or use most public toilets. Although alternative models, including those that brought in private partners (as seen in the case of Sulabh International) or community-based management, have been introduced in several parts of the country, large sections of urban India still suffer from lack of adequate sanitation facilities in public spaces.

There is a huge gap in provisioning of adequate water and sanitation facilities in public schools, markets, work sites and public spaces in general. This inadequacy, again, is higher for poor and vulnerable populations (including women, children, the disabled and the elderly).

3. Differential Impacts of Inadequate Water and Sanitation

The previous section highlighted the fact that while all sections of urban India suffer from poor public provisioning of water and sanitation, certain vulnerable groups face higher levels of exclusion —especially when measured against an expanded indicator set. This section seeks to present the result of such exclusions in terms of differential impacts. Absence of public provisioning forces all urban households to adopt some form of coping mechanism. While the middle class and rich households are able to afford alternate mechanisms to protect themselves from the lack of adequate water supply, poorer households are often unable to do so, leaving them vulnerable to diseases. Further, these poor and vulnerable households are the least able to afford adequate health care once they fall ill, as highlighted in the urban health chapter of the present volume.

3.1 Differential coping mechanisms and associated costs

Given the inadequate public provisioning, different households adopt different coping mechanisms.

The upper and middle class (Quintiles 3, 4 and 5) have managed to cope with inadequate supply and quality of drinking water through investments in bottled water and/or water purifiers. Almost 11 per cent of households in Quintile 5 use bottled water for drinking purposes compared to only 1 per cent in Quintile 1.[73] Fig. 2 clearly illustrates the differential ability to treat water: nearly two-thirds of households in the lowest quintile do not have any form of household treatment.

The urban poor also pay higher costs for coping

Fig. 2: Households by Method of Treatment of Drinking Water across Consumption Quintiles

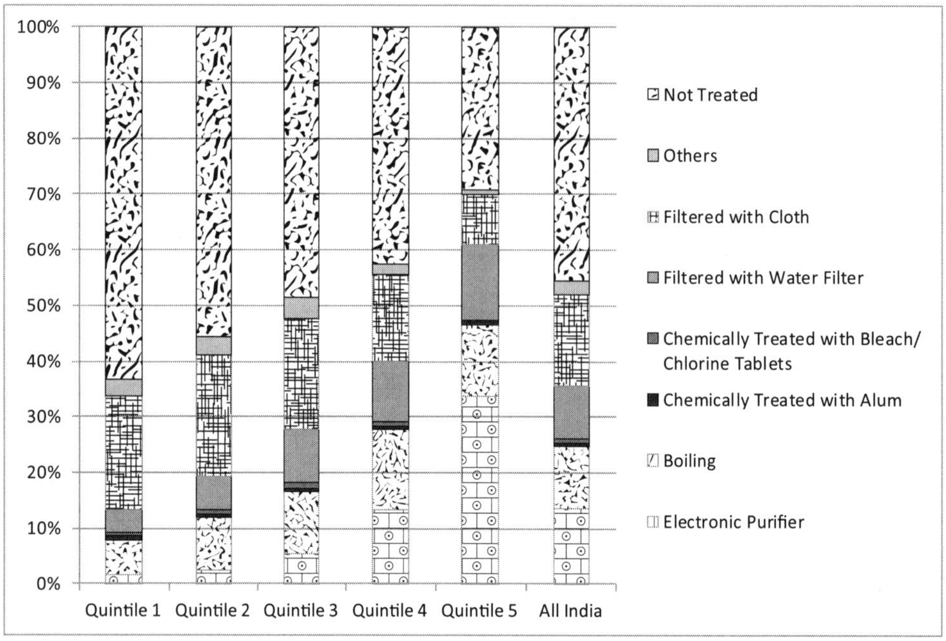

Source: NSSO (2013).

with the lack of public provisioning. In a case study in Delhi, while a typical middle-class household paid a bill of Rs 500 per year (Rs 2.7/cu.m), a household without access to public provisioning spent around Rs 4,000 per year (Rs 25/cu.m).[74] In another study in Dehradun, poorer households with access to public taps spent 6.7 per cent of their income on water, as compared to 1.6 per cent of income for households with access to individual household connections.[75]

Given that water is supplied for a limited period and often irregularly, another commonly adopted coping mechanism is storage of water. Households without financial and space constraints invest in large storage structures like underground sumps and overhead tanks while poorer households can only afford a limited number of pots/cans. Storage is easier for households with access to water within premises; those who fetch water from faraway places have a hard time carrying those pots and cans, and hence are forced to use less water.

In the absence of public provisioning, the burden of toilet construction falls on the households; those who can afford to do so build their individual household latrines based on their ability to afford them, while others resort to shared or public facilities, or to open defaecation. While there is considerable debate about whether individual toilets are a public or a private good, and who should take responsibility for them, the greater concern is that poor households might need to spend more money than rich and middle-class households to build toilets. This is because while overall costs (including household and public investments) of sewerage systems are higher than on-site systems, household investments for on-site systems might be higher.[76] In India, the combined cost of building a water closet and installing a sewerage connection is comparable to the cost of constructing a pit-latrine, and lower than that of a septic tank.[77] Furthermore, a majority of households (especially the poor) have to bear the burden of getting the pits/septic tanks cleaned on payment of charges, while sewerage services are provided almost free.

Urban households in the poorest quintile bear the highest per capita economic impact of inadequate sanitation—1.75 times the national average per capita losses and 60 per cent more than the urban average.[78]

3.2 Health impacts

Unsafe and inadequate water supply and sanitation facilities have severe health consequences. In 2004, 4 per cent of the global burden of disease and 1.6 million deaths in a year were attributed to unsafe water supply and sanitation, including inadequate personal and domestic hygiene.[79]

These diseases disproportionately impact certain sections of the population, particularly children. As stated earlier, diarrhoeal diseases are the second-largest killer of under five children. About 88 per cent of diarrhoeal deaths are attributed to inadequate sanitation, hygiene and the lack of quality water.[80] About a quarter of global under five diarrhoeal deaths occur in India.[81] Poor sanitation and unsafe drinking water cause intestinal worm infections, which lead to malnutrition, anaemia and retarded growth among children.

Diseases resulting from poor sanitation and unsafe drinking water often lead to children dropping out of school.[82] Meeting the MDG goal (Target 7c[83]) related to water and sanitation would add 272 million schooldays attended by children globally.[84] Each case of diarrhoea is assumed to lead to three days off from school.[85]

In case of women, if open defaecation is the only option available, women go to defaecate early in the morning or wait until nightfall. There is evidence to prove that this might lead to several health issues, such as urinary tract infections, constipation, and so on. Many women and girls also restrict their intake of food and drink to lessen the likelihood that they will need to go to the toilet. This affects their health, cognitive development and, if they are pregnant, the health and development of the unborn child as well. Infections due to inadequate water and sanitation are responsible for 15 per cent of maternal deaths. Girls and women face additional problems during menstruation.

Further, the lack of access to safe water and sanitation facilities can directly (e.g., trachoma) and indirectly increase risks of certain kinds of disability.

3.3 Economic impacts and loss of productivity

The total annual economic losses due to inadequate sanitation in India is estimated to be Rs 2.4 trillion ($53.8 billion), equivalent to about 6.4 per cent of India's gross domestic product (GDP) in 2006. The health-related economic impact of inadequate sanitation was Rs 1.75 trillion ($38.5 billion), 72 per cent of the total impact. Access time and water-related impacts made up the other two main losses.[86]

The lack of access to adequate water and sanitation can disrupt daily routines, and lead to loss of productivity. In low-income households that do not have access to water, time is spent in collecting water from the nearest water source. It is estimated that the time gained by appropriate access to water and sanitation if the MDG 7c is met would be nearly 20 billion working days.[87] There is also loss of productivity due to time spent in fetching water, or waiting in queues at community toilets. Nearly 40 per cent of households need to spend more than 30 minutes daily to fetch water. Conflicts are also not uncommon around public facilities, particularly when water supplies are irregular or limited (e.g., during summer or the pre-monsoon period).

Fig. 3: Time Taken to Fetch Water

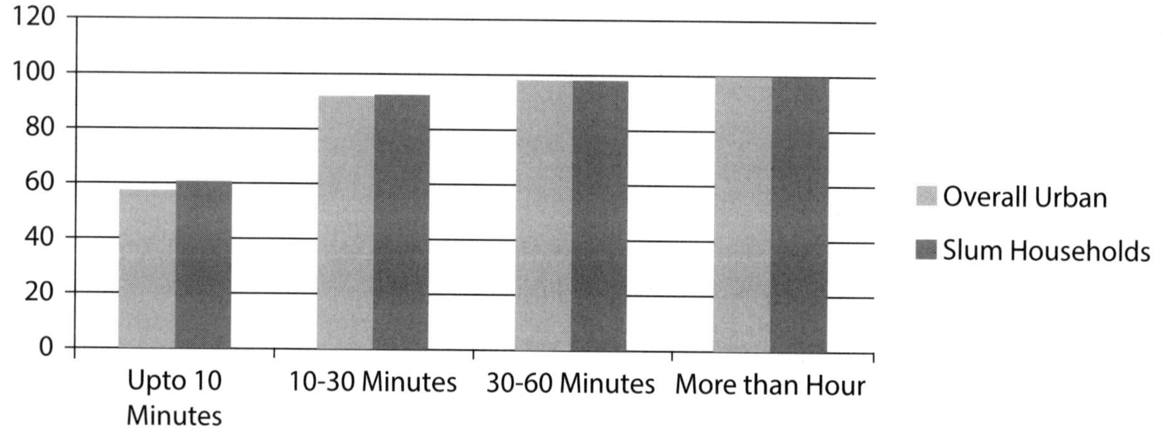

Source: IIHS Analysis of NSSO (2013)

Women play a very strong role in the management and handling of water at the household level. Table 3 shows the distribution of household members responsible for fetching water. In an overwhelmingly large number of households (68 per cent), women are responsible for fetching water. In examples of redeveloped settlements, while many households have access to private latrines, women often have to carry pots of water to the upper floors.[88] The time taken to fetch water can also lead to loss of livelihoods.

The lack of latrines in schools and absence of menstrual health management are impediments for girls attending school post-puberty and increase the likelihood of them dropping out of school.[89] Each year 23 per cent of Indian girls drop out of school due to the lack of functioning toilets and 66 per cent skip school during menstruation.[90]

3.3 Safety, dignity and convenience at risk

While travelling to fetch water or to defaecate, women and girls are exposed to the dangers of rape, assault and molestation.[91] There is evidence of physical injuries to neck and back because of hauling water over long periods of time.[92] In order to ensure privacy, women often prefer to defaecate after nightfall which in turn increases the risk of such dangers. The inconvenience of open defaecation is sharpened during menstruation. In addition, there are concerns about disposing sanitary napkins and other material discreetly. There have been instances of girls being teased and harassed by boys when spotted in the act.[93] The study conducted by Jagori (2011) noted that girls had learnt to control themselves since the school toilets were not clean, and since there was no provision of menstrual waste disposal.

The lack of access to adequate water supply and sanitation facilities that impacts everyone is likely to have a greater impact on disabled people. For instance, in a household with no access to toilet facilities, the disabled person is likely to experience greater discomfort and inconvenience while defaecating in the open. The lack of adequate facilities is also likely to create discomfort for the caregiver of the disabled person.

Table 3: Distribution of Household Members Fetching Water		
	Overall Urban	**Slum Households**
Male of Age Below 18 Years	1.86	1.58
Male of Age 18 Years or More	21.59	20.45
Female of Age Below 18 Years	3.57	3.95
Female of Age 18 Years or More	68.56	72.28
Hired Labour	2.26	0.1
Others	2.15	1.64
Total	100	100
Source: IIHS Analysis of NSSO (2013)		

3.4 Undignified work: manual scavenging and sanitary workers

A manual scavenger is defined as 'a person engaged or employed… for manually cleaning, carrying, disposing of, or otherwise handling in any manner, human excreta in an insanitary latrine or in an open drain or pit into which the human excreta from the insanitary latrine is disposed, or on a railway track or in such other spaces or premises... before the excreta fully decomposes in such manner as may be prescribed.[95] Despite being banned under the Indian Constitution via various laws since 1993, a variety of forms of manual scavenging still exist in Indian cities: cleaning dry latrines, manual cleaning of sewers, manual de-sludging, and so on. According to Census 2011, there are a total of 8 lakh dry latrines in the country that are serviced by humans; almost 2 lakh such latrines are in urban areas.[96]

Manual scavengers in India constitute a caste-based occupation group: these communities are at the bottom of the caste hierarchy as well as the Dalit

Box 3: Case Study of Adolescent Girls in a Bangalore Slum

The lack of sanitation facilities contributes to increased risk of harassment, assault and ill health, and also leads to multiple constraints on education, privacy and personal mobility.

The lack of access to sanitation facilities in schools leads to adolescent girls dropping out after they start menstruating. Girls were often found to be late for school because of long queues at the community toilet. All this is more pertinent given the fact that the literacy rate among females is 79 per cent as compared to the male literacy rate of 89 per cent. The task of collecting and managing water and its consequent responsibilities often gets gendered within households, where girls are responsible for numerous tasks at home while their brothers and males of the same age do not share the same burden and responsibility for household chores.[94]

Box 4

A municipal corporation worker, who has worked as a safai karamchari for the Bharatpur Municipal Corporation in Rajasthan since 2004, described her work:

'It is extremely dirty because the houses here flush the excrement from the toilets directly into the drains. I have to pick out the excreta, along with any garbage from the drains. I have to do it. If I do not, I will lose my job.' (HRW, 2014)

sub-caste hierarchy.[97] The taskforce constituted by the Planning Commission in 1989 estimated the number of scavengers belonging to Scheduled Castes as 4 lakhs (out of 7 lakhs in total) with 83 per cent in urban areas and 17 per cent in rural areas. There were another 3 lakh scavengers from other minorities including Muslims, Christians and tribals.[98] The Ministry of Social Justice and Empowerment in the year 2002–03 identified almost 6.8 lakh manual scavengers; of these, over 95 per cent were Dalits, who are forced to undertake this task in the garb of their 'traditional occupation.'[99]

Census 2011 reports that there are 750,000 families who still work as manual scavengers living mostly in Uttar Pradesh, Rajasthan, Bihar, Madhya Pradesh, Gujarat and Jammu and Kashmir. Surveys carried out by organisations working with manual scavengers estimate the number to be much higher, around 12–13 lakhs, especially because the official estimates do not include railway employees who have to clean excrement from the railway tracks.[100] [101]

Scavengers are also called *bhangis, dom, chura, chamar,* and so on, terms which are all considered very derogatory. The existence of this class of workers is closely associated with the Indian caste system which prevails even today, and therefore it is held that the hereditary occupation of scavengers has been scavenging.[102] A very high percentage of manual scavengers (almost 95 per cent) are said to be women.[103]

In many states, manual scavengers are employed by municipalities; it is estimated, as a matter of fact, that two-thirds of the manual scavengers in the country have been employed by municipalities while the remaining one-third still work in private houses. Sanitary workers, i.e., those employed by public or private agencies, often lack protective gear like gloves and proper equipment. Such direct contact with human excreta and other toxic waste has severe health consequences, often leading to vulnerability to faeces-borne illness. Exposure to harmful gases such as methane and hydrogen sulphide often leads to cardiovascular degeneration and other infections like tuberculosis, Hepatitis A, skin diseases and respiratory diseases.[104]

Apart from suffering the humiliation of being engaged in undignified work, these communities face social, political and economic discrimination, and are prohibited from accessing places of worship and basic services like water.[105]

3.5 Resource depletion and water pollution

There are several environmental impacts of the current urban water and sanitation situation in India. First, the lack of sufficient public supply has resulted in severe groundwater pollution in urban areas, particularly in core areas. Further, severe deficits in safe collection and treatment of waste water has resulted in widespread pollution of surface and groundwater. This environmental degradation affects everybody, but particularly the vulnerable groups because they may not be able to afford medical treatment, and since they are in any case located in vulnerable locations.

4. Structures and Processes of Exclusion

As discussed earlier, the level of service provision for water and sanitation in urban areas is inadequate, and hence these services need considerable improvement; urban sanitation needs greater attention than urban water provision. Addressing exclusion is only one of the goals for the urban water and sanitation sector, albeit an important one, while environmental and financial sustainability are other important goals. The reasons and processes for the under-performance of the sector are complex: historical neglect of Operations and Maintenance, the legacy of centralised capital-intensive schemes without institutional incentives, and the lack of context-specific solutions, to name a few. It is beyond the scope of this chapter to examine these causes in detail.[106]

This section turns to examining the structures and processes, and specific aspects of processes that are responsible for exclusion in urban areas.

4.1 Gaps in legal and regulatory frameworks

India is a votary to the UN resolution on the right to water. While the Constitution of India does not explicitly provide for the right to water, it is implied by judicial interpretation that the Right to Life and personal liberty includes the right to a clean environment[107] (Article 21), which is strengthened further by the interpretation of Right to Equality before Law (Article 14), and the responsibility of the State as a welfare state (Article 39). The Constitution (74th Amendment) Act, 1994, clearly articulates provisioning of water and sanitation as a responsibility of urban local bodies. These provisions have been used in progressive judgements to ensure the provisioning of these services to vulnerable groups (some of these are highlighted in the recommendations section below).

Box 5: Exclusionary Acts and Rules for Service Provision

At places, there is active discrimination in provision of water and sanitation services to certain sections of society.

For example, while the Delhi Jal Board Act, 1998 requires DJB to provide treated water, it explicitly mentions that the Board is *not* required:

> 'to do anything which is not in the opinion of the Board practicable at a reasonable cost, or to provide water supply to any premises which have been constructed in contravention of any law or in which adequate arrangement for internal water supply, including internal storage, as may be required by the Board, does not exist.' (DJB Act, Chapter 3, Clause 9.1A)

Another case in point is Mumbai. The Municipal Corporation of Greater Mumbai Water Rules, 2002 lays out conditions under which water (through stand posts) is supplied to unauthorised hutments and structures. These conditions include: preferably a minimum group size of 15 hutments (in any condition not less than 5); construction prior to 1995 or any other date notified by government in this behalf; and the ineligibility of footpath dwellers, even if they fulfil other criteria.

However, some legal gaps still exist, the single biggest being the provisioning of services to slums without security of title. Often, municipalities do not extend services to settlements located on land without a clear legal title. Three sets of Acts are relevant for ensuring services delivery to households: the relevant Municipal or Urban Local Body Acts, the Slum Acts, and the Acts that govern service delivery, especially when separate from the urban local body. Some of these Acts explicitly prohibit provisioning to properties or households that do not fulfil certain tenurial conditions, and these are in most cases the urban poor and other vulnerable groups. In other cases, the law does not mandate provisioning to such households and this legal gap needs to be closed. While there has been a push to delink tenure from service delivery in recent years, most ULBs find the lack of legal provisions a serious constraint on putting this into practice and hence progress has been limited.

There are other significant regulatory gaps with regard to the treatment of faecal sludge and waste management. The Indian legal system provides for the regulation of water and sanitation through the following acts: Water (Prevention and Control of Pollution) Act, 1974 and specific provisions of the Environment (Protection) Act, 1986. The Pollution Control Board, under the Water Act 1974, is responsible for monitoring safe treatment of waste water, and can take legal action against the municipalities for not treating waste water; however, enforcement is minimal. The 12th Schedule of the 74th Constitutional Amendment while listing 'public health, sanitation conservancy and solid waste management' as one of the responsibilities of the urban local bodies, does not explicitly mandate 100 per cent treatment of waste water. Various Municipalities' Acts also do not explicitly mandate 100 per cent treatment of waste water, or even regular cleaning or de-sludging of on-site installations.

Regulatory frameworks are also missing for private players like private water supply tanker operators, and de-sludging truck operators.

4.2 Inappropriate program design and budgetary constraints

Public provisioning in urban areas has usually been limited to constructing and expanding piped water supply networks, construction of water treatment plants, and to a lesser extent, expansion of sewerage networks and construction of sewage or waste water treatment plants. Under certain schemes targeted at slums, individual water connections and household toilets have been provided to slum households.

Low investment in water and sanitation since Independence has meant that provisioning has always fallen short of demand. Given this, the focus of the programme has often been on the expansion of coverage, using limited parameters and measures like water supplied in litres per capita per day. Except in recent times, little or no attention has been paid to the quality of service and the variations therein, which is especially critical considering how poor services are in settlements of the poor and in non-notified settlements.

While the overall low budgetary allocations to water and sanitation have been a concern, the available funds have been largely used for capital-intensive technological systems. Such programmes address the aspirations of select sections of city populations, and hence there is the contrasting demand for 24x7 water supply in cities, while even basic universal access remains to be assured elsewhere. The articulation of the Smart City paradigm is another such contradiction: the political economy of these divergent strands will play themselves out within a constrained financial envelope, thus potentially crowding out investments that are more equitable in favour of those that benefit a few.

In the absence of universalisation of services and the programmes and schemes providing for large network infrastructure creation, rather than towards defraying the costs of household' access (individual water connections or toilets), the poor suffer the most as private infrastructure and

Box 6: Government's Responses to Deficits in Water and Sanitation

In earlier years, urban infrastructure programmes focused on area-based development initiatives (like the Megacity scheme) targeted at the larger cities (mainly metros and State capitals), which focused on the development of infrastructure for the delivery of a basic service, for instance, water supply, sewerage or mobility services. The focus on large urban centres was broad-based during the Sixth Plan with the introduction of the Integrated Development of Small and Medium Towns scheme (IDSMT). This scheme has continued since then with adaptive evolutions over time. All these schemes were noted for the broad contours of design or planning required, mostly at the city level, and utilised the town- and country-planning ethos which had given birth to these programmes. Their progress over time indicates a predominant bias to networked solutions for waste water collection, conveyance and treatment; emphasis on physical infrastructure and not outcomes, thus resulting in inadequate networks; underutilised treatment facilities; and pollution of surroundings by waste water and faecal matter.

At the individual household level, a few schemes for poor households were developed in the earlier years (Government of Kerala in the 1970s, City of Bombay in the mid-1970s) by progressive city governments, and housing and slum development programmes necessarily aimed to cover sanitation deficits that needed correction. Apart from this, the Centrally Sponsored Scheme of Low Cost Sanitation for Liberation of Scavengers started from 1980–81, initially through the Ministry of Home Affairs and later on through the Ministry of Welfare. From 1989–90, it came to be operated through the Ministry of Urban Development and later through the Ministry of Urban Employment and Poverty Alleviation now titled Ministry of Housing & Urban Poverty Alleviation. This was perhaps the first national scheme that made provision for households to access sanitation, but the main objective of this scheme was to convert existing dry latrines into low-cost pour-flush latrines and to construct new ones where none existed. However, the new toilets were restricted to households from the Economically Weaker Section (EWS) category.

The launch of the Swachh Bharat Mission (2 October 2014) had the elimination of open defaecation as one of its objectives, and it aims for the coverage of all households without access to household sanitation through a combination of provisions like individual toilets, community toilets and public toilets. It pays attention to special focus groups like manual scavengers, the homeless and migrant labour, and seeks to prioritise households with vulnerable sections such as pensioners, girl children, and pregnant and lactating mothers. While SBM-Urban attempts to be inclusive, the subsidy offered (Rs 4,000 Central + 33% of central share as state share) for an individual household latrine might be insufficient to enable poor households to construct toilets, unless complemented by other sources.

connection costs become unaffordable for them. In sanitation, network systems have been the preferred options, and no attention has been paid to faecal sludge management, thus putting at risk a large section of society that is dependent on on-site sanitation.

The programmes focusing on individual/shared asset creation and service provision target households with a 'house'. In such situations, a lack of safe shelter becomes the primary reason for exclusion of homeless populations. As mentioned earlier, a majority of the homeless population do not possess documents like ration cards/voter cards, which have over time become prerequisites to access services or state benefits. In addition, a lack of public facilities like public standposts or public toilets, or high costs associated with these facilities, makes access to sanitation even more difficult.

4.3 Centralised funding and weak local institutions

Even while water and sanitation are state subjects, and the 74th Constitutional Amendment squarely places the responsibility for these subjects on urban local bodies, the Government of India plays a major role in decision-making related to them because it is responsible for the single-largest funding in the sector (excluding household investments).[108] Indeed, state governments usually look to the Government of India for funding these services, although a few states have made investments in improving infrastructure using their own budgetary sources. Urban local bodies, with the exception of a few larger municipal corporations, are typically under-funded and under-staffed, and hence dependent on the central and state governments for funding capital and O&M management. The local institutions that are perhaps most accessible to urban citizens are the weakest and most disempowered in these matters, severely affecting capacity and accountability for services delivery.

4.4 Lack of customer/citizen orientation and accountability in key institutions

Urban local bodies as well as water and sanitation utilities have historically been poor in being able to respond to citizen and customer demands and grievances. Lengthy and complex procedures for accessing services and expensive one-time connections often deter poorer households from attempting to access public services, and instead encourage them to seek alternative informal sector suppliers. Water and sanitation service delivery institutions have traditionally been technology-focused and engineer-driven, with little flexibility to accommodate the demands of constituencies that are not 'legal'. As explained above, poor capacities, accountability structures and processes dog the ULBs in taking cognisance of inequities and exclusions in services they provide.

4.5 Exclusionary planning and design features

There are two issues that cause exclusions. First, the planning norms (or lack thereof) do not provide for access in all the locations where sanitation facilities are needed. Sanitation facilities in public places are grossly inadequate but there are no norms to address these deficits. Most of the facilities in public spaces are not accessible for the elderly and disabled. While Town Planning rules specify norms for the provision of water supply and sanitation in institutional facilities, these are seldom enforced or the norms updated.

The second dimension is that of inappropriate design of water and sanitation facilities and fixtures that render them inaccessible for the disabled, elderly, and children, whether they are private facilities at home, or community and public facilities. Often, community toilets do not have facilities which are accessible to children. Similarly, toilets in schools are not accessible for disabled children. The biggest barriers in installing accessible facilities at home are the poor availability of accessible designs in the market and the inability of the households to afford these designs.

4.6 Social norms and discrimination

Access to water and sanitation may also be restricted because of societal norms and biases. Chaplin (1999) argues that the middle class has monopolised the provision of basic urban services (e.g., sanitation) by the state; as a consequence there is lack of interest in sanitary reform leading to the exclusion of large

Box 7: New Paradigms and Vision of Urban Development

One of the powerful reasons for low levels of inclusion (not only in water and sanitation, but other services) are the current paradigms and discourses that shape Indian cities. These urban imageries and visions, often borrowed from cities in developed countries, valorise cities as engines of urban growth, present the image of orderly and visually appealing structures, and prioritise urban development interventions that mimic them. These are also images that promise a new regime of cleanliness and public health without taking into consideration the complexity and diversity of Indian cities and communities, leading to particular priorities for urban development and kinds of infrastructure, which might benefit a few privileged urban citizens rather than all.

The current Smart Cities programme in the same way prioritises a set of technological solutions, and the development of specific portions of the city, even as large areas and populations are denied basic services. Will the technology-led smart solutions work for all citizens and enable them to enjoy continuous water and safe sanitation? Or will it just be for a sub-city of residents who can pay for it? Will sewerage systems remain a publicly-funded amenity for some areas while other areas depend on private informal arrangements for conveyance and disposal of their human excreta? These and many other questions have emerged even as we prepare for a new round of investments in Urban India under the Swachh Bharat, AMRUT, and Smart Cities Missions. Moreover, these paradigms result in far more attention being given to large metropolitan cities to the detriment of smaller towns and cities in India.

sections of society.[109] Social norms also impose the burden of fetching water disproportionately on women and girl-children, as already illustrated in earlier sections.

4.7 Physical and spatial constraints

While land tenure remains the single largest issue for provisioning in urban slums, there is also the issue of slum settlements being based in environmentally sensitive or vulnerable locations, for instance, near river-beds or other flood-prone areas. It becomes difficult to provide solutions for these settlements, and water and sanitation provisions have to be made at a distance at best. Further, seasonal flooding and related disruptions could effectively cut off supply of quality water or make sanitation arrangements dysfunctional.

Dense slum settlements pose another set of locational and design challenges: not only is there inadequate space for say, constructing toilets, but also access to these installations for periodic cleaning is near-impossible. The water pipes zig-zagging through many Indian slums are installed at low elevations to catch the meagre and intermittent supply, which also creates the hazard of water flowing in drains adjoining these pipes mixing with the water in them.

While many of the above exclusions can be traced back to deficits and gaps in physical planning and tenurial complexities, the fact is that generations may be held to ransom, and not even be ensured of basic water and sanitation services or a modicum of public health.

5. Making Water Supply and Sanitation Inclusive: Learning from Current Practices

There are sufficient examples in the country to illustrate exclusion from water supply and sanitation because of structural barriers and inimical processes. However, there are also a few successful initiatives that attempt to overcome these barriers through innovation: the introduction of a path-breaking national policy like NUSP, ensuring security of tenure within the Parivartan programme in Ahmedabad, community participation in Tiruchirappalli, institutional changes and rationalisation of tariffs in Bangalore, and so on. This section, by no means exhaustive, presents a few illustrative examples, which suggest learnings for inclusion.

5.1 National Urban Sanitation Policy, 2008

The NUSP (2008) aims to achieve open defaecation-free cities with all urban households having access to safe and hygienic sanitation facilities, including sanitary and safe disposal arrangements. The focus is on universal coverage, and also on the full cycle of sanitation. The policy stresses on the outcomes of universal coverage and 100 per cent treatment of waste, but does not prescribe a particular method. The emphasis in the policy on mandating universal access and 100 per cent treatment, and recommending delinking of service delivery from tenure security, are indicative of a positive break from previous policies. It also recommends looking beyond conventional sewerage systems, stresses process, and hence recommends the constitution of a City Sanitation Task Force for each city, and the preparation of City Sanitation Plans and a State Urban Sanitation Strategies.

5.2 Service Level Benchmarking, 2008

In 2008, the Government of India (MoUD) launched a Service Level Benchmarking initiative for environmental services: water, waste water, solid waste and drainage. It identified a minimum set of standard performance

Table 4: Service Level Benchmarks for Water Supply and Sanitation Sectors

Water Supply		Sanitation	
Coverage of water supply connections	100%	Coverage of toilets	100%
Per capita supply of water	135 lpcd	Coverage of sewerage network	100%
Extent of metering of water connections	100%	services	100%
Extent of non-revenue water	20%	Collection efficiency of the	
Continuity of water supply	24 Hours	sewerage network	100%
Quality of water supplied	100%	Adequacy of sewage treatment	
Cost recovery in water supply services	100%	capacity	100%
Efficiency in redressal of customer complaints	80%	Quality of sewage treatment	20%
		Extent of reuse and recycling of	
Efficiency in collection of water supply-related charges	90%	sewage	80%
		Efficiency in redressal of customer	
		complaints	100%
		Extent of cost recovery in sewage	
		management	90%
		Efficiency in collection of sewerage charges	

Source: MoUD (2010).

parameters for environmental services, defined a common minimum framework for monitoring and reporting on these indicators and set out guidelines on operationalising this framework in a phased manner. The SLBs include several dimensions of the expanded definition including coverage, quantity (sufficiency) and quality of water supply, and continuity of supply, among others. In the sanitation sector, SLBs include coverage of toilets, sewerage network services, collection efficiency, quality of sewage treatment, etc. (see Table 4). It is one of the first attempts at the national level to collect data for an expanded set of indicators.

The initiative aimed at enabling cities to benchmark their current status and measure their progress. It is expected that the initiative will create consensus on desired service standards, enable comparisons across time and cities, highlight and help address issues of data quality, and enable ULBs to self-report. Emphasis is placed on performance improvement planning based on the SLB data that is generated.[110]

5.3 Slum Networking Project (Parivartan), Ahmedabad

Parivartan was a slum upgradation project implemented in Ahmedabad. The initiative aimed at ensuring access to basic infrastructure and social services for the communities living in informal settlements. Launched in 1996, the initiative had two components: physical upgradation (water supply, sanitation, drainage, roads, etc.) and community development.

A key feature of Parivartan was that it had a strong multi-stakeholder partnership framework, and brought together the urban local body, NGOs (MHT, SAATH) and the community. The involvement of the community was critical for the success of the project. One of the key factors for ensuring the households' participation was security of tenure. Participating slums were provided an assurance by the Corporation that they would not be evicted for the next 10 years. Even though it had no legal binding, this helped facilitate community participation.

The ULB took a lead in financing the programme, ensuring integration with city-wide systems and also convergence with other schemes. The role of the NGOs in the community development aspect of the project was crucial and involved motivating residents to participate in the programme as well as to form community-based organisations (CBOs) and enabling access to livelihood opportunities and micro-credit. The community members contributed towards both capital and O&M costs, and also undertook supervisory responsibilities during construction.[111]

5.4 Community-managed toilets, Tiruchirappalli

The city of Tiruchirappalli has demonstrated that community toilets can be efficiently managed and run by community members and groups. Until 2000, all community toilets here were managed by the Corporation; however, due to poor maintenance, most toilets were dilapidated and defunct. In 2000, a group of NGOs, supported by Water Aid, started working with communities to renovate and take over these community toilets. Following the success of this initiative, the Corporation handed over these toilets to communities, directly or through NGOs.[112]

At present, 167 community toilets are managed by the community and 172 by the Municipal Corporation.[113] While the Corporation-operated toilets continue to be free of charge, the SHG-managed toilets charge a user fee, and are better in terms of cleanliness and usability.[114] The major outcome of the initiative has been that many slums in Tiruchirappalli have been declared open defaecation-free slums.

5.5 Water and sanitation services delivery in slums, Bangalore

Starting in 2000, the Bangalore Water Supply and Sewerage Board (BWSSB) started considering the urban poor as potential customers. It provided services to slum households, first through three pilot projects under an AusAID-funded project, and then through a newly created Social Development Unit (SDU). The SDU was an innovative institutional mechanism where personnel from other government departments with experience of working with the urban poor were deputed to the BWSSB to provide an interface between slum communities and BWSSB engineers. The unit focused on social development issues and undertook collaborative work with civil society organisations.[115]

A series of policy changes were further made in the Board to enable service delivery (WSP, 2009):

- Requirement of formal tenure documents for new connections was replaced with simple occupancy proof (to address concerns about land tenure).
- Connection fees were reduced and tariff structure for domestic water use was revised to introduce a lower minimum monthly charge (to address concerns of affordability).
- Shared connections were offered as an alternative.

6. Recommendations

According to a UN Resolution, the state has the primary responsibility to ensure right to water and sanitation, even while realising that the right to water and sanitation can only be progressively realised, given the capacities of the state. The state also has the central role in providing services, or ensuring that these are provided and regulated. The state's role becomes very important for the provision of basic services to marginalised populations since these would be the most vulnerable to unaffordable arrangements by formal and informal service providers. It is also the state's role to protect water sources from contamination. Further, it needs to protect individuals from violations of human rights by third parties, for instance, marginalised communities not being allowed to access certain water sources, or communities forced into inhuman vocations such as head-loading or manual cleaning of human excreta.

While there is a broader set of steps required for improvements in the water and sanitation sector in general, this section focuses on recommendations for the State to address specific concerns of exclusion.

6.1 Progressively deepen the framework for urban water and sanitation

While improvements have been made in urban water and sanitation over the past few decades, these have been along select dimensions like increasing the physical coverage of water supply through piped water to households, and constructing individual household toilets. There has been little improvement, or absence of data to track improvement, on certain other dimensions of service provision like reliability, quality and adequacy (e.g., hours of supply, timings, etc.) of water supply, safe conveyance and disposal (e.g., treatment of waste water) for sanitation, and so on.

To ensure improvements along all the dimensions outlined in the present chapter, the framework for water and sanitation needs to be deepened to first understand where the gaps are, prioritise the right set of actions, then measure improvements and increase accountability of the relevant public institutions. There is a need to detail what is measured and documented in the sphere of urban water and sanitation; collecting data on coverage is just the bare minimum requirement. There are initiatives like the Service Level Benchmarking (SLBs) that require self-reporting by ULBs on an expanded indicator set, but the initiative has not been institutionalised as mandatory, nor is this backed by necessary incentives for improvements along those indicators. To ensure a deepened framework, a series of steps—legal, programmatic, financial—are required, as described below.

6.2 Initiate necessary changes for legal and regulatory framework

Delink access to services from tenure security and land ownership

The most important legal and regulatory changes relate to tenure security, since lack of tenure security remains one of the key barriers to accessing services. As highlighted in the previous section, delinking service delivery from tenure security has been recommended in the NUSP and in the SBM-U guidelines. Further, there are examples of innovative solutions in different cities, for instance, the Parivartan programme in Ahmedabad, and the BWSSB initiatives in Bangalore. However, this delinking of tenure security and service delivery needs to be made explicit and mandated in the relevant Acts and regulations, including Municipal Acts, Slum Acts and Acts and rules governing the utilities responsible for water and sanitation services provision.

Mandate 100 per cent treatment of fecal sludge, septage and waste water

Mandating 100 per cent treatment of fecal sludge, septage and waste water, and ensuring enforcement, will be one of the critical steps likely to have maximum impact on public health. This again needs to be mandated in relevant Acts, with adequate backing in terms of investments as well as corrective or punitive actions for non-compliance.

Mandating adequate water and sanitation services in public spaces

Water supply and sanitation services are often associated with a house or a dwelling unit, leaving homeless and floating populations excluded, and others excluded in places other than homes, for instance, construction sites, schools, roads, railway stations, bus stations, and so on. The right to adequate water and sanitation needs to be extended, enforced, measured and monitored beyond the house as a unit of enquiry and intervention. Accessible, affordable and universal water and sanitation services must be mandated at the neighbourhood, cluster, market, public place, ward, and finally at the city level.

6.3 Re-design public programmes and reallocate budgets to ensure benefits for larger sections of urban population

The total investment in urban water and sanitation has not been commensurate with requirements since Independence, and there is an urgent need to increase overall funding. However, given the substantial gaps between current funding and projected investments, it is imperative to utilise the available funding prudently, and focus on extending services to the entire urban population, particularly to vulnerable groups who have the least coping capacities. This might require public institutions to be willing to adopt appropriate, less capital-intensive technological systems, for instance, non-networked systems as a complement to sewerage systems, or strong demand-management measures against wasting water, such as measures to discourage using potable water for car-washing. The focus of public programmes needs to be on improvements that will benefit all and not a select few, and hence, on building and operating infrastructure that does not create islands of high service levels and high maintenance management, but scaling infrastructure and services to serve equitably and economically. Invisible sections of society, for instance, the homeless, migrant workers and so on, need to be given due consideration while designing any public programme or scheme.

6.4 Strengthen local institutions

Local institutions which are accessible to urban citizens need to be strengthened. There is a need to increase accountability of service providers to citizens, particularly the urban poor, and local institutions are best placed to do so. In doing so, the legal, human resource and financial capacities of ULBs and local service providers need to be enhanced. One of the easier ways of strengthening local service delivery and accountability is to help de-concentrate utility or municipal functions with respect to water and sanitation, so that local units and offices are easily accessible and able to respond better to citizens' information and service delivery needs.

6.5 Enhance affordability of services

While universal access does not necessarily mean providing services for free, it needs to be ensured that services remain affordable. This means that there are lifeline water tariffs for the urban poor. Furthermore, de-sludging services need to be provided to the poor such that they are affordable for them. On the other hand, tariff structures need to signal incentives for conserving water and penalise wastage of water.

6.6 Remove supply-side constraints

The government should remove supply-side constraints for appropriate goods and services, for instance, disabled-friendly products, de-sludging services and so on, by putting appropriate regulatory frameworks in place that attract a larger pool of service providers. This is likely to augment the overall supply of services and products, making these affordable and accessible for the urban poor and vulnerable groups.

Annex 1A: SUMMARY TABLE OF EXCLUSIONS FROM WATER ACROSS DIFFERENT DIMENSIONS AND GROUPS

No.	Aspect	Indicator	All-India (Urban)	Economic Classes	Settlement Types	Caste/ Class	Religion	Gender	Region
1.	Accessibility	Location of primary source of water	Nearly 71% households have access to drinking water within premises; only 49% have treated tap water within premises	Stark differences are observed across economic classes; almost 56% Quintile 1 households have drinking water source within premises compared to almost 93% Quintile 5 households	Only 57% slum households have access to drinking water within premises	Significant differences are observed; 57% SC households and 55% ST households have drinking water within premises	No significant differences observed across religions	About 67% female-headed households have drinking water source within premises compared to 72 % male-headed households	Differences are observed across regions; only 60% eastern households have drinking water source within premises compared to almost 86% among households in western region
		Access levels to primary source of water (exclusive v. shared used)	Only 47% have access to source of water for household's exclusive use	More than two-thirds of Quintile 5 households have water source for exclusive use; the percentage drops to 33% in case of Quintile 1	At 35%, exclusive use is also lower amongst slum households	Exclusive use is also lower amongst SC/ST households; 35% SC and 39% ST households have water source for exclusive use	No significant differences observed	39% female-headed households have access to water source for exclusive use compared to 48% male headed households	Only around 35% eastern and southern households have water source for exclusive use compared to 55% and 62% in the North and the West respectively

Annex 1A: SUMMARY TABLE OF EXCLUSIONS FROM WATER ACROSS DIFFERENT DIMENSIONS AND GROUPS

No.	Aspect	Indicator	All-India (Urban)	Economic Classes	Settlement Types	Caste/ Class	Religion	Gender	Region
		Time taken to access water (if from outside premises)	On an average, more than half an hour (31 minutes) is spent to fetch water from outside (including waiting time)	Differences are observed; while on an average a Quintile 5 household takes 20 minutes to fetch water, Quintile 1 has to spend almost 36 minutes in a day to fetch water.	On an average, slum households take marginally more time than the national average to fetch water (33 minutes)	At 35 minutes daily, SC/ST households take slightly longer to access water from outside	No significant differences observed across religions		At 37 minutes, households in the West take longer than national average to fetch water
2.	Sufficiency	Quantity of water supplied	Average per capita supply of 73 lpcd in 1,493 cities						
3.	Quality	Quality of water supplied (Various indicators like turbidity, absence of pathogens etc.)							

Annex 1A: SUMMARY TABLE OF EXCLUSIONS FROM WATER ACROSS DIFFERENT DIMENSIONS AND GROUPS

No.	Aspect	Indicator	All-India (Urban)	Economic Classes	Settlement Types	Caste/ Class	Religion	Gender	Region
		Primary source of drinking water (availability of treated piped water supply)	Census 2011 reported that almost 62% households have access to treated tap water; NSSO 69th round reported that 69% households have piped water supply (assumed to be treated tap water)	Access to treated tap water increases with increase in MPCE; only 57% Quintile 1 households have treated tap water compared to 73% Quintile 5	On this indicator, overall slums are reported to be doing better than the national average; 65% households have access to treated tap water	Slight differences are observed; 59% SC households have treated tap water, while the percentage drops further to 54% for ST households	Almost 70% Hindu households have piped water supply compared to 64% Muslim households; amongst other minority religions, 72% have piped water supply	No significant difference is observed	Significant differences are observed; the West has 79% households with treated tap water while the percentage drops to 41% and 37% in case of eastern and north-eastern India
4.	Regularity	Duration of water supplied	Average duration of supply (1,493 cities) is estimated to be around 3 hours daily						

Annex 1A: SUMMARY TABLE OF EXCLUSIONS FROM WATER ACROSS DIFFERENT DIMENSIONS AND GROUPS

No.	Aspect	Indicator	All-India (Urban)	Economic Classes	Settlement Types	Caste/ Class	Religion	Gender	Region
		Frequency of supply of water	Almost a quarter of households are not supplied water daily	Slight differences across economic classes; 70% of Quintile 2 households are supplied water daily compared to 80% of Quintile 5; higher proportion of Quintile 1 households (76%) are supplied water daily but then they have to go outside to fetch water	Same as national average	No difference observed for SC/ST compared to national average			The North and West have higher proportion of households with daily water supply compared to other parts of the country
5.	Affordability	Average amount paid per month	Almost 55 % households are required to pay for water supply corresponding to limited public supply; an average of Rs130 is paid	Higher income groups pay more on an average	At Rs.110, average amount paid per month is marginally lower than the national average	Similar to national average			At Rs 160, northern households pay the highest for water supply while West and East pay the lowest (Rs 100)
		Costs of purchasing water (per litre)							

Annex 1B: SUMMARY TABLE OF EXCLUSIONS FROM SANITATION ACROSS DIFFERENT DIMENSIONS AND GROUPS

No.	Aspect	Indicator	All-India (Urban)	Economic Classes	Settlement Types	Caste/ Class	Religion	Gender	Region
1.	Accessibility	Location of sanitation facility	Almost 81% have latrine within premises; 6% rely on public latrines; 13% resort to open defaecation	While 98% Quintile 5 households have latrines within premises, the access is restricted to 63% Quintile 1 households	Only two-thirds of slum households have access to a latrine within premises; almost 15% rely on public latrines and 19% resort to open defaecation	Only two-thirds of SC/ST households have toilet facility within their premises; almost 10% rely on public toilets and almost a quarter resort to open defaecation	No significant difference across religions	Marginal difference observed; 78% female-headed households have latrine within premises compared to 82% male-headed households; at 14%, open defaecation is also slightly higher amongst female-headed households compared to male-headed ones (12%)	Almost 95% households in the Northeast have toilets within premises followed by the North with 87%; only 71% households in the central region have toilets within premises; open defaecation is also highest in central India (25%)

Annex 1B: SUMMARY TABLE OF EXCLUSIONS FROM SANITATION ACROSS DIFFERENT DIMENSIONS AND GROUPS

No.	Aspect	Indicator	All-India (Urban)	Economic Classes	Settlement Types	Caste/ Class	Religion	Gender	Region
		Access levels to sanitation facility (exclusive vs. shared)	Only 64% households have access to latrine for household's exclusive use	Exclusivity also decreases amongst lower income groups; while 80% Quintile 5 households have latrines for exclusive use, the percentage reduces to half (40%) in case of Quintile 1	Compared to national average, even lower proportion of slum households have latrines for exclusive use (38%)	Only 44% SC households and 57% ST households have toilets for exclusive use	No significant difference across religions	Almost 65% male-headed households have toilets for exclusive use compared to 57% female-headed households	Only 54% households in eastern India have latrines for exclusive use; at 72%, the percentage is highest in the Northeast
2.	Safety of Sanitation Facilities	Type of household arrangement for sanitation (connection to sewerage network/ septic tank/ improved pits/ etc.)	Only 33 % households are connected to piped sewer; another 45% depend on improved on-site system; 4% have insanitary latrines	Dependence on on-site systems increases with decreasing incomes; only 13% Quintile 1 households are connected to piped sewer compared to 57% Quintile 5 households	Slum households have poorer sanitation facilities; only a quarter are connected to piped sewer. Another 37% have improved on-site systems	Piped sewer connectivity is lower among SC/ST households with 27% SC and 24% ST households connected to it	Slight differences across religions observed; 37% Hindu households have piped sewers compared to 31% Muslim households	Almost 30% female-headed households are connected to piped sewer compared to 33% male-headed households	Access to piped sewers is as low as 12% in the East and the Northeast; the North and the West have better coverage at around 42%

Annex 1B: SUMMARY TABLE OF EXCLUSIONS FROM SANITATION ACROSS DIFFERENT DIMENSIONS AND GROUPS

No.	Aspect	Indicator	All-India (Urban)	Economic Classes	Settlement Types	Caste/ Class	Religion	Gender	Region
		Safe Disposal of Sludge							
		Treatment Capacity	Treatment capacity exists for about 31% of waste water in Class I and II cities; actual treatment is lower because of operational efficiencies of STPs; it is estimated that not more than 20% of waste in India is safely disposed.						
		Surface and ground water quality	CPCB reports suggest that most of the rivers in India are polluted; faecal coliform is the single largest point source of pollution						
3.	Acceptability	No information collected							

Endnotes

1. In alphabetical order by first name
2. In alphabetical order by first name
3. WSP (2013a), *Coming up Short without Sanitation.*
4. UN (2014), World Urbanization Prospects: The 2014 Revision, Highlights.
5. UN (2011), T*he Human Right to Water and Sanitation: Milestones,* UNW-DPAC
6. General Assembly resolution 54/175,(1999), The Right to Development, New York: UN General Assembly
7. UN General Assembly (1966), *International Covenant on Economic Social and Cultural Rights. New* York: UN
8. UN (2002), General Comment No. 15.
9. Ibid.
10. UN General Assembly (2010), *Resolution adopted by the Human Rights Council 15/9: Human rights and access to safe drinking water and sanitation,* New York: UN
11. General Assembly Resolution 15/9, (2010), Human Rights Council Resolution A/HRC/RES/15/9, New York: UN General Assembly
12. The three reports are the Annual Report 2014, Report on Violations of Right to Water and Sanitation, and a handbook for realising the human right to safe drinking water and sanitation.
13. UN (2014).
14. The indicators defined are: access to improved water sources, access to improved drinking water sources and, access to improved sanitation.
15. The public datasets measure mostly only at the household level. Accounts of intra-households disparities are available as case studies.
16. Census of India (2011), *Houselisting and Housing Census Data,* Office of the Registrar General & Census Commissioner, New Delhi: Government of India.
17. NSSO (2013), *Key Indicators of Drinking Water, Sanitation, Hygiene and Housing Condition in India - NSSO 69th Round,* Ministry of Statistics and Programme Implementation, New Delhi: GoI.
18. MoUD (2012), *Service Levels in Urban Water and Sanitation Sector: Status Report (2010-2011),* New Delhi: GoI.
19. Ibid.
20. NSSO (2013).
21. Census of India (2011).
22. NSSO (2013).
23. R. Bain, R. Cronk, J. Wright, H. Yang, T. Slaymaker, & J. Bartram, (2014), 'Fecal Contamination of Drinking-Water in Low- and Middle-Income Countries: A Systematic Review and Meta-Analysis' PLoS Med 11:5.
24. S. Varma (2014), *42% of urban, 60% of rural Indian households getting contaminated water: Study.* The Times of India.
25. Census of India (2011).
26. NSSO (2013).
27. J.E. Hardoy, D. Mitlin, & D. Satterthwaite (2013), *Environmental problems in an urbanizing world: finding solutions in cities in Africa, Asia and Latin America,* Routledge.
28. K. Wankhade, K. (2015), 'Urban sanitation in India: key shifts in the national policy frame', Environment and Urbanization 27:2, pp. 555-572.
29. CPCB (2009), *Status of Water Supply, Wastewater Generation and Treatment in Class-I Cities & Class-II Towns of India,* New Delhi: GoI.
30. AECOM & SANDEC (2010), *A Rapid Assessment of Septage Management in Asia: Policies and Practices in India, Indonesia, Malaysia, the Philippines, Sri Lanka, Thailand, and Vietnam.*
31. AIILSG (2011), *Urban Water and Sanitation in Maharashtra,* Mumbai.
32. WSP-TARU (2008), *Review of Sewerage and Sanitation Interventions in Urban India* New Delhi.
33. NSSO (2013).
34. Based on the monthly per capita expenditure (MPCE) data in the NSS dataset, all households are classified into five consumption quintiles, each quintile representing 20 per cent of the population. Quintile 5 represents households with the highest range of MPCE while Quintile 1 represents households with the lowest range of MPCE.
35. Census of India (2011).
36. NSSO (2013).
37. Ibid.
38. Census of India (2011).
39. Ibid.
40. NSSO (2013).
41. Ibid.
42. For easy, comprehensible analysis, the Indian states have been divided into seven regions as shown below (even while we recognise that there might be intra-state and intra-regional variations):
    1. Northern India—comprising Jammu and Kashmir,

Himachal Pradesh, Punjab, Haryana, Uttarakhand, Uttar Pradesh, Chandigarh and Delhi.

2. Central India—comprising Madhya Pradesh and Chhattisgarh.
3. Western India—comprising Rajasthan, Gujarat, Maharashtra, Daman & Diu, Dadra & Nagar Haveli and Goa
4. Eastern India—comprising Bihar, Jharkhand, West Bengal and Odisha.
5. Northeastern India—comprising Assam, Sikkim, Arunachal Pradesh, Meghalaya, Manipur, Mizoram, Nagaland and Tripura.
6. Southern India—comprising of Andhra Pradesh, Karnataka, Tamil Nadu, Telangana, Puducherry and Kerala.
7. Island groups—Lakshadweep and Andaman & Nicobar Islands.

43. Census of India (2011).
44. Ibid.
45. NSSO (2013).
46. Ibid.
47. Census of India (2011).
48. NSSO (2013).
49. Census of India (2011).
50. NSSO (2013).
51. Census of India (2011).
52. NSSO (2013).
53. Census of India (2011).
54. NSSO (2013).
55. Census of India (2011).
56. Commissioners of the Supreme Court (2008), *A Special Report on Most Vulnerable Social Groups and Their Access to Food,* New Delhi.
57. V. Walters (2014), 'Urban homelessness and the right to water and sanitation: Experiences from India's cities' Water policy 16:4, pp. 755-772.
58. Ibid.
59. Ibid.
60. H. Mander (2008), *Living Rough: Surviving City Streets.* New Delhi.
61. Walters, V. (2014).
62. Commissioners of the Supreme Court (2008).
63. V. Walters, (2014).
64. All figures mentioned for schools are aggregate rural and urban figures. There are two available sources to look at the water and sanitation status of schools across the country. One is NUEPA's District Information System for Education (DISE), which provides data that is self-reported annually by every school in India. The other is Pratham's Annual Status of Education Report (ASER), which is the largest sample survey of learning outcomes of rural children in the country. Thus, for urban areas only the DISE data is available, which also reports the status of water and sanitation services in schools at the national level.
65. NUEPA (2015), *Elementary Education in India - Where do we stand?: Analytical Report 2014-15.* New Delhi.
66. Ibid.
67. ASER (2012), *Annual Status of Education Report (Rural) 2011.*
68. NUEPA (2015).
69. D. Rajaraman, S.M. Travasso, and S.J. Heymann (2013), 'A qualitative study of access to sanitation amongst low-income working women in Bangalore', *Journal of Water, Sanitation and Hygiene for Development* 3:3, pp. 432-440.
70. The Factories Act and the Building and Other Construction Workers (Regulation of Employment and Conditions of Service) Act 1996 make it mandatory for employers to provide toilets for their employees.
71. S. Sharma (2013), *In the name of privacy,* The Hindu.
72. WSP (2006), *Mumbai Slum Sanitation Programme: Partnering with Slum Communities for Sustainable Sanitation in a Megalopolis.* New Delhi.
73. NSSO (2013).
74. World Bank. (2006), *Water Supply and Sanitation: Bridging the Gap Between Infrastructure and Service*
75. K. Choe, R. C. Varley & H. Bijlani (1996), *Coping with intermittent water supply: problems and prospects,* Environmental Health Project.
76. K. Wankhade (2015).
77. WSP (2013b), *Poor-Inclusive Urban Sanitation: An Overview.*
78. WSP (2010), *The Economic Impacts of Inadequate Sanitation in India,* New Delhi.
79. G. Hutton, L. Haller, & J. Bartram (2007), 'Global cost-benefit analysis of water supply and sanitation interventions' *Journal of Water and Health* 5:4, pp. 481-502.
80. UNICEF/WHO (2009), *Diarrhoea: Why children are still dying and what can be done, 2009.*
81. Ibid.
82. WHO (2012), *Global costs and benefits of drinking-water supply and sanitation interventions to reach the MDG target and universal coverage.*

83. 'Halve, by 2015, the proportion of the population without sustainable access to safe drinking water and basic sanitation'.

    See: http://www.un.org/millenniumgoals/environ.shtml

84. WHO & UNICEF (2005), *Water for Life: Making it Happen*.
85. WHO (2012).
86. WSP. *The Economic Impacts of Inadequate Sanitation in India*. New Delhi
87. WHO & UNICEF (2005).
88. A. Nallari (2015), "All we want are toilets inside our homes!" The critical role of sanitation in the lives of urban poor adolescent girls in Bengaluru' *Environment and Urbanization* 27:1, pp. 73-88
89. A. Adukia (2014), Sanitation and Education, Harvard Graduate School of Education.
90. ASER (2011).
91. J. Fisher (2006), *For Her It's the Big Issue: Putting Women at the Centre of Water Supply, Sanitation and Hygiene*. Water, Sanitation and Hygiene: Evidence Report.
92. Ibid.
93. Nallari (2015).
94. D. Joshi (2011), 'Caste, Gender and the Rhetoric of Reform in India's Drinking Water Sector' EPW 46:8, pp. 57-57.
95. Ministry of Law and Justice (2013), *The Prohibition Of Employment As Manual Scavengers And Their Rehabilitation Act, 2013*, New Delhi: GoI.
96. Census of India (2011).
97. R. Singh & Ziyauddin (2009), 'Manual Scavenging As Social Exclusion: A Case Study', EPW 44: 26/27, pp. 521-523.
98. B. Pathak (n.d.), 'Present Dalit (Scavengers) Situation in India'.
99. Safai Karamchari Andolan & Ors. vs. Union of India & Ors (Supreme Court 2003).
100. Ibid.
101. A. Masoodi (2013), *Manual Scavenging: The Worst Job in India; PS: Its Illegal Too*, Live Mint-The Wall Street Journal.
102. Pathak (n.d).
103. UNDP & UN Solution Exchange (2012), *Social Inclusion of Manual Scavengers*, New Delhi.
104. Rashtriya Garima Abhiyan (2013), *Manual Scavengers and Their Health*.
105. HRW (2014), *Cleaning Human Waste: "Manual Scavenging", Caste, and Discrimination in India*.
106. The authors have dwelt on these issues and made policy recommendations in another paper (IIHS 2014).
107. Attakoya Thangal vs Union of India 1990, KLT 580
108. IIHS (2014), *Sustaining Policy Momentum: Urban Water Supply and Sanitation*, IIHS - Rockefeller Foundation Urban Policy Papers, Bangalore: Indian Institute for Human Settlements.
109. S.E. Chaplin (1999), 'Cities, sewers and poverty: India's politics of sanitation', *Environment and Urbanization* 11:1, pp. 145-158.
110. MoUD (2010), Improving urban services through Service Level Benchmarking, New Delhi: GoI.
111. WSP (2009), *Global Experiences on Expanding Water and Sanitation Services to the Urban Poor*, New Delhi.
112. Ibid.
113. Ibid.
114. Gramalaya & WaterAid India (2008), *Tiruchirappalli Shows the Way: Community-Municipal Corporation-NGO Partnership for City-wide Pro-poor Slums' Infrastructure Improvement*. New Delhi: WaterAid India.
115. WSP (2009).

Women's Exclusion from Just Conditions of Work, and the Role of the State

*Shikha Sethia, Anamika Lahiri, Rajanya Bose, Radhika Jha, Coen Kompier, Harsh Mander**

*Sejal Dand, Sita Mamidipudi***

1. Just Conditions of Work for Women as a Public Good

In the India Exclusion Report 2013–14, we argued that decent work for all is an important public good and that it is the responsibility of the state to ensure equitable access of all persons to conditions of decent work. In this second Exclusion Report, we carry this argument further to underline that just conditions of work for women in particular, and not just of workers in general, is in itself a high-order public good.

We derive this view first from the *a priori* conviction that ensuring conditions in which women have equitable access to fairly remunerated, safe and dignified work, which is compatible with their aspirations and capabilities, is an absolute value in itself because of the intrinsic equal dignity and worth of women and men, and indeed of persons of other genders. Patriarchy, markets and the functioning of state laws, policies and institutions have created historically tall barriers to women's just access to work. These not only limit women's presence in what is considered the labour force, but severely impede and restrict the access of women and girls to fair conditions of work. We find empirically that these barriers continue to impede women's just participation in work in contemporary times, as we will illustrate briefly in the case of India in this chapter.

There is no doubt that some men, especially men who bear disadvantages due to class, caste, religious and ethnic identities, and different abilities, also face barriers of access to decent, fair and non-exploitative work. However, as gender deepens and consolidates these hindrances, we felt the need to underline these impediments and investigate the situation that pertains today relating to just conditions of work for women, and the role of the state.

India's Constitution mandates the state to adopt measures of positive action in favour of women and equality of opportunity in public employment. Article 39 of the Directive Principles of State Policy requires that states ensure that 'citizens, men and women equally, have the right to an adequate means of livelihood' and 'there is equal pay for equal work for both men and women'.

The United Nations Declaration of Human Rights, 1948, was perhaps the first articulation in international covenants of the rights of women to work, in using the phrase, 'all human beings…' as opposed to 'all men', when during the discussion of the drafting committee delegates pointed out that

* Leading authors

** Contributing authors

*** Research support provided by Srirupa Bhattacharya.
Reviewers and advisors: Rachel, Kurian, Navsharan Singh, Coen Kompier, Dipa Sinha

the latter did not necessarily include women.[1] The Declaration did not define any differential rights for women. In 1951, the ILO adopted the Convention on Equal Remuneration, incorporating the principle of equal pay for men and women workers for work of equal value and calling for rates of' remuneration to be established without discrimination based on sex.[2] Already in 1919, the year the ILO was founded, its first Maternity Protection Convention was adopted, entitling all women workers to maternity leave with cash and medical benefits.[3]

In 1967, the International Covenant on Economic, Social and Cultural Rights[4] explicitly laid down that women were to be treated as equal to men, with respect to standards of employment. Article 7 of the ICESCR states that 'everyone' has the right to enjoy just and favourable conditions of work, elaborated upon through the parameters of—fair remuneration, based on a minimum wage, which for women must be equal that paid to a male worker for the same work[5] and provide a decent standard of living for the employee and their families; a safe and healthy working environment where occupational accidents and disease (in realisation also of article 12 of the Covenant on the right to health) have been minimised and specific safeguards put in place to protect the safety and health concerns of women, for instance, during pregnancy; opportunities for advancement, based on considerations of seniority and competence and lastly, limitation of working hours to ensure time for rest, leisure and paid leave.

The strongest impetus to women's rights came from the Convention on the Elimination of all forms of Discrimination against Women (CEDAW),[6] adopted in 1979 by the UN General Assembly, which is still known as an International Bill of Rights for women.[7] In using the concept of discrimination, the convention affirms, as Diane Otto argues, that de jure equality is not an adequate strategy to address the 'institutionalized nature of women's disadvantage and change the cultural, religious, social, traditional beliefs that typecasts women as inferior to men'.[8] With respect to employment in particular, the convention recognises the right of women to the same employment opportunities and application of same criteria for selection in employment; equal remuneration and treatment in work of equal value; job security; opportunities for promotion and training; social security and the right to health and safety, including in reproductive functions.

The imperative to recognise unpaid care work has been also articulated in international frameworks, encouraging states to formulate inclusive and responsive policies. For instance, General Recommendation[9] 17[10] of CEDAW acknowledges that unremunerated domestic activities contribute to national development, and that states quantify and include these in the GNP. The ILO states that its 'understanding of the term "work" includes unpaid work in the family and in the community';[11] and its commitment to unpaid care work is reflected in ILO Convention no.156 on 'Workers with Family Responsibilities'.[12] Sustainable Development Goals on gender equality asks that states 'recognize and value unpaid care and domestic work through the provision of public services, infrastructure and social protection policies, and the promotion of shared responsibility within the household and the family as is nationally appropriate'.[13]

There are also more utilitarian reasons for regarding just conditions of work for women to be a public good, because exclusion of women from such work also denies society the benefits of their contributions that would have been possible and considerable, had they been able to realise their full potential. There is also some evidence from studies from many parts of the world which indicate that diversity in the workplace also promotes higher productivity of all workers.[14] It is a prerequisite for the worker's ability to sustain herself in employment and crucial in the enjoyment of other rights, for example, physical and mental health, by avoiding occupational accidents and disease, and an adequate standard of living through a fair remuneration.[15]

Women perform a variety of work, waged, non-waged, recognised and unrecognised. Of these, paid work has the greatest potential in terms of improving bargaining powers for women within the household, the ability to form social networks and the creation of assets.[16]

We recognise that the exclusions of women from just conditions of work are deeply rooted in the larger social context of patriarchy as also the direct consequence of the larger macro-economic context. However, as we have argued in the Introduction to this report, whereas we recognise that exclusion from public goods may and usually does arise from fundamental social and market exclusions, this report chooses to focus on the role of the state, because we believe it is the duty of a democratic state to prevent and correct social and market exclusions.

The state's role in ensuring the public good of just working conditions for women, must be in two distinct, inter-related spheres. First, in guaranteeing legal rights to women as workers in an employment relationship and extending the ambit of these guarantees to those women who work outside this relationship. In addition, for workers in the informal sector of the economy, and for those engaged in subsistence-level self-employment such as in farms, artisanal work, and in street-vending and rag-picking, where there is no clearly identifiable employer, the responsibility to ensure equitable social protection such as pensions and maternity benefits that are available to women in the formal sector, must rest squarely on the shoulders of the state.

2. Who is Excluded

There are very few women in any part of the world who are completely excluded from work itself. Women typically do more work than men, but much of this work is unremunerated, and often under-valued, unrecognised, unsafe and exploitative. In this section, we ask which women are excluded from just conditions of work.

Gender inequalities pervade different types of work across the world. As noted, women typically carry much higher burdens of unpaid work, especially unpaid care work, as compared to men. A greater proportion of women are typically concentrated in informal, precarious and low-end jobs, again compared to men. What distinguishes a woman's labour concerns, from that of a man, is that her ability to access work and just conditions of work is primarily determined by factors external to her own capabilities and income, and more by the social constructs within which she operates. In fact a woman's ability to work, especially for remunerated work outside her home, and her work choices, are often decided by her natal or partner's household members who wield decision-making power. The disparity between men and women's ability to bargain is evident in their highly unequal outcomes with respect to enjoyment of work under decent working conditions and their relative positions on the paid work-unpaid work continuum.

If we ask the question raised in this section—namely, who among women are excluded from just conditions of work—our conclusion would be the large majority of women, from every income decile and social category. But we will argue that exclusion is aggravated for certain groups of women, based on their social identity or due to the nature of the work they are engaged in, while recognising that the groups are not mutually exclusive. These are burdens carried by all women of every income decile, but more by women from excluded groups. The chapter focuses on women burdened by disadvantages of class, caste, religious and ethnic identities, and different abilities.

We find that there exists a whole range of dense, diverse and often overlapping categories of exclusion of women from just conditions of work. We start by speaking of the exclusions faced by women engaged in unpaid care-work mostly within the household, and also unremunerated work in family enterprises. The section goes on to underline the severe exclusions from just conditions of work faced by women in bonded, semi-bonded, forced as well as illegal work of various kinds: work which is outlawed such as work by children, or socially degrading work linked to caste such as manual scavenging (most of which is undertaken by women). Excluded women workers are also those in other socially devalued and stigmatised professions like sex-work. Sex work is nominally not unlawful but still illegalised and even criminalised in practice. Another category of exclusion that we cover in this section is of women in unsafe and exploitatively remunerated conditions of work. This covers again a large and diverse segment of women's work, and includes for instance work in brick kilns, construction and waste-picking, and also various kinds of factory and home-based work. We will also observe briefly that the burdens of unjust work are even higher for women who are burdened by social and economic disadvantages such as of class, caste and religious identity.

2.1 Unpaid workers

A majority of women, both in and out of the labour force engage in unpaid work, which, in a monetised economy, leaves them with multiple disadvantages.

Table 1: Females with various possible employment statuses, 2011-12 (all ages)

Usual principal activity status	Rural	Urban	Total
11 – Own account worker	2.9	2.8	2.8
12 – Employer	0.1	0.1	0.1
21 – Unpaid Family Worker	6.5	1.8	5.1
31 – Regular salaried Worker	1.3	6.1	2.7
41 – Casual Labour in Public Works	0.3	0.0	0.2
51 – Casual labour in other types of work	6.5	1.8	5.2
81 – Unemployed	0.5	0.9	0.6
91 – Attending educational institutions	25.1	26.0	25.4
92 – Attending domestic duties only	18.5	36.4	23.6
93 – Domestic duties + additional work	23.7	11.6	20.3
94 – Rentiers, pensioners , remittance recipients, etc.	0.9	1.5	1.1
95 – Not able to work due to disability	1.2	1.2	1.2
97 – Others (including begging, prostitution, etc.)	3.6	2.7	3.4
99 – Children of age 0-4 years	8.9	7.2	8.4
Total	100.0	100.0	100.0

*Domestic duties refer to codes 92 and 93
** Codes 11-81 refer to the labour force
Source: NSSO 2011–12

Unpaid work includes activities considered 'economic', i.e., production for the market, but also production or procurement of inputs and services for household consumption. While both of these are recognised in principle today in national accounts, they are hard to measure due to their social invisibility and the often unstructured engagement in them; for instance, they may be carried out in conjunction with other types of work, over short time-periods.[17] It is clear, however, that the participation of women in unpaid work is significantly higher than that of men, and women are also concentrated in unpaid work (see Table 1). Unpaid care, on the other hand, is often not considered 'economic'.

2.1.1 Unpaid care workers

Unpaid care work refers to the work done in the home and in communities, from the direct care of children, the ill and elderly and indirect care such as preparing food, cleaning, shopping and collecting water and fuel for the household. Far from being 'unproductive', it is necessary as it contributes to the development of children and maintenance of the labour force. Unpaid care workers subsidise businesses by providing services that would require the payment of a larger wage to workers to 'buy' care to maintain the same standard of living. They effectively also subsidise the state by providing health care, child care and filling gaps in infrastructure provisioning, for instance by travelling longer distances to fetch water and fuel.[18] While middle and high-income households with income and asset wealth are able to substitute or reduce their unpaid care work with paid domestic services and the purchase of market goods, problems of access to resources such as water, fuel and health care puts an additional burden on women from poor households, trapping them, in what Hirway refers to as 'income and time' poverty.[19]

Unpaid care work is highly unequally shared between women and men, to the detriment of the woman's ability to take up paid work or use time for leisure and self-development. Time allocation data (available only through a pilot time-use survey[20] carried out in 1998–99), showed that Indian men's contribution to unpaid care was 10 per cent that of women, across income groups. Participation in unpaid care work is significantly higher for women, compared to men: according to the NSS 2011–12 data, approximately 43.8 per cent of women of all ages were engaged solely in domestic work,[21] while for men, participation was negligible. These figures do not cover women involved in market work, who nevertheless continue to perform unpaid care work, bearing a 'double burden'.

Norms governing the sexual division of labour within the household and the hierarchy of work place unpaid care work at the very bottom; it is intensive, often repetitive and full of drudgery, and does not carry with it monetary rewards, opportunities for mobility or exposure to social and political life outside the household and is therefore relegated to women.

Policy has largely ignored unpaid care workers. Care has entered policy only in relation to paid work, through laws mandating paid maternity leave and through schemes such as the Rajiv Gandhi National Creche Scheme for the Children of Working Women. The Integrated Child Development Scheme (meant to address nutrition, infant and maternal mortality) developed a nominal care function over time. However, here too the state relies on the underpaid labour of women, who, as a consequence of being hired as 'honorary workers', are not entitled to standard minimum wages, pensions or insurance.[22]

In itself, measuring the extent of unpaid care work in an economy and shifting responsibility for certain components of care work to the market or state would not mitigate its under-valuation or lead to equitable sharing between men and women. Making this work visible, would however, reveal links between the paid and unpaid economy and enable the formulation of realistic macro-economic policies. Better state provisioning would also provide time to women from low-income households for education and skill-development, leading to better outcomes on the labour market.

2.1.2 Unpaid family workers

Unpaid workers in market work include those engaged within family enterprises (farms and businesses) owned by relatives living within the same household. They do not enjoy ownership and control rights over productive resources or capital (unlike self-employed or own-account workers) assisting the main worker, effectively as employees, but with no recognised employee rights and legal protection. Men are often accorded the status of 'owner' based on their position as the head of the household, while an unpaid family worker may be the main producer.

At present, it is difficult to estimate exactly how many are engaged in contributing family work as there appears to be a classification error between those contributing to the family's labour and those out of the workforce as a result of attending to domestic duties. According to 2011–12 NSSO estimates, 15.1 per cent of women between the age of 15–59 in rural areas are contributing family workers, relative to 6.6 per cent own-account workers. In urban areas, the share is only 3.5 per cent, relative to 5.1 per cent own-account workers–[23] the share of workers engaged only in domestic duties is a lot higher in urban areas, however. Available data suggests that women are shifting from waged employment to unpaid work, be it attending to domestic duties or contributing to family work.[24] Women are thus being pushed further down in the quality of employment hierarchy.

The large number of female unpaid family workers in the unorganised sector would clearly benefit from social security coverage; however, policy response in this regard has been paradoxical. They are not deemed beneficiaries under the Unorganised Workers Social Security Act, though counted as part of the informal sector workforce,[25] effectively excluding them from individual-based security provisions of the Act such as pensions and life insurance. The exclusion ignores intra-household inequities in resource distribution and re-inforces the breadwinner-dependent dichotomy.

2.2 Forced inclusion in illegal occupations

Certain exploitative and coercive labour arrangements are illegal under the Constitution, central and state laws. Articles 23 and 24 of the Constitution prohibit trafficking in human beings, forced labour and child labour. The central government in accordance has enacted the Bonded Labour Abolition Act (1976), the Employment of Manual Scavengers Act[26] (1993), the Child Labour Prohibition and Regulation Act (1986) as well as schemes for their rescue and rehabilitation. Social oppression was and continues to be the basis of such labour arrangements; Scheduled Castes, Scheduled Tribes and in particular, women and children from these communities are most vulnerable, due to low ascriptive status, recognised rights and consequently their access to resources such as education,[27,28] or assets like land.

Estimating the number of individuals in these practices is difficult, given that they are concealed and official surveys under-report their prevalence. In addition, practices such as labour bondage[29] have transformed, making identification difficult. Inter-generational bondage is increasingly giving way to short-term disguised bondage, in which workers labour against an advance or deferred wages, or both, at very low and exploitative remuneration. Identifying women may be even harder in such contexts as they are rendered invisible to a greater degree due to the working arrangements. Studies conducted in Andhra Pradesh, Tamil Nadu and Chhatisgarh[30] found that women and children in *bidi*-making were employed by contractors with an advance, under the promise of being paid the

Box 1: Girl Children in Labour: The Case of Sumangali

Tamil Nadu is one of India's most industrialised states. But its hidden face is the employment of several hundred thousand impoverished children and adolescents, mostly girls but also some boys, in conditions of months-long confinement and gruelling daily schedules of long hours of toil in the state's spinning mills. By employing what are called 'child camp coolies', their employers break many laws of the land with impunity, and damage tens and thousands of childhoods.

The state is the largest producer of cotton yarn in India and has emerged as a global sourcing hub for readymade garments. Tirupur district tops all hubs in terms of turnover (Rs 13,450 crore), with a total of 2,599 manufacturing units employing around 6 lakh workers, directly and indirectly.[38] More recent figures by SOMO and ICN estimate 4 lakh workers employed in some 1,600 spinning mills. Sixty per cent of the total labour force consists of women and girls.[39]

The tall walls of their factories, with often electrified barbed wire, serve not only to impound their young workers within their campuses, they also prevent public scrutiny of these factories by activists, unionists, journalists and researchers. But state officials are not prevented from entering these factories and enforcing the law. Their failure to do so makes them, and the political and administrative leadership of the state, gravely culpable in these many crimes against children.

Spinning mill owners invented *Sumangali,*[40] primarily to secure a steady labour supply of submissive adolescent female labourers. About two decades ago, with the help of contractors they started targeting young Dalit girls who had completed their basic education at the age of 14 years, and school drop-outs. 60 to 70% of the young women workers are Dalit.[41] Research carried out by SAVE between 2013 -15,[42] shows that 23% of all *Sumangali* workers were younger than 14 years of age and 26.85% of workers were between 12 and 14 years of age at the moment they were recruited, implying that a quarter of all workers are child labourers, in violation of, not only labour laws but also the right to free and compulsory education. During inspections, they are hidden in closets or closed rooms or doctors are brought in to certify that they are older than 14.[43]

They may join the mills due to their poor standing in the community, landlessness and lack of other assets, or discrimination in local schools limiting other livelihood options,[44] and about half of these girls are housed in dormitories or hostels managed by the mills. Although advertised as 'free' lodging and boarding, employers deduct these accommodation costs from wages without informing workers about the amounts.

The young women are offered a labour contract of 3 to 5 years. Upon completion, they receive a lump-sum payment which varies from Rs 35,000 to 70,000. Mill owners proclaim that the money could be used for dowry in the future, to attract parents, despite the fact that dowry is outlawed. During the contract period 'pocket money' is paid, rather than a regular wage. In reality, it is reported that the management discourages workers from completing their contracts towards the end of the contractual period, which would lead them to forfeit the lump-sum entitlement.[45] According to the SAVE study, while 90% of workers received the payment, 69% among them did not receive the entire promised amount.

Other malpractices include the depression of wages, by according workers 'apprentice' status on the one hand and compelling them to work overtime on the other. By law, apprentices cannot work overtime or be given incentives based on meeting production targets. In 2015, daily wages for eight hours of work were found to range between Rs 100 to 230, in contravention of the average minimum of Rs 282.40 set by the state in April 2015. Ninety per cent of the workers, however, worked more than 60 hours per week, with almost half working continuously for two shifts, without overtime payments. None of the interviewed workers reported paid leave wages, and 4% only had a weekly holiday. Mandatory breaks, of one hour daily for eight hours worked, were reported by 20% of the respondents.

Despite unhealthy working conditions, face masks and earplugs were seldom provided or used. Contrary to the advertised promise of 'round the clock medical services' a handful of workers reported free visits by medical doctors. Heavy penalties were levied for hours missed (Rs 50 to 60) making it difficult for workers to avail sick leave.

Verbal abuse and sexual harassment, including caste-based insults were reported by a majority of workers; sexual assault was reported by 6% of interviewees. No workers knew whether Workers Committees and Complaints Committees were established. Psychological trauma, resulting from these factors was reported by 65% workers. A fact-finding committee investigating the death of a young woman in a mill in Dindigul found that unions had no access to either factory or dormitory premises and none of the workers were affiliated to a trade union and speaking out against management was not tolerated.[46]

Sadly India's law still permits employment of children above 14 years. Though the Factories Act limits the hours of work of these adolescents to four and a half hours a day, in every factory, these children are made to work at least eight hour shifts, with additional hours for cleaning and filling in for other workers during their food breaks. They work night shifts and are denied weekly leave, in violation of the law, and conditions of work are unhealthy for children in contravention of the standards laid down by the law. Their net wages are well below the statutory minimum wage levels.

Even more culpably, the three criteria used to define bonded labour apply to the employment of the children and adolescents. Employment is legally deemed to be 'bonded labour' if work is done against an advance or deferred wages, remuneration is below minimum wages, and there are restrictions to freedom of workers to leave employment if they so wish.

What spurs tacit official support for this unlawful form of employment is the contemporary favoured model of globalised economic growth, in which the current god is global competitiveness, valued at all costs, even above compliance with the law and the well-being of our children. India's current aspirations to snatch from China the mantle of the 'world's factory' depends ultimately on its capacity to guarantee an unlimited reserve army of cut-price and compliant workers.

Sources: Case studies provided by Coen Kompier and Harsh Mander

remainder at the end of the term of employment.[31] But as it is largely home-based, it tends to be disguised as self-employment. Research on the silk-weaving industry in Varanasi noted that though both girls and boys worked as weavers, the former were confined to the home and their work could not be documented.[32]

In cases where the whole family is bonded, as in brick kilns, the employment contract exists between the contractor and the male head of the household, while women (and children) are not listed on muster rolls.[33] This could result in non-recognition of bondage of women (and children) by the state and a subsequent withholding of benefits upon rescue.[34] It is also important to note that while men are aware of the terms of the employment contract, women may enter them as a consequence of their spouse's employment.[35] The marked asymmetry in power relations, due to caste, gender and economic bondage makes women workers extremely vulnerable to sexual exploitation by contractors, which is reported in almost every sector where bondage exists.[36]

A 2010 study on 2.6 lakh rehabilitated bonded labourers from Madhya Pradesh, Orissa, Rajasthan, Tamil Nadu and Uttar Pradesh (over 43 per cent and 39 per cent were ST and SC, respectively and 16 per cent OBC) estimated that about 19 per cent of them were women,[37] indicating that a considerable number of women do find themselves in situations of bondage. However, numbers are likely higher, for reasons discussed above.

2.3 Women in stigmatised, unlawful, and illegalised occupations

Stigma is associated with 'unclean jobs', socially and culturally considered physically disgusting, morally offensive or undignified.[47] These jobs are often highly correlated with low-caste status and poverty as the marking of certain castes being ritually polluted (and consequent consigning of 'polluting' jobs to them), has been used as a strategy by upper castes to control 'clean', economically profitable trades and education.[48] Control could be exercised either overtly, through threats, economic or social boycott and active blocking of movement into other trades, as illustrated below, in the case of manual scavengers or could be couched in ideas of ritual and tradition. The *Devadasi* practice, for instance (described in detail in this report in a later chapter), validated the sexual access of upper caste men to girls and women from lower castes, outside of a marital relationship.

In the forms of unlawful and socially degrading work,[49] one that especially burdens women and girls, is manual scavenging (as well as men and boys). This involves the, gathering of human excreta from individual or community dry toilets with bare hands, brooms or metal scrapers into wicker baskets or buckets, and then carrying this on their heads, shoulders or against their hips into dumping sites or water bodies. Others are similarly employed to clear, carry and dispose excreta from sewers, septic tanks, drains into which excreta flows, and railway lines.

In 1976, almost three decades after India secured freedom, Section 7A was introduced into the Protection of Civil Rights Act, 1955,[50] to make the offence punishable by imprisonment, compelling any person on grounds of untouchability to scavenge. It took another 17 years, in 1993, for Parliament to pass the Employment of Manual Scavengers and Construction of Dry Latrines (Prohibition) Act,[51] which rendered even voluntary employment of manual scavengers for removing excreta an offence, and another four years for the act to be notified. The government also launched programmes for livelihood rehabilitation of freed manual scavengers and education of their children; and promoted flush latrines in place of dry latrines. However, these have not resulted in eradication, as governments have tended to look at this as an issue of sanitation rather than human dignity as guaranteed by Constitution. A much stronger law passed 20 years later the Prohibition of Employment as Manual Scavengers and Their

Rehabilitation Act, 2013,[52] has still not led to the end of the socially degrading practice.

While the practice of manual scavenging is easily identifiable, it persists despite legislation and civil society activism. Official estimates are based on self-identification or surveys that are limited to people hired to clean dry toilets, not those cleaning open defecation sites, public pour-flush toilets, healthcare facilities, sewers, septic tanks, drains, and railway tracks. In 2003, The Ministry of Social Empowerment and Justice reported that there were 6.76 lakh manual scavengers, but the Safai Karamchari Andolan estimates that the number is closer to 12 lakhs.[53] The problems with enumeration is that official agencies tend to deny the persistence of this outlawed practice, and in most places manual scavengers themselves do not speak out because of shame and fear of losing even this frequently insecure source of livelihood. Instead they remain trapped in a vicious cycle of intense stigma, segregation, poor health and education, destructive coping strategies like alcohol and drugs, all of which barred even more firmly options of other dignified vocations, which in any case are inaccessible by their birth in the most disadvantaged of all castes.

Civil society organisations working with manual scavengers, estimate that 95–98 per cent of individuals involved are women.[54] They belong to the most discriminated sub-castes such as of Valmikis, known regionally by different names—Bhangi, Chuhda, Mehtar, Madiga, Halalkhor, and Lalbegi, or the Muslim Hela sub-caste. They 'inherit' the work generation after generation, working for payments as low as a few rupees a month, daily rations of leftovers, old clothes, rights to use common/upper caste land for collection of free firewood, etc. Case studies indicate some degree of gender segregation in tasks and work arrangements, though it varies widely from state to state: in Gujarat, Rajasthan, and Uttar Pradesh, women clean dry toilets in households.[55] In Hyderabad, a study found that the Metro Supply and Sewerage Board hired only men and another municipal agency paid lower wages to women in both permanent and temporary employment.[56] The community is coerced into continuing the work by the local *Panchayats*, by being prevented from taking up other occupations despite having the requisite qualifications, threats of violence or eviction from their home and village.[57] In case families serving the area move in to other work, *Panchayats* are even known to hire individuals of the Valmiki caste from other areas. The absence of alternative employment for most individuals in the community is a pressing problem, as illustrated in the following narratives.[58]

In affidavits to the Supreme Court in a petition filed by the Safai Karamchari Andolan in 2001, Ramrakhi, who has worked since she was 10, says, 'The gas emitted by the shit has spoilt my eyes, and my hands and feet also swell. It sticks to my hands and makes me nauseous'. Chinta Devi, like many others, says she hates this work, but has to pursue it to raise her children. Kokilaben, a sanitation worker in Kadi municipality in Mehsana, Gujarat, testifies in an affidavit to the Court, 'The human excreta discharged by people on the road is collected by me in a large bowl with the help of a broom and tin plate and stored in a trolley. When the trolley is full, I drag (this with the help of) my daughter and my husband…. I carry the human excreta stored in plastic bucket on my head and while doing so the dirt falls on my body…. I fall sick frequently…. If I refuse to remove waste, I get suspended from duty by the Nagarpalika.'

Stigma can in some cases take the form of criminalisation of these workers by the state, as the case of sex workers illustrates. In 2010, based on information from state AIDS control societies, the Ministry of Health and Family Welfare estimated that there are almost 6.9 lakh registered female sex workers in the country[59]; actual numbers are likely to be much higher. Commercial sex work, unlike the work of women who are *Devadasis* or from the *Nat* community, is not initiated by their own community.

Sex workers may be forced to hide their occupation from their families and community. Their work exposes them to extreme physical violence and sexually transmitted diseases and erects barriers in access to housing and health care.[60]

Selling one's own sexual labour, while legal, is not recognised as work in India. The primary piece of legislation dealing with sex work, the Immoral Trafficking (Prevention) Act (1956),[61] conflates trafficking with sex work. Enacted to curb exploitation, it does not differentiate clearly between those consensually carrying out sex work and those coerced into prostitution. In fact, many women choose sex work, which may garner higher pay compared to other unskilled jobs,[62,63] and engage in it in addition to other work. Further, it illegalises brothels or establishments where sex work is carried out, leading to a *de facto* criminalising of sex workers.[64]

2.4 Women in hazardous occupations

Laws[65] protecting occupational health and safety in hazardous jobs or processes apply largely to formally registered enterprises, with a workforce above a specified minimum and prohibit the employment of women in certain sites such as underground mines, in processes such as cotton-opening, etc. Besides detracting from more effective workplace safety and health policies for all workers, these laws are unsuccessful in making workplaces safe for women. A 1996 World Bank report, in fact, noted that 'Indian women encounter health hazards in virtually all occupations',[66] including domestic work.

Home-based workers in such occupations, and their families, face a high degree of risk as the employer is absolved of the responsibility to maintain safety/hygiene standards or provide infrastructure. The *bidi* industry[67] is one such example; the government estimates that the industry employs about 45 lakh workers[68] a majority of whom are women, though exact numbers are unavailable. An NCW Report[69] estimates that in some states, about 80 per cent of workers in the industry are women. It reported that most of them worked in cramped spaces, without amenities like toilets and clean drinking water. The inhalation of tobacco dust, increases susceptibility to respiratory ailments like Tuberculosis and Asthma; posture and long working hours lead to chronic back pain and rheumatic pain. Though the workers are eligible for Employees State Insurance, contractors seldom provide the requisite identity cards. Contrary to expectations that home-based work enables a balance of paid work with care, most women reported not having free time as a combination of a piece-rate system with low wages requires that they produce lakhs of *bidis* a month, requiring 8–10 hours of daily work on an average.

Industries known to be hazardous, like construction and mining employ women for intensely strenuous tasks such as head loading. A case study from Tamil Nadu, quoted in an NCW, 2005 report on construction illustrates their intensity: loads of mud or bricks can weigh between 15 to 20 kilos and have to be carried to male workers about 180 times a day over the course of eight hours,[70] making them vulnerable to musculoskeletal diseases, chronic fatigue and undernutrition. A majority are hired at a young age, under 40, o wing to the taxing nature of work.[71] Labour laws are seldom implemented and organising is difficult as employment is transient. Pregnant and lactating women do not get maternity leave, neither do they have have access to crèche facilities at worksites, putting their reproductive health and the safety of their children at risk.

2.5 Women facing multiple social and economic disadvantages

Marginalised groups in India, while being varied and internally heterogeneous, have been marginalised through instituted practices that are similar. Gender-based discrimination is heightened when it intersects with caste or

Box 2: Women Subsistence and Unpaid Workers in Gujarat*

Like the rest of the country, over two-thirds of all tribal agricultural landholders in the district are small or marginal farmers, owning less than two hectares of land. However, being rain-fed, agriculture is at best a seasonal activity. Since produce from land is hardly enough for household consumption even for four to six months in a year[1], agriculture or agricultural labour in exchange for food grains provides at best a buffer against starvation. There are no consistent sources of wage labour, leading to distress migration.

Basic infrastructure for water, sanitation and subsidised cooking fuel are absent in Dahod. 84 per cent of the people have no water sources within their premises; 78.1 per cent have to depend on firewood for fuel. Women's unpaid work within the household therefore becomes more tedious, time-consuming and tiring.

During the agricultural season, women sow food grains for sustenance such as maize, pigeon peas and paddy, which are locally grown, labour-intensive crops. Women are engaged in the production of major grains and millets, land preparation, seed selection, sowing, applying manure, fertiliser and pesticide, weeding, transplanting, threshing, winnowing and harvesting as well as the collection of non-timber forest produce. However, their contribution is neither recognised nor compensated in subsistence production in family farms[19]?? by the state or in farm production by the markets.

Almost all of the women in the study supplement agriculture with agricultural labour, wage labour, forest produce, distress migration or by community work that pays an honorarium. Wage and migratory work includes agriculture and forest work as well as high-risk labour such as construction, laying telephone lines, electricity transformers and railway tracks. Women and men migrate to Saurashtra for agriculture and to cities (Baroda, Ahmedabad and Rajkot) for construction. Women earn between Rs 150 and Rs 200, whereas men earn Rs 300 per day. Migration increases women's vulnerability economically as well as to physical or sexual violence.

A leader of the Devgadh Mahila Sanghatan, a community-based organisation in the district articulates, 'Why will we migrate if we get enough from our own fields? If we have enough *saak-sabji* (greens and vegetables) to eat and to sell, we can live comfortably. But if we have to go to someone else's field for agricultural labour or somewhere outside the village for wage labour, we have to face dangers and risks. We don't have a decent place to live, and there is also the risk of violence and sexual assault. If women have a place to live, land to cultivate and enough water, they can live their lives independently with dignity.'

* This case study, written by Sejal Dand and Sita Mamidipudi, is based on evidence collected from a larger study conducted by the Collective for the Advancement of Action on Women's Livelihood Rights (CAWL Rights) in Gujarat, Madhya Pradesh and Maharashtra. It is based on in-depth interviews with 15 women in Dahod who have claimed their rights to land and livelihoods from their families, non-tribals or the state upon dispossession.

religious disadvantages, although it must be highlighted that the experience of discrimination faced by women from each group is distinct. The combination of low household ownership of assets, such as land[72] and marketable skills means that women from these groups are pushed into low quality work in the unorganised sector, are most adversely affected by economic or job-market fluctuations.[73] Dalit, Tribal and Muslim women have the lowest levels of education among social and religious groups, even in comparison to men from the same groups. Data from the NSS 2009–10 shows that in rural areas, 58.1 per cent Dalit, 58.3 per cent ST and 52.6 per cent Muslim women were illiterate, compared to the average 43.9 per cent and only 1.1 per cent Dalit, 0.9 per cent tribal and 0.9 per cent Muslim women were graduates. In urban areas, while average proportion of graduate women was 14.7 per cent, only 7.2 per cent of Dalit women, 9.8 per cent of tribal women and 4.8 per cent of Muslim women were graduates.

Due to poverty and lower restrictions on mobility, the participation of Dalit and tribal women on the labour force has always been higher than that of upper caste and Muslim women, but, not surprisingly, casual wage work is the predominant source of paid employment for them. An analysis of NSS data from 2009–10 shows that over 31.5 per cent of Dalit women and 35.5 per cent of tribal women in urban areas were in casual labour, compared to 5.8 per cent of upper caste women. In rural areas as well, the proportion of upper caste women in casual labour was 19.4 per cent, compared to 56.3 per cent for Dalit women and 43.8 per cent for tribal women. Further, the highest decreases in labour force participation over the past decade have been for these groups in rural areas, which in the absence of an improvement in household wealth, is especially worrying.[74] Muslim women are concentrated in self-employment, in home-based sub-contracted work with low earnings.[75] While cultural restrictions on mobility may be partly responsible (as with upper caste Hindu women), the claim needs to be examined in the context of the insecurity created by repeated episodes of targeted violence and everyday experiences of discrimination, which could potentially impact women's access to public life.[76,77]

In a patriarchal society, women who live by choice or circumstance independent of adult men, as single women, face particularly strong barriers to just work, as reflected in a subsequent chapter of this report devoted to single women. Another highly vulnerable category of women workers are women with disabilities, who are denied opportunities for dignified work both as women and as persons who are culturally seen to be 'without abilities'. Their limited access to education, health care, and aids to mobility, necessary for pursuing dignified labour are compounded by the social isolation and stigma they face. Their contributions to household labour also tend to be undervalued. Only 16.1 per cent of working age women with disabilities were employed in 2002, although just 29 per cent of the same group were recorded as being 'unable to work owing to disability.[78]

Another major social barrier to access to just work is created by age. Unlike women in the working age, elderly men and women should see a declining need to participate in the workforce with economic growth and progress in social security coverage. On the contrary in India, they continue to work well past their retirement age. NSSO data shows that participation rates for rural elderly women have fluctuated around 20 per cent between 1983 and 2011–12.[79] While urban participation of elderly women has declined from historical levels, no such pattern is visible in rural areas. Far from the expectation that the elderly would be doing low intensity work, most of the elderly are working full-time, for more than four hours every day[80] while being paid lesser than younger workers for the same work.[81] If this work by aged persons is voluntary, then it can add to their sense of social and self-worth. But if work is forced by conditions of penury and the absence of social protection, their high work intensity[82] is indicative of their economic insecurity.

This workforce of older women faces multiple vulnerabilities, both in their access to work and to adequate social security. Almost 70 per cent of all elderly workers and 93 per cent of all elderly women are either illiterate or have not completed primary education.[83] This elderly workforce is therefore primarily engaged in low-end, unskilled work, with elderly women more downwardly classified as compared to men—39 per cent of elderly women work in elementary occupations, as compared to 26 per cent elderly men[84] and receiving lower wages than men, regardless of whether they are engaged in regular or casual employment. In addition, the largely informal nature of India's labour market means that few workers manage to avail of employer's pension—only 3% of elderly women receive it and 15% elderly men.[85] With no control over resources, elderly women are also likely to face abuse in hands of family members. One in 10 elderly persons reportedly face some form of abuse after 60 years of age and, in the case of women, the perpetrators are usually family members.[86]

3. Processes of Exclusion

In looking for the causes of these exclusions, we recognise first that these stem most of all from the hegemonic social and cultural contexts of patriarchy, in which normative beliefs that privilege men over women result in their oppression and denial in work and the ownership of land and capital. There are also exclusions by markets, because the macro-economic context of neo-liberal globalisation has created a permissive framework in which women and girls are often preferred as workers because they can be paid less, denied more basic rights in the conditions of work, and are denied opportunities to organise themselves. We also find the state wanting, both in the design of its policies for the rights of women workers, but even more in the institutional bias that plays out in the implementation of these laws and policies.

We shall consider each of these by turn in this section.

3.1 Exclusion by patriarchy

Patriarchy is a social-political system that maintains the superiority of men over women.[87] The overarching context of enduring, indeed dominant cultures of patriarchy, denies women social and economic power both within and outside the family, denies them ownership and inheritance of economic assets like land, withholds from them political voice, regards them as subordinate to men in both domestic and work spaces, denies them equitable education and health care, and restricts them to domestic roles.

As Jacqui True argues in her influential work, 'The Political Economy of Violence Against Women',[88] the gendered household division of labour, supported by gender ideologies place the primary responsibility for unpaid work 'private realm' leading to unequal bargaining powers in the household. Care work on the labour market is shaped by this hierarchy and devalued, both within nations and transnationally, as women from poorer regions migrate to provide care services for families in the wealthier regions. True[89] points out that 'in a mutually constitutive way, the strict division of roles in the domestic sphere constrains women's public participation and their access to education and economic opportunities in the market, in turn creating hierarchal structures that entrap many women into potentially violent environments at home and at work. Some women, especially in the developed regions, evade patriarchal and potentially violent situations in the family/private sphere by contracting out caring work to poor women.' Further, it is evident that opening up of the economy has brought about a significant movement in the location, occupation and social position of women. It has expanded women's economic participation but it has left unchanged the underlying patriarchal structures that perpetuate women's inequality with men and their susceptibility to violence. Despite the fact that women's labour is mobilized by the dynamic of globalisation, the majority of women workers in the informal economy, care sector and unpaid work lie outside the ambit of recognised labour standards and the human rights system.[90] They are stuck in 3D jobs—dirty, dangerous, and demeaning—often with a fourth D: degrading.

Kabeer[91] deploys the useful analytical constructs of 'gender-specific constraints' and 'bearers of gender' to understand structural constraints in relation to women in the labour market. 'Gender-specific constraints' refer to 'norms, customary beliefs and values that allocate certain roles to men and women based on ideals/models of masculinity and femininity, while also attributing a lower value to roles and labour deemed feminine'.[92] This would shape, for instance, the expectations that a community or society has of women in terms of the distribution of paid and unpaid work.

The sexual division of labour starts in the household, with women bearing primary responsibility for unpaid domestic work and care in most societies. Participation in paid work is, further, determined, by cultural restrictions for women from certain socio-economic backgrounds. Studies have documented that concerns about status restrict participation in work outside the home, for upper caste women.[93] On the other hand, although paid work is necessary for women from poorer households, their position in the social hierarchy may push them into other forms of culturally-determined work roles. Bardhan[94] and Mencher and Saradamoni[95] note, for instance, that in the rice-growing regions of Eastern and Southern India, the concentration of women, especially Dalit and Adivasi women is very high in wet cultivation of rice. Wet cultivation has traditionally been done by those at the lowest rung of the social hierarchy as it is considered polluting. Rice (wet) cultivation consist of ploughing, applying cow-dung, transplanting, weeding, fixing bunds (these activities are often done in knee-deep mud and water), followed by harvesting, carrying it to the site of processing and processing. The work requires women to remain with their backs bent for hours at end, making them vulnerable to waterborne infections, mosquito and leech bites.

This is also a reminder that women are not a homogenous group; caste, religion, sexuality, class and other axes of stratification interact with gender to produce distinct forms of disadvantage for women as they engage with work. The market and state carry and reproduce these gendered ideologies through 'practices, processes and rules', to become 'bearers of gender'. Stereotypes about women, such as their 'natural' affinity for caring tasks, subservient temperament, inability to perform intellectual or physically taxing tasks, etc., are used as reasons to keep them in low-status and low-paid jobs.[96] On tea plantations in West Bengal, Assam, Tamil Nadu and Kerala, women are hired as tea-pluckers as they have 'nimble fingers' and then paid low wages as they are 'tire easily'.[97] Men seek employment in other work in the plantation that is better-paid, less intensive and require lesser hours, etc., like office staff, security guards, drivers, electricians, typists, pharmacists, teachers, supervisors, etc.

Constraints can be reproduced in formalised modes, through gender-blind and gender-unjust laws, for instance, as a forthcoming section shows. Further, they can be reproduced in routine processes that reinforce existing hierarchies. Labour statistics, for instance, under-report women's work as they may engage in several kinds of unpaid and paid work in a single day or week, effectively reinforcing the idea that women are not as 'productive' as men.

Also, given social and economic contexts, individuals and households may be making ostensibly rational choices that nonetheless have a greater disadvantageous effect on women, due to their vulnerability. The unavailability of decent employment for individuals with lower-than-graduate-level education may prompt families to educate boys rather than girls if returns from the labour market are higher for the former. In turn, these act as feedback mechanisms, perpetuating lower access to resources and lower bargaining power for women.

3.2 Exclusion by macro-economic processes

The barriers to women accessing just conditions of work erected by social and cultural contexts of patriarchy are further reinforced by the larger macro-economic context of neo-liberal policies. Jayati Ghosh reminds us of the fact that women are not excluded from the economy by neo-liberal policies, but are unjustly included. 'A basic feature of economic development in India', she points out, 'has been exclusion of the bulk of the population: exclusion from control over assets; exclusion from the benefits of economic growth; exclusion from the impact of physical and social infrastructure expansion; exclusion from education and from income-generating opportunities; even exclusion from such basic needs as adequate nutrition. This exclusion has been along class, asset ownership and income lines, by geographical location, by caste and community and by gender. However, exclusion from benefits has not meant exclusion from the system—rather, those who are supposedly marginalized or excluded have been affected precisely because they have been incorporated into market systems. India thus has a process of exclusion through incorporation. This process of simultaneous incorporation and exclusion has been especially marked in the recent phase of rapid accumulation of capital over the past two decades, when the Indian economy has been viewed globally as "a success story".'[101] In the contemporary neoliberal globalisation system, where the domestic policy environment has led to the expansion of women's employment, it has also led to the intensification of their workload in the market and at home. At the same time, neo-liberal policies have reduced the state's capacity to regulate and tax capital, resulting in an enforcement problem and difficulties in generating expenditure for social provisioning that could alleviate women's poverty and vulnerability. Social provisioning of housing and child benefits which might provide better options for women are rarely on the political agenda.

As observed in a UN Women Report, 'At the global level, women's labour force participation rates (LFPR) have stagnated since the 1990s. Currently, only half of women are in the labour force compared to more than three quarters of men. Despite considerable regional variations, nowhere has this gender gap been eliminated. Nor have improvements in access to education closed the gender gap in pay. Globally, women earn on average 24 per cent less than men. The cumulative result of gender gaps in labour force participation, in earnings and in social transfers is substantial. A study of four countries estimates lifetime income gaps between women and men of between 31 and 75 per cent.'[98] Although macro-economic policy is generally considered to be gender-neutral, there are a number of ways in which it impacts women's work. Macro-economic policies affect not only the availability of paid employment but also the resources needed to implement social policies. The recent trend in women's workforce participation of a declining proportion of women in paid work or in work where they are counted as 'workers' are to a large extent a result of the macro-economic processes that India has been experiencing in the last three decades. Along with a neo-liberal economic framework, rigid gender norms result in women not being able to access decent employment. While these processes affect men as well, the underlying patriarchal norms result in an unfair or unequal impact on women.

Macro-economic policies therefore have an impact on women's work in a number of ways. The quantity and quality of work available as well as the sectoral distribution of work gets affected by macro-economics policies. Different sectors get affected in different ways and in turn there is an unequal effect on women as they are differently concentrated across sectors. As mentioned earlier, macro-economic policies also affect the burden of unpaid care and domestic work via their impact on employment, household incomes and living standards. Demands on unpaid work may intensify during times of economic stress, increasing the burden on women. The UN Women Report on Progress of Women also talks about other ways in which macro-economic policies have a gendered impact. It mentions, for example, the distributive consequences—through taxation, for instance—that affect women and men differently which can either reinforce the extent of women's socio-economic disadvantage or, potentially, promote a redistribution of resources towards women. Another aspect which is also related to the burden of unpaid work on women is the influence the quantum of resources that are made available to governments to finance social policies and social protection programmes that can be used to reduce women's socio-economic disadvantage are often determined by prevailing macro-economic framework.

We can identify three processes which have led to women being excluded from equitable and decent work in India: (1) Processes leading to overall 'jobless growth' in the Indian economy; (2) greater flexibilisation and feminisation of labour and; (3) inadequate social protection policies and declining social sector investments that reduce the unpaid work burden on women and therefore free up their time making them available to participate in paid employment.

In India, high growth of around 8 per cent[99] per annum between 2003–4 and 2011–12, did not create commensurate employment, leading many analysts to term this period as one of 'jobless growth'. In fact, the employment elasticities of growth have declined over time. Employment elasticity fell from 0.44 during 2000–05 to 0.01 during 2005–10 though rising to 0.2 during 2010–12.[100] Aggregate rates of growth of employment in India have been very low with total employment having grown faster when the economy was growing more slowly. Rural employment has been more affected than urban employment, with the number of workers in rural areas actually showing a decline in absolute numbers (a reduction of 35 million) and urban employment growing by only 2.5 per cent annual compound rate between 2004–05 and 2011–12.[101] Along with the new entrants in the workforce, the total employment generated by the non-farm sector was 49 million.[102]

Although there is an increase in non-farm employment, this has not been in high productivity and regular manufacturing jobs but mainly in the low productivity construction sector. Manufacturing actually saw a decline in its share of non-farm employment. Also, almost two-thirds of new non-farm jobs in rural areas were as casual daily wage workers, with no addition in regular employment.[103] Much of the decline in employment has been because of decline in female employment.

When women are 'pushed' into the labour market because of economic distress, they are often employed in precarious, informal and low-paid activities. When a crisis triggers women's withdrawal from paid employment, they return to dependent positions within the household with less autonomy and less access to incomes of their own. This is the phenomenon that has been seen in India as well where women's employment increased during the period between 1999–2000 and 2004–05, which has been attributed to distress[104] and later a decline in women's employment has been seen in the post-2004 period which has been at least partially attributed to the improvement in living standards in rural areas.

While female labour force participation rates in India have been historically low, it is still counter-intuitive that despite three decades of economic growth, these rates have not only not gone up but have in fact decreased in the last 10 years, with the decline being particularly sharp for rural women.

It is widely believed that the decline in women's work participation rates is because of an increasing participation in education, which is to be welcomed. It is certainly true that female participation in education has increased in both rural and urban areas,[105] and especially so since 2007. However, it still does not explain fully the total decline in female labour force participation.

The decline in work participation has been among self-employed workers,[106] including (but not only) those involved in agriculture. One of the factors that has played a role in reducing the demand for women's work in agriculture has been the growing mechanisation in this sector. Further, due to environmental degradation and particularly a decline in access to forests and common property resources, there has been a fall in many of the rural activities earlier performed by women, such as the collection of minor forest produce. On the other hand, the increased time that now has to be spent in activities such as collecting fuel and water (because of declining availability and inadequate social services to provide these) has led to women spending more time on these unpaid activities at the cost of their ability to participate in the labour market.

These changes are also aided by existing social norms in society about the work that women can do. Therefore, roles such as driving a tractor or a harvester is seen as a man's job even though the labour these machines displace are primarily of women. Similarly it is the prevailing gender norms that result in the burden of unpaid work related to the household falling disproportionately on women. New jobs that are generated are in the low productivity services sector; here women are employed (home-based, etc.) because of gendered norms of employment.

Particularly in times of crisis, the effects of macro-economic policies on social hierarchies can become pronounced, which can intensify stigma, stereotypes and violence. The macro-economic framework within which other policies are implemented either enlarges or constrains their scope to advance substantive equality for women.

3.3 Exclusion through design and implementation of law

Application of labour laws in India for enforcing workers' rights is the exception rather than the norm. The India Exclusion Report of 2013–14 shows how the State is gravely culpable in condoning and fuelling this culture of non-application of labour legislation.

This neglect by the state is even more acute for women workers. A brief analysis of various labour laws will show that labour laws in India do not cover the vast majority of working women because they are engaged in informal working arrangements. The 2008 Unorganised Workers Social Security Act, while in some ways a positive attempt to correct this, excludes unpaid family workers without a sound rationale, neglecting that household-based social security does not ensure fair intra-household resource allocation between men and women. In addition, the laws do not address women's concerns in work adequately, even in the organised sector, where they are applicable.

In this section, we will examine a few major labour laws from the perspective of women workers' rights.

3.3.1 Factories Act, 1948

One of the oldest labour legislations, the Factories Act lays down the necessary conditions of work to be ensured by an employer in manufacturing units. In the absence of any umbrella legislation on occupational health and safety (OSH) (other than those specific to certain sectors like mining and ports), it is the only set of OSH standards. The Act excludes home-based workers, sub-contracting and self-employed women by defining the factory in terms of the number of people employed.[107] In addition to working condition provisions directed at all workers like working time, payment of overtime wages, holidays and facilities, the Act addresses women specifically in protective provisions related to separate toilets, crèches, night work restrictions and additional safety measures.[108]

This protectionist stance towards women results in clubbing them with other vulnerable categories; for instance, in regulations regarding the operation of machinery in motion women are clubbed together with young persons,[109] presupposing that gender renders women incapable of dealing with machinery in motion. The proposed amendments in the 2014 Factories (Amendment) Bill[110] seek to limit the restriction to specific groups, such as pregnant women and adolescents. Nevertheless, this approach separating women workers from categories of vulnerable workers is not maintained on the use of dangerous machinery. The unjustified blanket restriction against women continues to hold under Section 87. The proposed amendments are inconsistent, and safeguards should be put in place for all workers, irrespective of sex.[111] The Factories Act contains a provision for the instating of committees to decide on health and safety safeguards, in units using hazardous substances. Participation of women on these committees would allow them greater choice in the matter of engaging in 'unsafe operations'. However, it does not mandate that women be part of the committee, constituted of representatives from workers and management.[112]

Contrary to promoting shared care work between men and women, the Factories Act makes women workers responsible for child care including washing, changing their clothes and feeding, and stipulates that crèches are mandatory only in factories with 30 or more women workers.[113] Several trade unions,[114] as well as the National Commission of Women suggest an amendment removing references to 'women' workers specifically.[115] This would be in line with an ILO Convention dealing with workers with family responsibilities.[116] While the implementation of the provisions of the Act overall remains poor, employers frequently evade providing for child care[117] through strategies such as under-reporting the number of female workers in the muster roll of the factory.[118]

One of the most controversial provisions bars women from working except between 6 am and 7 pm, also mandated by the ILO Convention No. 89 from 1948, putting a blanket prohibition on night work for women. India ratified this convention in 1950. By a 1976 amendment, state governments were given the power to remove this restriction by official notification, provided that such variations do not authorise women to work between 10 pm to 5 am. The prohibitions obviously resulted in a decrease in employment of women workers.[119]

In 1990 the ILO adopted two new instruments on night work doing away with the blanket ban but still ensuring that working at night for women remained safe. In its Night Work Convention No. 171,[120] it provided for a special compensation and regulation for men and women alike in night shifts. Several High Courts have struck it down as unconstitutional and discriminatory, violating Articles 14, 15 and 16 of the Constitution. The Madras High Court in Vasantha R. v Union of India[121] and the Andhra Pradesh High Court in Triveni KS v Union of India[122] also stipulated guidelines to ensure the safety and welfare of women workers in night shifts.

The other ILO 1990 night work instrument, a Protocol amending Convention No. 89, was ratified by India in November 2003. It implied the same consequences, no longer a prohibition of night work for women as long as the safety of women workers could be guaranteed. This ratification prompted the need to amend Section 66 of the Factories Act.[123] In the face of demands for gender parity, in 2014, the Government of India permitted state governments to lift the ban and allow night work for women as long as transport is provided from a women worker's homestead to her workplace. In addition, workplace facilities such as separate toilets must enhance women's options to work at night, provided the consent of women workers, workers, employers, the representative organisation of the employers and the representative organisation of the workers of the concerned factory has been taken. The amendment was expected to benefit workers in SEZs, and sectors like IT, garments, textiles and handicrafts.[124]

The removal of the ban without instating regulations and safeguards is naturally detrimental to the health and overall welfare of women workers.[125] In fact, night work could have detrimental medical effects if performed regularly, for both men and women. Further, it could add to the time-poverty experienced by women in low-paid jobs, who cannot afford private household help or work in multiple jobs.[126]

3.3.2 Equal Remuneration Act, 1976

Enacted to implement Article 39(d) of the Indian Constitution and the 1951 ILO Convention No. 100 on Equal Remuneration,[127] this Act postulates the principle of payment of equal remuneration to both men and women for performing work of a similar nature'. By a further amendment in 1987, discrimination against women during 'any condition of service subsequent to recruitment, such as promotion, training or transfer' was prohibited.

The Act has been criticised for using the phrase 'equal work of a similar nature' rather than 'work of equal value', the principle used in ILO Convention No. 100. This could encourage employers to classify jobs for women of inferior nature, justifying a lower wage. The ILO's Committee of Experts[128] recommends the development of objective and neutral job evaluation systems to 'avoid prejudices or stereotypes based on sex'.[129]

Courts have frequently ruled in favour of women, upholding the seniority of female staff, for example in the India Forest Service[130] and in airlines.[131] In Mackinnon Mackenzie & Co. Ltd. V Audrey D' Costa 1987,[132] where a woman stenographer filed a case for wage arrears in lieu of being paid a lower salary than male stenographers on the pretext that she was a 'confidential stenographer', the court emphasised that work should be evaluated based on whether *real* differences exist in the '...duties actually performed, not those theoretically possible'.[133] In Democratic Rights & others v Union of India,[134] discrimination in payments of construction workers on the basis of sex was held to be a violation of Article 14 of the Indian Constitution.

Lower wages and barriers to promotion persist even in formal employment; women's average earned income (PPP) is US$1,304, whereas men's earnings are US$4,102 and they occupy only 3 per cent of senior and management positions.[135]

3.3.3 Industrial Disputes Act, 1947

This Act seeks to make provisions for the investigation and settlement of industrial disputes, and safeguards workers' rights against arbitrary dismissal from service. The Act was amended in 2010, and even this version speaks about 'workmen', proof of its archaic gender setting. Only a single provision mentions the word 'woman', on the Grievance Settlement Authority and its possible membership of women representatives.

Several landmark judgements have broadened the meaning of the term `industry'[136] to include institutions such as hospitals,[137] and have established criteria for the determination of whether a workplace is an industry or not.[138] However, the restriction of applicability to industries employing as high as 50 or 100 workers, means that it does not apply to the large proportion of the country's workforce in the unorganised sector where workers have no assurance of labour law protection.[139]

3.3.4 Sexual Harassment at Workplace (Prevention, Prohibition and Redressal) Act, 2013

In 1993 India ratified the 1979 United Nations Convention to Eliminate all forms of Discrimination Against Women (CEDAW), which paved the way for the landmark 1997 Supreme Court judgement of Vishakha & others v State of Rajasthan.[140] The case resulted from a Public Interest Litigation (PIL) regarding Bhanwari Devi, a social activist who was brutally gangraped for opposing child marriage in her village. Invoking CEDAW for its justification, the Supreme Court mandated the government to establish sexual harassment legislation.[141] The court also came up with specific guidelines which made it compulsory for employers to set up internal sexual harassment complaint committee. The case of Medha Kotwal Lele and others v Union of India (2013)[142] extended the obligation to nursing homes, and to law, architecture and engineering firms.

A 2010 survey brought out that an overwhelming 88 per cent of women working in information technology (IT) and business process outsourcing (BPO)/knowledge process outsourcing (KPO) companies had suffered some form of workplace sexual harassment. It showed a paucity of trained personnel to implement the policies and handle cases of workplace sexual harassment (Sharma 2010).[143] Surveys conducted by organisations across India over the years have revealed that employers either choose to ignore the guidelines or not take them seriously.[144] Sexual harassment at the workplace remains the most under-reported form of gender discrimination[145] and the private sector has been very reluctant to acknowledge its existence.

It took the State of India 15 years after Vishakha to enact the Sexual Harassment (Prevention, Prohibition and Redressal) Act, 2013. However, the Act is seen by many as a watered-down version of the Vishakha Guidelines. The definition does not include, for instance, students in educational institutions, who while not being workers, frequently suffer coercive sexual harassment on campus or otherwise. This concern was also voiced by the Justice Verma Committee.[146] The most controversial provision of the Act is Section 14 which punishes a 'false or malicious complaint'. To premise an Act on the assumption that women are potential liars about their human rights abuses reflects stereotyping of women and for that reason would be constitutionally untenable,[147] and further discourages women from filing complaints. The Act vests too much power in the hands of the employer and the district officer without an appropriate accountability mechanism.

Another critique of the Act as raised by several theorists is its skewed premise in attempting to reach a 'conciliation' at the first instance, as laid down in Section 10 of the Act. This approach negates the criminal nature of the perpetrator's acts as well as the devastating effect of sexual harassment for women employment opportunities. Not to mention the stigma, violence, powerlessness and character assassination forced upon women workers.

The field experience of the New Trade Union Initiative (NTUI) in the garment industries of Haryana shows that most of the Local and Internal Complaints Committees had either not been set up or were dysfunctional until the filing of RTIs asking for details of these committees.[148] Moreover, the external member of the Internal Complaints Committee, as stipulated in the Act, should be a member of an NGO committed to the cause of women or a person familiar with the issue of sexual harassment; in the best of situations, this is a vague definition. There is also the need to ensure that members of these committees are trained in basic issues regarding sexual harassment such as confidentiality and non-conflict of interests, which are often seen to be flouted.

Poor implementation of the Act and the laxity with which it is being dealt with by the authorities raises serious doubts regarding its effectiveness. In 2014, 526 cases of sexual harassment were reported by the Ministry for Women and Child Development.[149]

With a new government in power it turns out that this trend is independent from political parties representing the State. In its flagship NREGA programme of which women workers are a major recipient, the previous government did set minimum wage levels below the statutory minimum wage requirements, undermining its own rule of law. The current government does not fare any better. On the one hand, it is betting on employment creation by making labour laws more flexible and their monitoring a voluntary undertaking, fully aware of the fact that maximum flexibility had already been achieved through a total disregard for labour law application, overseen by a defunct labour inspectorate. On the other hand, policy intentions like the illegal NREGA wage levels continue. One such example of taking the law for a ride is given by Finance and Corporate Affairs Minister Arun Jaitley. Under the 2013 Sexual Harassment Act, companies are obliged to set up Internal Complaints Committees investigating sexual harassment complaints. Their functioning must be disclosed in a yearly report. The Women and Child Development Minister Menaka Gandhi suggested making it mandatory for companies to reveal whether they had appointed Internal Complaint Committees under the 2013 Companies Act. Minister Jaitley however deemed this unnecessary, stating that industry representatives were against 'enhanced disclosures under the Companies Act, and adding to these may not be desirable'.[150] In another development, Menaka Gandhi, in the Indian Labour Conference of 2013 promised coverage under ESI (health insurance) and EPF (pension) for unorganised women workers in education and health services delivery like ASHAs and Anganwadi workers.[151] The subsequent session of the Indian Labour Conference shut down this intention,[152] withholding dues to thousands of working women on the basis of a simple technicality. Under such an insecure and uncertain labour law regime, the exclusion of working women from just and favourable conditions of work is likely to be the only rule in force.

3.5.5 Criminalising women's work: the example of sex work[153]

Collectives of women sex workers, speaking for an estimated 3 million-strong workforce, are emerging slowly from the shadows across India. We met sex worker representatives in Chennai, Delhi and Kolkata, and encountered everywhere women of substance, filled with a newfound and hard-won confidence as they battle stigma, violence, criminalisation and citizenship denials that routinely plague their difficult lives. 'We are women first, and sex workers only after that', they said to us. 'We want you to recognise sex work as work. Instead of viewing us through the lens of social morality, we wish you would see us for what we are. Many of us are single women workers, supporting our children and old parents. We are informal, unprotected women workers. Why should you and the police treat us as criminals?'

Their biggest complaint is against the law which regulates sex work in India today: the Immoral Traffic (Prevention) Act (ITPA), 1956. This does not criminalise sex work *per se*, but, as the Lawyers' Collective which works for sex workers' rights points out, it results in '*de facto* criminalisation through prohibition of soliciting, brothel and street work', and this 'has effectively undermined sex workers' ability to claim protection of law'. The law is defended as being necessary to prevent trafficking and child prostitution. But there should be specific robust laws to curb these evils, and not the deployment of a statute which is widely misused to harass adult women who voluntarily pursue this profession.

The law, to begin with, prohibits brothels, or declares premises shared by sex workers illegal, including their residences. Often sex workers are evicted from the only shelter they have with their children in the name of 'closing down brothels'. The law also punishes adults who live off the earnings of sex workers. In all the consultations I attended, women complained that this criminalises even their children as soon as they cross the age of 18, and old parents and younger siblings who many sex workers support.

However, sex workers are beaten down the most by Section 8 of ITPA which punishes soliciting, or drawing the attention of potential customers from a visible, conspicuous site, whether in a street or private dwelling. As the Lawyers' Collective explains: 'The criminalisation of soliciting is one of the most obvious legal problems for sex workers…. Sex workers are arrested even when they're not soliciting. Most plead guilty finding themselves in a vicious cycle of criminalisation.'

This law also arms the police with wide powers to search and raid premises suspected of serving as brothels. The raid by Delhi's Law Minister Somnath Bharti in 2014 on the homes of some African women in the South Delhi enclave Khirki was an unusual example of police restraint, but the Minister angrily demanded that the police raid the women's apartments nonetheless. Somnath Bharti is a lawyer by training, but he seemed unaware that even if sex work were indeed under way, it is not barred by law. Magistrates are authorised to order arrests and removal, close down brothels and evict sex workers, and involuntarily house them in official rescue and rehabilitation homes which are most often low-resourced, undignified and violent spaces, where they are forcefully and abruptly separated from their children.

Sex workers want this law which unjustly criminalises their work and exposes them to violence from police and sometimes vigilante groups to be repealed. They also seek the basic rights of citizens and workers. Most citizenship entitlements bypass sex workers, except sometimes in ironical ways. Paradoxically, the fear of the spread of HIV/AIDS led governments to open health clinics in red-light areas. But sex workers point out that these clinics only offer treatment for sexually transmitted diseases. 'Are we not women, and human beings? Do we not contract other illnesses which also should be treated? But the government only wants to treat us for sexually transmitted diseases, not for our sake, but for the sake of protecting the rest of society!'

Many sex workers spoke to us of their difficulties in getting their children admission in schools, because the school form has a column requiring them to indicate the child's father's name. They do not want to have to acknowledge their profession to school authorities in order to protect their children from the accompanying stigma. Indeed, many children themselves are unaware what work their mothers do to warn a living, unless their mother works from a brothel. A long overdue reform is that school forms across the country should require only the child's mother's name. What brothel-based sex workers want most for their children are special night-care child centres where the children can sleep protected during their mothers' work hours. As the children grow older, admission in residential schools would enable them to pursue further education.

4. Consequences of Exclusion

We have found that the consequences of these hydra-headed forms of exclusion of women from just conditions of work are also multiple and profound. The non-recognition and devaluation of women's care work renders women at a further disadvantage when they enter the remunerated workforce. It also subjects them to double burdens of exclusion, unfairly and disproportionately burdened in both care work and remunerated work. It further deprives or inhibits women from accessing other public goods, such as health care, education and training, self-fulfilment and self-actualisation, and power in domestic, work and community spheres.

Drawing on the work of Chen et al.,[154] consequences on work for women can be understood, broadly, as follows. First, informal employment, with lower likelihood of stability, earnings and legal protection accounts for a relatively larger share of female than male employment. As an NCEUS report from 2009 estimated, 91 per cent of women are in informal jobs without contracts or legal protection, compared to 86 per cent of men. Women are also typically represented in segments with lower earnings. NSS findings from the 68th round estimated that on an average, daily wages from regular salaried work were twice the wage-amount from casual wage labour in rural areas and almost three times the amount in urban areas[99] and the same report states that only 5.6 per cent of women on the labour force in rural areas were in regular employment, compared to 10 per cent men.[156] In urban areas, data shows that regular waged work has seen an increase, but official and independent research suggests also that this is mainly attributable to a rise in numbers in the highly feminised sector of paid domestic workers.[157]

Analysis of NSS data over several years also shows that the persistent trend in women's self-employment is their concentration in unpaid work in rural and urban areas,[158,159] perpetuating financial dependence on the head of the household.

Second, within employment statuses, women's earnings are lower than men's. This occurs, in part at least due to the segregation of women in jobs that are deemed relatively unskilled and of low value, which therefore garner lower wages. In construction, for instance, they are largely engaged in manual jobs,[160] carrying cement, bricks and concrete to skilled male workers and are not trained or upgraded from these positions, despite years of experience. In agriculture, similarly, transplanting and weeding, which are women-dominated tasks, do not have fixed minimum wages unlike ploughing and harvesting, which are the domain of men.[161] Further, female wages for casual work across operations are 20–50 per cent lower than male wages.[162] This 'vertical segregation' manifests also in health, where care roles are overwhelmingly carried out by women, as nurses and midwives, while men form a greater proportion of physicians and in the rural education sector, where women are concentrated in pre-primary education and men in higher education.[163] In addition, as Ghosh,[164] points out, 'Gender-based differences in labour markets and the social attitudes towards women's paid and unpaid work are also reflections of the broader tendency to keep wages low. The widespread perception that work is an addition to household income and thus commands a much lower reservation wage[165] is common to both private and public employers.'

Third, unpaid care work limits time available for paid work. While it is possible to choose to perform unpaid work for the household, evidence suggests that in fact this does not hold for many women workers. Based on an analysis of NSS statistics over several years, Maitreyi Bordia Das[166] points out that 92 per cent of the women primarily doing unpaid work[167] reported doing these activities out of compulsion, due to the unavailability of other family members, social and religious constraints, or the inability to afford hired help. About two-thirds cited the absence of others to share responsibilities as the primary cause.

It is interesting to note that, a third of the women engaged only in unpaid work for the household also expressed willingness to engage in paid work despite the intensity of unpaid work for the household (which includes not only cooking, cleaning and care of people, but also the production or free collection of goods for household use). Of these women, 70 per cent stated that they would prefer part-time work.[168,169] This preference could indicate (in addition to economic compulsion) that women feel unable to shed themselves of responsibility of certain unpaid work duties but aspire to balance these with limited participation in paid work roles. Constraints on time can therefore lead to further segmentation of the labour market, impelling women to take on work that offers flexibility, such as paid domestic work and home-based work. Additionally, in an unequal labour market, where returns to labour for women are much lower, working on agricultural or non-agricultural subsistence activities represents a rational choice for women as it helps increase the household income.[170]

The result of concentration in low-value and precarious employment on the one hand and the inability to redistribute domestic responsibilities, is an intensification of the totality of women's work.

The Time Use Survey carried out in 1998–99, showed that on an average, women's participation in productive work was higher than for men. Extremely poor, poor and even non-poor women spent between 8–10 hours more on work, compared to men from the same households.[171] Time for rest and leisure is therefore, limited; women's leisure time is more likely to be fragmented and secondary, i.e., broken up into shorter periods and often conducted simultaneously with other activities, such as cooking, neither of which allows complete 'immersion'.[172]

The intensification of work can be the result of speeding-up of production processes to keep pace with demand, facilitated in factories by mechanisation and assembly line production. A study involving 134 workers from garment manufacturing factories in Bangalore,[173] of whom three-quarters of line employees were women, concluded that a rise in exports led to greater flexibility of work contract and an increase in workload. There was little reported difference between permanent and temporary employees as both could be dismissed without notice. Having to work 10 hours rather than the normative eight, without overtime, was frequently reported. Management also deducted wages for each Sunday when workers rested. Employment thus structured neither accommodates the unpaid care work families have to undertake, nor are they adequately remunerated to enable the purchase of care services.

At times, responsibilities carried out by men can shift to women, increasing their load of paid and unpaid work as well as leading to a diversification of tasks. In recent years, agricultural distress, stagnation of real wages, mechanisation and job generation in the urban areas (of a kind) have resulted in steady and increasing migration out of rural areas in search of non-farm livelihoods. However, this has followed a gendered pattern as men have largely been the ones to migrate (due to several factors: the lack of availability of jobs and lower wages for women, socio-cultural norms and costs of migration). In Bihar, a study found that the groups of women, from different communities and class backgrounds reported having to perform both, farm work as labourers or sharecroppers and take care of animals, or take complete responsibility of hiring and overseeing the work of agricultural labourers on family farms, after men migrated, in addition to childcare. This applied to marginal or subsistence workers who engaged in their community's traditional occupation. Women from the Dhobi community had to take responsibility for delivering clothes to clients, besides washing and ironing. Mallah women worked in multiple jobs, making and selling snacks, bananas, processed flour, etc., in markets or as vendors.[174]

The lack of decent work, combined with unpaid work burdens means ultimately that poor women have fewer options in terms of responding to and moving out of poverty, which results not only from the absence of or inadequacy of income, but also from a dearth of social security.

Recommendations

While we recognise that just conditions in work for women would require the battling and dismantling of patriarchy, as well as the neo-liberal framework of the globally dominant economic model, our recommendations focus on the role of the state, or national and state governments, to ensure justice to women as workers.

We call for the state first to recognise and measure unpaid care work, and to accord it the value that is due to it. We also call for the state to share women's burdens of care-work, such as by establishing crèches and day-care centres for children and the aged, and supporting professional home-based care of the ailing aged.

We call for an extensive review and reform of labour laws with a much clearer recognition of the fact that women constitute about half the work-force. They should be permitted to undertake night work, under safe conditions of work and transport. Work outsourced as home-based work should also entail the same responsibilities for safety, health, minimum wages, social security and overtime payments as for factory-based work.

We would like to see the ban on child labour to extend also to adolescent children until they have attained their required education levels, and the recognition that culturally sanctioned practices such as caste-based sex work are actually forced labour in unacceptable forms of work. We call for a much stronger enforcement mechanism for laws that ensure justice and safety of women in work, such as those against sexual harassment in the workplace, against forced and bonded work and child labour, for equal remuneration and conditions in the work-place, the comprehensive decriminalisation of sex work voluntarily undertaken by consenting adults, even as sex work by children and trafficking are more effectively halted; and the ending of undignified and illegal vocations such as manual scavenging.

We call for a much stronger framework of social protection, which is individual based, and therefore accessible to women workers. We call for a strengthening of the legal safeguards underlying the MGNREGA to ensure that it is actually demand-driven, and women are able to secure work for at least 100 days a year and receive timely wage payments. And finally, beyond the chosen scope of this chapter (we propose to devote the next India Exclusion Report to this) we also recommend stronger rights of inheritance for women, and promoting their ownership of land and capital.

Endnotes

1. Devaki Jain (2005), 'Women, Development and the UN: A Sixty Year Old Quest for Justice.', Bloomington: Indiana University Press, p. 20
2. ILO Equal Remuneration Convention, 1951 (No. 100) was ratified by India in 1958. Out of 186 ILO member states, 171 countries have ratified this Convention. See: http://www.ilo.org/dyn/normlex/en/f?p=NORMLEXPUB:12100:0::NO::P12100_ILO_CODE:C100
3. Maternity Protection Convention, 1919 (No. 3). This Convention was revised twice. First in 1952 by the Maternity Protection Convention (Revised), (No. 103) and in 2000 by the Maternity Protection Convention, (No. 183), the latter covering all employed women, including those in atypical forms of dependent work. India did not ratify any of these conventions. See: http://www.ilo.org/dyn/normlex/en/f?p=NORMLEXPUB:12100:0::NO::P12100_ILO_CODE:C183
4. For details of the Convention, see: http://www.ohchr.org/EN/ProfessionalInterest/Pages/CESCR.aspx
5. The ICESCR actually uses the narrower concept of 'equal pay for equal work', rather than recognising the value of work performed based on the effort and skills required. Draft General Comments on Article 7 state that national governments should try to determine objective criteria for valuation progressively and implement equality in pay for equal work immediately.
6. For the Convention, see: http://www.ohchr.org/Documents/ProfessionalInterest/cedaw.pdf
7. Ratified by India in 1993.
8. Quoted in Devaki Jain, (2005), *Women, Development and the UN*, p. 88
9. General Comments provide orientation for the implementation of human rights, with criteria for evaluating the progress of states in their implementation of these rights, but are not legally enforceable.
10. http://www.un.org/womenwatch/daw/cedaw/recommendations/recomm.htm

11. See, for instance, ILO (2009), 'Gender Equality at the Heart of Decent Work.' International Labour Conference, 98th Session, 2009, Report VI. Available at: http://www.ilo.org/wcmsp5/groups/public/@ed_norm/@relconf/documents/meetingdocument/wcms_105119.pdf

12. Workers with Family Responsibilities Convention, 1981 (No. 156), ratified by 44 countries, but not by India. See: http://www.ilo.org/dyn/normlex/en/f?p=1000:12100:0::NO:12100:P12100_INSTRUMENT_ID:312301

13. See: http://www.undp.org/content/undp/en/home/mdgoverview/post-2015-development-agenda/goal-5.html

14. Ankita Saxena (2014), 'Workforce Diversity: A Key to Improve Productivity.', Procedia Economics and Finance, 11, Elsevier, pp. 76–85

15. UN Economic and Social Council (2015), 'Right to just and favourable conditions of work (article 7 of the International Covenant on Economic, Social and Cultural Rights)', presented at the 54th session of the Committee on Economic, Social and Cultural Rights. Available at: http://www.ohchr.org/en/hrbodies/cescr/pages/cescrindex.aspx

16. Naila Kabeer (2012), 'Women's Economic Empowerment and Inclusive Growth: Labour Markets and Enterprise Development', CPDR and SOAS, Discussion Paper 29/12, p. 17

17. Indira Hirway, and Rania Antonopoulous (2010), 'Introduction' in Indira Hirway and Antonopoulous (eds) *Unpaid Work and the Economy: Gender, Time Use and Poverty in Developing Countries*, Palgrave Macmillan, p. 4

18. Hirway and Antonopoulous (2010), *Unpaid Work and the Economy*, pp. 7-9

19. Indira Hirway (2010), 'Understanding Poverty: Insights Emerging from the Time Use of the Poor', Hirway,. and Antonopoulous (eds), *Unpaid Work and the Economy*, p. 29

20. The pilot survey was conducted in six states—Meghalaya, Gujarat, Tamil Nadu Orissa, Madhya Pradesh, Haryana . It employed three classificatory categories of SNA (market-oriented work), non-SNA (care) and personal time (leisure, sleeping, education, etc.).

21. Refers to NSS codes 92 (attended only to domestic duties) and 93 (attended to domestic duties and was also engaged in free collection of goods (vegetables, roots, firewood, cattle feed, etc.), sewing, tailoring, weaving, etc., for household use).

22. The average honorarium paid to Anganwadi workers and helpers ranges from Rs 5,000-7,000 and Rs 3,000–Rs. 4,500 respectively. The central government's share is limited to Rs 3,000 for Anganwadi workers and Rs 1,500 to the honorarium for Anganwadi helpers. Organised collectives of Anganwadi workers and helpers in some states have raised demands for an increase in pay, as well as pension.

23. Estimates provided by analysis of NSSO 2011–12 data by Ruchika Chaudhary.

24. Steven Kapsos., Andrea Silberman, and Evangelia Bourmpola (2014), 'Why is Female Labour Force Participation Declining so Sharply in India?', ILO Research Paper No. 10. ILO. pp 14 Available at: http://www.ilo.org/wcmsp5/groups/public/---dgreports/---inst/documents/publication/wcms_250977.pdf

25. Neetha N. (2006), notes that an NCEUS 2006 report advocating universal social security as right for all informal workers who are not provided insurance or pensions by the employer recommended the exclusion of unpaid family workers, seemingly without rationale. See: "Invisibility' Continues? Social Security and Unpaid Women Workers', *Economic and Political Weekly*, 41:32, (Aug. 12-18, 2006), pp. 3497-3499

26. Manual scavenging is the caste-based practice of removing human excreta from dry latrines by hand, or with simple tools.

27. Anecdotal evidence from case studies shows that most women engaged in manual scavenging, for example, never had the opportunity to go to school and a negligible number completed high school. See: http://in.one.un.org/img/uploads/Socio_Economic_Status_of_Women_Manual_Scavengers_Report.pdf

28. A Planning Commission study on the socio-economic status of rescued bonded labourers, of whom about a fifth were women, shows that three-quarters were illiterate. See: http://planningcommission.nic.in/reports/sereport/ser/ser_bon0405.pdf

29. In India, the traditional system of labour bondage, in agriculture, was based on the exploitation of the erstwhile untouchable caste groups and extended beyond a single generation, trapping families in a cycle of indebtedness. The practice has transformed in some respects; declines have been seen in long duration and inter-generational bondage and the compulsion to enter relationships of bondage is usually economic, rather than social. However, certain aspects of the practice, such as indebtedness and the participation of SCs and STs persist. Although the practice is most visible in agriculture, it has been adopted in the unorganised sector, specifically in industries that have a high incidence of intermediaries or contractors.

30. Ravi Srivastava (2005), 'Bonded Labour in India: Its Incidence and Pattern.' ILO Working Paper No. 43, Geneva; ILO, p. 27.

31. For a review of conditions of employment in the *bidi* industry, see: CWDS (undated), 'Survey of Studies on Beedi Industry -With Special Emphasis on Women and Child Labour', Available at: http://www.cwds.ac.in/researchPapers/survey_studies_beedi_industry.pdf

32. Alakh N. Sharma and Nikhil Raj (2000), 'Child Labour in Sari Units of Varanasi' (draft report), Institute for Human Development and V.V. Giri Institute of Technology as cited in Human Rights Watch (2003), 'Small Change: Bonded Child Labour in India's Silk Industry.' Available at: https://www.hrw.org/reports/2003/india/India0103-02.htm

33. Srivastava(2005), 'Bonded Labour in India', p. 18.

34. CEC Uttar Pradesh Report (2005) as cited in Krishna Upadhyaya (2008), 'The Reality of Bonded Labour in India, Nepal and Pakistan.' Anti-Slavery International, p. 15. Available at: http://www.antislavery.org/includes/documents/cm_docs/2009/p/povertydiscriminationslaveryfinal.pdf

35. Jen Lerche (2007), 'A Global Alliance against Forced Labour? Unfree Labour, Neo-Liberal Globalization and the International Labour Organization', *Journal of Agrarian Change* 7:4, pp. 425–52.

36. See, for instance, Srivastava, 'Bonded Labour in India: Its Incidence and Patterns'.

37. SEEDS (2010), 'A Report on Bonded Labour Rehabilitation Scheme under Centrally Sponsored Bonded Labour System (Abolition) Act, 1976 in the state of Madhya Pradesh, Orissa, Rajasthan, Tamil Nadu and Uttar Pradesh', New Delhi: Planning Commission, p. 16. Available at: http://planningcommission.nic.in/reports/sereport/ser/ser_bon0405.pdf

38. National People's Tribunal (2012), 'Living Wage as a Fundamental Right of Indian Garment Workers' Bangalore, 22-25 November, p. 5

39. P. Overeem and M. Theuws (2014),'Flawed Fabrics: The Abuse of Girls and Women Workers in the South Indian Textile Industry', SOMO and ICN. Available at: http://www.somo.nl/publications-en/Publication_4110?set_language=en

40. A Tamil word which refers to the state of happiness a woman attains once she is married and cared for by her husband.

41. See: ASK (2014), Addressing Modern Slavery in Tamil Nadu Textile Industry – A Feasibility Study Report , Freedom Fund, p. 25 or; see READ (2015) *End All Forms of Forced Labour in the Garment Sector*, p.8. Available at: http://www.indianet.nl/pdf/EndAllFormsOfForcedLabourInTheGarmentSector.pdf

42. Findings based on interviews conducted in two rounds with a sample of approximately 500 workers. See SAVE (2014), '*Sumangali* Trend Analysis January 2013–June 2014'; SAVE (2015) '*Sumangali* Trend January 2015'.

43. Harsh Mander, 'Child 'camp coolies' in Tamil Nadu ' 12 January 2016, *Times of India*. Available at: http://www.livemint.com/Opinion/ZpH9hN76b27t74BBgFPc7K/Child-camp-coolies-in-Tamil-Nadu.html

44. Ibid.

45. In sum, the following labour acts are being violated: factories act, apprentice act, payment of bonus act, sexual harassment act, bonded labour act, trade union act, equal remuneration act, payment of wages act, minimum wages act, ESI act, PDF act, contract labour act, worker's compensation act, The Tamil Nadu industrial establishments (national & festival holidays) act, weekly holidays act, prohibition of dowry act, juvenile justice act, and industrial disputes act.

46. Fact finding on suspicious death of mill workers, SSM Spinning Mill, Vedasandur, Dindigul district, 26 February 2015. Mill management did not interact with the mission members.

47. E.C. Hughes (1951), 'Work and Self' in J. Rohrer and H.S. Muzafer (eds), *Social Psychology at the Crossroads; the University of Oklahoma Lectures in Social Psychology*, Oxford, England: Harper, pp. 313–23

48. Selig Harrison (1960), *India: The Most Dangerous Decade*. Madras: Oxford University Press.

49. This section on manual scavengers draws heavily on the work of Harsh Mander. [See for instance, Harsh Mander, 'India's Great Shame', 17 November 2012, *The Hindu*. Available at: http://www.thehindu.com/opinion/columns/Harsh_Mander/indias-great-shame/article4097808.ece]

50. For the Act, see: http://tribal.nic.in/WriteReadData/CMS/Documents/201211290238513271484pcract955E2701676142.pdf

51. See: http://indiacode.nic.in/ fullact1.asp?tfnm =199346

52. See: http://indiacode.nic.in/acts-in-pdf/252013.pdf

53. Kalpana Amar, Bejwada Wilson, Ishwarbhai Patel, D.C. Lakha, Bipin Mallick (undated), 'Report Of Sub Group on Safai Karmacharies', p. 9 Available at: http://safaikarmachariandolan.org/docs/Report%20to%20the%20Working%20Group%20on%20Safai%20Karmacharies.pdf

54. See: Rashtriya Garima Abhiyan (RGA), National Campaign on Dalit Human Rights (NCDHR) and the International Dalit Solidarity Network (IDSN) (2014), *Violations of the Right to Water and*

Sanitation, p. 4. Available at: 'http://idsn.org/wp-content/uploads/2015/12/Joint-Submission-SR-on-water-and-Sanitation-RGA-NCDHR-and-IDSN.pdf and Jan Sahas Social Development Society (2014), *Socio Economic Status of Women Manual Scavengers* [Baseline Study Report -2014], p. 9. Available at: http://in.one.un.org/img/uploads/Socio_Economic_Status_of_Women_Manual_Scavengers_Report.pdf;.

55. Human Rights Watch. (2014), 'Cleaning Human Waste: "Manual Scavenging", Caste and Discrimination in India', p. 40. Available at: https://www.hrw.org/report/2014/08/25/cleaning-human-waste/manual-scavenging-caste-and-discrimination-india

56. D. Joshi., J. Morgan and B. Fawcett (2007), 'Sanitation for the Urban Poor: Whose Choice – Theirs or Ours?' Unpublished research report prepared for DFID. Available at: http://www.dfid. gov.uk/r4d/PDF/Outputs/ Water/R8028-FTR.pdf

57. See: Human Rights Watch, 'Cleaning Human Waste: "Manual Scavenging", Caste and Discrimination in India'

58. Harsh Mander, 'Scavenging Dignity', *The Hindu*, 29 June 2008. Available at: http://www.thehindu.com/todays-paper/tp-features/tp-sundaymagazine/scavenging-dignity/article1437393.ece

59. D. Dash,. (2010). '6.8 Lakh Sex Workers In India, Delhi Red-Light Capital'. *Times of India*, 10 July 2010. http://timesofindia.indiatimes.com/india/6-8-lakh-sex-workers-in-India-Delhi-red-light-capital/articleshow/6193566.cms

60. http://www.unaids.org/sites/default/files/media_asset/06_Sexworkers.pdf

61. See: http://www.hyderabadpolice.gov.in/acts/immoral-traffic.pdf

62. R. Sahni. and V. Kalyan Shankar. (2013) Sex Work and its Linkages with Informal Labour Markets in India: Findings from the First Pan-India Survey of Female Sex Workers. IDS Working Paper 2013, No. 416. Available at: http://www.ids.ac.uk/publication/sex-work-and-its-linkages-with-informal-labour-markets-in-india

63. S. Rao. and C. Sluggett. (2013) ' Sex Work, Trafficking and Human Rights' in Laxmy Murthy and Meena Seshu (eds), *The Business of Sex*, New Delhi: Zubaan, pp. 148–74

64. R. Shukla (2013), 'A Walk Through the Labyrinths of Sex Work Law' in Murthy and Seshu (eds), *The Business of Sex*, pp. 212-42

65. Factories Act, 1948, Mines Act, 1952, Dock Workers (Safety, Health and Welfare) Act, 1986, Plantation Labour Act, 1951, Dangerous Machines (Regulations) Act, 1983, etc.

66. World Bank (1996), *Improving Women's Health in India*, Washington: World Bank, pp 41. Available at: http://www.wds.worldbank.org/external/default/WDSContentServer/WDSP/IB/1996/05/01/000009265_3961214180613/Rendered/PDF/multi0page.pdf

67. *Bidi* production in the late 19th and early 20th centuries was distributed between factories, smaller branches of factories and homes (through contracting). The adoption of the Beedi and Cigar Workers (Conditions of Employment) Act, 1966 prompted a shift in production to homes and with it developed a new system of contracting. The contractor sold raw materials and purchased the finished products, effectively disguising the employer-employee relationship.

68. Ministry of Labour and Employment estimates cited in ILO (2004), *ILO's Pilot Action Project for Beedi Women Workers in India*, p. 2. Available at: http://www.ilo.org/wcmsp5/groups/public/@asia/@ro-bangkok/@sro-new_delhi/documents/projectdocumentation/wcms_125467.pdf

69. Kusum K. (2005), *Women Beedi Workers: A Report*, New Delhi: National Commission for Women. Available at: http://ncw.nic.in/pdfReports/Women%20Beedi%20Workers.pdf

70. S. Madhok (2005), *Report on the Status of Women Workers in the Construction Industry*, New Delhi; National Commission for Women, p. 11. Available at: http://ncw.nic.in/pdfreports/women%20workers%20in%20construction%20industry.pdf

71. Ibid., p. 30.

72. 'NSSO (2012) *Employment and Unemployment among Social Groups in India*, Coen Kompier et al., 'Labour markets: Exclusion from Decent Work'.this reference is not clear Centre for Equity Studies(2014) India Exclusion Report, New Delhi: Books for Change, p. 116

73. N. Neetha (2013), 'Inequalities Reinforced? Social Groups, Gender and Employment'. *CWDS Occasional Paper*, 54

74. Ibid., p. 8

75. See for instance: Government of India (2006), *Social, Economic and Educational Status of the Muslim Community of India*, New Delhi: GOI, pp. 95–96

76. Ibid.

77. Sameera Khan(2007), 'Negotiating the *Mohalla*: Exclusion, Identity and Muslim Women in Mumbai' *Economic and Political Weekly*, 42:17.

78. Sophie Mitra and Usha Sambamoorti (2006), *Economic and Political Weekly*, 41,: 3 (21–27 January), p. 200.

79. A. Bheemeshwar Reddy (2014), 'Labour Force

Participation of Elderly in India'. (Conference paper presented Population Association America 2014 Annual Meeting) Available at: http://paa2014.princeton.edu/papers/141609

80. UNFPA (2012), *Report on the Status of Elderly in Select States of India,* New Delhi: UNFPA, p. 33
81. Reddy, 'Labour Force Participation of Elderly in India'.
82. UNFPA, *Report on the Status of Elderly in Select States of India,* pp. 33–34
83. Ibid.
84. Reddy, 'Labour Force Participation in India'
85. UNFPA, Report on the Status of the Elderly, pp. 22
86. 86. Ibid, pp 90-93
87. http://imaginenoborders.org/pdf/zines UnderstandingPatriarchy.pdf
88. Jacqui True (2012), *The Political Economy of Violence against Women,* New York: Oxford University Press
89. Ibid., p. 31
90. Ibid., p. 33
91. Kabeer, 'Women's Economic Empowerment and Inclusive Growth', pp. 12–14
92. Ibid, p. 12
93. For instance, see: Eswaran Mukesh, Bharat Ramaswami, and Wilima Wadhwa (2013), 'Status, Caste, and the Time Allocation of Women in Rural India', *Economic Development and Cultural Change* 61.2, pp. 311–33
94. Pranab Bardhan (1982), 'Agrarian Class Formation in India.' *The Journal of Peasant Studies* 10.1, pp. 73–94
95. Joan Mencher. and K. Saradamoni (1982),'Muddy Feet, Dirty Hands: Rice Production and Female Agricultural Labour', *Economic and Political Weekly* 17:52, pp. 149–67
96. Richard Anker (1998), *Gender and jobs: Sex Segregation of Occupations in the World.* Geneva: International Labour Office.
97. Mita Bhadra (2004). 'Gender Dimensions of Tea Plantation Workers in West Bengal', *Indian Anthropologist* 34:2, pp. 43–68
98. UN Women (2015), *Progress of the World's Women 2015-16: Transforming Economies, Realizing Rights,* p. 68
99. Himanshu (2015), 'The Livelihood Question' Mint, 29 April 2015,. Available at: http://www.livemint.com/Opinion/Dk2OPASLtOibQTCI2gK13M/The-livelihood-question.html
100. Santosh Mehrotra et al. (2014) 'Explaining Employment Trends in the Indian Economy: 1993-94 to 2011-12.' *Economic and Political Weekly* 49:32, pp. 49–57
101. Jayati Ghosh and C.P. Chandrasekhar, (2014), 'Growth, employment patterns and inequality in Asia: A Case Study of India' (No. 486985). International Labour Organization, p. 19 Available at: http://www.ilo.org/wcmsp5/groups/public/---asia/---ro-bangkok/documents/publication/wcms_334063.pdf
102. Himanshu, 'The Livelihood Question'.
103. Ibid.
104. Vinoj Abraham (2013), 'Missing Labour or Consistent "De-feminisation"?' *Economic & Political Weekly* 48:31, pp. 98–108
105. Geeta Gandhi Kingdon (2007). 'The Progress of School Education in India', *Oxford Review of Economic Policy,* 23:2, pp. 168–95
106. Jayati Ghosh (2011), 'The Challenge of Ensuring Full Employment in the Twenty-first Century', *The Indian Journal of Labour Economics* 54:1, pp. 51–68
107. State Governments have the power to declare a manufacturing unit not meeting the above criteria also as a 'factory'.
108. 48 hours of work per week (Section 51) or a 9 hour work-day (Section 54), intervals of half-hour after every 5 hours of work (Section 55), payment of overtime wages of double the wage beyond 9 hours of work per day (Section 59), weekly holidays (Section 52), washing facilities for males and females (Section 42), facilities for storing and drying clothes (Section 43), facilities for sitting (Section 44), first aid appliances (Section 45), canteens (Section 46), shelters, rest rooms and lunch rooms (Section 47), etc.
109. Section 22(2), Section 27 and Section 87.
110. The Factories (Amendment) Bill, 2014.Accessed at http://labour.nic.in/upload/uploadfiles/files/latest_update/what_new/53994ae87860bBriefforNIC.pdf on 6 November 2015.
111. A. Kaiwar (2014), 'Women Workers in the Factory', *Economic and Political Weekly,* 49: 33.
112. Section 41G.
113. Section 48 deals with crèches.
114. One of the national trade union centres, NTUI, included this in their Workers' Charter for the General Elections. See http://ntui.org.in/images/articles/Workers_Charter_2014_Web_version.pdf, accessed on 13 November 2015
115. Review of Laws and Legislatures Affecting Women by National Commission for Women, No. 15, The Factories Act, 1948. http://ncw.nic.in/frmReportLaws15.aspx Accessed on 12 November 2015 at 1558 hours.

116. Workers with Family Responsibilities Convention, 1981 (No. 156), not ratified by India. See in particular Articles 1 and 5b.
117. Vikram Singh (2014), 'Employees Awareness towards the Welfare Provions of Factories Act 1948 and its Implementation in the State of Haryana', *IRACST-International Journal of Commerce, Business and Management,* 3: 2.
118. A. Abraham, D. Singh and P. Pal (2014), *Critical Assessment of Labour Laws, Policies and Practices through a Gender Lens.* National Resource Centre for Women, National Mission for Empowerment of Women, Ministry of Women and Child Development, Government of India.
119. Ibid.
120. http://www.ilo.org/dyn/normlex/en/f?p=NORMLEXPUB:12100:0::NO::P12100_INSTRUMENT_ID:312316 Accessed on 16 November 2015.
121. 2001 II LLJ 843.
122. 2002 (5) ALT 223.
123. Introduced in Lok Sabha in 2005.
124. The Rajasthan government has already permitted these changes, the Maharashtra Cabinet has recently moved the amendment. Mansi Phadke (2015), 'Maharashtra Cabinet Gives Nod to Night Shift for Women Workers',. *The Indian Express*, 21 May. Accessed here: http://indianexpress.com/article/india/india-others/maharashtra-cabinet-gives-nod-to-night-shifts-for-women-workers/ on 17 November 2015.
125. See for instance one of many such stories at http://timesofindia.indiatimes.com/city/bengaluru/BPO-employee-gang-raped-inside-moving-van-in-Bengaluru/articleshow/49234065.cms
126. Source: Submission dated 1 July 2014 by the Garment Labour Union to the Ministry of Labour.
127. Ratified by India in 1958.
128. The ILO Committee of Expert on the Application of Conventions and Recommendations (CEACR) was established in 1926 and the main and independent ILO supervisory body. Its recommendations are non-binding on member-states.
129. International Trade Union Confederation (ITUC) (2011), *Internationally Recognized Core Labour Standards in India: Report for the WTO General Council Review of the Trade Policies of India.* Geneva, September. Accessed at http://www.ituc-csi.org/IMG/pdf/final_India_TPR_Report_3.pdf on 13 November 2015.
130. AIR 1979 SC 1868.
131. LPA No. 122-125 of 2006, Delhi High Court.
132. 2 SCC 469.
133. 'the authority should take a broad view;...in observing whether any differences are of practical importance, the authority should take an equally broad approach for the very concept of similar work implies differences in details, but these should not defeat a claim for equality on trivial grounds. It should look at the duties actually performed, not those theoretically possible.'
134. Ibid.
135. International Trade Union Confederation (ITUC). Internationally Recognized Core Labour Standards in India: Report for the WTO General Council Review of the Trade Policies of India. Geneva, September 2011. Accessed at http://www.ituc-csi.org/IMG/pdf/final_India_TPR_Report_3.pdf on 13 November 2015
136. DN Bannerji v PR Mukherji : AIR 1953 SC 58.
137. State of Bombay v Hospital Mazdoor Sabha 1960 AIR 610, 1960 SCR (2) 866.
138. Bangalore Water Supply and Sewerage Board v R. Rajappa where the court developed a 'triple test' and the 'dominant nature test'.
139. P. Goswami (2009). 'A Critique of the Unorganized Workers' Social Security Act', *Economic and Political Weekly*, 44:11, March.
140. The Vishakha Guidelines made employers responsible for the prevention and deterrence of the commission of acts of sexual harassment, which included 'physical contact and advances; demands or requests for sexual favours; sexually coloured remarks; showing pornography; sny other unwelcome physical, verbal or non-verbal conduct of sexual nature'. See: http://www.mgu.ac.in/files/Microsoft%20Word%20-%20Vishaka%20Guidelines_doc%20-%20Vishaka-Guidelines.pdf AIR 1997 SC 3001.
141. The Court derived its authority to invoke CEDAW from the Bangalore Principles of Judicial Conduct. These guidelines encourage judges in Common Law countries to apply international law directly where lacunae exist in domestic law.
142. 1 SCC 297.
143. Pankaj Sharma (2010). 'India's First Sexual Harassment at Workplace Survey Reveals Startling Revelations'. Accessed through Anagha Sarpotdar (2013).'Sexual Harassment of Women: Reflections on the Private Sector', *Economic and Political Weekly,* 48:40.
144. Ibid.
145. Seema Shukla (2002), 'Indecent Proposal', *Business Today,* 1 September. Accessed at http://archives.digitaltoday.in/businesstoday/20020901/cover1.html .
146. Ayesh Kidwai (2013). 'Sexual Harassment in the Workplace: The Verma Committee and After', *Economic and Political Weekly*, 48:6.

147. Naina Kapur (2013), 'Workplace Sexual Harassment: The Way Things Are', *Economic and Political Weekly*, 48 :24.

148. Society for Labour and Development (2014), *Struggle Within the Struggle: Voices of Women Garment Workers*. Also based on author's conversations with Anannya Bhattacharya, dated 5 November 2015.

149. Mayurpankhi Choudhary, 'Arun Jaitley, Here's Why Committees To Tackle Sexual Harassment Won't 'Burden' Companies', *Youth Ki Awaaz*, 12 December 2015. Available at: http://www.youthkiawaaz.com/2015/12/sexual-harassment-committees-wont-burden-companies/

150. Shalini Nair, 'Harassment at Workplace: Jaitley says No to Maneka Request on Disclosure of Probe Panels', *Indian Express*, 8 December 2015. Available at: http://indianexpress.com/article/india/india-news-india/harassment-at-workplace-jaitley-say-no-to-maneka-request-on-disclosure-of-probe-panels/#sthash.0AwuUReV.dpuf'

151. See under item 1 in minutes of 45th Session of Indian Labour Conference, pp. 1–3, Available at: http://pib.nic.in/newsite/PrintRelease.aspx?relid=96048

152. See under item 2 in minutes of 46th Session of the Indian Labour Conference, pp. 16–17. Available at: http://labour.gov.in/upload/uploadfiles/files/latest_update/what_new/ 52df954c39a8c46 thSessionof StandinglabourCommitteeAgendaitems.pdf

153. Section contributed by Harsh Mander.

154. M. Chen, J. Vanek, F. Lund, J. Heintz, R. Jhabvala and C. Bonner(2005), *Progress of the World's Women: Women, Work and*, pp. 36–57

155. NSS 68th Round; pp. 19, 21

156. Ibid., p. 111

157. NCEUS, *Report on Conditions of Work and Promotion of Livelihoods in the Unorganized Sector*, and Jayati Ghosh (2013), 'Women's Work in the India in the Early 21st Century' *Conference Paper, presented at: India Today: Looking Back, Looking Forward*

158. N. Neetha (2009): 'Women's Work in the Post Reform Period: An Exploration of Macro Data', *CWDS Occasional Paper No. 52*, New Delhi: Centre for Women's Development Studies.

159. Neetha, 'Inequalities Reinforced? Social Groups, Gender and Employment'

160. A case study on the construction sector in Ahmedabad by SEWA found that about 92% of women were in jobs like carrying cement, bricks and concrete, compared to 36% of men. A study from Tamil Nadu found that notwithstanding years of experience, women continue in physically intense jobs and are never trained or upgraded from these positions. See: A. Barnabas, J. Anbarasu, and C.S. Paul(2009), 'A Study on the Empowerment of Women Construction Workers as Masons in Tamil Nadu, India', *Journal of International Women's Studies*, 11:2, pp. 121–41. Available at: http://vc.bridgew.edu/jiws/vol11/iss2/8

161. Nisha Srivastava and Ravi Srivastava(2010), 'Women, Work and Employment Outcomes in Rural India', *Economic and Political Weekly* 45:28.

162. Government of India (2010), Wage Rates in Rural India. (2008-9), Table 1(a). http://labourbureau.nic.in/Wage_Rates_Rural_India_2008_09.pdf

163. See: National Commission for Employment in the Unorganized Sector. 2007; *Report on Conditions of Work and Promotion of Livelihoods in the Unorganised Sector*. New Delhi; NCEUS.

164. Ghosh, 'Growth, Employment Patterns and Inequality in Asia', p. 24.

165. The lowest **wage** rate at which a worker would be willing to accept a particular type of job. A job offer involving the same type of work and the same working conditions, but at a lower **wage** rate, would be rejected by the worker.

166. Maitreyi Bordia Das (2006), 'Do Traditional Axes of Exclusion Affect Labour Market Outcomes?' *Social Development Papers: South Asia Series*. Paper no. 97, p. 6

167. Calculated using descriptive statistics from NSS rounds on females out of the labour force for various reasons, focusing especially on codes 92 and 93.

168. Das, "Do Traditional Axes of Exclusion Affect Labour Market Outcomes?'

169. An NCEUS Report confirms this, using NSS data from 2004-5. See: NCEUS, *Report on Condition of Work and Promotion of Livelihoods in the Unorganised Sector*, pp 78-79 http://www-wds.worldbank.org/external/default/WDSContentServer/WDSP/IB/2006/08/11/000310607_20060811102524/Rendered/PDF/369630sdp970web.pdf

170. Sonalde Desai and Devaki Jain (1994), 'Maternal Employment and Changes in Family Dynamics: The Social Context of Women's Work in Rural South India', *Population and Development Review*, 20:1, pp. 115–36.

171. Hirway and Antonopoulous, Unpaid Work and the Economy', p. 34

172. Alaka Basu (2011), 'Gender and Leisure', *The Telegraph*, *4 July. Available at: http://www.telegraphindia.com/1110704/jsp/opinion/story_14107905.jsp*

173. A. Kalhan(2008), 'Permanently Temporary Workers in The Global Readymade Garment Hub of Bangalore', *The Indian Journal of Labour Economics*, 51:1.

174. A. Datta and S. Mishra (2011), 'Glimpses Of Women's Lives In Rural Bihar: Impact Of Male Migration.' *The Indian Journal of Labour Economics*, 54:3, pp. 459–77

Part II – Budgets and Planning

Towards a Tax System for Inclusive Development

Some Aspects of Tax Incidence and Tax Mobilisation in India

Rajeev Malhotra and Sridhar Kundu[*]

Overview

The magnitude of tax revenue and the manner of its mobilisation, in terms of its composition and incidence with regard to different segments of the population, is of direct consequence to the development process and human well-being in society. While a higher tax-Gross Domestic Product (GDP) ratio[1] based on high tax rates (and narrow tax base) could be detrimental to the growth of economic activity, giving rise to black economy and encouraging the flight of capital (both physical and human) from the country, a high tax-GDP ratio with moderate tax rates (and a broad tax base) could spur growth through improved scope for provisioning of public goods in the economy. It could also support the State's capacity to create a social protection floor and, if required, specific entitlements, especially for the poor and the vulnerable to help create more equal outcomes in the society. Similarly, a progressive tax system, where taxes levied take into account the ability of an individual to pay, is a potent redistributive tool, which could potentially support a more inclusive and equitable development process.

In India's case, unlike some other emerging economies, neither is the tax-GDP ratio adequately favourable to create the required fiscal space i.e., the fiscal capacity for augmenting the supply and quality of public goods and essential social services (primarily on account of the narrow tax base and weaknesses in tax administration), nor is the tax system progressive enough, particularly at the state level, to address equity and inclusion in the development process. Furthermore, since there is inadequate production of public goods, inefficient delivery and uneven access of the poor and the marginalised to those goods, the development process has resulted in rising inequalities in social outcomes and the exclusion of significant segments of people from the economic and social mainstream of the country.

Direct taxes (i.e., the taxes imposed on incomes of individuals and businesses) in India are more or less progressive in their impact. However, that is not true of indirect taxes (i.e., the taxes imposed on the production, trade and sales of goods and services), which are regressive in nature as they do not distinguish potential tax payers on the basis of their ability to pay or, in other words, on the basis of their incomes. At the aggregate level (centre and states together), India collects only one-third of its total tax revenue from direct taxes; most developed

---

* The views reflected in the paper do not necessarily reflect the position of the authors' organisations. The authors acknowledge the support extended by CBGA for the study; the chapter has benefited from an ongoing research project in CBGA analysing the impact of India's fiscal policy on poverty and inequality. They can be reached at: rmalh1@hotmail.com and sridhar@cbgaindia.org, respectively.

** The chapter has been reviewed by Arjun Bedi and Charmaine Ramos countries and a few developing countries (like South Africa and Indonesia) depend on direct taxes to a much higher extent. In all fairness, the tax system is more regressive at the state level than at the level of the central government. While the central government has managed to invert its tax system from an overt reliance on indirect taxes (nearly 80 per cent in the 1970s–80s) to a situation in recent years where nearly 55 to 60 per cent of tax collections are accounted for by direct taxes, the situation with respect to state governments has only deteriorated. This is largely due to the fact that state governments have a limited capacity to raise resources from the direct taxes allocated to them and even those taxation avenues (such as on account of property tax or wealth tax) have not been adequately tapped. Instead, state governments often find it easy to raise resources from indirect taxes such as state excise duties (on alcohol) and sales taxes (i.e., the value added tax or VAT). The situation is symptomatic of the fiscal profligacy largely due to the practice of politics of appeasement at the state level. Inadequate assessment of resource availability and mobilisation efforts, especially at the time of assessment undertaken by the Finance Commission, along with populist pressures linked to electoral cycles, have often led to public spending being increasingly financed by levying state-level indirect taxes. As a result, there is a disproportionate incidence of indirect taxes on the poor when the commodities involved are necessities and occupy a significant share in their consumption baskets.

The study presented in this chapter undertakes a limited analysis of India's fiscal policies, primarily the government's tax policies and the tax system, at the centre and the state levels, and the consequences it has on the development process and its outcomes. Although the government's expenditure policy can typically overcome the weakness in its tax policy to support inclusive outcomes in a society and therefore should be considered in tandem with the tax policy framework for assessing the inclusiveness of fiscal policies, the scope of this chapter has been restricted to a limited analysis of the tax policy framework in India. More specifically, it seeks some preliminary answers to two broad questions. First, does the Indian government mobilised tax revenue commensurate with its level of development? The chapter does not engage with the normative or political economy discussions around the appropriateness of tax policy and tax rates in India. Given the current direct tax policy regime, it focuses on assessing the extent to which incomes are being under-reported, thereby limiting the growth of the income tax base in the country. Second, the chapter explores the extent to which the tax policy, with its reliance on indirect taxes (at the state level), is exacerbating poverty and inequality?

A rigorous quantitative analysis to address these issues is handicapped by the fact that India does not collect income data[2] and the data on tax mobilisation, at the required level of disaggregation, is also not available in the public domain. In the face of these limitations, this study uses the unit-level National Sample Survey Organisation's (NSSO) household consumer expenditure distribution for 2011–12 (NSSO 68th round) and a methodology that is only a second-best option to address the identified issues for the study. While there is practically no analytical literature available on the subject that addresses these issues in the Indian context, this study has been inspired by Lustiget et al.[3], which is among the forerunners in the field. It established a causal relationship between fiscal policy (both tax and subsidy policy) and its implications on poverty and inequality for Argentina, using the model described as a 'Commitment to Equity (CEQ)'. Over the years the model has been replicated for several Latin American, African and Asian countries. The Centre for Budget and Governance Accountability (CBGA) has also made some progress in estimating this model to analyse the fiscal policy implications on poverty and inequality in India.[4]

Does the Government Mobilise Adequate Revenues for Provisioning of Public Goods?

Given the extant tax policy regime, a short answer to the above question is no. In comparison to many developing and developed economies, the Indian government (both centre and states together) is mobilising less revenue, mainly the tax revenues, than what it could perhaps do. In the process, it can be argued that the government is not able to spend as much as it should on the supply of public goods directed at strengthening India's social and physical infrastructure capacity for its rapid development transformation. For a developing economy with a high incidence of poverty, the widespread deprivation and exclusion of population from the economic, social and political mainstream, the provision of and improved access to public goods, especially for the most marginalised sections in the society, has to be a key element of the development strategy. Well-directed public expenditure creates a platform to step up investment, to support economic activities and sustain growth. It is important for building human capabilities for a productive participation in the market and in scaling up the factors that contribute to human resource development. A low rate of tax revenue mobilisation, and thus, a lower rate of growth in public expenditure, constrain improvement in the supply of public goods and services in pursuit of inclusive development.

This section considers three different datasets to analyse India's performance in mobilising revenues, especially tax revenue. The first one relates to the cross-country dataset on government finances. The second uses the NSSO consumer expenditure data to estimate (based on certain assumptions) the potential number of income tax payers in the country in 2011–12, as against the actual income tax payers who filed income tax in that year and the consequence that this has on the government's revenues. The third examines the trend in tax expenditure or tax revenue foregone by the government on account of tax concessions extended to the industry, primarily through concession in excise tax and custom duties. Between the three datasets, the study explores the aggregate picture reflecting the overall tax efforts, and separately for a part of the direct taxes and indirect taxes, respectively. The analysis helps in explaining the government's under-performance in the mobilisation of tax revenues, given the size of India's economy and its level of development.

India's comparative performance on revenue mobilisation

A cross-country analysis of public finances shows that India mobilises comparatively less revenue with respect to its GDP. In 2013, India's total revenue (tax and non-tax) was 20 per cent of its GDP and its tax revenue was around 16 per cent of the GDP. A much smaller economy like Kenya (with about half of India's per capita income both in USD and Purchasing Power Parity) also raised about the same magnitude of revenues. Although there is no defined upper limit or desired level for this ratio, a higher level of revenue mobilisation or more specifically, a higher (and rising) tax-GDP ratio for a growing economy is typically indicative of improved tax administration and tax policy, and consequent scope for improved supply of public goods and services. It creates the fiscal space for the government to expand and qualitatively improve its public expenditure to support inclusive development outcomes. Figure 1 shows the revenue and total expenditure as a proportion of country's GDP for India and few developing and developed countries. France generates revenue equal to 53 per cent of its GDP as compared to USA's 31 per cent (2014 figure). Accordingly, government expenditure figures in France and USA are 57 per cent and 37 per cent of their respective GDP.

In India, agricultural income is not taxed and over the past two decades, the share of agriculture in the total GDP has come down from nearly 30 per cent to around 15 per cent. Yet there is no significant change in its tax-GDP ratio. It has varied, for most of the last decade-and-a-half between 10–12 per cent of the GDP for the central government and between 14–16 per cent for the central and state governments combined. This is despite a spurt in the GDP growth rate averaging about 8.5 per cent per annum in the first decade of this millennium; a steady growth of the tax base in the service sector, which now accounts for nearly 58 per cent of India's GDP; considerable improvements in tax administration, particularly in

Figure 1: Government Revenue and Expenditure as a Proportion of GDP in 2013

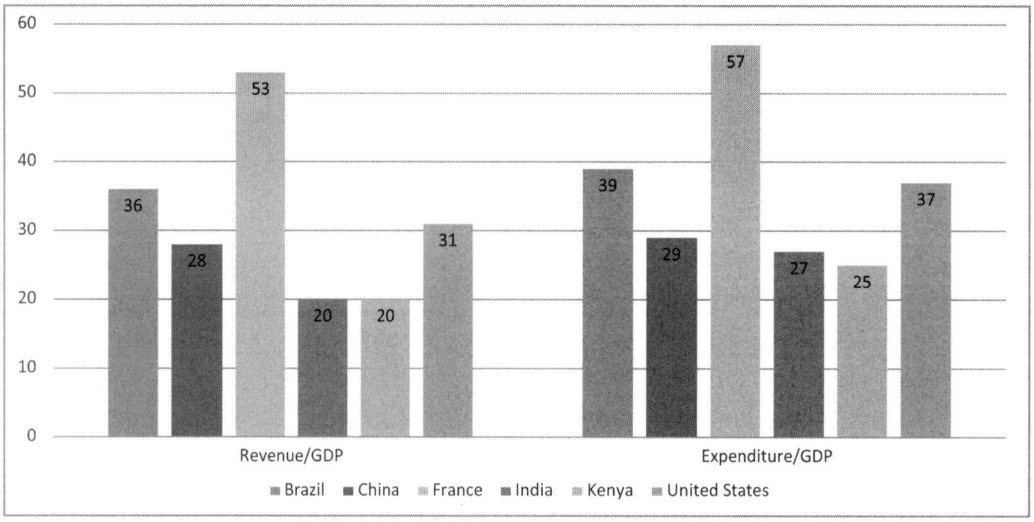

Source: IMF World Economic Outlook Database, 2015
Note: Revenue consists of taxes, social contributions, grants receivable, and other revenue.

Figure 2: Tax-GDP Ratio and Tax Buoyancy in India

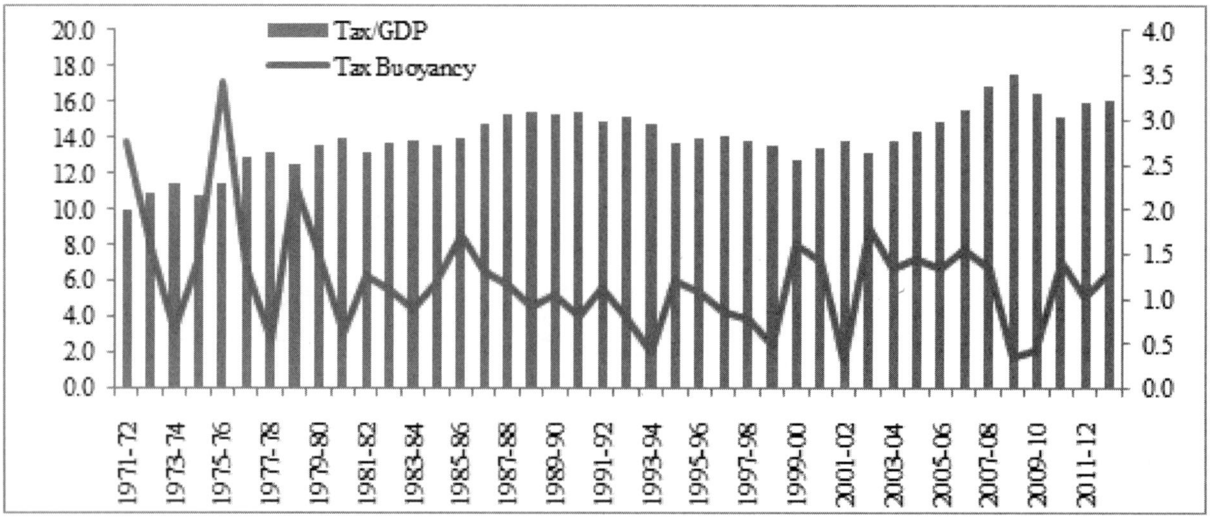

Source: Reserve Bank of India, Database of Indian Economy

the ease of filing tax returns; interface with the tax authorities; and some reforms in tax policy. In other words, there is little, if any, growth in tax revenues in response to the growth in GDP. Indeed the time-series data over the last four decades shows that tax-buoyancy or the ratio of the growth in tax revenue and GDP growth exhibits periodic fluctuations around a stable trend (Figure 2). The growing tax avoidance by under-reporting incomes and a proliferation of tax expenditure or tax concessions in tax policy (in respect of indirect taxes) helps in explaining the near stagnancy in tax buoyancy and tax-GDP ratio. The momentum in the improvement of the tax-GDP ratio (primarily on account of an expansion in the service tax base and improved tax administration) that was briefly observed during the high growth phase of 2004–8 (Figure 2), was perhaps derailed due to the fiscal stimulus measures administered as indirect tax cuts in the wake of global financial slowdown, the delay in rolling them back when the economy recovered, and the subsequent slowdown in GDP growth and political logjam on tax policy reforms.

Estimating under-reporting of income and income tax payers in India

The government data for 2011–12 shows that 3.24 crore income tax payers contributed nearly Rs 2 lakh crore of the income tax revenue. There is ample anecdotal evidence to suggest widespread under-reporting of incomes in India, especially among the non-salaried, unorganised sector workers and the self-employed. As a result, only a small proportion of people who ought to pay income tax actually do so, and others who file tax returns pay less than what they should. The fact that agricultural income is not taxed implies that nearly 45 per cent of the country's population dependent on agriculture for livelihood is not part of the country's income tax base and only a minuscule proportion of the remaining rural population may be filing income tax.[5] Indeed by keeping the agricultural income out of the tax net there is a 'legitimate' channel available for those who essentially earn non-agricultural incomes but also engage in some agriculture activity (at least on paper) to hide or under-report their taxable income. In order to assess the extent of under-reporting of incomes, and the implication of this on the number of potential tax payers and the potential income tax collection in the country, this study makes use of the NSSO consumer expenditure unit-level data for 2011–12. The study focuses on estimating the urban income distribution followed by the number of tax payers and their potential income tax contribution.

Before proceeding further, it is important to recall a few considerations that underpin the analysis of this exercise. On an average, other than for the extremely poor households, consumption levels are necessarily less than income levels, the difference between the two being savings. Second, both theory and cross-country evidence suggest that the inequality measure for consumption expenditure distribution (i.e., the Gini coefficient)is much lower than that for the corresponding income distribution. In other words, consumption inequality in a society is significantly less than its income inequality. There could be several reasons for that, including a general tendency in a developing country to under-report consumption expenditure in surveys. It could also be that the nature of consumption expenditure captured in the surveys itself introduces a bias towards greater equality, unlike in the case of income distribution, especially based on administrative data. Further, apart from the definitional distinction, there is a significant difference in the NSSO direct estimates of household consumption expenditure, over the successive rounds, and the estimates of private consumption expenditure, for the corresponding years, derived from the National Accounts Statistics.[6] That also suggests a lower consumption inequality for the NSSO consumption distribution than the estimates for income inequality in the country. Finally, with relatively high household saving rates in India and a significant proportion of population (up to one-third) living in extreme poverty, income inequality will have to be necessarily higher than consumption inequality. Therefore, in generating an income distribution based on the consumption distribution, it becomes necessary to have a robust conceptual and empirical basis for the inequality attribute of the estimated income distribution. Indeed, the consequence on the number of income tax payers and their potential tax contribution hinges critically on the inequality of the estimated income distribution.

In the first instance, assuming that all the income tax payers are residing in urban areas for reasons elaborated earlier, an attempt is made to estimate the distribution of income for the urban population (totalling 31.6 crore in 2011–12). After examining the consumption distribution, the highest 0.1 percentile of the population, which has very high consumption levels, is removed from the consumption distribution. This is to prevent the outliers at the top of the highly skewed consumption distribution from exploding the income distribution based on it. It then turns out that the average per capita consumption expenditure for the urban population is Rs 28,790 per annum and the maximum consumption expenditure of the highest person in the truncated consumption distribution is Rs 6,73,664 per capita, per annum. In other words, the highest per capita consumption expenditure is 23.40 times the average consumption expenditure for the urban population. The per capita income for the urban population is estimated at Rs 92, 804 (applying the NSSO ratio of the urban consumption to the total consumption expenditure for 2011–12 on the per capita (national) income of Rs 61,855, derived the National Accounts Statistics). Thus, the average per capita income of the urban population is 3.22 times the average per capita consumption of the population. At the top end, although the highest per capita income is likely to be several times the average per capita income, the said multiple is limited to 23.40, the same as the difference between the average per capita consumption and the highest per capita consumption of the truncated urban consumption distribution. Assuming the consumption distribution series follows a trend of arithmetic progression, the relation between two open end values in an arithmetic progression series is established using the relationship:

$$t_n = a+(n-1)*d,$$

where, t_n is the end value in the series, a is the first value in the series, n is the number of values and d is the difference between two successive values. In this case it turns out that t_n= 23.4, a = 3.22, n =15,834 (number of observations corresponding to about 31 per cent of the population above the urban average per capita income) and d= 0.0012. Using the series so estimated, the income distribution of the urban population is estimated from the corresponding consumption distribution.It is then subjected to the prevalent tax rates for different income slabs to arrive at the total number of tax payers and their potential income tax. It turns out that (Table 1) the total number of tax payers goes up by 2.6 times from 3.24 crore to 8.4 crore, and the potential income tax

Table 1: Estimate of Potential Income Tax Payers and Income Tax for 2011-12

Table 1				
S. No.	**With respect to tax Slabs**	**No. of Tax Payers**	**Tax Rate**	**Estimated Income Tax Revenue (Rs. Crore)**
1	180000 – 500000	34,365,645	10%	5E+11
2	500000 – 800000	17,007,234	32,000+20%	1E+12
3	>800000	32,256,832	92,000+30%	1.25253E+13
		83,629,711		1.40253E+13

Source: Authors' own estimation of individual household income from the NSS National Household Consumption Expenditure Survey, 2011–12.

revenue could go up by as much as 7 times from Rs 2 lakh crore recorded to Rs 14 lakh crore in 2011–12. Also the inequality coefficient (Gini) deteriorates from 0.285 in case of the consumption expenditure distribution to 0.512 in case of the estimated income distribution.[7]

Alternately, just for the sake of completing and argument, we could assume that the number of income tax payers in 2011–12 is correct, i.e., all those who need to pay income tax are filing tax returns, but they are all under-reporting their incomes. In that case also we can estimate the extent of under-reporting of incomes and hence, income tax revenue. Using the same methodology as described above, and by restricting the analysis to the top 3.24 crore persons in the urban consumption expenditure distributed, their corresponding income distribution can be generated. It turns out that the potential income tax revenue in that case could be as high as Rs 12.5 lakh crore or just over 6 times the income tax revenue collected in 2011–12. The inequality parameter (Gini) for this subset of the population would deteriorate from 0.254 for their consumption expenditure to 0.310 for their income distribution.

The question is how appropriate is the methodology employed to estimate these results and, therefore, how seriously should one consider the estimated figures on the potential tax payers and the potential income tax revenue. We have already noted earlier the sensitivity of this exercise to the differences between the average consumption and income levels, and how those differences are distributed among the people, in other words, on the inequality of the estimated income distribution. The consumption expenditure distribution for 2011-12 is highly skewed, with the consumption expenditure of the top 0.1 percentile of the population influencing the overall inequality of the consumption distribution. By dropping this segment of the distribution a smoothened consumption distribution has been used for estimating the income distribution, which is methodologically desirable for an exercise like this. Similarly, the maximum per capita income used to derive the income distribution is a reasonably conservative number and the inequality parameters for the estimated income distribution vis-à-vis the consumption distribution in each case turns out to be in line with the expectations and evidence from other survey-based studies in India and from other countries. However, some of these assumptions to estimate the income distributions need to be validated with the government's income tax data, which is not available in the public domain but will have to be accessed at some stage, and with some large sample-based independent estimates of income distribution in the country.[8] Indeed, the National Council for Applied Economic Research's India Human Development Survey data suggests that the Gini for household income in India is around 0.52 for 2004–05.

While there is scope to further refine the methodology used for this analysis, a most conservative conclusion from the analysis would be that the number of eligible income tax payers could be up to two times the number of those who filed income tax returns in 2011–12, but for the fact of under-reporting their incomes. And the income tax revenues could be anything between 2 to 3 times the amount collected in 2011–12, or anything between 4 to 7 per cent of the GDP. In other words, the amount of additional income tax revenue would have easily absorbed the fiscal deficit of the central government in 2011–12, or made available that amount of additional resources for augmenting the supply of public goods. A consideration that guides the said conclusion is the likelihood that under-reporting of incomes is more at the income levels in and around the income tax thresholds at the lower end of the tax rates and among the middle-income-range earners. However, a significant amount of tax actually comes from high networth individuals at the top 0.1 percentile of income/consumption distribution, who may have little incentive to significantly under-report their incomes.

Implications of tax expenditure or tax concessions for tax mobilisation

A lower proportion of tax revenue mobilisation with respect to GDP in India is not because its tax rates are low. Rates of taxation on personal incomes and corporate bodies in India are comparable to many developing and developed countries. Corporate tax rate in Brazil is 34 per cent, which is more or less similar to the rate in India (though a gradual reduction to 25 per cent over the next four years has been announced by the government during the budget 2015–16). In China, the corporate tax rate is 25 per cent while in USA, the rate stands at 40 per cent.[9] One of the reasons for the lack of improvement in India's tax buoyancy, despite tax policy and tax administration reforms, is the significant tax expenditure undertaken by the government or tax concessions extended to the industry. It results in the effective tax rate for the relevant tax payers becoming considerably lower than the statutory tax rate. Tax expenditure is an implicit tax subsidy given to certain tax payers as per the preferences exercised by the government of the day. It is implemented through a range of measures such as special tax rates, tax exemptions,

Table 2: Estimated Revenue Foregone (Rs Crore)

Heads	2005-06	2006-07	2007-08	2008-09	2009-10	2010-11	2011-12	2012-13	2013-14 (R)	2014-15(p)
Corporate Income Tax	34618	50075	62199	66901	72881	57912	61765.3	68720	57793	62398.6
Personal Income Tax	13550	15512	38057	37570	45142	36826	39375.4	33535.7	35254.1	40434.6
Excise Duty	66760	99690	87468	128293	169121	192227	195590	209940	196223	184764
Customs Duty	127730	123682	153593	225752	195288	172740	236852	254039	260714	301688
Total Revenue Foregone	242658	288959	341317	458516	482432	459705	533583	566235	549984.1	589285.2
Total Tax Revenue	270264	351182	439547	443319	456536	569869	629765	741877	815854.22	977258.4
Revenue foregone as a % of Tax Revenue	89.8	82.3	77.7	103.4	105.7	80.7	84.7	76.3	67.4	60.3

Source: Budget documents of the Central Government

Table 3: Effective Corporate Tax Rates

Sector	2008-09	2009-10	2010-11	2011-12	2012-13	2013-14
Public	27.14	25.36	22.28	22.21	21.49	19.33
Private	21.56	23.03	24.61	23.10	22.78	24.44
Manufacturing	21.97	23.40	24.83	22.01	21.10	21. 96
Services	23.53	23.77	23.40	23. 70	23. 71	24.37
Overall effective tax rate	22.77	23.58	24.10	22.85	22. 24	23.32
Statutory tax rate	33.99	33.99	33.99	33. 99	33. 99	33.99

Source: Budget documents (Receipts Budget) for various years.

Note: The effective tax rates are based on sample companies and include surcharge and education cess for the indicated financial years. With dividend distribution tax, effective tax rate for 2009–10 was 25.06.

deductions, rebates, deferrals and credits. It impacts the overall magnitude of tax collections and the tax incidence. In principle the use of tax expenditure as an instrument for incentivising economic activity (savings, exports, infrastructure investment, charity, scientific research and technology development) and to encourage tax compliance is desirable (and enshrined in the relevant taxation Acts). However, its indiscriminate use has compromised resource mobilisation efforts of the government and created the scope for exercising patronage and corruption. Tax exemptions and concessions also violate the principle of equity in taxation, primarily because of the process underpinning their implementation. It favours the well-off who are in a better position to negotiate with the government.

Table 2 reflects the tax concessions under various heads. In 2013–14, the total tax concession was 67.4 per cent of total tax collections of the centre. In 2014–15, it was estimated at Rs 5.9 lakh crore, which is 60 per cent of total tax revenue. The implementation of corporate tax preferences (in terms of the tax concessions extended) has also ensured that the effective tax rate at sectoral and overall levels remains well below the statutory tax rate (Table 3). Moreover, based on the effective corporate tax rates, it can been seen that the tax expenditure incurred by the government in respect of the private sector companies until the last few years turns out to be higher than that for the public sector companies. Thus, the mobilisation of tax resources falls short of the intended levels on account of the government's implementation of its tax preferences and tax policy.

Tax Burden: Does it Come in the Way of Inclusive Development?

Tax is inevitably a burden on every person who has to pay it. It impacts an individual's expenditure and behaviour in a number of ways. An income tax generates an income-effect by making an individual's disposable income necessarily less than her income. A commodity or service tax creates a substitution effect, which often results in a reallocation of resources between competing goods and services for the consumer as well as the producers in an economy. By virtue of being included as a part of the price of a good, an indirect tax also generates socio-economic exclusion, especially for the poor

Figure 3: Per capita Tax Collection in India

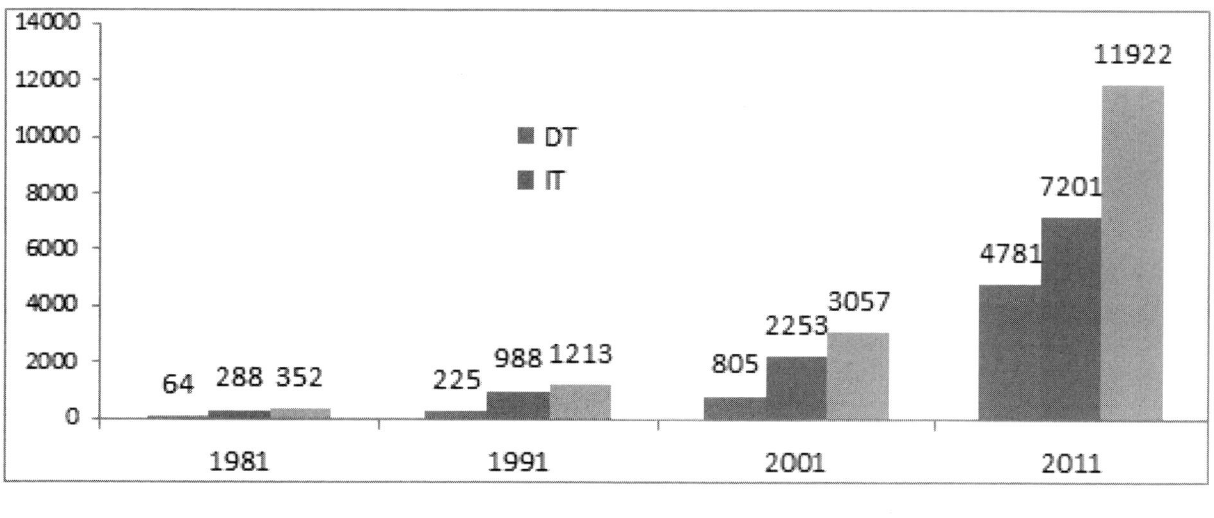

Source: Estimated from data collected from RBI Statistics and Census of India; DT stands for direct taxes and IT for indirect taxes.

consumer. Finally, as in the case of direct taxes, the mobilisation of indirect taxes in India also suffers from significant leakages, principally because of the nature of the economy which continues to rely on cash transactions, numerous petty traders and malpractices in business, all of which creates scope for corrupt practices. The nature and overall trend in India's tax collection, in particular, the relationship between indirect taxes and poverty and inequality in the country, is explored in the rest of this chapter.

Is the tax system becoming more progressive in India?

Per-capita tax collection has been rising over time. It is estimated that between 2001 and 2011, the per head tax burden in India increased from Rs 3,057 to Rs 11,922, amounting to over 28 per cent growth in tax collection during that period. There is a shift in favour of direct tax collection compared to the indirect taxes (Figure 3). Per capita direct tax collection has increased from Rs 805 to Rs 4,781, recording 49 per cent growth, compared to 22 per cent growth per annum, in indirect taxes during that period. In the interest of having a progressive and an inclusive tax system in the country this trend needs to be further consolidated.

The increase in per capita tax collection in the last decade (2001–11) is accompanied by relatively lower rate of growth in per capita income in the country. The per capita income growth is estimated at 22 per cent per annum as compared to 29 per cent in per capita tax collection for the period 2001–11. In the same period, both rural and urban inequality in India has increased. Although the positive correlation between the two is not independent of other factors that contribute to poverty and inequality, *prima facie* it can be established that the incidence of (indirect) taxation has increased at the lower end of income distribution. Therefore, it plays a role in contributing to the incidence of poverty and deterioration in inequality. With the rise in tax incidence, the purchasing power of the lower income strata gets adversely affected, undermining their standard of living. This has increased the gap between the poor and the rich in both rural and urban India. The trends in per capita income, per capita tax collection and inequality are reflected in Figure 4.

Figure 4: Trends in Per capita Income, Per capita Tax Collection and Inequality

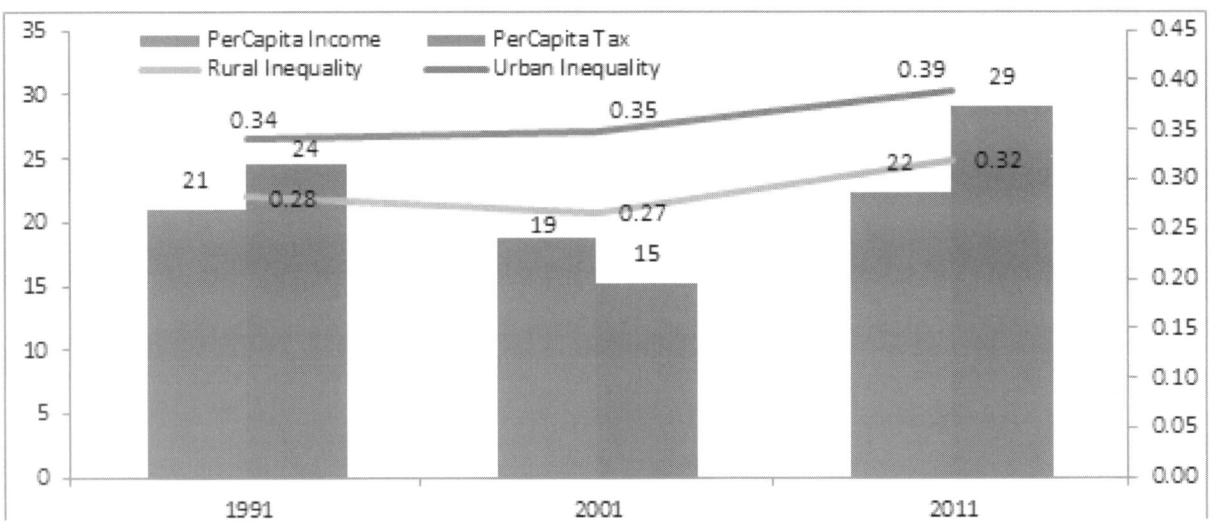

Source: Estimated from RBI Statistics and NSSO Consumption expenditure surveys from various rounds.

Is the tax incidence contributing to poverty and exclusion?

In an attempt to measure the actual tax burden (incidence) on the living standard of a family, the state-specific household consumption baskets (from NSSO 68th Round) for a few selected states and state level (indirect) tax rates on various commodities that comprise a household's consumption basket have been analysed. Indirect taxes constitute a major share in total tax revenue in the states. More than 80 per cent of tax revenue of the state governments comes from indirect taxes. The most important component of indirect taxes at the state level has been the state sales tax, which in the post-2005 period has been replaced by Value-added tax (VAT) in all the states. Guided by their respective fiscal policies and political compulsions, VAT rates differ for commodities across states. Therefore, incidence of VAT on the households also differs from state to state. This incidence also depends on differences in the consumption baskets across states.

Many government and non-government agencies have made an effort to estimate the average VAT rates to facilitate cross-country comparisons. The United States Council for International Business (USCIB) suggests that the average VAT rate in India should be 13.5 per cent.[10] Trading Economics estimates the all-India average VAT rate in 2014–15 to be 12.44 per cent.[11] Boomerang at Carnet shows the all-India VAT rates to be 13.5 per cent.[12] The World-wide Tax Agency estimates India's VAT to be in the rage of 5 per cent to 15 per cent. KPMG suggests that the all-India average indirect tax rate in India is 14 per cent in 2014–15.[13] The Royal Malaysian Customs Department made a cross-country comparison of VAT rates where India's VAT rate was estimated at 12.5 per cent.[14] For this study, an average VAT of 12.5 per cent for the country as a whole has been used for estimating tax incidence on the people. If each household is subjected to an average 12.5 per cent VAT on the estimated all India monthly household consumption expenditure of Rs 7,210 in 2011–12, the net purchasing power (post-VAT) of the consumer would be Rs 6,306. In other words, a state government collects an average Rs 900 from every family out of its consumption expenditure in a month.

In order to refine the analysis of VAT incidence, there is a need to move from the average all-India rates to state-specific VAT rates and allow for the consumption baskets to change across population segments and states. Accordingly, five states, namely, Andhra Pradesh, Bihar, Odisha, Punjab and Maharashtra, were randomly selected for this study. These states differ in terms of their socio-economic standards. The mean monthly

Table 4: State-level Mean Monthly Tax Burden on Households

States	MPCE (Rs)	Tax burden (Rs)	Tax burden as Percentage of Mean Household Consumption Expenditure
Andhra Pradesh	6675	632	9%
Odisha	4261	183.7	4.3%
Bihar	5285	311	6%
Punjab	10655	943	9%
Maharashtra	8923.7	581	6.5%

Source: Estimated from NSS Household Consumption expenditure survey 2011–12

expenditure of a family in Punjab is almost twice that of the monthly household expenditure of families in Bihar. Similary, although Maharashtra's mean monthly household expenditure is less than that of Punjab, it is twice that of Odisha. Andhra Pradesh falls in the middle among these five states in terms of its monthly household consumption expenditure. Table 4 presents the mean per capita consumption expenditure (MPCE), tax burden and share of tax burden on an average household for the selected states. An average household in Punjab and Andhra Pradesh ends up paying around 9 per cent, Rs 943 (out of Rs 10,655) and Rs 632 (out of Rs 6,675) respectively, of their MPCE in indirect taxes. In case of Maharashtra and Bihar this share is 6.5 per cent (Rs 581 out of Rs 8,924) and 6 per cent (Rs 311 out of Rs 5258), respectively. Odisha with its tax share of 4.3 per cent (Rs 183.7 out of Rs 4,261) ranks lowest in the group in terms of the VAT incidence.

As a next step, the tax burden on households (HHs) living below poverty line (BPL) is estimated at the state level for these five states. The poverty line as defined by the Planning Commission, Government of India (based on the methodology recommended by the Expert Group headed by Suresh Tendulkar) has been used to estimate the household level poverty line. The household poverty line is defined as the product of poverty line (at an individual level defined by the Planning Commission for each state) and the average size of the households in that state.

Indirect taxes do not differentiate between a poor and a non-poor family. They are included in the price of a commodity and whoever is the end-consumer bears the burden of the tax. In Table 5 it can be seen that a family living below the poverty line also pays taxes to the governments and in some instance not too different from the rest of the households. In many instances, although the tax burden for the poor households varies, it could have serious consequences on their consumption expenditure and the standard of living. In Andhra Pradesh 4.06 million households live below the poverty line. The average tax a BPL household pays is Rs 188 which is 8.6 per cent of the mean expenditure of all the BPL families. In Odisha, 3.3 million households live below the poverty line. The average tax collected from families living in this bracket is Rs 82 which is 4.1 per cent of their mean consumption expenditure. In Bihar, 6.8 million families live below the poverty line. The average tax paid by them is Rs 153 per month. This constitutes 5 per cent of the mean consumption expenditure of BPL households in Bihar. Families living below the poverty line in Punjab pay a larger share of their expenditure in terms of taxes among the five states considered in this study. Each BPL household in that state pays 8.6 per

Table 5: Incidence of Tax Burden on BPL Households

States	Household Poverty Line (Rs/ month)	No. of BPL Households (million and per cent)	Tax burden (Rs) on BPL Households	Tax burden Percentage of Mean BPL Households Consumption Expenditure
Andhra Pradesh	3195	4.07 (17.9%)	188	8.6
Odisha	2928	3.3 (36%)	82	4.1
Bihar	4126	6.8 (37.7%)	153	5
Punjab	4906	0.89 (15.67%)	306	8.6
Maharashtra	4338	5.8 (23 %)	202	6.9

Source: Estimated from NSS Household Consumption expenditure survey 2011–12

cent of their mean consumption expenditure, i.e., Rs 306 per month in terms of taxes. In the case of Maharashtra, BPL families pay 6.9 per cent of their consumption expenditure in terms of taxes, which is equivalent to Rs 161. Thus, among the five states, Odisha is the least exclusionary in terms of the VAT incidence on the BPL households.

Figures 5 (A to E) present the distribution of BPL households (HHs), reflecting the impact on the level of poverty incidence if the VAT imposed on the BPL household is withdrawn. The cumulative distribution of the BPL households between the household poverty line (HH Poverty line, upper line) and the net household poverty line (Net HH Poverty line, lower line) reflects the proportion of the households who would come out of poverty should the VAT currently imposed on the goods

Figure 5: BPL Households Overcoming Poverty if VAT is Withdrawn

Andhra Pradesh

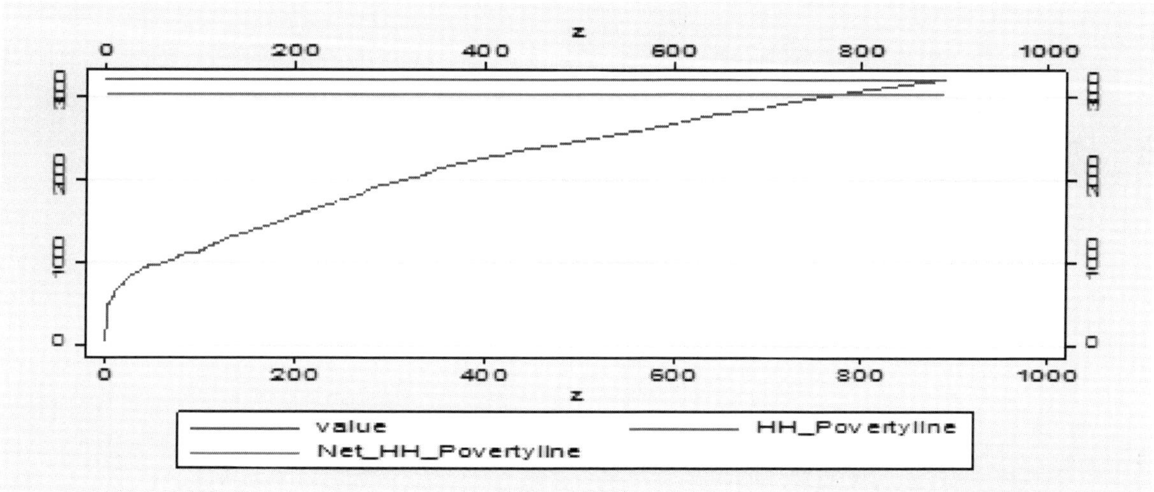

Bihar

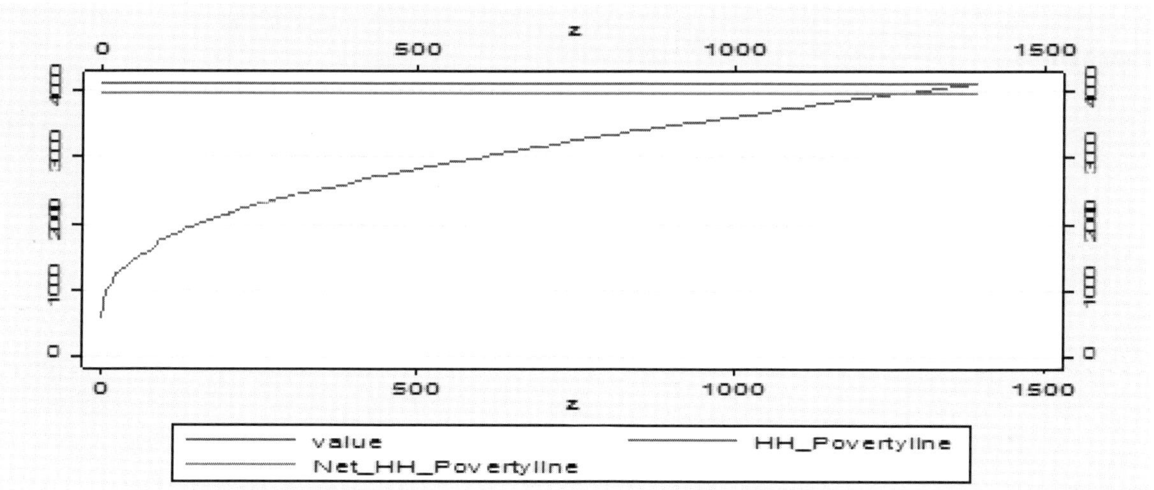

Odisha

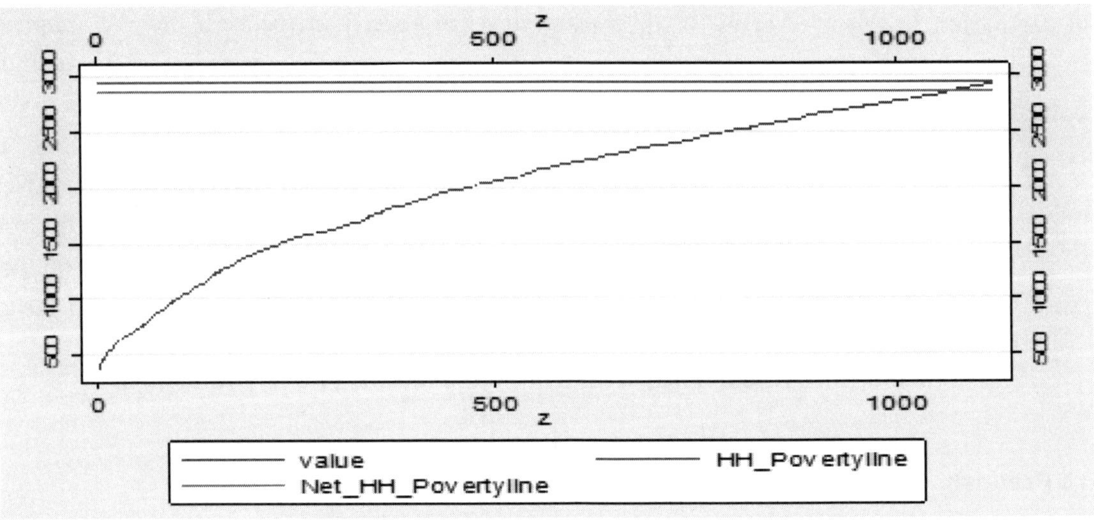

Punjab

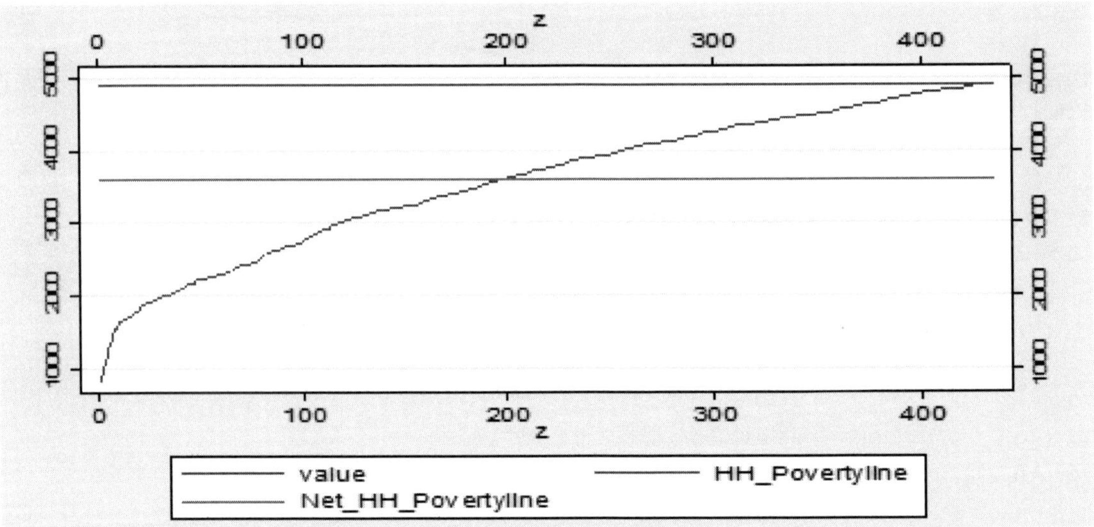

Maharashtra

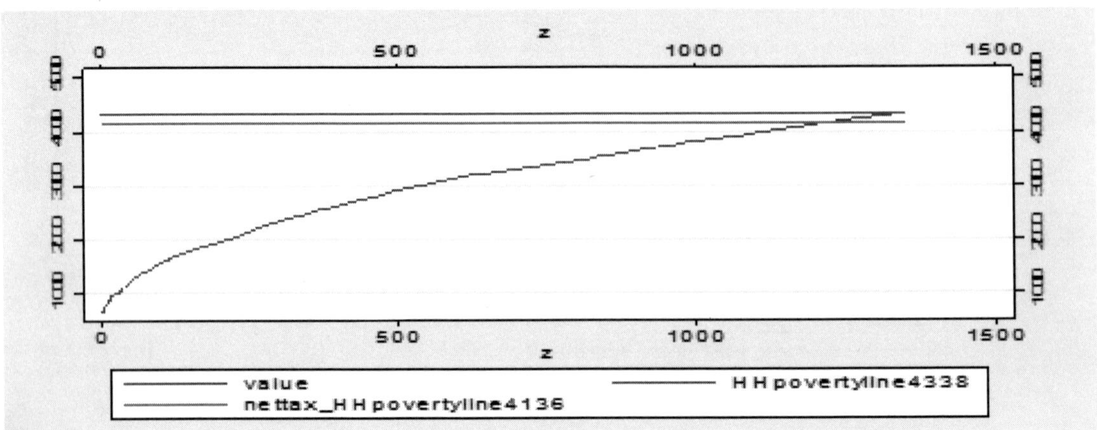

in their consumption basket be withdrawn. Table 6 summarises these results.

It can be seen from Table 6 that for Andhra Pradesh reduction in poverty incidence, when VAT is withdrawn, is most significant at nearly 14 per cent, followed by Punjab at nearly 12 per cent, and it is least for Odisha where it drops by just over 4 per cent. The other two states, Bihar and Maharashtra also show significant reduction in poverty incidence. The net impact of VAT withdrawal is a function of the distribution of BPL households (how dispersed or concentrated they are around the household poverty line) and the magnitude of the tax burden, which in case of Odisha was the least, at 4 per cent of the mean BPL HHs average consumption expenditure.

The exclusionary consequences of indirect taxes (VAT) could also be examined in terms of the tax burden imposed on the consumption of merit goods like education and healthcare, particularly for the poor and the marginalised of a society. The supply of and access to the goods that underpin these merit goods is critical for equalising opportunities and development outcomes in a society over time. The NSSO household consumption expenditure survey 2011–12 shows an average household spending on education to be Rs 404 out of its total spending of Rs 7210. An average family is therefore spending 5.6 per cent of its total expenditure on education. In rural areas, this share is 3.9 per cent and in urban it is much higher at 8 per cent. For the BPL HHs also it is 2 per cent of its total consumption expenditure. Education is not a freebie at all. Even when there are no tuition fees to be paid for acquiring elementary education in public schools (or for the entire school education for a girl child in many states), there is a price to be paid when a family purchases books, paper, pencils, pens, school uniforms or engages private tuitions for the children. While prices of these education goods are rising, in many instances the government's taxation policy on those goods is also adding to the household burden.[15]

Most state governments do not hesitate to impose VAT on education goods and services, such as books, periodicals, journals, pens, pencils, private tuitions, etc. It affects the price of these products and thus, impacts a family's expenditure. There is no uniformity in the manner in which they impose VAT: Tamil Nadu levies 12.5 per cent VAT on erasers, scales and colouring kits, but ball pens and pencils are exempted from VAT.[16]Among the states chosen for this study the average VAT on education goods for households is 2.5 per cent in Andhra Pradesh and 5.3 per cent in Odisha. The BPL HHs in Odisha also face VAT at the same rate as an average household. Similarly, in the case of healthcare goods and services consumed by households, Andhra Pradesh has an average VAT of 14.5 per cent and Odisha 5 per cent. The former also levies an average VAT of 5 per cent for BPL HHs in the state.

Table 6: BPL Households Overcoming Poverty if VAT is Withdrawn

States	Proportion of Households below poverty line (%)	Number and Percentage of BPL Households escaping poverty if VAT withdrawn	Percentage reduction in poverty
Andhra Pradesh	17.9	567931 (2.5)	13.99
Bihar	37.7	583974 (3.2)	8.59
Odisha	36	142752 (1.6)	4.34
Punjab	15.67	106605 (1.9)	11.98
Maharashtra	17.46	518780 (2.1)	8.94

Source: Based on NSS Consumption Expenditure Survey 2011–12.

Conclusions and Policy Takeaway

The study presented in this chapter has made an attempt to address two questions: whether India is mobilising tax revenue commensurate with its level of development, given its extant tax policy regime, and is the state-level tax policy framework, with its reliance on indirect taxes (mainly VAT) to raise resources, exacerbating poverty and inequality? Notwithstanding the limitation on account of data availability for the analysis required to undertake this enquiry, the study comes to a conclusion that there is significant under-reporting of incomes when it comes to filing income tax returns in India. It implies that there are fewer persons filing income tax returns than those who should be and that the income tax revenues of the government could be a multiple of the realised amounts. Thus, given the extant direct tax policy regime, India is certainly not collecting tax revenues in keeping with the size of its economy and the growth in average per capita incomes that it has witnessed in the recent decades. In the process, the study provides some quantitative evidence to support the popular perception on tax avoidance behaviour of Indians. Besides the fact that indirect taxes are regressive in their impact, as they don't distinguish a poor from a non-poor tax-paying person, the study provides evidence to suggest that significant proportions of population, both in the better-off and the backward states, are being pushed into poverty (i.e., into household consumption expenditure levels below the official poverty line) on account of the indirect tax burden they face on their consumption expenditure.

On a conservative count and based on the methodology used, the analysis suggests that the number of eligible tax payers could be up to two times the 3.24 crore persons who filed income tax returns in 2011–12, and the income tax revenues could be anything between 2 to 3 times the amount collected in 2011–12, or between 4 to 7 per cent of the GDP. In respect of the analysis undertaken on the burden imposed by VAT on the households and based on the random sample of five states, the study concludes that between 5 to 10 per cent reduction in poverty incidence can be brought about in most states if the VAT burden were removed for the BPL HHs. The study also notes that there is widespread leakage in the collection of indirect taxes as well. This is mainly on account of malpractices in business transactions, including the under-invoicing and non-invoicing of retail-level transactions, where VAT is levied and is collected.

The policy response to address these concerns has to do with minimising and even discouraging cash transactions. But that is easier said than done because of the nature of India's economy. India's labour market is predominantly in the informal or unorganised sector where cash transactions are the norm. Its retail markets are mostly unorganised, run by petty traders, too numerous to be effectively regulated. A major challenge in reducing the cash economy in the country is the low level of financial inclusion (i.e., access to banking services) and financial literacy among the people, and weak oversight and enforcement of business practices. Despite steady reforms for simplification of procedures to file income tax returns, constantly improving IT interface to support that process and rationalisation of tax-related litigation to improve overall mobilisation of tax revenues, there is still some distance that remains to be covered, particularly in respect of the administration of indirect tax (VAT) policy. It is also true that VAT incidence cannot be entirely eliminated for the poor households because of the difficulties in targeting it, but there is scope to rationalise VAT and compensate BPL HHs with well-directed social transfers to help them overcome poverty. At the same time, under the Finance Commission awards, a greater devolution of tax revenues collected by the central government to the states would help state governments in reducing their dependence on indirect tax revenues. While there is policy movement in most of these action areas of reforms, the process needs to gather greater momentum.

A potential game changer in that context is an

early implementation of the Direct Tax Code (DTC) and establishing a harmonised Goods and Service Tax (GST) regime in the country. These initiatives have been in the works for the past several years but have become a casualty of political wrangling and posturing. It has been argued that the GST would provide the economy with a modern, broad-based, equitable and non-distortionary tax system to promote allocative efficiency along with sustained growth in tax revenues. As per reported estimates, the implementation of GST alone could add up to 2 per cent to India's GDP growth rate and therefore to its tax revenues as well.[17] Indeed, there is a strong case for an early implementation of the proposed DTC and the GST regimes with emphasis on few and lower tax rates, and minimal tax concessions and exemptions. While some provisions of the DTC have been implemented in the successive budgets over the past few years, GST continues to be on the drawing board with a consensus between the centre and state governments proving elusive. Depending on the actual format of its implementation, as and when that happens, including the rates of taxation and the list of commodities exempted from taxation, the implications of the GST burden on the poor household would have to be reassessed. It is however well understood that the implementation of GST and DTC in its proposed totality is necessary to curb the revenue forgone or tax expenditure being undertaken by the government, year after year without the desired impact on revenue mobilisation outcomes. A complete overhaul of the tax regime, direct as well as indirect, is necessary for a sustained improvement in the tax buoyancy and tax-GDP ratio of the Indian economy. That, in turn, would help in improving the government's fiscal space and the resulting capacity to improve the supply and quality of public goods in the country.

Appendix-1

A1. Value Added Tax (VAT) Rates for Various Education Goods and Services

States	Education goods and services	VAT rate(%)
Andhra Pradesh	Books, periodicals and journals including maps, charts, globes and atlases	Exempted
	(1) Exercise notebooks including graph books and laboratory notebooks, office stationery including computer stationery, writing pads and account ledgers. (2) Paper of all kinds and news print, excluding wall papers. (3) Diary, calendar, annual reports, application forms and similar printed materials. (4) Printing ink excluding toner and cartridges. (5) Writing instruments, writing ink, geometry boxes, colour boxes, pencil sharpeners and erasers	5%
	All goods not mentioned above	14.50%
Odisha	Books, periodicals and journals, slate, slate pencils, educational maps, globes and charts	Exempted
	Exercise book, graph book and laboratory notebook Printed material including diary, calendar, etc. Printing ink excluding toner and cartridges. Writing instruments	4%
	All other goods	12.50%

States	Education goods and services	VAT rate(%)
Bihar	Books, periodicals and journals excluding those specified elsewhere in this schedule or any other schedule but including Braille books, maps, charts and globes; Newspaper; Slate and slate pencils	Exempted
	Printed materials including diary, calendar and letter pad. Printing ink excluding toner and cartridges; writing instruments such as lead pencils, pen of all varieties and descriptions, refill, cartridges, nozzles, nib; geometry boxes, colour boxes, crayons, erasers, pencil sharpeners and writing ink other than those specified elsewhere in any other schedule	4%
	All other goods not specified here to be charged 12.5 %	12.50%
Punjab	Books, periodicals and journals including maps, charts and globes, slate and slate pencils and chalks	Exempted
	Computer stationary; exercise books, graph books and laboratory note books. Printed material including diary and calendar; printing ink excluding toner and cartridges; school bags; writing ink; writing instruments, geometry boxes, colour boxes, brushes for colour boxes, crayons pencil, pencil sharpeners and erasers	4%
	Goods not mentioned above	13.00%
Maharashtra	Books, that is to say, every volume or part or division of a volume including almanacs, panchangs, time tables for passenger transport services and periodicals, maps, charts, orreries and globes, but excluding annual reports, application forms, account books, balance sheets, calenders, diaries, catalogues, race cards, publications which mainly publicise goods, services and articles for commercial purposes and publications which contain space exceeding eight pages for writing. Chalk Stick. Slate and slate pencils but not including writing boards	Exempted
	Exercise book, graph book, laboratory note books and drawing books. Paper, news print, paper board, waste paper. All types of paper stationery for computer, carbon paper, ammonia paper; printing ink and writing ink excluding toner and cartridges; writing instruments, ball point pens, felt tipped and other porustipped pens and markers; fountain pens, stylograph pens and other pens; duplicating stylos, propelling or sliding pencils; pen holders, pencil holders and similar holders; parts (including caps and clips) of the foregoing articles; mathematical instrument boxes including instruments thereof, students colour boxes, crayons and pencil sharpners.	4%
	All goods not mentioned above	12.50%
Tamil Nadu	Mechanical pencils, pencils lead, sharpener, wooden pencils, colour pencils, wooden roller ball pen, wooden roller pencil refill, ball pen, geometry box, mathematical box, ball pen refills, etc.	Exempted
	Writing and colour kit, wax crayons, plastic crayons, drawing boards	4%

States	Education goods and services	VAT rate(%)
	Paint marker pen, eraser, scales, sketch pends, tex liner pens, multi marker pen, permanent marker pen, white board marker pen, self inking stamp, text liner pen inks, child safe scissors, stamp pad, glue/gum, poster colour, white board marker pen ink, oil paste,	12.50%

A2. Value Added Tax (VAT) rates for various health goods and services

States	Health goods and services	VAT rate(%)
Andhra Pradesh	Aids and implements used by handicapped persons. Condoms and contraceptives. Human blood and blood plasma. Semen including frozen semen	Exempted
	Bulk Drugs. Drugs and medicines whether patent or proprietary, as defined in clauses (i), (ii) and (iii) of section 3 (b) of Drugs and Cosmetics Act, 1940 (Central Act 23 of 1940), and hypodermic syringes, hypodermic needles, perfusion sets, urine bags, catguts, sutures, surgical cotton, dressings, plasters, catheters, cannulae, bandages and similar articles, but not including, (a) medicated goods (b) products capable of being used as cosmetics and toilet preparations including toothpaste, tooth powder, cosmetics, toilet articles and soaps (c) mosquito repellants in any form, veterinary medicines, medicinal water	5%
	All goods not mentioned above	14.50%
Odisha	Aids and implements used by handicapped persons.Condoms and contraceptives. Human blood and blood plasma. Semen including frozen semen	Exempted
	Bulk drugs. Drugs and medicines.	4%
	All other goods and services	12.50%
Bihar	Aids and implements used by handicapped persons. Condoms and contraceptives. Human blood and blood plasma.	Exempted
	Bulk Drugs. Drugs and medicines, whether patent or proprietary, including vaccines, disposable hypodermic syringes, hypodermic needles, catguts, sutures, surgical dressings, medicated ointments produced under the license issued under the Drugs and Cosmetics Act,1940 but excluding any cosmetics, perfumery, toiletry and hair oil, whether or not such cosmetics, perfumery, toiletry and hair oil is manufactured under any Drug License and whether or not such cosmetics, perfumery, toiletry and hair oil contains any medicinal properties. Medical Diagnostic Kits. Medical equipments, devices and implants. X-Ray film and other diagnostic films.	5%
	All others	12.50%

States	Health goods and services	VAT rate(%)
Punjab	Aids and implements used by handicapped persons. Condoms and contraceptives. Human blood alongwith its components like platelets, red blood corpulscles (RBC), plasma, anti hemophilic factors, albumin and gamma golobulin. Semen including frozen semen	Exempted
	Drugs and medicines including vaccines , syringes and dressing, mediated ointments produced under drug license, light liquid paraffin of IP grade, medical equipments/devices and implants	6%
	Goods not mentioned above	13.00%
Maharashtra	Aids and implements used by handicapped persons. Contraceptives of all types. Human blood and its components and products thereof.	Exempted
	Drugs (including Ayurvedic, Siddha, Unani, Spirituous Medical Drugs and Homoeopathic Drugs), being formulations or preparations conforming to the following description:- Any medicinal formulation or preparation ready for use internally or on the body of human beings, animals and birds for diagnosis treatment, mitigation or prevention of any diseases or disorders, which is manufactured or imported into India, stocked, distributed or sold under licence granted under the Drug and Cosmetics Act, 1940 but does not include mosquito repellants in any form. Medical Oxygen and Nitrous Oxide manufactured under licence granted under the Drugs and Cosmetics Act, 1940. Bandages and dressings manufactured or imported into India, stocked, distributed or sold under licence granted under the Drugs and Cosmetics Act, 1940. Syringes. Glucose-D	5%
	All others	12.50%
Tamil Nadu	Aids and implements for physically challanged persons as notified by the Government, Condoms and contraceptives , Gauze and bandage,	Exempted
	Drugs and medicines including vaccines, syringes and dressings, medicated ointments produced under drugs licence, light liquid paraffin of IP grade	4%
	All others	12.50%

Endnotes

1. Tax-GDP ratio is the total tax revenue as a proportion of the GDP.
2. With nearly 90 per cent of the labour engaged in the non-formal or unorganised sector, it is not surprising that India does not collect income data through administrative means. Only a few limited income surveys are available.
3. Lustig Nora, George Gray Molina, Sean Higgins, Miguel Jarakillo, Wilson Jiminez, Veronica paz, CladiniePerrera (2012), 'The impact of taxes and social spending on inequality and poverty in Argentina, Bolivia, Mexico and Peru: A synthesis of results' Commitment to Equity Working Paper No. 3.

4. For an estimation of indices of poverty, inequality and polarisation using NSS HH Consumption Expenditure survey, see

   Sridhar Kundu (2011), 'Inequality Vs. Polarisation: Trends and Patterns in Indian States' in *Economic Development and Poverty in India*, Chapter 6, New Delhi: New Century Publications

   Sridhar Kundu (2007), 'Poverty, Inequality and Social Development: An interstate analysis of trends and patterns in India' in *Rural Development and Social Change*, NIRD, Ministry of Rural Development, pp. 131–165

   Thomas Piketty (2014), *Capital in the Twenty First Century,* Harvard University Press

5. It is another matter that an overwhelming proportion of the agriculture-dependent population is too impoverished to qualify as income tax payers under the prevalent income tax law of the country.

6. See, for instance Rajeev Malhotra (1997), 'Incidence of Poverty in India – Towards a Consensus on Estimating the Poor' in The *Indian Journal of Labour Economics*, 40:1, pp. 67–102,

7. If the same exercise is repeated with the entire consumption expenditure distribution and not just the urban distribution (assuming that everybody including those dependent on agriculture incomes and residing in rural areas have to pay income tax), it turns out that the total number of tax payers shoots up to 22.7 crore (10 times the number of income tax payers in 2011–12) and the potential income tax revenue also jumps up by 10 times to 20 lakh crore. The inequality parameter (Gini) deteriorates from 0.282 for consumption to 0.513 for estimated income distribution.

8. The Organisation for Economic Cooperation and Development (OECD.org/els/social/inequality) study on emerging economies suggests that India's income inequality (Gini) deteriorated from about 0.35 in the early 1990s to about 0.40 in the early part of the first decade in the current millennium. Another study by the Boston Consulting Group and Confederation of Indian Industry [Sinha and Aggarwal (2011)] estimated the number of households with income more than 2 lakh per annum (well over the income tax threshold) to be over 4.3 crore. Full reference for Sinha and Aggarwal (2011) is as follows

   Janmejaya Sinha and Neeraj Aggarwal (2011), 'Financial Inclusion: From Obligation to Opportunity', a survey report prepared from the finding of the Household Survey Conducted by Boston Consulting Group and Confederation of Indian Industry

9. Accessed at: kpmg.com/global/en/services/tax/tax-tools-and-resources/pages/corporate-tax-rates-table.aspx in October 2015, NewDelhi, India.

10. Accessed at http://www.uscib.org/valueadded-taxes-vat-ud-1676/ in October 2015.

11. Accessed at http://www.tradingeconomics.com/india/sales-tax-rate in October 2015

12. Accessed at http://www.atacarnet.com/vat-duty-rates in October 2015

13. Accessed at http://www.kpmg.com/global/en/services/tax/tax-tools-and-resources/pages/tax-rates-online.aspx in October 2015

14. Accessed at http://gst.customs.gov.my/en/gst/Pages/gst_ci.aspx in October 2015.

15. Private sector has made major inroads into the education sector in rural India. The District Information System for Education (DISE) report indicates that Kerala, Tamil Nadu, Puducherry and Goa have more than 60 per cent of enrolment atthe primary levelin private schools. In Tamil Nadu, Andhra Pradesh, Maharashtra and Karnataka that proportion is 40 per cent, and in UP it is 50 per cent.

16. Commercial Tax Department, Government of Tamil Nadu.

17. Rajeev Malhotra (2012), 'Refocusing the Union Budget: Fiscal Imperatives and Some Other Issues', in Rajeev Malhotra (ed.), *A Critical Decade: Policies for India's Development*, Oxford University Press

OXFAM

Part III – Highly Excluded Groups

Living Single

Being A Single Woman in India

Kanchan Gandhi[*]

Harsh Mander, Agrima Bhasin, Radhika Jha, Sejal Dand[**]

Introduction[1]

Dr Ginny Shrivastava, the founder of the National Forum for Single Women's Rights, notes: 'The stories [of single women] are not "nice" stories—they tell of human cruelty, of wicked superstition, of systemic corruption, of age-old cruel caste customs. Women "discarded", "abandoned", murdered. But generally, women have survived, and brought up their children, through the sweat and blood of their labour. They are strong women, not weak women!'

Society is profoundly troubled by women who survive—by choice or circumstance—independent of male control, support and patronage. Martha Nussbaum observes that women 'are treated as mere instruments of the ends of others—reproducers, caregivers, sexual outlets, agents of a family's general prosperity'.[2] In a patriarchal society such as India, a woman's identity is necessarily perceived in relation to a man (father, husband, brother, son), whom she is subservient to and dependent on for survival. Single women, alone or with their dependents, therefore have remained, through history right into the present day, an extremely oppressed category of people in most parts of the world. In India, as in all of South Asia, historically the cultural anxieties, neglect, oppression, denials, cruelties, exclusions and violence of overarching patriarchy towards single women has been dramatic and extreme, and a great deal of these socially embedded exclusions continue into the present day, reflected also in the State, in the design and implementation of law and policy. It is noteworthy that in the nature of patriarchy single men face no such disabilities.

Singleness is a socially and culturally constructed category, wherein the disadvantage is manufactured by virtue of the patriarchal societal setup. In the way that gender is done to people, so is 'singleness'. Women who choose to remain or become single owing to a range of circumstances find themselves in locations of often multiple

> According to the 2001 census, 7.4 per cent of the female population of India is 'single'. There were 3,43,89,729 widows in India, and 23,42,930 divorced/separated women—a total of 3,67,32,659 single women.[5] 'This figure is likely to increase with the inclusion of "customarily" separated women and women whose husbands are missing.'[6]

* Lead author

** Contributing authors

*** Research support: Caitlin Mackridge and Emily Davey
Reviewers: Amrita Chacchi, Aparna Chandra

disadvantage as a result of social and cultural, and also often legal and administrative, constructions of singleness. This has been exemplified further with the aid of case studies that attempt to bring to the report the voices and the lived realities of women who are single.

This chapter discusses primarily the four categories of single women identified by the National Forum for Single Women's Rights (hereinafter referred to as the National Forum), which is: widowed, divorced, never married and 'abandoned'/separated women. In the first part, the chapter attempts to look at these categories, and build through them an understanding of 'singleness' in the Indian context. It then moves on to portray life histories, varying contexts and societal perceptions of the different categories of single women, as experienced by them. Subsequent sections look at public policy measures and the legal debates surrounding this category, finally concluding with some preliminary recommendations. One limitation of this chapter is that there isn't an explicit discussion around transgendered persons and sex-workers as categories of single women.[3] Since the chapter draws heavily from the CES study on single women carried out with the Ekal Nari Shakti Sangathan (ENSS) between 2013–15 in the three states of Punjab, Gujarat and Assam, voices of single women from these three states may appear more prominent in the empirical examples provided below.[4]

Singleness: A Diverse Spectrum

Singleness is not a static, rigid or homogenous category. It is porous, a wide spectrum, and extremely heterogeneous. The conventional dictionary definition of a 'single' woman is an adult female person who is not married. The National Forum however complicates the definition of a single woman as a 'woman who is not living with a man in a marital-like relationship' and includes widows, divorced and separated women and unmarried women above the age of 35 (these are its qualifications for becoming members of the single women's collectives).

The social, demographic or administrative category of 'single' is a slippery one to work with, since there exists wide diversity within this group, all of which needs to be accounted for in constructing a social understanding as well as while framing policies. As singleness is seen as a 'troubled' (or troubling?) category in society, and in opposition to marriage which is strongly associated with 'wellbeing' in the western world as much as in Asian societies, the careful unpacking of categories of singleness becomes very important.[7] Within each category of single women, too, there exists diversity in living conditions depending on their class, race, ethnicity, caste, or age positions in a given context.

In India the heteronormative family model is still widely considered socially and culturally to be the ideal model for societal organisation, and singleness is seen as a deviation from normal. Having said this, there exists possibly significant rural-urban differences in social constructions and acceptance of single women. Writing in the context of America, Fuguitt et al. (1989:192)[8] argue: 'The greater representation of single, ever-divorced, or ever-widowed women in urban areas is the result of migration of such women from rural areas to urban .... For women supporting themselves, cities have offered more opportunities.'

This finding could hold true also in the Indian context. Cities produce many challenges for dignified and safe survival, but they are also sites of escape from the often cast-iron bonds of caste and gender. Urban areas generally offer more opportunities for work for single women. In contexts of dwindling community and familial support, single women may prefer to migrate to urban areas in search of sustenance.

Marriage and child-bearing are important markers of respectability for women in India, and hence, being a 'single' woman is also considered to be a 'problem' by the state and society alike. By being single, a woman is thought to be more 'available' and hence more susceptible to sexual violence, social oppression and economic exploitation. In the absence of 'male protection', single women—especially multiply disadvantaged ones—are at the receiving end of several forms of injustice.

It is hard to capture the diversity of single women. For instance, to understand 'singleness' in any region of India, we need to appreciate the social, economic and political dynamic in that region. For instance, the corporatisation of the tribal heartlands of India is creating unique conditions for singleness among tribal women by driving them out of their forested habitats into the city, or the military action against militant uprisings in Jammu and Kashmir has created a localised category of single women: 'half widows'. Based on this understanding, we suggest that policy interventions must be culturally informed and should come from the women themselves.

Journeys in Singleness and Multiple Vulnerabilities

Studies reveal that the journey and causes underpinning their identity as single women is different depending on whether they were widowed, separated, divorced or remained single by choice or circumstance, and those who belong to variously oppressed and dispossessed groups. While the death of the husband due to accident, alcoholism, suicide or illness were the primary reasons for widowhood, the dominant cause for why women separated or divorced their husbands was mental and physical violence, bigamy and adultery (wherein husbands left their wives for other women).[9] Among women who did not marry or remained single by choice or circumstance, the motivation or compulsion to support poor parents and siblings in childhood was the foremost reason.

Most single women either stayed by themselves, or with their children, or with their natal/parental family. In almost all cases, the women contributed substantially to household care work and also worked to earn money to support themselves. This financial independence was often borne out of a necessity to ensure their own sustenance, and at times it also serves to earn some goodwill and respect from the family. A number of reasons contributed to the lack of family support and acceptance of single women. Marital family members shrugged the responsibility as they were often concerned about widows making a claim to their husband's property, in addition to the financial support cost. Even support from one's natal family was often not forthcoming because of economic circumstances, and sometimes fears of social stigma.

The physical and social barriers for poor and differently-abled single women in rural and urban areas in terms of accessing services and livelihoods, and also for marriage, are much higher than for able-bodied single women. As a woman with disability mentioned, while a man with a disability may get a non-disabled wife, for women the spouse is typically more disabled, a drunk or unemployed person, or a divorcee looking for a second wife. Probably as a result of such discrimination in the family, there are a substantially higher proportion of never-married women among women with disabilities, as compared to other groups. A study of rural disability[10] revealed that most disabled women were either single or forced to marry in highly unequal situations, as second wives to older men, widowers or divorced men. The large majority of women surveyed reported that they were treated mainly as unpaid domestic labour and sexual objects, and suffered high levels of physical and psychological domestic abuse, sometimes desertion.

The CES study in Punjab showed that elderly widows who contracted HIV from their late husbands, hid this fact from their sons and daughters-in-law for the fear of being disowned and 'abandoned' by them. A volunteer at an HIV treatment centre mentioned the case of a single woman who would not take medication from the link centre in her village because she was afraid people would find out and that it would affect the prospects of her daughter's marriage. Further HIV+ widows are often accused by their parents-in-law for infecting their sons and are forced to leave their marital homes after their husband passes away. Typically if the child does not have HIV, the marital family will want to keep the child, but will otherwise refuse to care for the child.

Women who leave or flee from their homes mainly due to violent spouses and sometimes extreme economic distress, mostly stay alone on city streets, frequently falling prey to unremitting sexual violence. Further, the lack of sanitation facilities, healthcare and education for their children adds to their difficulties.

Sangrur is an area in Punjab that has witnessed a large number of farmer suicides. The reasons are many from cut in subsidies and low agricultural productivity to increasing debt. Women whose husbands committed suicide face multiple disadvantages that cause them profound psychological distress. As they struggle to overcome the loss of a loved one, these women are blamed for abetting suicide—stigmatised as 'suicide widows', burdened with the responsibility of relieving the family of debt, expected to work in the fields and at home and raise their dependents. The police often do not register a case of death but further harass the women by denying compensation in the absence of a death certificate. Despite a Supreme Court order that mandates compensation for families of farmers who committed suicide after 2000, a woman had received compensation eight years too late, that too in the run-up to elections.

In some states where ethnic conflict is rife and the army is in conflict with separatist groups, categories such as 'half-widows' have emerged as a manifestation of the poignant predicament of women whose husbands have gone missing. These are women whose husbands were picked up by security forces, and then 'disappeared.' The women do not know if they are dead (eliminated by security forces) or alive (in custody) to return one day. Kashmir and Manipur are states where several years of conflict have created many *de facto* women heads of households. Their singleness is contested and they cannot claim their entitlements as 'single' women.

Similarly women who survive 'natural disasters' are often in precarious positions and their varied situations may not be accounted for by policy makers. For example, after the 2004 Tsunami in Tamil Nadu, some women became the *de facto* heads of their households since their husbands were critically injured in the disaster. The NGOs working with widows however did not consider these women eligible for aid. Like many state policies, the NGOs prioritised *de jure* women heads of households and neglected the *de facto* ones (see Gandhi, 2010).[11]

Apart from these glaring disadvantages, single women face substantial social pressure and condemnation in everyday life. Neighbours and family members constantly raise questions about their activities, even if it is to attend self-help groups or meetings of the single women's *sangathans*. People also tend to pass comments if they wear colourful clothes or jewellery, or if a man comes to a single woman's house. They face constant harassment from men, who regard them as an easy target.

To an extent, such forms of discrimination have been internalised by single women and many do not feel societal pressures. Others said that wearing white clothing, which is associated with widowhood, constantly reminded them of their husband's death, leading to guilt and depression. However, some younger women said that they followed the restrictions around dressing and jewellery because of fears about what the family and community would say if they chose not to.

While most widowed women agree that the restrictions on their participation in marriages is unfair, particularly since the same does not apply to widowed men, very few have been able to challenge these norms and participate in their children's marriages. Most single women, and not just widows, reported that during weddings, festivals and other social functions, if invited, they were not given the same respect and dignity as others.

There is also substantial inequality between men and women on the question of remarriage as well. While it is generally acceptable for a divorced or separated man to remarry, women who do so face a lot of social censure. Most single women reported that they would find it difficult to marry again, even if they wanted to do so. However, Dalit and tribal single women, and particularly widows, generally have greater freedom to remarry than their upper-caste counterparts. In some states there are regressive practices such as the '*chaadardalna*', also known as '*chadarandazi*' ritual in Punjab whereby widows are forced to marry their brothers-in-law.[12] This is done largely to prevent the widow from claiming her share in the property of her late husband's family.

As a consequence of this societal rejection and control, single women experience extreme economic distress and credit unworthiness. Very few single women we spoke to had assets like land or a share in family property. As women point out, having to earn one's own money, most often in the absence of assets and without any support in the form of a pension or BPL ration card, means that money is always tight, and this also forms the basis for other kinds of vulnerabilities and exclusions.

While there may be no explicit discrimination against single women joining a micro credit collective, their inability, without a steady income or assets, to regularly contribute to the pool excludes such single women in a practical sense. This drives them into the hands of extorting moneylenders, which creates a further cycle of debt. Often the women take loans from people in the village for small expenses and then work as daily wage employees to pay them off; they don't have to pay interest on this amount if they are doing housework. For large sums, they must approach the moneylender, who charges 10 per cent interest. Even if they have the same earning capacity as a man or a married woman, they find it more difficult to get a loan, as a consequence of lack of collateral in their name.

Single women often find themselves alone in their struggle, but if organised, it was observed that single women coped positively, that is, as members of *sangathans* or collectives that enabled them to recognise their oppression and offered them the acceptance, encouragement and motivation they were otherwise denied.

In this chapter we try to penetrate the multiple layers of oppression and resistance that surround the lives of single women in the Indian context, by employing intersectionality as a tool. Singleness impacts different women differently, depending on their socio-economic and cultural contexts. But we do not claim to have captured the complexity and diversity in its entirety. The categories used, such as 'dalit single', 'differently-abled single', 'aged single' and so on, were required to complicate singleness with other layers of disadvantage in the Indian society. We, however, realise that these intersectional categories are unstable and evolving, needing continuous review and challenge. In the following section, we try to understand how these vulnerabilities play out for different categories of singleness by bringing out the voices and experiences of the women themselves.

Stigmas of widowhood

Widows face the most severe forms of social stigma and discrimination from the family and the wider community across the states of Punjab, Assam and Gujarat included in the CES study. Traditional biases towards widows remain intact as they frequently continue to be held responsible for the death of their husbands. They are routinely subjected to the wrath of the community and blamed for any misfortune. The model of a chaste and subservient widow still dominates consciousness, denying them a life of dignity.[13]

Many widows cannot participate even in their children's marriage ceremonies since they are perceived as inauspicious. Instead, other relatives perform these ceremonies. Family members avoid seeing the widow's face before the beginning of a journey, wedding or other happy occasions. A woman related the story of her nephew, who saw her before he was about to leave for an interview and then rushed back into the house to be 'purified.' People also spit in the way of widows crossing the path and rebuke them for ruining the day.

In Rauni village in Khanna block, we met Pinder Kaur, a 42-year-old widow who was married 29 years ago and widowed six years later. She had two daughters and a son. The children had completed school. She had three brothers-in-law—one older and two younger. Her father-in-law divided the house into four parts and gave them a portion each, so she had a roof over her head. She brought up her children by sewing clothes for people in the village. She stitched salwar-kameez for women. Her son was training to be an electrician. She said that the village people helped with her daughters' weddings and gifted them clothes and utensils. Her brothers-in-law, however, were not helpful at all. They were drunkards and struggling to support their own families. They sold the flour mill they owned, and spent their money on drink. Her mother-in-law worked as a cook. Her brothers-in-law had been abusive towards her. Eleven years ago her younger brother-in-law got drunk and demanded money from her; he smashed her head with a glass bottle. She bled profusely and had to get 32 stitches on her head (the injury marks were still visible). The village people helped her by admitting her to the hospital. She was able to recover and live on due to the kindness of her neighbours, she said. There had been no state action to ameliorate her situation. She did not receive a widow's pension and had to stay on with her marital family but managed to get her daughters married.[14]

Tribal women in Gujarat and Assam said they were ill-treated, both in their natal and marital village, largely on account of property disputes, and were forced out when seen as a threat. Attempts to silence their claims to land and property often also led to arbitrary torture, violence and cold killings justified in the name of *dayani/dayanpratha* or 'witch-hunting', a superstitious social evil that has widespread social sanction in Assam and Gujarat. Women are publicly tortured by the community till they break down and are forced to admit to being a witch. The traumatised woman, if she is not lynched to death, is perforce displaced or compelled to migrate. The Partners for Law in Development (PLD) has published an important report on the targeting of women as witches.[15]

Widows are usually 'abandoned' both by their in-laws and adult children, who come to view them as a burden. Those who find some kind of support in either their children or their in-laws are mostly reduced to a living arrangement best described as 'adjacent living', sharing as little as possible of available resources.

Separated, divorced and 'abandoned' women

A woman in Sonitpur (Assam) who was separated from her husband said that she starves for 7–8 days every month. She earns Rs 50 in a day and can only afford rice and salt. She can't afford to eat meat or fish. If she ever skips work, she has nothing to take home to feed her daughter. On days she works in someone else's house, they give her the leftovers from their meals—she lies to them that she cannot eat it as it has too much chilli powder, just so she can save it and take it home to her daughter.

Women who are alone despite living spouses are even more discriminated against in a patriarchal society.[16] 'They are described as women "even more despised... in a twilight zone of neither being respectably married nor widowed—especially those who have themselves left their partners".'[17]

Many married women are victims of abuse, or tolerating violence, physical and mental cruelty, unable or under-confident to rescue themselves from such a situation.[18] The few women, who are able to muster the courage to escape such dehumanising conditions, rarely receive any support from the larger society or even their natal families. 'Parents are often unwilling to accept a married daughter who leaves her husband, and therefore, a woman is trapped having nowhere to go if she breaks ties with her husband's home.'[19] Some women, however, may altogether be deprived of choice if they are 'abandoned' by their husbands. Remarriage amongst such women is also rare as a consequence of the dictates of customary practices, which seek to control women's sexuality while allowing men free access to remarry for the sake of their progeny and lineage.[20] In some cases, women do not get remarried for fear of having to leave behind their children from the first marriage.

A Tiwa tribal woman in Assam, aged 35, looked older than her age. She separated from her husband after he married another woman, and used to work as a daily wager in the house across from her own. One day, in the absence of his wife and child, the owner of the house sexually assaulted her and made her pregnant. Five months later, when she was visibly pregnant, the villagers learnt of the incident and forced him to marry her. The night they were married, he and his first wife took her to the hospital and made her undergo an abortion. They would beat her and starve her, not allowing her to leave the house.

She bore this for seven months, until she finally managed to leave, and came home to her natal home. She works as a daily wager now and can support herself but her humiliation continues. When she passes by her ex-husband's house, his first wife and he spit at her and taunt her, encouraging others to do the same. They even filed a case against her for stealing their household utensils. Even her father and brothers blame her for what happened and ask her repeatedly to leave but as she is earning for herself, she has managed to remain in her natal home.

The ability of women to negotiate the option of a formal divorce and compensation is severely constrained by their unequal position within the family unit and the larger society as well as due to their marginal awareness of the court procedures and prohibitive litigation cost. Moreover, society at large continues to view divorced men and women differently, according vastly greater acceptance and freedom to the former.

One woman in Darrang, who had separated from her husband, shared that she earns between Rs 20 to Rs 100 a day and survives by working in the agricultural fields in the summer and raising chickens in the winter. She worked for 10 days straight before Eid to earn Rs 150 a day so she could buy clothes and sweets for her son and daughter. She borrows money for her medical expenses from some rich families who live nearby. She then works for them to pay off the debt.

Never-married women

Many of the women who remain single do so out of personal choice or as a consequence of family circumstances or a mixture of both.[21] The early death of parents and the need to educate younger siblings or to look after children of widowed siblings have also been identified as contributory factors. Irrespective of whether the reasons for their unmarried status are circumstantial or voluntary, these women are routinely condemned for defying the conventions of society.[22]

The status of both employed and unemployed never-married women is poor and characterised by insecurity. Employed women, despite their financial contributions, often perceive themselves to be a burden on their families. Women belonging to this group contribute a bulk of their earnings towards the maintenance of their families, reserving little for themselves.[23] Unemployed unmarried women on the other hand face more problems as a consequence of their financial dependence. They are made to feel like an economic burden and are often subjects of castigation and ill treatment. Outside the home, society either sees them as sexually available or socially unequal, or both.[24]

In Assam, a group of women who had remained single explained that it was a marked sense of responsibility towards family after the loss or illness of a parent or sibling that compelled them to discontinue schooling or higher education. Living either with their parents or brothers, they manage the affairs often as unacknowledged breadwinners of the house.

A woman, after a dominant-caste lover spurned her, spent her life educating her brothers but the brothers were ungrateful. A sense of betrayal and hurt among these women routinely demoralises them. Even if they so desire, thinking about marriage is not an option. 'There is a *right age* to marry. Once you cross that, society mocks you, they call you "*boodhi*" (old), "*besha*" (prostitute)!' said one woman.

Aged 30 years, a quarry worker in Assam was a victim of this socially prescribed 'right age.' Given the prevalence of child marriage in Assam, the young woman, who did not initially marry at 18, was later deemed unworthy of marriage altogether. Through her adolescent years, she had assumed responsibility of the natal family after her mother's death and had lived with her brother. The woman was deeply traumatised and expressed a wish to marry in order to escape the sexual violence her brother was inflicting on her.

Perception of Single Women in Public Policy and Planning[25]

Discussing the shadow that marriage casts on the well-being of single women in the context of the state of New York, Dubler (2003)[26] argues that single women have been traditionally excluded by law-makers and implementers of public policy since marriage is considered to be the most important marker of social respect and 'protection' for the women in that society. The state thus absolves itself from the responsibility of providing for single women.

While widows have received some attention in public policy from the earlier days of formal planning in India, other groups of single women scarcely found a mention in social policies until recently. Single women are largely constructed as 'vulnerable' or as 'women in distress' in policy language, depriving them of their agency and imagining them as passive recipients of state and societal charity. The Delhi government, for instance, has a scheme called the 'Delhi Pension Scheme to Women in Distress' (widows, divorced, separated, destitute, 'abandoned').[27] The monolithic construction of single women as 'vulnerable' and 'distressed' is in danger of becoming a tool to control women's lives and bodies by a paternalistic state. Even more tellingly, the Government of Delhi has another scheme for 'Widow Daughter Marriage'[28] with the stated aim of 'providing financial assistance to the poor widows for performing the marriage of their daughters (upto two daughters).' The emphasis is yet again on marriage as the defining institution of 'settling' women's lives.

In the same spirit, the early national plans were directed at single women perceived as eligible for welfare on account of their 'handicapped' status, that is, being outside the ambit of the family. Shelter homes, short stay homes, and measures for the rehabilitation of destitute women were some of the measures adopted for single women during this period.

A National Plan of Action for women was prepared in 1980, but this did not focus on single women as a separate category. Such schemes still only addressed the manifestations of the problem. Consequently, the impact of such efforts was limited and piecemeal.

In the aftermath of the 1984 riots, the state

announced death pensions to the widows of those who had died during the anti-Sikh riots. This was similar to the response of the state in the period immediately following Independence, when the state provided for the rehabilitation and training of the widows of men who had died during the Partition. The state thus conceived itself as having a responsibility to widows only if their husbands had been killed in conflict situations, i.e., situations in which the state was unable to protect its citizens.

The 1990s ushered in the neo-liberal era of economic reforms, which was accompanied by a discourse that championed the role of the market as being the most efficient in resolving economic problems of scarcity, and called for the retraction of the state from the economic and social spheres. Consequently, during this period the state's policy toward women also underwent a change and unlike the previous welfare model under which women's conditions was described as being handicapped and marginalised, under the neo-liberal discourse, women were encouraged to participate in the formal economy, but without any attempts to address the inequities of power in both the public sphere and private sphere that discouraged such participation. Simultaneously, the emphasis on the market economy also led to fiscal austerity—public spending on social sectors such as health, education, social welfare, poverty reduction programmes was reduced, as economic growth increasingly came to be equated with development. Spending on programmes benefiting women, in particular single women was drastically curtailed during this period.

Although the 12th Five Year Plan working group did acknowledge that the situation of women is diverse and touched upon the intersectionality of identity, it placed single women in the extremely 'deprived and vulnerable' group along with 'minorities, scheduled castes, scheduled tribes, including particularly vulnerable tribal groups, internally displaced groups, migrants, urban poor communities, women vulnerable to or victims of abuse, violence, exploitation, trafficking and commercial sex work, affected or infected by HIV/AIDs, single women, widows, the elderly, women with different abilities, among others' (p. 106). It failed to acknowledge that 'singleness' is a cross-cutting theme among all these different 'vulnerable' groups of women.

Similarly, patriarchy limits women's access to the legal justice system. Due to the fact that the police stations and courts are largely male-dominated

Box 1: Dalit Women and Panchayati Raj System in Punjab

The research team at the Centre for Equity Studies conducted a field study on the status of single women in rural Punjab, Gujarat and Assam. The primary fieldwork revealed that government schemes channelled through the panchayats failed to reach out to the most vulnerable group in the village—the Dalit single women. In most villages that were visited during fieldwork, these panchayats had Jat sarpanches who were not interested in changing the caste status-quo in the villages. During the Focus Group Discussions with Dalit women, several of them complained about oppression by the sarpanches and the other members of the panchayat. In Otala village of Khanna district, the researchers witnessed an argument between Dalit women and the Jat sarpanch on the matter of the non-payment of MNREGA wages over two months. The argument was non-conclusive since the sarpanch refused to acknowledge his lackadaisical approach and passed on the blame to the Block Development Officer (BDO).

Source: Field Report from Punjab by Agrima and Kanchan, CES

spaces, women, especially those who are single, feel constrained to visit these places. The multiple disadvantages of caste, religion and tribe work in this case too. For example, in the CES study on single women in Gujarat, the team of researchers found that Muslim women could hardly access the criminal justice system. While Muslims have generally faced more discrimination in Gujarat after the riots of 2002, being a woman, and especially one who is single, creates other barriers of access. Many of the divorced single women reported difficult battles in court in either securing a divorce itself, or consequent alimony payments. Muslim divorces are covered under Muslim personal law, where many women say religious leaders tend to side more with men.

The examples from Gujarat and Punjab show that multiple disadvantages lead to the exclusion of single women from social, economic, political and legal spaces. Male-led *panchayats*, *khap-panchayats* and *jamaats* tend to side with men and punish women as observed in different states in India. Dalit women face sexual exploitation and abuse from upper castes on a regular basis.

Budget 2015-16: An analysis of the Union Budget 2015–16 by the Centre for Budget and Governance Accountability (CBGA),[29] especially an assessment of the Gender Budget Statement (GBS) 2015–16 and the allocations to the Ministry of Women and Child Development (MWCD), reflects a reduced priority for women and withdrawal of several important schemes for women. Crucial schemes implemented by the MWCD have either been withdrawn or have witnessed steep declines. These schemes include the Women's Helpline; assistance to states for implementation of the Domestic Violence Act, 2005; One Stop Crisis Centre (meant to be set up in each district); and the scheme for Restorative Justice for Rape Victims; among others.

Meagre honorariums for Anganwadi workers, among them several single women, deprive them of the opportunity to live a life of dignity. With the proposed change in pattern of cost-sharing between the centre and states in the Union Budget 2015–16, the Integrated Child Development Services Scheme, among other schemes, has been transferred to the states. In effect, this would mean that once the Union Government meets the infrastructural needs under ICDS through capital expenditure (say, on construction of Anganwadi Centres, etc.), the recurring or revenue expenditure (on honorarium to Anganwadi workers), which would constitute the

Box 2: Appraisal of Schemes and Benefits Available to Single Women.

There are no major central schemes for widows in particular or single women in general. The only specialised scheme is the Swadhar Scheme run by the Ministry of Women and Child Development.

1. Swadhar Scheme

'It is a shelter based scheme and caters to the requirements of diverse groups of women in distress, including destitute widows. The package of services made available under the scheme include provision of food, clothing, shelter, health care, counselling and legal support, social and economic rehabilitation through education awareness generation and skill up gradation and behavioural training.'[31]

The training offered to women in these homes however is squarely focused on tailoring and cooking (skills traditionally associated with women), and women are not being taught other skills. As per the report of the MWCD, 2007, the number of such homes across the country was 208—not even one per district.[32] Besides, these homes are unevenly concentrated in very few states like Andhra Pradesh and Orissa.[33]

2. Short Stay Homes

'These homes are meant primarily for those women and girls who are either exposed to moral danger or are victims of family discord. The scheme focuses on women and girls from disadvantaged and underprivileged groups. Case files are developed for all women seeking refuge in these homes. Services offered in the home include medical care, psychiatric treatment, casework services, occupational therapy, social facilities of adjustment, educational, vocational, recreational and cultural activities etc., according to individual requirements.[34]

According to a study conducted by the Centre for Market Research and Social Development, the functioning of the scheme is also crippled by the untimely release of funds, dated financial norms and ineffective monitoring.

3. National Family Benefit Scheme

The national family benefit scheme benefits widows who possess BPL cards by providing them with a one-time cash assistance of Rs 10,000 upon the death of the primary breadwinner. 'This scheme provides immediate relief to those who have lost their husbands and are suddenly left to support their families.'[35]

The cumbersome process of application, however, limits access to the scheme. 'The bereaved family is required to present several supporting documents (including a death certificate), which are hard to obtain.'[36] It also suffers from abysmally low levels of implementation.

4. National Old Age Pension Scheme

'The scheme is available to all persons above the age of 65 years. Under the NOAPS, the central government contributes Rs 200 per pensioner per month and the states are urged to contribute an equal amount.'[37] As per the guidelines the beneficiaries are supposed to get benefits regularly each month before the 7th of the month.[38]According to the 9th report of the Supreme Court Commissioners,[39] many states including Andhra Pradesh, Bihar, Orissa, Jammu & Kashmir, Assam, Madhya Pradesh, Uttar Pradesh and Chhattisgarh are currently paying a monthly pension of less than Rs 400 per month.

Evidence suggests that NOAPS has benefited sections of the vulnerable population, in the data obtained from the Ministry of Rural Development: in 1998–99, 30 per cent of the women benefited while in 1999–2000, 36.7 per cent of the women benefited. A gender breakup also indicates that 13 states had 30 per cent or more coverage of women in the scheme in 1998–99 and 1999–2000.

However, those women who receive an old-age pension are often denied widow pension. This greatly affects the capacity of widows who are also heads of households to support themselves and their families.

5. Widow Pension

Widow pension schemes have been functional in India since the 1960s. In 2002, the Government of India introduced a new scheme, the Indira Gandhi National Widow Pension scheme, which increased the amount of financial assistance given to widows to Rs 400 per month. This scheme covers widows between the age group of 40–64 years, from families with incomes below the poverty line. Like the old age pension scheme, the centre contributes 50 per cent of the funds, i.e., Rs 200, with the rest being contributed by the states.[40]

A 2007 study, *Destitution of Widow in Rajasthan* by the Budget Analysis Rajasthan Centre, found that almost 50 per cent of BPL widows did not get pensions.[41]

Till 2001, four of the north-eastern states had failed to introduce the scheme. In other states, a ceiling has been imposed on the maximum number of person to be covered under the scheme.[42] Tamil Nadu and Kerala, however, have been unique in this respect, by totally eliminating the ceiling.[43]

It is undeniable that procedural bottlenecks prevent women from accessing welfare schemes they are entitled to and most states lack the political and bureaucratic will to execute pro-women programmes.[44]

Though it has the lowest widow pension, the Kerala government is among the first state governments to have introduced an exclusive Single Women Benefit Scheme for destitute and marginalised widows, separated and divorced women, unwed mothers and unmarried women belonging to the BPL category. The scheme, run by the state's Social Welfare Department/Kerala State Women's Development Corporation, provides a one-time grant-in-aid of Rs 10,000 to enable women to establish small enterprises.[45] Goa's Dayanand Social Security Scheme offers a pension of Rs 1,000 to senior citizens, the disabled, and single women through electronic transfers to bank accounts. An amount of Rs 2000 per year under the Himachal Pradesh government's education scheme called the Mother Teresa Matri Sabal Yojana, for children (5–14 years) of impoverished mothers, is available for all divorced, widowed, separated and 'deserted' women.[46]

6. National Rural Employment Guarantee Scheme

MGNREGA 2005 guarantees 100 days' paid work each year for every rural household whose adult members volunteer to do unskilled manual work. In this way, it envisages improving the livelihood security of rural households.

For single women in particular, this act is extremely critical. It guarantees statutory minimum wages, and ensures better and more dignified working conditions. For single women, the availability of work also means that they no longer have to wait or migrate in search of work. Widows who are no longer getting widow pension now have a way of sustaining themselves. Consequently, NREGA has been envisaged as a gender-sensitive scheme which allows for crèche facilities on worksites, and 'insists that one-third of all participants are women, and wages do not discriminate between the sexes.'[47] The act also ensures the participation of single women by recognising a single person as a 'household.'

In spite of the provisions aimed at improving the participation of women, the MGNREGA survey 2008 revealed large variations in the participation of women across states.[48] The overall participation of women in NREGA was found to be only 32 per cent. The survey also found that women are often deterred from attending Gram Sabhas, which are responsible for the implementation of the projects.[49] Since one job card is issued per household, typically in the name of the male member, to whom wages are usually paid, single women who are a part of a larger household are not provided with an independent job card, and are often denied access to their own wages.[50]

Women are usually the first ones to be turned away, required to work in pairs or refused employment if they come to work wearing a burqa.[51] Women are also found to face routine harassment at the worksite. The NREGA survey was also unable to identify the operation of even a single crèche facility in the worksites. The lack of these facilities are particularly crippling for women, especially for those with infants who cannot be left behind for long hours.[52]

In addition to the abovementioned factors, women are also paid less than men and the schedule standard of rates makes women's work invisible. 'While the extent of digging and soil conditions forms the basis of the payment for men's work, the carrying of load, its weight, the underfoot conditions and its distance do not figure in wage calculations.'[53]

7. Targeted public distribution system

The targeted distribution system entitles all BPL, AAY and APL cardholders to 35 kg of rice/wheat at subsidised rates. The Below Poverty Line (BPL) families are identified by the state governments and about 40 per cent of these families receive an additional subsidy under the Antodaya Anna Yojana (AAY) which entitles them to the same quantity of food grains but at roughly half the price of that which is sold to the other BPL families.[54]

However, the TPDS is a household-based scheme and that is obviously problematic, as it does not address intra-household inequities; the ration card is usually in the name of the husbandand the wife is not given another card in the event of a separation.[55]

Despite the Supreme Court order which mandates the inclusion of widows and other single women with no support in the scheme, the selection of beneficiaries continues to be arbitrary. States such as Bihar, Delhi, Gujarat, Jammu & Kashmir, Maharashtra, Uttarakhand and West Bengal have more than 1 lakh undistributed cards. West Bengal is the worst with more than 5 lakh undistributed AAY cards. Kerala is perhaps the lone state to have included all female-headed households in the BPL list alongside other vulnerable groups such as the fishing community and all SC and ST households.[56]

8. Integrated Child Development Scheme

Health care, nutrition and pre-school education of children upto the age of six as well as the nutrition of adolescent girls, and pregnant and nursing women are part of this programme flagship scheme.[57]

A six-state study on inclusion within the ICDS discovered that not a single women recipient attributed to these rations any role in improving their own nutrition. Dry rations that they carry home from the state are simply consumed by the rest of the family.

Moreover, like other government programmes, the nutritional requirements of the mother are of secondary importance. Besides, the allocations to ICDS in the Union Government Budget 2015–16 stand at Rs 8,754 crore as against Rs 18,391 crore in BE 2014–15.[58]

bulk of expenditure, will have to be provided for by the state governments.[30]

There have, however, been some positive measures in public policy in the context of single women. The inclusion of single women in the 12th Five Year Plan, despite its limitations, represented an important attempt to create space for single women and foreground their entitlements, without subsuming them under the heteronormative family category. Creating a quota for them, reserving a certain percentage of jobs for single women under centrally sponsored schemes (Indira Awas Yojana and Mahatma Gandhi National Rural Employment Guarantee Scheme), provisioning of legal aid and establishing and strengthening federations of single women at the block and district levels were among a few significant suggestions in the Plan.[59]

Two Expert Committees were appointed by the Government of India to suggest ways to identify vulnerable households eligible for state assistance. One set up by the Ministry of Rural Development under the Chairmanship of Dr N.C. Saxena critiqued the earlier approaches of conducting the rural BPL census (in the years 1991 and 2001) and suggested the 'automatic inclusion' of households headed by single women in the BPL list. The other set up by the Planning Commission and chaired by Prof Hashim to recommend a detailed methodology for families living below poverty line in urban areas made an identical suggestion for urban poverty.

The National Social Assistance Programme (NSAP) across many states includes a pension for widows but does not provide it for other groups of single women. A Task Force chaired by Mihir Shah corrected this with the following recommendations.[60]

- Single women and divorced/abandoned/separated women face the same kind of discrimination as widows especially stigmatisation leading to social exclusion and imposition of restrictions on socio-economic development. Therefore, the pension may be extended to single, never-married women above 40 years and divorced/abandoned/separated women above 18 years.
- In addition there are women whose husbands are 'missing' / disappeared but not formally proved to be dead. Such 'half widows' should be treated at par with widows. In such cases the 7 years, condition for 'missing' / disappeared persons should be reduced to 3 years. It must be noted that cause of disappearance / missing / death of the husband shall not be a reason for denial of pension.
- Pension to divorced/separated women (18 years and above) and never-married women (40 years and above) in below-poverty-line households will benefit 12 lakh beneficiaries with additional expenditure of Rs 428 crore (assuming that on par with widow pensions, the pension amount will be Rs 300 per month until the age of 80 years, and Rs 500 per month thereafter).

The government, in a reply to the Standing Committee on Social Justice and Empowerment, has said that it has accepted these recommendations 'with certain modifications'.[61]

Similarly the MNREGA notifications issued by the Ministry of Rural Development, GoI in December 2013 discuss the inclusion of single women in productive work. For instance, point number 15 of the MNREGA notification (p. 10) suggests that: 'Priority shall be given to women in such a way that at least one third of the beneficiaries shall be women who have registered and requested for work. Efforts to increase participation of single women and the disabled shall be made.'

While this point calls for greater participation of single women in the programme, it does not suggest any concrete measure for the same.

The Programme Advisory Group of the Ministry of Rural Development recommended that:

(i) The MNREGA should focus on equity, including women-headed households, single women who are widowed, never-married women above the age of 35, and divorced/abandoned/separated women above 18 years. These should also include women whose husbands are 'missing' / disappeared but not formally proved to be dead.

(ii) Every adult single woman and her dependents, and adult disabled person and his/her dependants should be treated as a separate household for purposes of entitlement to a job card, even if they share a common kitchen with other members of a household who have a job card.

(iii) Single women, aged persons and persons with disability coming to work on common worksites would be given a choice of being part of any workers gang at the site and/or could form their own collectives at work. They should also be given preference in managing work site attendance, facilities such as provisioning of drinking water and running the child care centres.

The National Food Security Act 2013 contains an important provision (Section 13(1)) which designates the eldest adult woman member of a household to be the head of household for purposes of the Act. This is important to protect the rights of separated women, as well as single women-headed households.

The Justice Verma Committee (JVC) Report was significant for its recommendations for preferential opportunities for single women within wider concerns of rehabilitation for destitute women, overhaul of 'nariniketan' or shelters for women, skill development and livelihood opportunities for their growth.[62] The Report also proposes a 'Bill of Rights', outlining constitutional guarantees for women. This enlists a host of sensitive and practical rights with respect to securing bodily integrity, dignity, sexual autonomy of women; every woman's right to free education till under-graduate level; freedom to marry of their choice; and right to access housing, nutritious food and transportation facilities.

Legal Debates

The Constitution of India, and the Convention on Elimination of All Forms of Discrimination against Women (CEDAW), which India ratified in 1993, firmly enshrine the principle of gender equality—to enable and oblige the state to proactively adopt positive discrimination measures in favour of women to overcome the multiple disadvantages they face.

Despite these constitutional safeguards in India's legal framework, perhaps nowhere is the inequality so stark as in the case of the inheritance and divorce and maintenance laws, which have a strong bearing on the legal rights of single women. Most personal laws, be it Hindu, Muslim, Christian or Parsi, are inherently unequal and discriminate against women.

Both, in Hindu and Muslim law, especially in the Northwest states, 'women are still seriously disadvantaged in relation to both agricultural land and joint family property'.[63] These laws also do not recognise a woman's right to marital property for divorced and separated women.

Deininger et al.[64] examined the impact of the Hindu Succession Act (1994) on the status of women in India and concluded that the HSA significantly increased women's likelihood to inherit land, although it did not fully compensate for the underlying gender inequality. However, other analysis of the success of HSA shows that not much has changed for Hindu women in terms of inheritance even after the significant amendment in the year 2005 since it only entitles women to ancestral properties and not their fathers' self-acquired ones. A report by the Times of India[65] provides the barriers that exist for women to claim their property rights. The article argues that Muslim daughters are better-off than the Hindu ones since they can claim half of the share in the family property including father's self-acquired properties. But in reality Muslim daughters may also forgo their rights to maintain cordiality within their families.

In a survey undertaken by Kirti Singh on the economic status of separated and divorced women, it was learnt that women were disillusioned with the legal system and the police. Singh finds that accessing the limited right to maintenance is often fraught with difficulties for women. When awarded, maintenance is usually not substantial but a symbolic amount paid haphazardly, or not paid at all. The survey found that most women had no knowledge or documents in their possession about the husband's assets or income, when bylaw they were expected to prove their husband's income.

Husbands continue to escape the obligation of payment of maintenance and of disclosing their incomes. Additionally, in Indian law (under Sub-section of Section 125 of CrPC), maintenance is made dependent on the conduct of the wife and not viewed as an entitlement that accrues to a woman because of her past contribution to the marital home.[66]Allegations of adultery and immorality can be hurled against women, which can challenge the legitimacy of women's claims to maintenance.[67]

Under the criminal procedure code, Section 125 says that no woman can be entitled to receive an allowance if she is living in adultery.[68] However, such considerations, in determining maintenance support, are regarded as invalid in many countries of the world such as Canada.

Aspects such as inordinately lengthy delays, insensitive divorce procedures, inability of the judiciary to view maintenance as an amount that can substantially assist the woman and her children after separation, overburdened and fewer number of family courts, discretionary powers of the courts to grant maintenance, burden of proving husband's income and linking of maintenance with custody and morality issues, special problems of women from minority communities governed by patriarchal customary laws,[69] are barriers to accessing legal justice.

Another ploy, which is a barrier in availing maintenance, is the husband's refusal to validate the marriage. This not only results in the loss of maintenance for the woman, but also her status as a 'wife', and thus renders her vulnerable to scorn and social stigma as a 'mistress'.[70] Since the law only recognises monogamous marriages, this especially disadvantages women trapped in polygamous relationships. Agnes argues that in cases of bigamy, since the husband could escape conviction after years of litigation, refusal to validate the marriage was particularly crippling for the first wife in case she is unable to furnish a proof of Brahmanical ritual ceremonies with regard to the husband's second marriage.[71] In contrast, it is difficult to refute Muslim marriages, which are reflected as a contract in the form of a signed *nikahnama.*

The rights of women who were duped by men into sexual relationships with a false promise of marriage were further eroded in a parochial 2010 Supreme Court judgement by Justice Markandey Katju, who, while denying a woman her due maintenance also excluded women in polygamous relationships from the purview of the Protection of Women from Domestic Violence Act, which had thoughtfully included the term 'marriage like relationship' to offer relief to 'women who were denied rights when their husbands pleaded that they are not "wives," as they already have a valid marriage subsisting'. The judge had held that: 'If a man has a "keep" whom he maintains financially and uses mainly for sexual purpose and/or as a servant, it would not, in our opinion, be a relationship in the nature of marriage... (paras 34–35).'[72]

Apart from its content, the use of the sexist term 'keep' was regrettable. In another judgement, however, two other judges [Justices Ranjana Desai and A.K. Sikhri] breathed life into the spirit of the Constitution when they, in 2014, upheld the right of a Hindu woman who had been duped into a bigamous marriage and thwarted the attempt of her husband to subsequently deny her maintenance.[73] Yet, this judgement is limited in its application since it only covers women who have been 'duped' into a bigamous marriage and does not take into consideration any other situations, circumstances or contexts of the second wife. The law does not recognise the multiplicity of the forms of marital or marital-like relations that exist in society. The burden lies squarely on the second wife to prove that she has been 'duped' into marriage. Moreover, it often becomes difficult for the second wife to prove in court that a 'valid' marriage ceremony has taken place.

Agnes hails the above judgement, which further cited 'as a classical example the journey from *Shah Bano* to *Shabana Bano*,' which guaranteed post-divorce maintenance rights of Muslim women by carving out new sets of rights within established principles of Muslim personal law. Such favourable developments within Muslim personal law have been reflected in other rulings (*Daniel Latifi, Shabana Bano, Shamim Ara*) as well.[74]

According to Kirti Singh (2013), it should not be the responsibility of the wives to fight another round of litigation to retrieve maintenance once the courts have ordered it. A special fund to disburse maintenance amounts and an enforcement agency to recover maintenance from husbands should be established; other reforms should seek to shift the burden of proof on the man to prove his income and assets and amend the law to curb the judiciary's discretion in the award of maintenance amounts.[75] 'Apart from getting a token maintenance, married and separated women in India have no ownership rights to the home and assets accumulated during the marriage' through the monetary and non-monetary contribution of both partners in the household.[76] That the productive nature of women's household work remains unrecognised both in law and in the household deems her to a subordinate position, which is most often the cause for domestic violence and women's marginal decision-making power. Working women too are similarly vulnerable and allow their spouses and in-laws to dictate how their salaries are spent.[77]

Moreover, after separation, women become asset-less, since most of the marital property is in the husband's name.[78] 'The right to divorce without a right to equal division of marital property is violative of a woman's right to equality and results in further oppressing her.'[79]

Kirti Singh advocates a Community of Property legislation for India in which marital property becomes common property to be divided between spouses in diverse ways. However, in an impoverished context like India, there may be no property/income to divide and a woman upon separation/desertion/divorce may be left destitute. 'In situations where the woman is "deserted" by a man who disappears or who becomes alcoholic or is chronically unemployed, it becomes impossible to obtain maintenance from him'.[80] Thoughtful and adequate social security support in such situations becomes imperative to enable single women and their children to live a life with dignity. It is therefore critical that women's economic rights are written in law so that denial of such rights can be challenged as violation of the law of the land.[81] Another factor that needs to be considered is that although 'irretrievable breakdown of marriage' has not been recognised in the Hindu marriage Act, 1955, but the court has been increasingly using this as an argument for providing divorce, such as in Dastane vs. Dastane[82] and in Varalakshmi vs. N.V. Hanumanth Rao.[83]

This concept needs to be understood in greater detail, particularly in the Indian context. The government has, on several occasions, attempted to introduce 'irretrievable breakdown of marriage' as a valid ground for divorce under Section 13 of the

Hindu Marriage Act, 1955, such as in 2010,[84] and the Maharashtra government in 2012.[85] If accepted in their bare form, these laws would abdicate men of the civil and criminal consequences of the violence inflicted on their wives by citing an irretrievable breakdown of marriage as a ground for being granted divorce.[86] In such a context, the concept of 'Community of Property' as advocated by Kirti Singh becomes even more relevant. It has also been urged by the court in B.P. Achala Anand vs. S. Appi Reddy[87] for the legislature to bring in a law to protect women's interest in matrimonial property.

In her compelling scholarship, Barooah highlights that women whose spouses leave them are entitled under the Hindu Adoption and Maintenance Act, 1956, to live separately from the husband without forgoing their right to maintenance. But for a divorced woman to get alimony from the husband for herself and her dependents is difficult. Most often the husband wants to shirk the responsibility or he is financially constrained to make regular payments.[88]

Recommendations

The recommendations for improving the status of single women are based on the premise that the central focus of the state of viewing marriage as the quintessential unit of society needs to change and women need to be identified as an individual category, rather than in relation to others. We therefore challenge the notion of the patriarchal set-up of the modern state. Consequently, many of these recommendations would be applicable to all women, but are particularly important for single women.

1. Focusing on schemes for *de facto* women heads of households in the realm of policy

The policy focus in social security schemes, especially the pension schemes, has been the BPL widows. The policy needs to be expanded to include other varied groups of single women, including also those whose husbands are ill and invalid. Thus, policy has to look beyond heteronormative societal and familial assumptions and reach out to other women who have been neglected in this scheme of things. The good practice established in the National Food Security Act of recognising the oldest adult woman in the household as the head of household should be universalised. In that case for instance, if a woman is separated from a living husband, the ration card or other household entitlement would remain with the woman, rather than with the man as is the case otherwise.

2. Prioritising access to land and credit for women to pursue shared livelihood opportunities

Independent land rights continue to be important for women's right to live with dignity. Given that the large population of rural women in India are dependent on agriculture for their existence, working on land without rights increases their vulnerability to poverty.[89] This is particularly relevant for the category of single women as economic deprivation and lack of assets, as seen above, hugely impacts their societal and familial status.

Bina Aggarwal urges us to shift our focus from just non-land related income-generation activity to facilitating an environment in which women collectives are engaged in community-based farming. With its imperative focus on poor, rural women, such an approach reserves the potential to revive land reform, joint farming and community cooperation. Successful examples include the Deccan Development Society's (DDS) women-led collective farming initiative in Andhra Pradesh. They even prioritise financial support for single women. Kerala government's community-centred, women centred, poverty-reduction programme, Kudumbashree, is another noteworthy example.

3. State and civil society should recognise the merit in outreach and mobilisation activities and budget for it

Organising and collectivising women is an important act of solidarity. It rouses in women a political consciousness about their rights that enables them to combat violence and injustice. As observed during the CES fieldwork, single women's claim to their rights become strengthened when voiced through collectives, especially owing to their lack of other forms of social support. The act and effort, with dignity and respect, of organising women around issues of shared concerns must be distinguished from micro-credit driven Self Help Groups (SHGs), where economic concerns take primacy over women's personal suffering. Organisations like the National Forum for Single Women's Rights, MahilaSamakhya (Assam), networks for persons with disability and HIV AIDS have reached out to the most marginalised individuals. The state governments should also consider collaborating with women's organisations in their jurisdictions to further reach out to single women in India.

4. Eliminating official requirement of father's/husband's name

Single women and their dependants are often excluded from accessing government programmes, or suffer humiliation, because all official documents require a person to specify her/his father's name or husband's name. This especially burden's single mothers and their children, or separated women. This requirement should be replaced by the requirement to specify only one's mother's name.

5. Institutionalising the practice of gender budgeting[90]

It has long been recognised that public policies, rather than being 'gender neutral', need to address gender inequalities in a purposeful and direct manner. There is a necessity of institutionalising the practice of gender budgeting to address women's specific vulnerabilities within each ministry, rather than just the Ministry of Women and Child Development focused solely on SHGs as the only transformative model.

An intersectional understanding of multiple disadvantages that single women face necessitates that schemes/laws and allocations are not gender neutral but specially focused on women who face crippling socio-cultural, economic and political discriminations not only because of their gender but also because of their identity as Muslim, Dalit, tribal, disabled, transgender women. To ensure scrupulous implementation of women-related welfare services and laws, the governments should effect better allocation of funds, utilisation of resources and robust monitoring mechanisms (such as gender audits, not just of the schemes and policies specifically targeted at women, but also those which indirectly affect the status of women in general, and single women specifically).

6. Removal of barriers that deny women access to welfare services

Most single women in this study described corrupt, profiteering and gender-discriminating panchayats, local authorities and police/judicial officers as the greatest barriers to accessing basic services, presumably due to the lack of 'family' backing. This obliges central ministries and state governments to collaborate with civil society organisations to organise human rights and gender sensitisation trainings for these service providers as well as state-level officials. Service providers should be sensitised to recognising single women as independent head-of-households, to be provided (price indexed PDS, ICDS, pension) entitlements in their name.

7. Adult education, legal aid cells and awareness campaigns

Single women often forgo their share in property and are unwilling to move court in the case of divorce and maintenance claims. While on one hand this is rooted in socio-cultural propriety that discourages them from asserting their rights, on the other hand, it stems from none to very low levels of literacy, lack of adult education and minimal awareness of formal court/government procedures for accessing justice/entitlements. To make quality education available for young, middle-aged and old single women who have not had the opportunity to learn, the government needs to deepen investment in adult education facilities which can robustly assist women in qualifying for tests conducted at existing Open Schools/IGNOU and pave the road for greater learning.[91] District legal aid services departments should endeavour to constitute legal aid cells and hold awareness camps for single women jointly facilitated with women's groups and local NGOs.

8. Ensuring substantive political participation of women in Panchayati Raj Institutions (PRIs)

In the experience of the National Forum for Single Women's Rights, PRIs have a great potential to present women with a platform to challenge and change existing power relations. More often than not, women's active and democratic participation in local politics stems from their experience in grassroots advocacy with *sangathans*. There is a need to actively address the host of difficult challenges elected women face—they are routinely discriminated, harassed by local elites and dominant castes, and given token representation, but not actual decision-making powers. Further, state amendments requiring a minimum eligibility criteria, such as a minimum educational qualification[92] or the two-child limit,[93] for contesting elections disparately impact women who have little to no say in these matters, further weakening their political agency.

9. Right to marital property, inheritance, maintenance: the need to implement a Uniform Civil Code[94]

Legislations that seek to alter unequal and patriarchal social relations need more proactive implementation to bear results on the ground. The state needs to encourage property ownership and inheritance rights of women. Unjust aspects of personal laws that deal with marriage, divorce, maintenance and inheritance have to be challenged and amended to secure equal rights for women. It is important to bring in legislative amendments so as to ensure the right to maintenance and property to women who may not be legally qualified, by virtue of not having a 'valid' marriage in law or through other disqualifications as mentioned above.

10. Eliminating the practice of witch-hunting

State governments of Bihar, Rajasthan, Jharkhand and Chhattisgarh have laws outlawing this custom, however, the state of Assam and Gujarat, where this custom receives widespread social sanction, no laws exist to eliminate the practice. This should compel state governments to put in place legislations that identify and hold accountable the perpetrators of the crime. The state should also provide affected women with access to hospitals, rehabilitation and compensation as well as livelihood opportunities.

11. Survivors of ethnic/communal violence

This requires adequate training and payment to state police, legal authorities, concerned government departments so that they are capable of responding to these situations. As has been recorded through various studies, compensation is provided to survivors of mass violence often in an ad-hoc manner,[95] and often not as an entitlement but ex-gratia payment, significantly crippling the situations of single women who are survivors of such violence. Receiving large monetary compensation immediately after the violence which may have killed not just the woman's husband but also many other family members often becomes a reason the woman being harassed, especially by her husband's family members, in order to access the large compensation amounts. An alternate could be to institute a monthly pension for each family member who is killed.

12. Gaps in data related to single women's issues[96]

The availability of appropriate, reliable and timely data is critical to processes of informed decision-making and determining effective policy choices, plans, budgets, schemes as well as their implementation. Large-scale surveys like NSSO and pan-India household surveys on employment and unemployment inaccurately capture and reflect women's workforce participation, thus under-reporting their contribution to the economy and making them statistically invisible as workers. There is a need, therefore, to not only identify single women as a separate category and to map their contribution to the workforce, but also to research their particular vulnerabilities for future policy measures.

Endnotes

1. This chapter derives substantially from a major year-long study undertaken by the Centre for Equity Studies (CES), New Delhi, on the lived experiences of single women from three Indian states, namely, Punjab, Gujarat and Assam. The research was undertaken in close collaboration with the extraordinary collective of single women in many Indian states, the National Forum for Single Women's Rights, or the Rashtriya Ekal Nari Adhikar Manch. The fieldwork for this study was undertaken in 2013 and the findings analyse the personal and group narratives of economically impoverished and socially disadvantaged single women. Some life histories are also drawn from a CES study *Living with Hunger*. This chapter also learns from an earlier study undertaken also by the National Forum (2011) on the status of low-income single women in India, undertaken by single women themselves as researchers, titled 'Are We Forgotten Women?'
2. Martha Nussbaum (2000), 'Women's Capabilities and Social Justice' in *Journal of Human Development*, 1:2
3. The 2014 issue of the *India Exclusion Report* however, has a chapter dedicated to transgender people and this Report has a chapter on 'devadasis' which will touch upon issues that relate to the category of sex-workers.
4. National Forum for Single Women's Rights (2011), 'Are we forgotten Women? A Study on the Status of Low Income Single Women in India'
5. National Forum for Single Women's Rights (2009),'Our Lives, Our Struggles'
6. A. Dhar (2012), 'Good news for single women in 12th plan' in *The Hindu*. Accessed here: http://www.thehindu.com/news/national/good-news-for-single-women-in-12th-plan/article3867569.ece
7. J. Reynolds and M. Wetherell, (2003), 'The discursive climate of singleness: the consequences for women's negotiation of a single identity' in *Feminism & Psychology*, 13:4, pp. 489–510.
8. G.V. Fuguitt, D.L. Brown and C.L. Beale (1989), *'Rural and Small Town America,* New York: Russell Sage Foundation
9. In her book, *Single Women in Assamese Hindu Society,* Jeuti Barooah (1993) classifies the causes of dissolution of marriage into bigamy, adultery, cruelty, unwed motherhood, disappearance of husband and unknown. We found this a useful break-up of causes. Her book also discusses cases where adultery on the part of the woman led to a broken marriage.
10. H. Mander, M. Kumaran, A. Rai, and A. Tulsyan, (2013), *Living with Hunger,* New Delhi: National Book Trust
11. Kanchan Gandhi (2010), 'Identity Politics, Power and Resistance in Disaster Response: A Case Study of the 2004 Tsunami Relief, Rehabilitation and Recovery in Tamil Nadu' (PhD thesis), National University of Singapore. Accessed here: http://scholarbank.nus.edu.sg/handle/10635/22061
12. S.C. Bhatt and G.K. Bhargava (2006), *Land and*

*the people of Indian States and Union Territories: Punjab,*Volume 22, New Delhi: Kalpaz Publications

13. Gayatri Sahgal (unpublished), 'Social Protection and Single Women', New Delhi: Centre for Equity Studies
14. Kanchan Gandhi (2015), 'It is Better to Die Than to Live Like This: Experiences of economic denial and violence among widowed women in rural Punjab, in Anidita Dutta (ed.), *Re Orienting Gender Geographies of Resistance, Agency, Violence and Desire in Asia,* New Delhi: RK Books
15. Partners for Law in Development (2012), 'Women as Witches: Trends, prevalence and the law in northern, western, eastern and north-eastern regions of India', New Delhi: Partners for Law in Development . Accessed at http://pldindia.org/wp-content/uploads/2013/02/WH-Report-.pdf
16. Harsh Mander (2012), 'Lone Warriors' in *The Hindu,* 6 February. Accessed at http://www.thehindu.com/todays-paper/tp-features/tp-sundaymagazine/lone-warriors/article2933814.ece
17. Kirti Singh(2013), *Separated and Divorced Women in India: Economic rights and entitlements,* New Delhi: Sage Publications, International Development Research Institute, p. 1
18. Ibid.
19. Harsh Mander, (2012), 'Lone Warriors'
20. Ibid.
21. N. Krishna Kumari (1987), *Status of Single Women in India,* New Delhi: Uppal Publishing House.
22. Ibid.
23. Ibid.
24. Sahgal (unpublished), 'Social Protection and Single Women', Centre for Equity Studies
25. Ibid.
26. Areila R Dubler (2003), 'In the Shadow of Marriage: Single women and the legal construction of the family and the state' in, *The Yale Law Journal,* Volume 112, pp. 1641-1715
27. Delhi Government - Scheme for Financial Assistance to Widows. Accessed at: http://wcddel.in/faw.html
28. Government of NCT of Delhi—Scheme for Financial Assistance to Widows. Accessed at: http://wcddel.in/faw.html
29. Centre for Budget and Governance Accountability (2015), 'Of Bold Strokes and Fine Prints: An analysis of Union Budget 2015-16', New Delhi: CBGA Accessed at http://www.cbgaindia.org/files/recent_publications/Analysis%20of%20Union%20Budget%202015-16.pdf
30. Ibid.
31. Programmes for Women, Ministry of Women and Child Development. Accessed here: http://wcd.nic.in/ar0304/chapter2.pdf
32. Y.M. Jhamb (2009), 'An Assessment of UPA-I through a Gender Budgeting Lens', in *Economic and Political Weekly* , XLIV (35), August
33. Ibid.
34. Sourced from, 'Short stay home for Women and Girls—(Aashray')'. Accessed at http://www.cmmpune.org/aashray1.php
35. Eighth Report of the Commissioners of the Supreme Court. Accessed here: http://www.hrln.org/hrln/pdf/rtf/reports/Eight%20report%20.harsh%20tanveer%20final%20aug%2020%2008.pdf
36. Ibid.
37. B.P. Remesh, 'Rethinking Social Protection for India's Working Poor in the Unorganised Sector'. Accessed here: http://www.umdcipe.org/conferences/policy_exchanges/conf_papers/Papers/1931.pdf
38. Sourced from http://www.sccommissioners.org/Reports/Reports/Gujarat_Report_0110.pdf
39. Accessed here: http://www.sccommissioners.org/Reports/Reports/SCC9_0909.pdf
40. Remesh, 'Rethinking Social Protection for India's Working Poor in the Unorganised Sector',
41. Singh, *Separated and Divorced Women in India: Economic Rights and Entitlements,* , p. 198.
42. Ibid.
43. Ibid.
44. Ibid.
45. Ibid.
46. Ibid.
47. J. Poonia, 'Critical Study of MGNREGA: Impact and women's participation' in *International Journal of Human Development and Management Sciences,* 1 (1). Accessed here: *http://journalshub.com/mrp-admin/journal/pdf/3.jyoti.pdf*
48. Reetika Khera and Nandini Nayak. (2009). 'Women Workers and Perceptions of the National Rural Employment Guarantee Act' in *Economic and Political Weekly,* XLIV (43). Accessed here: http://www.righttofoodindia.org/data/women_workers_and_perception_of_NREGA.pdf
49. Ibid.
50. Eighth Report of the Commissioners of the Supreme Court.
51. Ibid, p. 196.
52. Khera and Nayak. (2009). *Women Workers and*

perceptions of the National Rural Employment Guarantee Act

53. Eighth Report of the Commissioners of the Supreme Court
54. Ninth Report of the Supreme Court Commissioners. (2009)
55. Eighth Report of the Commissioners of the Supreme Court
56. Singh, *Separated and Divorced Women in India: Economic Rights and Entitlements*, p. 197.
57. NC Saxena, Sheila Vir and Harsh Mander (2014), 'Review on Food and Nutrition Security: India's domestic story and scope to build global partnerships.' Knowledge Partnership Programme—PIE Global, UK Aid. Available online at http://ipekpp.com/admin/upload_files/Report_1_15_Review_4510453616.pdf
58. CBGA (2015) 'Of Bold Strokes and Fine Prints: An analysis of Union Budget 2015-16'
59. Dhar, 'Good news for single women in 12th plan'
60. Ministry of Rural Development (March 2013*)*. 'Proposal for Comprehensive National Assistance Programme: Report of the Task Force'. Accessed here: http://rural.nic.in/sites/downloads/latest/Report_Task_Force_Comprehensive_NSAP.pdf on 10 November 2015.
61. Sourced from http://articles.economictimes.indiatimes.com/2015-03-15/news/60137538_1_minimum-pension-monthly-pension-task-force Accessed on 10 November 2015 .
62. Full text of Justice Verma Committee Report: http://www.prsindia.org/parliamenttrack/report-summaries/justice-verma-committee-report-summary-2628/
63. Bina Agarwal (2003), 'Gender and Land Rights Revisited: Exploring New Prospects via the State, Family and Market' in *Journal of Agrarian Change*, 3 (1, 2), pp. 184–224. Accessed here: http://www.uky.edu/~tmute2/geography_methods/readingPDFs/Agarwal-JAC-paper.pdf
64. Klaus Deininger, Aparajita Goyal and Hari Nagarajan (2010), 'Inheritance Law Reform and Women's Access to Capital Evidence from India's Hindu Succession Act', World Bank, Policy Research Working paper No. 5338 Accessed on 13 July 2015 at https://openknowledge.worldbank.org/bitstream/handle/10986/3823/WPS5338.pdf?sequence=1
65. Manoj Mitta (2015), 'Property: Daughter has share but father has will'. Times of India online edition 15 June. http://timesofindia.indiatimes.com/india/Property-Daughter-has-share-but-father-has-will/articleshow/47684675.cms?utm_source=facebook.com&utm_medium=referral&utm_campaign=TOIAccessed on 16 June 2015.
66. Ibid.
67. Flavia Agnes, (2009), 'Conjugality, Property, Morality and Maintenance', Economic and Political Weekly , XLIV (44). Accessed here: http://www.careerlauncher.com/lstcontent/plansuppliments/attachments/40/64/conjugality,%20property,%20morality%20and%20maintenance.pdf
68. Ibid.
69. Singh *Separated and Divorced Women in India: Economic Rights and Entitlements*, p. 191, 200.
70. Flavia Agnes(2015). 'Liberating Hindu Women'. Economic and Political Weekly , L (10), Accessed at http://majlislaw.com/file/Liberating_Hindu_Women_EPW_Mar_15.pdf
71. Ibid.
72. Ibid, p. 16.
73. Ibid.
74. Agnes, 'Liberating Hindu Women', p. 16. ShamimAra: '...Which curtailed the rights of a Muslim husband to arbitrary talaq by stipulating strict quranic conditions for pronouncing talaq under Islamic law. But these landmark rulings lie buried in law books'.
75. Singh, *Separated and Divorced Women in India:* Economic Rights and Entitlements, p. 191, 201.
76. Ibid.
77. Ibid.
78. Ibid.
79. Ibid, p. 192.
80. Ibid, p. 201.
81. Ibid.
82. AIR 1975 SC 1534
83. 1978 HLR 246
84. The Marriage laws (amendment) Bill, 2010. Accessed here http://www.prsindia.org/uploads/media/Marriage%20Laws/Marriage%20Laws%20Bill%20 2010.pdfon 10 November 2010.
85. Matrimonial Property (Rights of women upon marriage) Bill, 2012.
86. Flavia Agnes (2012), 'His and Hers', *Economic and Political Weekly*, Vol XLVII no. 17, 28 April 2012
87. 2005 3 SCC 313
88. Jeuti Barooah(1993), *Single Women in Assamese Hindu Society,* New Delhi: Gyan Publishing House, p. 191
89. Bina Aggarwal (2003), 'Gender and Land Rights revisited: Exploring new prospects via the State, Family and Market'. Accessed here: http://www.uky.edu/~tmute2/geography_methods/readingPDFs/Agarwal-JAC-paper.pdf

90. G.R. Yamini Misra (ed.) (2009), *Human Rights and Budgets in India*, New Delhi: Human Rights Law Network and Centre for Budget and Governance Accountability. Accessed here: https://books.google.co.in/books?id= HLw2zN_gHf4C&pg=PR8&lpg=PR8&dq=Human+ rights+and+budgets+in+India&source= bl&ots= ovf GwHr_Pu&sig= UvDKSckgzWumAm UtkOQw-7eN_S4&hl =en&sa= X&ei= LfU9 VeurJo6Juw TA0Y GoDg&ved = 0CEIQ6AEwAw#v = onepage&q = Human%20rights%20 and % 20 budgets % 20in % 20 India&f = false
91. National Forum for Single Women's Rights (2011), 'Are We Forgotten Women? A Study on the Status of Low-income Single Women in India'
92. http://www.thehindu.com/news/national/other-states/rajasthan-passes-bill-on-eligibility-for-panchayat-polls/article7041483.ece Accessed on 10 November 2015 .
93. http://indianexpress.com/article/india/india-others/those-with-more-than-2-children-not-allowed/ Accessed on 10 Novembver 2015 .
94. National Forum for Single Women's Rights (2011), 'Are We Forgotten Women? A Study on the Status of Low-income Single Women in India'.
95. See S. Chopra and P. Jha (2014), *On their Watch*, New Delhi: Three essays collective
96. A.K. Mehta and D. Arora(2014), 'Base Paper on Availability of Data and Data Gaps for Situation Analysis of Well-being of Children and Women', New Delhi: Indian Institute of Public Administration (IIPA)

Survivors of Mass Communal Violence in Muzaffarnagar

Profiles of loss, dispossession, and recovery

*Sajjad Hassan**

1. Introduction

In September 2013, as the country was getting ready for General Elections scheduled for the following April, large-scale communal violence engulfed Muzaffarnagar and Shamli districts of western Uttar Pradesh. A BBC report described the violence as 'the worst in India in a decade'.[1] By the time the violence had abated later that month, 52 persons lay dead, over 60 had been grievously injured, and scores of houses, destroyed in fires, across 14 villages in the two districts. This was the official count—many instances of deaths, injuries, sexual violence, and destruction of property remain uncounted to this day. The violence mostly targeted Western UP's Muslims, especially the ones from poorer backgrounds. Additionally, the violence affected 74 villages in Muzaffarnagar and Shamli, and surrounding districts, as Muslim families here, especially where they were in minority, fled fearing violence, in the tens of thousands, resulting in one of the largest violence-induced displacements in the country in recent years. Estimates vary but a figure of 50,000, at its peak, has been widely accepted.[2]

This paper tries to understand, from the perspective of violence survivors, the dynamics of bias-motivated violence towards minorities, and more specifically the loss that violence survivors suffer. Of course, immediate loss on account of death and destruction is just the start. Loss induced by displacement, of dislocation from homes; the resultant anomie and breakdown of family and of social ties; the impermanence and uncertainties stretching for months in relief camps, in many cases years on end, of a life in limbo; the loss of livelihood and education; and the particular losses suffered by women and girls that follow in the wake of episodes of mass communal violence, is an untold story.

> We are but poor. What did we do that they (the perpetrators) snatched our homes and our livelihood? They made us homeless, and forced terror and displacement on our children. All this is a big conspiracy. Why did they come after us? Why did they destroy our lives?
>
> (An old man, name unknown, Ailum Village, Muzaffarnagar, 6 March 2014)

---

* A much shorter version of this paper has appeared in MRG's State of the World's Minorities Indigenous Peoples' Report, 2014. (See: Sajjad, (2014), 'Understanding the Dynamic of Communal Riots against Muslims in Muzaffarnagar and Shamli districts, Uttar Pradesh, India', in *State of the World's Minorities and Indigenous Peoples Report, 2014*. London: Minority Rights Group International, pp.121–24.)

** Research Support: Akram Akhtar of Afkar India Foundation and Asghar Sharif, as well as numerous volunteer researchers

*** This chapter was reviewed by Navsharan Singh, Jan Breman and Apoorvanand.

For long since Independence, Muslims in India have been the target of right-wing Hindu mobilisation, resulting in their frequently suffering physical violence. Called 'communal riots' in India, such violence is increasingly taking the form of organised pogroms by those aligned to right-wing Hindu organisations, including political parties such as Bharatiya Janata Party (BJP) that use violence instrumentally, both to consolidate Hindu support behind them, and counter Muslim mobility.[3] In the final analysis however, it is the state that must guarantee its citizens the basic rights of security, justice and opportunities. These underlie the notions of citizenship that are inscribed in the Constitution. 'Communal violence'; the losses suffered by minorities; and the absence of much accountability of state actors, failing in their duties to provide security and justice, are failures of the state.

This paper tries to describe then, using the specific case of the Muzaffarnagar mass violence, how victim communities are denied that citizenship—equal treatment in terms of protection from violence, besides access to legal justice, and reparation and resettlement. This is situated within the larger discussion of the dilemma: how are certain communities repeatedly and variously subject to violence and atrocious crimes and what can they do about it? Lastly, the paper attempts to highlight ways out of the trap by providing examples of how particular survivor communities are coping. These include attempts at rights-based grassroots collective action for justice.

The study is based on participatory research conducted over the course of over a year from January 2014 to the present, as part of the ongoing work of Muzaffarnagar Adhikaar Jan Manch (Muzaffarnagar Rights Forum - MAJMA), a civil society collective for survivor rights that the author helped set up and led in Muzaffarnagar and Shamli districts.[4] The research prioritised, as key respondents, poorer sections among victims in the relief camps, resettlement sites and villages in the two districts, although there was some interaction with the rest of society, including the dominant Jats, to better understand violence dynamics. Methods used were participant observation, unstructured interviews, group discussions, and some desk research. The relief camps covered included those in Rotan, Mansura and Bibipur Hatia in Shamli district; and Bassi Kalan, Sanjhak, Joala and Loi, in Muzaffarnagar district. The villages included Kiwana, Ailum, Simbhalka, and Nalla in Shamli district, and Kharar and Kheda Mastan in Muzaffarnagar. In each camp, we conducted at least one group discussion with the victims. This happened more in the villages and discussions were held with different sections—Jats as well as separately with women. The research team itself was large (too many to name here), with student interns as well as young professionals, drawn from different social and religious backgrounds.

The paper is organised as under: we start, in Section 2, with an account of the violent events in Muzaffarnagar, their drivers, and the immediate sparks that triggered the violence. This is followed (in Section 3) with an account of the nature of violence, especially the displacement caused by it. In Section 4, we touch upon the impact of the violence on survivors and the various forms of losses suffered. The next section (5) deals specifically with how victims have been denied legal rights, an urgent issue needing rectification. Section 6 briefly addresses the question of civil society's response to the violence, concluding with a short exposition of the MAJMA collective and its work. Before we get to Section 8 on Conclusion and Recommendations, in Section 7, we try to situate Muzaffarnagar within the wider context of the poor record of the Indian State to provide justice and hold its agents accountable in the many cases of massacres since Independence.

2.1 Muzaffarnagar and Shamli districts are part of the agriculturally rich western UP region that benefited from the Green Revolution of the 1970s and 1980s, with landowning middle-caste Hindu Jat farmers being the main beneficiaries of the large productivity gains in farming. Prosperity and favorable public policies have helped Jats in public employment too, resulting in Jat control over much of the bureaucracy and police in the region.[5] Our research revealed how the twin political formations of Rashtriya Lok Dal (RLD) and Bharatiya Kisan Union (BKU) that wholly monopolises the political space in the region, successfully protected and promoted Jat interests, while also providing some space for better off non-Jats, including Muslims.[6] The region was, quite uncharacteristically, bereft of communal violence so common in Uttar Pradesh due to the influence of this elite platform. It was rather the poorer sections, both Hindus (including Dalits) and Muslims, who were the object of the elite's exploitation. The anti-Muslim violence of September 2014 therefore came as a surprise. 'A hundred years of mutual bonds were shattered in five days! In that time, friends and neighbours turned enemies.' (Neeshoo, 32, male, Sanjhak relief camp, Muzaffarnagar district, 30 January 2014)

Our respondents, among victims as well as other social groups including Jats, spoke of how BJP's bid to power at the Centre in the upcoming elections to the national parliament in April–May 2014 was behind much of this sudden explosion of anti-Muslim violence. One explained:

> BJP's bid for power rests a great deal on good performance in UP (accounting for 80 of the total 545 seats in Parliament). 14 of these come from the western UP region, the Jat stronghold, including Muzaffarnagar and Shamli districts. Canvassing Jat votes, by breaking up the monopoly of RLD, and consolidating Hindu votes behind it, has been for BJP, the strategy of choice, regardless of its social costs.
>
> (A local Muslim businessman, male, 53, Muzaffarnagar, 29 January 2014)

Pointing to how the violence was politically motivated is the response of a local Jat notable, when asked how the divide between communities could be bridged:

> Just wait for two months, let the elections get over, things will get back to normal.
>
> BJP wants to sweep up Hindu votes as does (the ruling) Samajwadi Party (SP), which wants all Muslims behind it. This is a deal between the two parties.
>
> (Udaivir Singh, 56, Chairman, Ailum Municipal Council, 6 March 2014)

2.2 Journalistic and scholarly writings have shown that in this political game, BJP was using its tried and tested strategy of communal polarisation and violence (by Jat Hindus on Muslims) as the vehicle.[7] But that begs the questions: why this particular region? This, as it turned out, was because divisive ideology found ready grounds in the local context, primarily rooted in the Jat grouse against recent trends of lower-class mobility among Muslims.

This is how a local Muslim activist explains the situation:

> Muslims, along with Dalits, are the underclass in these villages, mostly semi-bonded helps and farm hands in Jat households, or brick kiln and other daily wage workers, all landless. Recently, a new breed of Muslims is emerging due to the political patronage of the ruling Samajwadi Party (SP) that relies on Muslims, among others, for votes. Many elected offices in the two districts have recently gone to Muslims. They are not dependent on Jats, in a patron-client relationship, as they were in the past.
>
> (Akram Akhtar, male, 27, Shamli, 4 March 2014)

Muslims are also doing better in trade and commerce, as artisans, petty traders, and itinerant cloth hawkers (*pheriwallahs*). These changes in the political and economic spheres threaten Jat control, eroding the latter's hold over traditional authority, already undermined by Dalit assertion and are thus deeply resented.

> They (Jat) do not want to see us do well. They want us to remain subservient to them. They are resentful of Muslims who are doing well or of the new leaders among Muslims, who do not toe the Jat line.
>
> (Muslim Elder, name with held, 63, Kharar Village, 15 March 2014)

We found resonance in this acknowledgment of loss of authority among the Jat community too. A Jat teacher from Kheda Mastan village confided candidly:

> Jats controlled local institutions in the past. People came to us for resolving disputes, and for other help. Now people go rather to the new leaders, for getting the benefits of public schemes and help with police and the bureaucracy. These new SP leaders do not recognise our authority. In the past during election time, we were able to control voting outcomes through 'booth capturing'. Now everyone is free to vote who they decide.
>
> (Jat teacher, name withheld, male, 50, Kheda Mastan village, 15 March 2014)

The violence then, was a case of a political idea (of BJP polarising Hindu and Muslim votes) finding local resonance in Jat grievance around the erosion of their traditional hold over society.[8] Poor Muslims, especially in minority rural pockets, were easy targets.

2.3 The trigger for the violence itself was provided by a scuffle between young men that resulted in the death of a Muslim boy and two Hindu Jats. BJP, with other Hindu right parties, quickly lent the incident communal colour, claiming that Jat pride had been hurt because Muslims boys were luring Jat girls into marriage. In an environment of deep misogynistic patriarchy, this sense of offence to Jat honour helped BJP whip up adverse sentiments, mobilising Jats to teach the 'upstart' Muslims a lesson through targeted violence.[9] As an old man at Sanjhak relief camp put it:

> 'they used lies and untruth, all, to whip up Hindu sentiments against Muslims'.
>
> (Mohammad Yusuf, 67 years, Sanjhak, 30 January 2014)

A victim at the same camp, from the village of Qutba, the site of large-scale violence and arson, laments how hate speeches, recruiting the services of traditional Jat leadership (*khap panchayats* or traditional courts), and print media and IT-based social media particularly (through SMS and fabricated MMS) to spread hate messages were mobilized to devastating effect.[10] Local BJP leaders openly incited violence.[11]

The fact that Jats dominate frontline positions in the police and bureaucracy helped the hate-mongers have a free run of the streets going on an unrestrained rampage. As a victim at another relief camp said:

> Administration's and Police's attitude towards us has not been helpful. They did not provide us security when we needed it. And now all question our loss and suffering. No one shows us any sensitivity. We have been given little relief or support. Rather the government have tried to drive us out of relief camps on one pretext or another.
>
> (name withheld, male, Rotan relief camp, Shamli, 27 January 2014)

3. Violence and Dislocation—The Calamity!

3.1 Official records recognise only nine villages as violence-hit, where much of the killings, burning, destruction of property, and other forms of crime against minorities took place. Minor incidents, burning and looting as well as attacks also took place, according to official records, in another five villages. But the violence and the environment of fear that was created affected a total of 74 villages not only in Muzaffarnagar and Shamli, but also in the adjoining districts of Baghpat, Meerut and Karnal.

A unique aspect of the violence was its rural character, and its disproportionate impact on the largely poor and weaker sections among the Muslim community. Although better off, landowning Muslims too were not spared.

'Most of the rioting happened in villages dominated by Jats, with only a small Muslim presence. Victims are almost all poor families - farm hands, labourers, and local artisans.' (Group discussion with victims, at MBF brick kiln, Kiwana village, Shamli, 5 March 2014)

The landowning Jat community among Muslims in Muzaffarnagar, the Mulay Jats, mostly found in Kharar village, have suffered considerably less than the other Muslims: they were displaced, but were not the victims of any major attacks. The Mulay Jats attribute this to the fact they are socially powerful with means and resources unlike the hapless poor Muslims.

3.2 The violence led to large-scale displacement. According to official sources, in the first waves, during and immediately after the incident, some 1,700 families from nine villages that saw large-scale rioting, escaped to safer locations. There was also an exodus of Muslims from nearby villages, prompted by the fear of escalating violence. At its peak, official estimates of the displaced were at 50,000, mostly those who were now in relief camps in the two districts.[12] By February 2014, this figure remained at an estimated 24,000.[13] Many families, especially extended ones, were torn apart.

Life in the camps was, and continues for those still there, to be insecure, with the state government providing little relief, rather actively seeking to shut down the camps. When asked what victims sought the most, a survivor answered:

> We don't like to live on charity, and are happy to live by our own labour. But without a home of our own, all that is not possible. We worry every day, if we will still have our tents and camp, or we will be forced out on the streets. But we do not want

Table 1: Numbers of displaced

S. No.	District	Open Camps	Families	Those on rent/ relatives	Families
1	Shamli	20	1785	10	539
2	Muzaffarnagar	6	785	11	580
3	Baghpat	-	-	3[15]	115
TOTAL		26	2570	24	1234

Source: Afkar India, for MAJMA (March 2014)

Table 2: Survey of the displaced (March 2015)

Persons in district	Relief Camps	Resettlement Colonies
Shamli	2329	6410
Muzaffarnagar	1996	2200
Total	4325	8610

Source: Afkar India, for MAJMA (March 2015)

Box 1: Mapping Displacement in Stages

Stage I: Immediately, on onset of violence, from village to:

- Relatives, in safer areas, mostly urban
- Community-organised shelters, families/madrasas/Idgah (for security)

Stage II: From first few days to few weeks of the violence:

- Movement/exchange of families across sites (in search of long-term habitation)
- Movement to relief camps—set up OR recognised by State (where relief is available)

Stage III: From few weeks to few months, when the dust has settled

- Those who can, return to their villages
- Those who can't (from directly affected villages; complainants in cases; fear)
  - move to rented accommodation, locally; those who receive compensation buy plots and start to build.
  - Others move further afield (cities/other), in search of work and a life.
  - The poorest continue living in makeshift camps.

Stage IV: Few months to beyond

- Those with means (own or compensation) move to resettlement colonies.
- Those who don't, carry on in camps or move on to join the ranks of the homeless.

> to go back to our villages as we do not know what awaits us there.
>
> (Anwar, male, 43, Rotan relief camp, 27 January 2014)

Seven months after the violence, an overwhelming majority of poor labouring families remain displaced, living either in makeshift camps in deplorable conditions (many children died during the cold months[14]) or in houses of relatives in nearby urban centres. A survey conducted by MAJMA in March 2014 recorded 3,804 displaced families making up about 15,000 persons.

An earlier survey by MAJMA, of families who had returned to six villages partially affected by the violence, found victims to be further marginalised with regard to access to entitlements, services and livelihood opportunities, and living in constant fear. A more recent MAJMA survey in March 2015, to track down the displaced in relief camps and rehabilitation colonies, found a total of 13,000 displaced still, spread over Muzaffarnagar and Shamli districts (Table 2). Those in relief camps do not even find mention in official sources.

This does not include those who have moved on, out of the theatre of violence and joined the ranks of the homeless or of migrants in nearby urban centres of Delhi, Ghaziabad, etc. Of them, there are no records.

4. The multiple dimensions of victims' loss

4.1 Violence against women and girls

Sexual violence, including rape and molestation, has been widely reported.

Inflammatory speeches and frenzied slogans of 'bahu bachao, beti bachao' and 'beti bahu ki izzat bachao' were used to mobilise men of the dominant castes by convincing them that 'their women' were in imminent danger. The notion of protecting community honour was invoked to justify a direct call for targeted violence against minority women. A wave of sexual violence was unleashed against women immediately after the Mahapanchayat held on 7 September 2013. Women and girls were chased down as they tried to flee the mobs, and subjected to rape and gang rape. Young girls were singled out for particularly humiliating and degrading forms of violence. [16]

According to a delegation of the AMU Lawyers Forum, as many as 27 victims confirmed instances of rapes but only seven were ever reported.[17]

Our discussions with women victims in Kharar and Kheda Mastan villages in Muzaffarnagar and Shamli districts respectively, revealed how violence has had other marginalising effects on women; the continuing fear has led to women's movement outside their homes being severely restricted.

> We had to flee our homes at night to safeguard the honour of our daughters and daughters-in-law. After all the honour of our daughters is more precious than our lives. All adult men are outside the village, only adult girls at home. Their protection is our prime concern.
>
> (Muslim woman, 45, Kharar village. 15 March 2014)

Fear and insecurity affected schooling, with large incidence of drop-out cases in senior classes, as well as access to employment among other things. Concerns about 'family honour' and fear of further violence resulted in a large number of under-age girls among survivor families, especially those in relief camps, being married off, ironically with the state government fuelling the push by subsidising weddings with cash incentives. According to one estimate, 398 marriages were solemnised in this way.[18] These, the report notes, have tended to end up later in largescale separations. The specific gender aspect of the loss must be seen in the context of the overall adverse gender prospects in the region–the skewed sex ratio of 889 females to 1000 males (against State ratio of 912 females), and child sex ratio of 863 girls to 1000 boys (against all India ratio of 914 girls) as per 2011 Census.

4.2 Children and education

Education is another area, where the impact has been severe.

> Initially, in camps there were no teachers, and children just spent time playing. Later an NGO started a make-shift school in the camp, hiring a local instructor. A madrasa has also been running, for sometime. But how can this make up for the months of lost schooling?
>
> (Nawab Pradhan, Muslim, 62 years, Mansura camp, 28 January 2014)

There was large-scale exclusion of Children from education—many joined the ranks of child labour, helping their families in brick kilns or in other odd jobs in towns. There were no schools in camps, and it has been difficult to link the camps to nearby schools for a variety of reasons, the most important being the indifference of the local education affairs bureaucracy to the children in these camps and their inability to continue education there. Indeed, most displaced children in higher classes were unable to sit for their classes IX and X examinations, and only strong pressure by MAJMA constituents and other civil society groups prompted school and college administrations to integrate them. Girls have been specially excluded, poor perceptions of security being a chief factor in parents' eyes.

For those who have been able to return, this has not meant guaranteed resumption of pre-violence schooling. The head teacher of the boys' middle school in Simbhalka village informed us of how out of the 11 Muslim students (out of 40 in all) before the outbreak of violence, only two have returned to school since. Factors like the months-long gap in schooling due to displacement, loss of books and uniform which were destroyed in the violence, and insecurity and uncertainty weighing heavy on victim families have meant that schooling has been severely compromised. The drop-out rate is highest among girls.

4.3 Livelihoods

Victims informed us about how their livelihoods have been affected severely. As a victim from Kheda Mastan village said:

> We came back to our village because life in the camps was desperate. But here we face the same problem of absence of employment. We were dependent on Jat patronage for much of our livelihood, as farm hands, ironsmiths, barbers and the like. We also feel insecure going into many Jat villages in the affected areas. All this affects our trade. We are now forced to sell off our belongings at throwaway prices to make ends meet.
>
> (Kheda Mastan group meeting, 14 March 2014)

Another victim told us:

'We cannot leave our children alone and go out in search of work further afield. This has reduced our livelihood choices.' (Kiwana village brick kiln meeting, 5 March 2014)

Kiwana has seen a large number of victims joining large gangs of labourers at the brick kilns in the village. This is not the work of choice for most, given the exploitative conditions and the need to press entire families into work. However, public wage employment schemes do not work, particularly for Muslims, thus offering no escape from the trap. In Kheda Mastan village, Muslim residents claimed not to know anything about NREGS—the flagship national wage employment scheme—showing how little public programmes work for them.

Overall, the violence and breakdown, and dislocation in survivors' lives has resulted in their pauperisation: those who were mobile shop owners, cloth merchants, artisans and other artisanal classes were reduced to taking up unskilled work, in agricultural fields, brick kilns and the odd daily wage to make ends meet. For women who were engaged in agricultural work or home based activities (sewing/tailoring) before the violence, even these options have been closed due to security and dignity concerns.[19] Furthermore, there is a poor social safety net to compensate for this loss of livelihood. There is weak uptake of NREGA among women (due to reasons ranging from low wages, patriarchy, poor awareness, and a broken NREGA administration) and the situation is not much better among men as well.

4.4 Inter-community relations

Finally, the violence has left a permanent divide between communities. Given the largely rural context, pre-violence relations between 'victims' and 'perpetrators' were intimate. Violence, in such a situation, has left a deep imprint on people's psyche. Trust has been destroyed.

'We have been betrayed. We have lost faith in the Jats. Those whom we considered our own, our neighbours, attacked us. How can we forget that?' (Muslim victim, name unknown, Bassi Kalan relief camp, 29 January 2014)

Box 2: Profiles of the displaced

	In Resettlement Colonies	In Relief Camps	Returned to village
Profile	From villages violently affected; mostly those who received relocation compensation, and other support also from non-government agencies. Bought plots and built houses. Many complainants in cases. Not returning to villages.	From different districts, including outside MN-Shamli. The poorest victims, mostly not from directly affected villages. Little property, security or trust to return to.	Mostly those from villages not directly affected; had property to go back to. Many still keep part of family in safer urban locations.
Housing	Bought plots and built houses in their own names, mostly resettlement colonies close to Muslim majority areas.	In make-do tents/ jhuggis, in open space; constant threat of eviction. The homeless!	Back to own houses, but a slow migration out to 'safer' places/distress sale.
Public infrastructure/ services	Poor infrastructure—water, electricity, etc. Most colonies not linked to GPs and wards for public service purposes.	No roads, electricity, water, toilets. Or services—schools, Anganwadi, PDS.	Same as before, but worsening situation in terms of high drop-out rate of girls due to fear.
Government scheme	Slow process of linking IDPs to schemes and services.	No I-Cards (or acceptance as victims by the state), hence excluded from all schemes.	Returned, but access to schemes is a challenge. The slow process of building this up through mobilisation.
Overall	The camps themselves have turned ghetto-like, with communities segregated, and education and livelihood options, especially for girls, much restricted.		Increasingly, Muslim sections of villages have tended to become ghettoised, with poor interaction and exchange and that much exclusion of Muslims from village-level processes/ institutions.

(Source: Based on Afkar India's survey of survivors, March 2015)

'The damage has been so high that I am afraid relations will not be better for a long time. Maybe never. Political parties, both BJP and SP, have played politics with us.' (Devi Singh, Secy., Jat Mahasabha, Simbhalka village, 7 March 2014.

Along with this has come homogenisation of habitations, with Muslims moving into Muslim majority areas and mixed habitation pockets divested of Muslims, resulting in greater polarisation.

'These riots have shown me how perfectly normal people can become stubborn Hindus and Muslims. The community has been badly polarised. We were not like this. This is not good for society.' (Muslim businessman, Muzaffarnagar, 29 January 2014)

Box 2 provides a snapshot of the life of survivors (categorised here into three groups, by type of habitation) and their access to services, a year after the devastation.

5. Denial of Rights—Law, State and Mass Communal Violence Victims

International law lays down that states owe victims of gross human rights violations reparation. Reparation includes (a) access to justice in the form of criminal prosecution, and (b) access to truth, and material and non-material restitution.[20] How have victims fared on this? How about access of survivors to their rights?

5.1 Criminal justice

According to available official records, the police filed a total of 566 cases, of which 59 were for murders, six for rape, and the rest for dacoity, arson and other crimes. But for survivors to pursue criminal prosecutions and get justice has been an uphill task, especially given the context of a criminal justice system that is not supportive of legal justice for the poor. The local state being skewed in favour of Jats further hinders post-violence delivery of justice (investigation and prosecution), as well as access to public goods for victims of the violence.

> Peace committee has been set up, with Pradhan and other Jat leaders, but with no Muslim members. They held many meetings to discuss how to get us to withdraw cases against Jat youth. They say they will see to it that no untoward incident now happens. But how can we trust them?
>
> (Old man, name unknown, Muslim, 65, Kharar village, 30 March 2014)

Jat domination of frontline positions in the police and bureaucracy also means that the administration is perceived as being biased.[21]

Table 3: Financial assistance to survivors—Number of beneficiaries

	Murder	Grievous Injury	Injury	Relocation
Muzaffarnagar	34	14	27	901
Shamli	16	9	16	768
Other	13	10	-	-
Total	63	33	43	1669

Source: Tabulated by author from Supreme Court judgement, dated 26 March 2014

'Those responsible for the violence are roaming about freely. The police knows who they are, but is not arresting them. This gives the Jats the opportunity to put pressure on us to withdraw cases.' (Joala relief camp, 1 February 2014)

The denial of legal rights has taken many forms. FIRs were recorded inaccurately; police action for arresting and apprehending the accused was tardy; investigations have been slow and shoddy; a large number of cases have simply been dropped, without giving any chance to the defendants to question this; and cases against politicians and powerful hate-mongers have not been taken up at all. Cases are only very slowly coming up for hearing before trial courts. As a result, no convictions have been made yet; rather a large number of the accused have been released on bail.

There are multiple reasons for these failures; among them, the fact that perpetrators are rich and powerful members of local society and often act as gatekeepers controlling the return of survivors to their villages, thus able to influence complainants to withdraw cases or weaken them. These sections also have access to caste and other networks enabling them to influence the police and courts in their favour. As for the survivors, criminal justice is not high on their priority list given the poor level of trust in the law, and the victims' immediate post-violence scramble for life and survival. It is only as a result of the work of human rights activists and civil society groups, strengthened by the intervention of the Supreme Court for victim rights, that there is now pressure on the administration, police and courts to keep up the work of criminal justice for violence victims.

5.2 Compensation

The government has made awards for compensation—for loss of life, limb, property and habitation. These were, compared to the compensation provided to victims of other episodes of mass violence, reasonably generous. Besides the Rs 15 lakh that was awarded as compensation for murder, Rs 1 lakh was provided to those grievously injured, Rs 20,000 for non-grievous injury and a flat rate of Rs 25,000 for loss of immovable property. Those injured were also granted pension (at Rs 400 per month) under the Rani Laxmi Bai Scheme. The next of kin of the deceased have been given government employment, as per their qualifications. New categories of compensation have emerged, most prominently for the relocation of affected families at Rs 5 lakh each). Further, under orders of the Supreme Court, the state government has also provided Rs 5 lakh to victims in rape cases; and Rs 2 lakh to parents of children who died in relief camps during the winter months. As many as 40 children were reported by media outlets as having died in relief camps.

However, the administration of compensation has been a big problem, with complaints of exclusion of deserving cases being widespread; as well as complaints of widespread corruption in identification and award.

'District administrations did not devise a clear definition and transparent process to determine the family unit eligible for separate compensation and the process was conducted very differently in the two districts.' [22]

Some of these state-led compensatory schemes have also been self-defeating for victims. For instance, for relocation, awarding each family from the nine directly affected villages, a sum of Rs 5 lakh to move to another place is quite evidently not adequate for a family to set up home elsewhere. However, once the victims are awarded this inadequate compensation, the rest of society feels they have little claim to return to the village. There are other problems too with these schemes, especially with regards to their effect on intra-family conflicts, over how the money would be divided, for instance. The award of compensation for supporting survivor families has faced similar trouble. The money has acted as an incentive for parents to get their daughters married even if the girls are underage. Many of these girls have now been deserted by their husbands, who clearly married for money.[23]

5.3 Resettlement

Last, the matter of the displacement of victims, their taking shelter in camps, resettlement colonies or other locations, and their access to basic services and social security schemes—all of it falls under the rubric of citizenship services. The displaced in the refugee camps and later in resettlement colonies have found it difficult to access the most basic of services—individual entitlements, such as voter I-cards, pensions and PDS rations, as well as services such as education for children. This has been on account of procedural bottlenecks in accessing rights, that make access to entitlements contingent upon inclusion of names in village registers or Gram Sabha-approved village lists, and the rigid rules and procedure that exist if families wanted to withhold or change theirs names. Another hurdle has been the reluctance of both host villages and administrative units (panchayats) to accept the displaced among them, as well as the insensitivity of officials towards victims. It has only been after much sustained effort, by victims' collectives, supported by the advocacy efforts of civil society groups with state and national agencies, that small gains on access to entitlements for victims have been achieved.[24]

Additionally, displacement-induced influx of refugees, especially in Muslim-dominated pockets of the districts (Kairana, Kandhla, and blocks of Shamli, besides Shamli and Muzaffarnagar towns) has meant additional pressure on urban services already under severe strain in these localities—housing, roads, power, water supply and sanitation. There has been very little serious effort by the government to improve services in these urban pockets to cope with the significant rise in their populations.

The influx has also resulted in changing the demographic profile of Muslim-dominated areas; these have become large ghettos, with homogenised settlements. Adding to that is an increasing trend of spatial segregation between Muslims and Jats (and other Hindu groups). This ghettoisation has been fuelled partly by the absence of any attempt by the administration to resettle families in original villages. Peace Committees formed after the violence to bring back families were driven, we were informed by survivors, by the urge to evacuate relief camps. The same applies for recent evictions of remaining relief camps in the forest lands in Shamli. There has been no serious effort at settling the displaced people in their original villages despite assurances of security and a sincere attempt by the government at peace-making. Relocation compensation further divides society, giving victims the financial incentive to move away, buy plots of land and settle down in Muslim ghettos (even though the amount is too small for any meaningful 'relocation').

6. Civil Society Response to Survivor Loss—Victimhood to Empowerment

6.1 Whilst it is true that the state has the primary responsibility to respond to mass communal violence, non-governmental organisations, too have responsibilities. How did civil society fare in the case of Muzaffarnagar? Immediately after the violence began, there was much outpouring of civic action, mostly by local community, led by Muslim individuals and religious charities. This was focused on provision of relief—including food, rations, temporary shelter, clothing, medicines—all of which went into filling the gap left by the government, at least in the initial days. Later local action was supplemented by national

Box 3: How Does the State Provide for Mass Violence Survivors?

Right	Summary of provisioning
Security	Poor ability to provide security to minorities. Public officials mostly not held to account. Commissions of enquiry reports not implemented. State-government set up V. Sahay Commission on Muzaffarnagar violence; yet to be tabled in state assembly, and made public.
Relief, Rehabilitation, Resettlement	No national norm for victims of mass violence. Arbitrary across episodes and states. Most of schemes are narrowly defined and limited to 'reparations principle', the international norm on this.
Criminal Justice	'...the criminal justice system consistently fails victims of communal violence.' This includes poor filing of complaints, poor and biased investigation, and weak-kneed prosecution. Widespread impunity of perpetrators and officials.
Rebuild peace and inter-community relations	Little serious effort, by state or others, to rebuild relations, after they have broken down. Mostly organising peace committees that are episodic, and do not keep victims' concerns in focus. Weak efforts, not sustainable in the long term.

Source: Tabulated by author from among others, Chopra & Jha (2014) and media reports.

level organisations, mostly Muslims charities, intervening with further relief, but also services such as housing colonies, and provision of water and sanitation facilities.

Apart from this, there was only limited civil society effort, especially for resettlement and rehabilitation. Missing particularly was the kind of civil society effort one sees in cases of natural calamities, with only a handful of non-denominational development agencies entering the field. Many entered late, and very quickly exited the field. Taken together, civil society response to the communal violence in Muzaffarnagar was a tame affair. And as an observer has noted, the deficiencies of Muslim/community organisations (in terms of religious appeal and poor professional ethics), and the unavailability and unwillingness of 'corporatised' NGOs to network with the former, meant among other things, that a 'broad-based and long-term vision for resettlement of the people could also not be developed'.[25]

6.2 In this context, the the intervention by a collective of national and local civil society organisations for victim support under the platform of MAJMA acquires significance. MAJMA was established in January 2014, when state and national advocacy bodies, international development agencies, and grassroots activists and community-based organisations of survivors agreed to come together to collectively respond to the calamity and displacement. The driver was the realisation that there had been little concerted effort to engender a civil society response. MAJMA's approach to the work was to empower the survivors—support them in their attempts to cope with the calamity and in their struggles to organise and work for obtaining justice and entitlements whilst re-building inter-community relations. The nub of the MAJMA effort has been the building of the community capacity of survivors. This has been done through the Afkar India Foundation, established as a local facility for mobilisation, capacity-building and advocacy for victim rights. Afkar's work, supported by MAJMA, has focused on:

i. Organising survivor groups into collectives, around rights and entitlements—compensation, education, basic services, and legal rights;

ii. educating and capacity-building survivor groups on laws, services and schemes, and mobilising them to demand the same;

iii. advocacy with local, state and other actors, governmental and non-governmental, to aid in the process of obtaining rights; and

iv. fostering cross-group dialogue and understanding, by organising activities to bring the survivor community and the rest of society together—including Jats, but particularly the deprived sections— on common platforms, to enable dialogue and long-term peace.

Afkar has had many successes since its inception, prominent being the ones with regard to compensation, admissions to schools, legal justice, and access to services and schemes. But given the enormity of the challenge, these successes remain modest. The silver lining, however, is that as a result of the mobilisation, everywhere among the survivor community, 'aspiration for equal citizenship (is) being articulated'[26] and this in itself is a significant gain.

7. Muzaffarnagar in Wider Perspective

India, and other similar democracies, pose a particular challenge to studying and improving rights of minorities and their protection in the face of violence. They are established democracies, with a set of laws and mechanisms for protecting minority lives and interests. These are also countries that enjoy political stability overall and not the conflict situation which create conditions for mass violations of minority rights. Yet, discrimination, marginalisation, and indeed violence against minorities persist in here.

State authorities argue that the Indian state is committed to protecting minority rights. But the acid test whether indeed the state is playing its part in this regard is whether those responsible for the violence are prosecuted and the victims are delivered justice. India's record on this front is poor—one commission of enquiry after another looking into cases of violence have documented in great detail the failures of state actors to protect during episodes of violence against minorities. Indeed, these very official enquiries have often found particular state actors themselves having, in some cases, encouraged, and in others, participated in the violence against minorities.[27] Yet, as our treatment of the Muzaffarnagar case shows, there have been alarmingly few prosecutions against offenders.

8. Conclusion and Recommendations

Our research with survivors of mass communal violence provided us insights on ways to counter hate-inspired violence and move towards struggles for justice. Some of these are catalogued below, grouped by their desired audience:

8.1 For state actors and agencies

i. First and foremost is the issue of strengthening the rule of law, ensuring that the accused are prosecuted and justice delivered. Related to this is also the demand for ensuring security of life and property, both in relief camps and villages.

> Those responsible for the violence are roaming about freely. The police knows who they are, but is not arresting them. This gives the Jats the opportunity to put pressure on us to withdraw

cases. We must have the assurance of security. Without that how will we survive?

(Muslim member, Joala relief camp, 1 February 2014.)

ii. Legal action must also include countering the politics of hate and polarisation, through prosecution of those who make hate speeches and action against irresponsible media reporting , both of which played a big role in the violence in Muzaffarnagar.

iii. Relief, compensation and rehabilitation is an area that needs significant focus in Muzaffarnagar, as well as generally for violence survivors everywhere. The following recommendations are important in this regard:

Need for a national policy on compensation, so that it becomes a right that survivors are entitled to automatically, rather than the system of awarding compensation which is usually an outcome of political negotiations between the government and survivors; and to work towards establishing uniformity among the types and quantum of compensation across states and groups affected.

Survivors of mass violence need to be included in the definition of IDPs (as understood for victims of natural disasters and displacement), so that they are entitled to at least the same rights which individuals affected by disasters and displacement are entitled to, especially in terms of immediate relocation and long-term rehabilitation. Displaced survivors should automatically be able to access all the citizen services (education, ICDS, PDS rations) that they were enjoying in their homes.

iv. Additionally, in our group meetings with survivors we repeatedly heard villagers urging dialogue across communities.

'Peace committees can be helpful, if they are used honestly, to bring the two communities together. Where village elders have been responsible and tried honestly to resolve issues, peace has been maintained, and miscreants kept at bay.' (Muslim member of municipal council, Ailum village, 6 March 2014.)

Connected to this is the point about expanding common spaces and undoing ghettoisation, by bringing victims back to their villages, providing them with security and creating a sense of inclusion by providing public goods equally to all.

'Everyone has rights. If all get their share of what is due, things will be fine. If on the other hand people are denied their rights, just because they are smaller in number, that is neither just nor good for society. (Muslim elder, 63, Kharar village, 15 March 2014.)

v. Any systematic fight against violence on minorities must be grounded in efforts to undo discrimination against them in the provision of services (and in society generally) and countering the impunity of officials and service providers who fail to deliver for minorities. This must also include promoting greater minority participation in decision-making processes, at sub-state and local levels.

8.2 For Civil Society

To this must be added the point about the need, in the long run, to strengthen inclusive political formations—interest groups with cross-cutting membership, workers' organisations and parties—that will act as bulwarks against polarisation, while standing for justice for all. These efforts, aimed at managing and promoting diversity, in society and in the provision of rights, are crucial to inoculate the society against communal polarisation and conflict. A society that cherishes diversity, and where different groups, faith-based and otherwise, are engaged across boundaries in their struggles for life, opportunities and dignity, is a resilient society. MAJMA's brief work with survivors of violence in Muzaffarnagar and Shamli districts, particularly supporting them with their struggles for justice, entitlements and peace building, has thrown up many learnings about the need for building cross-group solidarities for justice outcomes. It is therefore crucial to build local-level alliances of violence survivors, as well as of other deprived groups (Dalits, backward sections, women, labourers and the like) working together to educate, empower, and mobilise victim (and deprived) communities, on common social justice agendas, and making demands on the state for justice. This is the MAJMA way!

But for pluralistic solidarities to emerge, victims themselves need to be mobilised; they need to acquire the agency for collective action, including forging alliances with pro-poor movements and groups. This requires educating, organising and mobilising 'victims' around rights and citizenship, so that they are able to voice their grievances and make demands on the state. This transition from 'victimhood' to 'empowerment' is the critical necessary condition for rights to be realised, and for inclusive and robust pro-poor alliances to be forged. Rights-based groups and community-based organisations (such as Afkar India Foundation, in this case) can play an important facilitating role in this transition.

Endnotes

1. BBC. 2013. Muzaffarnagar: Tales of death and despair in India's riot-hit town. Web edition, 25 September 2013. Available at: http://www.bbc.co.uk/news/world-asia-india-24172537
2. The Supreme Court of India, *Judgement in the Writ Petition (Criminal) No. 155 of 2013*. 26 March 2014, p37. State Government admitted to a figure of 50,955 made homeless.
3. Brass, Paul. 2003. *The Production of Muslim-Hindu violence in Contemporary India*. Seattle: University of Washington Press. Available at: http://www.paulbrass.com/the_production_of_hindu_muslim_violence_in_contemporary_india_16681.htm
4. Muzaffarnagar Adhikar Jan Manch (MAJMA), (2015), 'Report of the Aftermath of Violence in Villages in Muzaffarnagar and Shamli districts of Western Uttar Pradesh, India; and Civil Society Response for Survivors' Struggle for Justice, Rights and Peace' (September 2013–June 2014). Mimeo. February 2015. Available at: http://centreforequitystudies.org/wp-content/uploads/2015/06/MAJMA-Report-180215-2.pdf
5. On the construction of Jat dominance in the region, see Jefferey, Chris. 2008. 'Kicking Away the Ladder: Student Politics and the Making of an Indian Middle Class. *Environment and Planning*, vol. 26, pp. 517-36). Available at: http://www.arnold-bergstraesser.de/cms2/images/stories/Downloads/Jeffrey.pdf.
6. *The Hindu*. 13 September, 2013. 'Meltdown of the MAJGAR alliance'. Available at: http://www.thehindu.com/opinion/op-ed/meltdown-of-the-majgar-alliance/article5120950.ece
7. For an example of this analysis, refer to *Sanhati Web Edition*, 22 September, 2013, 'Death, Destruction and the Electoral Calculus: A Report on Muzaffarnagar Riot'. Statement by Shramjivi Pahal,. http://sanhati.com/articles/8034/
8. Refer to this article with similar conclusions. http://www.rediff.com/news/special/special-how-muzaffarnagar-riots-will-impact-2014-elections/20130919.htm
9. Rao, Mohan, Ish Mishra, Pragya Singh, and Vikas Bajpai 2014. 'Fact Finding Report: Independent Inquiry into Muzaffarnagar "Riots"'. *Economic and Political Weekly* vol. XLIX no. 2 January 2014. Available at: http://www.epw.in/web-exclusives/fact-finding-report-independent-inquiry-muzaffarnagar-%E2%80%9Criots%E2%80%9D.html
10. Interview with Neeshoo, (32), a male resident of Sanjhak village on 30 January 2014.
11. See Sajjad Hassan,'BJP legislators Hukum Singh, Sangat Singh Som, Suresh Rana and Kunwar Bharatendu;

former Congress MP Harendra Malik; Bharatiya Kisan Union leaders Rakesh Tikait and Naresh Tikait accused of making incendiary speeches and inciting violence'. *14 September, 2013.* http://www.countercurrents.org/hussain140913.htm

12. Supreme Court of India, 2013. Judgement in the Writ Petition (Criminal) No 155 of 2013, Md Haroon and Others vs Union of India and Another. (26 March 2014, p. 37). The state government, in its submission, admitted that at its height, the total figure of the displaced stood at 50,955 (27,198 persons in 41 camps in Muzaffarnagar and 23,757 persons in 17 camps in Shamli district).
13. Based on information provided to civil society groups in meeting with District Administration, Muzaffarnagar, 10 February 2014. The state government in its submission to the Supreme Court (March 2014) noted that of all the relief camps, only two along with four satellite camps remained operational in Shamli district, housing 2,618 persons in all. Ibid pp. 25
14. Indian Express, 5 December 2013. 'At least 40 children dead as UP riot relief camps brace for a long winter'. Available at:

    http://archive.indianexpress.com/news/at-least-40-children-dead-as-up-riot-relief-camps-brace-for-a-long-winter/1203511/
15. Asara (60), Badaut town (35), Baghpat town (20)
16. WSSNET, 1 December 2013. *Women's Bodies are Not Political Battlefields!* http://wssnet.org/2013/12/01/womens-bodies-are-not-political-battlefields/
17. Verma, Sushmita, and Jenny Sulfath. 'Less Evident Forms of Violence: Muzzafarnagar riots'. February 6, 2014. http://sanhati.com/articles/9144/
18. Oxfam India. 2015. A Study on the Status of Women Riot Survivors: State & Non-State Efforts towards Response & Rehabilitation. New Delhi.
19. Separately, Muslim religious organisations, also solemnised 156 marriages on its own, with its own incentives to parties, of Rs. 15,000. (Ibid, pp :21)
20. Chopra, S. and P. Jha (eds) 2014. *On their Watch: Mass Violence and State Apathy in India.* New Delhi: Three Essays Collective.
21. A notable exception is that of the of Officer in Charge of Budhna Police Station, Shailendra Lal, a Jat himself, who, it is claimed saved close to 200 lives in Hasanpur Majra of Lisarh village. It is reported that people from that neighbourhood in Joula camp carried photos of Lal in their pockets, and made it a point to tell people about him when they visited the camp.
22. Ghazala Jamil, 2014. 'Internally Displaced Muslims of Western Uttar Pradesh'. *Economic & Political Weekly,* 49:51, pp. 10-13.
23. Oxfam, A Study on the Status of Women Riot Survivors: State & Non-State Efforts towards Response & Rehabilitation.
24. An example of a success here came in the form of recent orders by the state government to provide basic services to those in resettlement colonies.
25. Ghazala Jamil, 2014, 'Internally Displaced Muslims of Western Uttar Pradesh', pp. 10
26. Ibid, pp 12
27. Notable here are: Tewary Commission (Assam, 1983); RN Mishra Commission and Nanavati Commission; (Delhi 1984); RCP Sinha Commission (Bhagalpur, 1989); and Sri Krishna Commission (Bombay, 1993).

Survivors of Ethnic Conflict

Sanjay (Xonzoi) Barbora and Saba Sharma[*]

1. Brief Description of the Excluded Group

1.1 Size and location of the group

Political violence in a particular area of western Assam has resulted in the death and displacement of several thousand persons of different ethnic groups since the early 1990s. The areas in question constitute the Bodo Territorial Areas Districts (BTAD), an entity that covers four districts—Kokrajhar, Baksa, Udalguri and Chirang—and is home to several ethnic groups who differ from one another in terms of language, religion and culture. The very existence of BTAD is contentious; the nomenclature suggests that it is the home of the Bodo-speaking community, while in reality several other language-speaking groups have an equal claim to the territory.

It would be best to begin with a reflection on the basis of social and political exclusion in India, as well as to engage with the discontinuities that emerge when one looks at the Northeast region. Social movements and organisations in South Asia as well as advocacy groups have relied on three historical modes of exclusion to work on strategies of dissent and political programmes: (a) caste, (b) religion and (c) language. When it comes to caste, there has been a long history of mobilisation (and persecution) in South Asia. Religion too has been an important source of political mobilisation, resulting in the partitioning of British India and the persistence of faith-based politics. Language, on the other hand, has been one of the main drivers behind movements to create new countries and states after the partitioning of the British Empire. Taken together, these three sources of conflict and cooperation have yielded a robust body of literature and documentation that one can draw from in order to understand the social realities in India. They also serve as a basis for interventions for enabling social inclusion and exclusion alike. It is easier, therefore, to map people according to their position within the different matrices that are created by the three modes of exclusion.

However, all three modes are insufficient to understand the peculiarities that exist in Northeast India. One needs to add a fourth mode of exclusion here: *territory*. It is true that caste, religion, and language too played a role in social exclusion in the region and there is literature that underscores their importance. Historians have shown how caste played a significant role in the segregation of communities in Assam[1] . Premier educational institutions, such as Cotton College, continued with the early 20th-century policies of separate dormitories and dining areas for tribal, Muslim, and upper caste students,

* Lead authors

** This chapter has been reviewed by Sajjad Hassan and Jan Breman

until relatively recently. Though some might argue that this, in itself, might not constitute a basis for exclusion (as all dormitories and dining areas could theoretically be offered similar amenities), the existence of such practices are significant.

Similarly, religion too has been the basis for exclusionary practices in Assam. Pre-colonial historical chronicles show the tensions that existed between emerging Vaishnavite Xatras and the Ahom rulers of eastern Assam, especially when the latter's corvée labour practices were challenged by the monasteries[2]. In contemporary times, there have been interesting works that allude to religion being an important social schism in Assam[3]. This is especially true in the context of conflicts that have emerged after political milestones such as 1947 (Indian independence) and 1971 (Bangladesh war of liberation). There has been a significant body of literature—especially from the 1950s to 1960s—that focus on various language movements in the Brahmaputra and Barak valleys of Assam[4,5]. The contestations between predominantly Assamese- and Bengali-speaking educated youth in both valleys have been important events in the eventual framing of political positions in Assam. Despite the occurrence of episodes that highlight the importance of caste, language, and religion in the narratives of exclusion, it is in questions of territory that the dynamics of exclusion are most pronounced.

Thus, the details of groups that are excluded by the territorial political discourse and dispensation are subject to several caveats. The first is a note of caution in accepting census definitions to fix a sense of belonging of groups to territory. In his critical analysis of the census in colonial Sudan, Mahmood Mamdani draws attention to the complex dynamics involved in the colonial state's classificatory politics and also the manner in which the colonised responded to this regime[6]. The situation in BTAD mimics Sudan in many ways: it is home to several language-speaking and religious groups. The last census (2011) data for the four districts shows a consolidated population of 3,151,047 people. Within it are several ethnic and religious groups, including Scheduled Tribe groups such as the Bodos and Rabhas, other tribal groups or Adivasis (not classified officially as STs) such as the Santhals, Oraons, Mundas, the Bengali Muslims, as well as smaller numbers of Koch Rajbongshis, Bengali Hindus, Nepalis, etc. Data from the 2011 census on religions and tribes indicates the Bodo population to be 29 per cent in the BTAD, while the proportion of Muslims is around 19 per cent. Other groups are not disaggregated.

1.2 Historical context of exclusion and discrimination

The nineteenth century was in fact the era of expansion of capital to hitherto untrammelled landscapes such as Assam. This supposed discovery

Table 1

District	Total Population	No. of Muslims	Percentage of total	No. of Bodos	Percentage of Total
Kokrajhar	887,142	252,271	28%	225,041	25%
Chirang	482,162	109,248	23%	167,888	35%
Udalguri	831,668	105,319	13%	218,581	26%
Baksa	950,075	135,750	14%	288,397	30%
TOTAL	3,151,047	602,588	19%	899,907	29%

Source: Census 2011, Table C-01, *Population by Religious Community (India and States/UTs/District/Sub-Distt/Town Level)*; Census 2011, Table A-11, *Individual Scheduled Tribe Primary Census Abstract Data and its Appendix.*

precipitated a move towards a fundamentally different type of economy, where the movement of populations became a condition for growth and colonisation.[7] The process of creating frontiers became a condition peculiar to the type of economy introduced. Hence, a complicated process of mapping the region within notions of centre-periphery was undertaken. Those inhabiting regions that were not immediately earmarked for expansion of capital and colonial administration were clearly subjected to a position of marginality precisely because they constituted a new periphery. It is in the interplay between spaces and peoples that ethnicity becomes an important factor in defining subjects.

The Bodo are an ethnic community comprising a number of groups speaking a more or less common dialect or language and claiming a common ancestry. They have been referred to as *Kachari* in the pre-colonial historiography of Assam. Until the 12th century, these groups controlled much of present-day Assam. They are considered aborigines of the Brahmaputra valley. Though there is some dispute as to how many sub-groups actually constitute the larger Bodo group, it is widely accepted that 18 different groups are part of the larger family mentioned above[8]. The question of their homogenous ethnic identity is widely contested by ethnographers and administrators alike. A census conducted by the colonial British government in 1881 listed 12 sub-groups who were collectively termed as 'Bodo-speaking groups', whereas others like Endle[9] counted as many as 15 such sub-groups.

It is generally believed that these groups inhabited the fertile plains of the Luit (Brahmaputra) river in the 12th century and due to frequent skirmishes with waves of migrating groups of people, like the Tai-Ahom from the east and the Indo-Aryan groups from the west, they moved to Karbi and North Cachar Hills in the 16th century. According to Nath, the Aryanisation of these groups began in the royal houses and the process ceased to hold much sway after the 16th century, at least among the masses[10]. The acceptance of Hinduisation by certain sections of the predominantly swidden[11] agricultural society, did create some degree of difference among the people who live in the region and many traces of this are seen even today[12]. Using a mix of anthropology and probabilities arising out of myths and oral history, Ajoy Roy says that following '[...] intelligent guess work [one] does find some physiognomic and temperamental similarities between the Bodos and the present Kham tribes of Tibet.'[13] Other refrains about the possible origin of Bodo people lead to further confusion, typical of any myth of origin that sees the Bodo as Mongoloid aborigines of the Luit valley.[14] This is not as bewildering a position as it appears. The region known as Assam today was once considered a crossroads for several cultures and peoples. It was home to corporate groups of migrants, traders, and smaller subsistence-agriculture-based ethnic groups. These groups moved constantly between South Asia, Southeast Asia and inner Asia.[15] In such cases, it is important to conjure a sense of the geography of resource use among the denizens of the 'crossroads', with the Bodo-speaking group being one among many.

The colonial encounter transformed the social and political structures of the region. Trade routes into Southeast Asia and China were closed and new routes opened. In order to monitor and regulate the trade activities in the region, the colonial authorities constructed an all-weather road from Mangaldoi to Udalguri and moved some troops to Udalguri. In addition to these measures, they also began according obligatory rights to tribal chiefs who lived in the hills. The idea was to pay them to maintain some degree of law and order along the trade route. Hence, seven hill-chiefs, known as *Sath Rajahs* (seven kings) were to be paid an annual amount in return for their services as surveillance agents of the state[16]. With law and order established just the way the colonial authorities desired, traders started making inroads into the region. Soon, barter gave way to monetary transactions and balance of trade favoured those who used the currency of the British administration. Unlike the older generation of traders, the new traders were from different parts of the subcontinent and belonged to communities whose access to and use of capital were legendary. They controlled the wholesale trade in the Udalguri market.

All communities that lived in this region underwent a profound change during this period. Pushed away from agriculture and trading, the Bodo peasants were compelled to fall back on the thickly forested areas north of Udalguri. Adjacent to the forests there were vast grasslands where a variety of long, thatched grass grew. The peasants became substantially dependent on the forest and grasslands. This survival strategy worked for a while, as the Bodo-speaking farmers traded small quantities of lac and rubber obtained from the forests. However, the northward push by merchants meant that commercial interests threatened even the livelihood arising from small-scale dependence on the forests. By the time the authorities began getting revenue from the forests, non-Bodo merchants from north India had taken control of what had become a lucrative timber trade. The Bodo-speaking peasants were thereafter barred from felling trees and extracting any resources from the vast forest region north of the river.[17] Much of the forested areas north of the Brahmaputra were declared reserved forests or wildlife sanctuaries in the early 20th century and this substantiated the notion that Bodo-speaking people had been pushed out of areas that the colonial state had claimed for itself.[18]

By 1947, two simultaneous processes were seen to be working among the indigenous, non-caste Hindu people (including the Bodo) peoples of the region.[19] First, these societies were poised at the brink of tremendous change. Education and social reform had created enough aspirations for democratic rule. Many tribal intellectuals sympathised with the anti-colonial struggle. Second, tribal societies were relatively weakly positioned with respect to the aggressive decolonising nationalist ethos prevalent at the time. This meant that while a section of tribal society was optimistic about the changes that were to come, it was still a matter of concern as to just how they would be able to negotiate their place in the postcolonial sun and seek coherence as communities within a (new) nation-state.

Following the transfer of power in 1947, the interim government of India appointed a sub-committee of the Constituent Assembly, called the North-East Frontier (Assam) Tribal and Excluded Areas Sub-committee under the chairmanship of the Assamese political leader, Gopinath Bordoloi. Ostensibly, this happened because the leaders of the anti-colonial struggle were sensitive to the need for adequate understanding of the situation in the Northeast, especially with regard to the growing aspirations of the tribal people. The sub-committee, also known as the Bordoloi Committee, sought to '...reconcile the aspirations of the hill people for political autonomy with the Assam government's drive to integrate them with the plains.'[20] The instrument of this integrative devolution of powers was embodied in the concept of the 'Autonomous District Councils' designed by the committee. This instrument was thereafter passed by the Constituent Assembly *with certain modifications* and it now constitutes the Sixth Schedule of the Constitution of India. Originally, the Sixth Schedule was to apply to the 'tribal', essentially hill areas of Assam. On 25 January 1950, the Indian Constitution came into force. As would be expected from such an ambitious nation-building project, the Constitution tried to build in some safeguards for the marginalised and oppressed groups in the country. For the people of the Northeast frontier, this safeguard came in the form of the Sixth Schedule of the Constitution. The provisions in the Sixth Schedule dealt mainly with the issue of safeguarding the land and customs of the hill tribes of the region. It drew upon the erstwhile 'excluded and partially excluded areas' legislation of the colonial state. Yet again, the Bodo people and others were left outside the ambit of Constitutional protection. The communities categorised as hill tribes by the colonial census did get a semblance of territory but the Sixth Schedule was not equipped to handle immigration. As other issues like cultural and social hegemony of dominant ethnic groups continued to eat away into the fabric of political discourse in Assam, the realities of the day seemed to lead the tribal people into yet another long series of confrontations with not just the state apparatus, but also with the dominant groups associated with the state.

Educated Bodo youth had already begun to feel the need for more say in the political and economic distribution; they were of the opinion that these 'belts' and 'blocks' were just not enough. As early as 1933, when the All Assam Plains Tribal League was formed under the initiative of the Bodo leader Rupnath Brahma and his counterpart Bhimbor Deori, the need to reassess the condition of the Bodo-speaking peoples in the region was of utmost importance. Continuing with the formation of a consolidated political collective, the Bodo Sahitya Sabha (BSS) was formed in 1952. The Forum's main activities were to promote and protect Bodo culture and identity in the face of what they perceived as a growing threat to their survival as a people. It also aimed to devise a 'standard Bodo language', which could be a link for all the Bodo-speaking peoples in the region.[21] Some years later, in 1967, the educated Bodo youth also formed a student body known as the All Bodo Students Union (ABSU). In the years to come, these civic organisations would try to steer Bodo political discourse through several challenges, both from within and from external forces.

The Plains Tribal Council of Assam (PTCA), a body representing the various tribes living in the plains, including the Bodo, sent a memorandum to the President of India in 1967, stating:

> ...the bitter experience of the last 20 years of independence has given rise to a firm conviction among the tribals of Assam that the Assam government is not interested in giving adequate protection to tribal land. It has deliberately rehabilitated refugees from East Pakistan in tribal Belts and Blocks areas, given settlement to the non-tribal encroachers...(in) gross violation of provisions of the Belts and Blocks.[22]

The main demand of the PTCA was the federal re-organisation of Assam. Symbolic of the fact that the decision to rationally allow for democratic federalism could not be taken by the denizens of the region, the central government in Delhi rejected the plan submitted to them. Over the next few years, this demand took concrete shape in the agitation for a homeland for the plains tribes of Assam. This homeland was called 'Udayachal'. Almost immediately, the Koch-Rajbongshi community who shared the same spaces with the plains tribes struck a discordant note and opposed the demand for a separate state for the Scheduled Tribes, in this case the Bodo and the Mishing. The Koch-Rajbongshi community was not among the Schedule Tribe list and the fact that they had been Hinduised seemed to weigh against them. Soon after, dissent among the PTCA leaders led to a split in the movement, with one section renaming itself the Plains Tribal Council of Assam (Progressive) with a broader position on which communities ought to be considered indigenous communities in such a proposed state.

Here, it is interesting to also note the differences and similarities of political mobilisation in the areas where tribal communities claim to enjoy a statistically contentious demographic advantage over others. It is a matter of concern for most Bodo academics and activists that the Bordoloi Commission chose to leave the Bodo-inhabited areas outside the purview of the Sixth Schedule, choosing instead to implement the ineffectual 'tribal Belts or Blocks' for the plains tribes of Assam.[23] Hence, a discussion on the Sixth Schedule of the Indian constitution is warranted here.

The Sixth Schedule provides that for any area notified as an autonomous region by the Governor of the state, a district council comprising 30 members will be elected. Of these, the Governor of the state appoints four. Thereafter, it is the Governor who makes the rules for the first constitution of councils in consultation with the tribal representative organisations. As may be noticed, it is the Governor who has the final say in the creation and dissolution of the council. As for finance, the autonomous district council gets a meagre amount from business and commercial enterprises and some land revenue. A district and regional fund, endowed and managed by the Governor, is the main source by which the autonomous body is financed. The powers of the autonomous council are varied, but it is in their capacity to regulate land transfer that their discretionary powers are most interesting. Following the colonial policies of allowing land in the hills to be under 'community ownership' and not bringing such land under its revenue scheme, the Sixth Schedule also mentions that tribal land is not to be sold to anyone and that it belongs to the community. However, by 1979, the overwhelming logic of doing away with community property was visible in a notification wherein private property was not only acknowledged but also encouraged.[24] In that sense, the councils and village chiefs became the most likely figures of authority to be able to grant and renew leases and land titles. Furthermore, this created opportunities for political manipulation, wherein it was known that village chiefs, who belonged to one or the other political party, would try and push the leases (or titles) of their party members if a friendly party dominated the executive council. This discrepancy between formal rules of the game and informal occurrences, the tension between valorising 'tribal tradition and community' and undermining the community by extending the logic of private property, all contributed to the reaction which was sometimes violent and always aggrieved. This was the architecture adopted for the two hill districts and subsequently grafted on to the multi-ethnic, polyglot districts that comprise BTAD; naturally, such a move had disturbing consequences.

In 1999, leaders of an armed opposition group—Bodo Liberation Tigers (BLT)—declared a unilateral ceasefire with the government and said that it was ready to be part of talks. In response, the government announced that it would create a territorial council under the Sixth Schedule for an area demarcated in consultation with representatives of the Bodo groups and the government of Assam. Almost immediately, non-Bodo groups launched a massive agitation claiming that such a move would not only encourage more ethnic clashes, but also lead to evictions and population transfers from the proposed area. The story, however, predates the 1999 ceasefire announcement. In 1988, the Bodo Peoples, Action Committee (BPAC) was formed to try to incorporate all the different tendencies within the Bodo movement. However, this could not stop the rupture within the ranks of the Bodo movement with the All Bodo Students Union (ABSU) scaling down its 92-point demand to just three, which included the creation of a full-fledged state on the North Bank (of the river Luit), the creation of autonomous districts for the Bodo on the South Bank, and the inclusion of non-Karbi tribals of Karbi Anglong in the Sixth Schedule. This position was obviously not acceptable to other tribal groups and the government of Assam. The central government intervened and initiated a tripartite round of talks with the ABSU-BPAC combine and the government of Assam in 1989.

After eight rounds of talks, the government of India proposed a three-member expert committee in 1990 to examine and demarcate the areas of the Bodo and other plains tribes of Assam and submit its report within 45 days to make recommendations on autonomy. The committee submitted a report with a proposal to grant maximum autonomy to the Bodo, short of a separate state within the Indian union, which the BPAC-ABSU leaders resolutely rejected. However, the recommendations did foreground some concrete points over which the leaders would possibly soften their stand and accept a compromise. The main issue that remained was one of the inclusion of a certain number of villages within the proposed homeland. While a section of the Bodo leaders insisted on as many as 4,443 villages to be included in the proposed territory, the state government offered another sop saying that it would be the contiguity of the region that would determine the basis of the creation of an autonomous Bodo territory, i.e., villages in which the Bodo constituted even a mere one per cent of the tribal population would be included within a compact territorial area. A section of the BPAC-ABSU leadership debated the issue and came up with a counter-demand where an additional 1,035 villages were to be added to any proposed autonomous territory. The issue was referred back to the central government.

In 1993, the central government herded together the Bodo leaders, who had sent friendly and frequent feelers for an honourable resolution of the conflict, as well as the government of Assam, to sign what came to be known as the 'Bodo Accord' in Kokrajhar. The accord created the Bodoland Autonomous Council (BAC), that was to comprise an area covering 2,000 villages and 25 estates stretching from the Sakosh river to Mazbat Pasnoi on the north bank of the river Luit (Brahmaputra), via a government of Assam notification (No. TAD/BAC/26/93/18).[25] The area also included reserved forests as per the guidelines of the Ministry of Defence and the Ministry of Environment, Government of India. The actual difficulty in the demarcation of the boundary continued to be the vehement opposition of the non-Scheduled Tribe population living in the area. A considerable number of people residing in the said area are actually classified as Scheduled Tribes outside Assam. This is especially true of erstwhile indentured labourers who had left the tea plantations. Hence, there are large pockets of Santhal, Munda and Oraon villages and these ethnic groups are considered Scheduled Tribes as per the Central list. The government of Assam has not included these tribes in its list of Scheduled Tribes in Assam.

On the other hand, there was also an internal split within the broad spectrum of political discourse in the Bodo community, with an armed section of the movement declaring the accord to be a "sell-out" of the original goal of an ethnic homeland for the Bodo community. A more militant armed opposition group called the Bodo Security Force denounced the accord and vowed to continue 'the resistance to colonialism.'[26] This organisation was later renamed the National Democratic Front of Bodoland (NDFB) and continues its armed activities against the state. Importantly, the armed oppositional activities had begun to articulate the idea of self-determination for the Bodo-speaking people. This included complete and total secession from India. The rejection of the Indian Constitution marks an epistemological break of sorts in the movement. Both armed factions, the Bodoland Liberation Tiger Force (BLTF) and NDFB, repudiated the formation of the BAC, though their positions were considerably different. Both had an ideological problem with a 'deal' that diluted the movement for self-determination. Since the year 1996, the BLTF and NDFB had been engaged in a series of internecine wars in which both sides took extreme steps to target each other's cadre and sympathisers. The fault-lines between the two groups spilled over into the public sphere as well. It was obvious that a section of Bodo political opinion, especially the students and literary bodies, favoured a settlement brokered by the central government. In this settlement, they saw the beginning of a barter where they gained more resources, and which made it possible for them to control the ethnic competition that would arise with other groups. Indeed, one of the most disturbing aspects of the armed struggle for any kind of autonomy in the Bodo-inhabited areas is that successive episodes of violence have made it look like a campaign for ethnic cleansing of the area. There is a continuing debate on what constitutes the historically demarcated Bodo areas and the contemporary demographic realities. This adds a potentially intractable angle to the question of who 'belongs' to a particular version of national space.

Echoing a concern along these lines, Biswas and Bhattacharjee state that '(ethnic) movements in the Northeast can be understood in terms of a contest over greater social, political and cultural spaces, the spaces in which the ethnic communities were not hitherto represented. This non-representation is further explained within the contexts of rights, power and authority, which cause ethnocentric concerns to find their expression in contestations in many possible ways.'[27] Here, contestation against the 'other' assumes the most explicit form in social spaces, for purposes of mobilisation. The 'other' is characterised in terms of an undifferentiated concept of citizenship, as enshrined within the Constitution of India, which does not recognise the claims of any identity to override others represented within the nation and the state. This contradiction between the statist view and collective aspirations is sharpened through a number of unsuccessful mediation measures (undertaken by the State) that seek to negotiate the variation in representations of identity and space between communities. One wishes to locate the ethnic polarisation in the Bodo areas within this context, especially in the absence of an effective mediation process that can accommodate different responses.

Splits within the movement are a prime example of the kind of ad-hoc policies that are taken up by the state apparatus in containing the problem posed for the nation-building process by ethno-national projects. The persistence of colonial tones in political structures in the region only accounts for one aspect of the 'ends' to which governments strive—that of political and territorial unity. In the process, the Indian state's propensity to carve out states to satisfy the political elite might suggest that it is more 'tolerant' of ethnic aspirations. However, the fact that it has a definite 'ethnic agenda' of its own—an agenda that is shaped by policy machines that are not 'ethnically neutral'—is a condition that negates the provisional safeguards in its Constitution.[28,29]

There seems to be a pattern to ethno-nationalist demands for autonomy in the Northeast, and a lack of institutional capability to handle these demands. Most political demands for self-determination are centrally linked to the idea of the distinct identity of an ethnic group. The manner in which this identity consciousness is articulated is precisely the subject of discussion here. It is against this backdrop that much of what appears as guarantees of autonomy compatible with the aspirations of given groups of people within the framework of the Constitution, or even within international law, can actually be seen as a condensed body of intricate political negotiation. In essence, these negotiations are supposed to appear as processes that lead to further democratisation of society and politics. In the Indian context, this idea was supposed to form the core of the federal ethos of the republican tradition. Hence, provisions like the Sixth Schedule, Article 371A and the recent Panchayati Raj Bill are seen as efforts to ensure the devolution of powers of administration and governance to the grassroots. In each case, legislative, resource mobilisation and executive powers are supposed to somehow address the complex web of people's aspirations. Yet in the manner in which they filter down, they leave more questions than answers in their wake. One senses the overwhelming assertion of the concern of the (centralised) state at losing its locus as the sovereign fount of law and administrative processes. Indian democracy is defined by its constitution, inasmuch as it is defined by a particular notion of the rule of the 'majority'. On one hand, a 'statist' view asserts that it is the individual citizen, rather than seemingly amorphous collectives, who is the backbone of the state. This view evoked the tensions between notions of citizenship and communitarian collectives, and reiterated that the state 'was above all gods.'[30] The view that the individual's loyalties as a citizen of the state supersede her or his loyalty to other identities is constantly being challenged by a second discourse that is articulated against the backdrop of inadequate representation in matters of governance and administration. It would be tempting to see the persistence of primordial identity in the shaping of demands for autonomy in such a situation. Perhaps it would help to see some semblance of political leverage at work here. The definitions of an indigenous collective self is meant to challenge a 'settler' nation-state. In both cases, indigenous cultures within postcolonial societies find themselves excluded from the decision-making processes that are central to the state. Their subsequent declaration of separation from a 'mother body' is based on an implicit declaration of *people-hood* emerging from genealogy and descent ties which function 'not only as other sub-national units do in, say, the assertion of ethnicity, but point to the history of pre-contact and raise questions about legal and moral legitimacy of the present national formation'.[31] In this significant development, one sees that ethnicity and notions of ethnic contiguities begin to change almost as soon as the community sees itself as the purveyor of a smaller national space. In just a matter of two or three decades, the organic solidarity of the groups classified as plains tribes, against caste-Assamese society, changes to one of mutual distrust and competition between groups who are placed on the same social and economic plane.

Central to both discourses are certain principles that govern the quest for autonomy. Autonomy and autonomous institutions have not delivered justice. Hence, it is rare to find an instance where autonomy has sought to work on the principle of restitution, by acknowledging that an injustice has been committed or that some form of reconciliation has to be undertaken. Moreover, autonomy—as framed within a statist discourse—does not address the issue of control of resources, finances and costs of running autonomous territories in a comprehensive manner. When they do, as in the Sixth Schedule, they seem ineffectual and laden with contradictions that make the principle of custodianship appear more like a managerial policy. As long as autonomy arrangements are seen as a tool to manage the political demands of people in the region, there will always be problems with their implementation. For every instance where an ethnic group is promised autonomy, there will remain others who will claim to be aggrieved by that arrangement.

1.3 The broader excluded group(s) they belong to

The Bodo Territorial Council is a unique place where most ethnic groups feel some sense of exclusion. In this, the BTAD is a little like the former Yugoslavia, where contentious histories, discordant narratives, and an unfavourable political vocabulary for re-imagining territorial belonging created a tragic series of upheavals and social strife. For many, it might seem as though the Bodo people have managed to push out other communities who seek to claim a place in the area.[32] Nothing could be further from the truth.

As mentioned earlier, BTAD is home to several linguistic and religious groups. Many feel disturbed by the terms on which autonomous institutions have been set up in the area. In districts like Baksa, local communities have come together to form Land Rights Committees (LRC), *Gaon Unnayan* Committees (Village Development Committees), in addition to the Village Development Councils (VDC). The VDC is possibly the smallest administrative unit of the BTC and is formed as part of the BTC's mandate. The other two units—LRC and *Gaon Unnayan* Committees—are voluntary. As voluntary bodies, they bring together different ethnic groups from a block or group of villages. In BTAD, most villages are mixed, to the extent that different groups live in close proximity to one another. Within the larger village, there are smaller, more homogenous enclaves of ethnic groups. Almost all these groups have a claim, either seasonal or on longer-term leases, on the forests and grazing reserves of the BTAD. The LRC and *Gaon Unnayan* Committees therefore have the difficult task of creating a common platform for all the ethnic groups. They also carry out surveys, sometimes with the help of developmental non-government organisations (NGOs), focusing on the social and economic indices of the villages.

These voluntary associations are indicative of the networks of solidarity that exist between different ethnic groups. Their work extends beyond conducting surveys: they also undertake unofficial cadastral surveys of landholdings, assess the requirement of individual members for access to grazing land, and most crucially, negotiate with functionaries of the BTC. None of these activities are as cut-and-dried as one might imagine. They are exercises in solidarity-building and grassroots diplomacy that unfortunately do not have much say in policy matters. After all, when it comes to dealing with the land and revenue department (that has now been transferred from Dispur to Kokrajhar for the BTAD), LRCs and other voluntary associations are at best seen as pressure groups, or else as irritants.

However small and statistically insignificant, the existence of such voluntary associations that bring together different ethnic groups is *ideologically* of utmost importance. They allude to class-based solidarities among collectives that are clearly aware of the precariousness of their claims to resources in the BTAD.

2. Analysis of Exclusion

In this section, we examine the kinds of exclusion that stem from dealing with violence as a regular occurrence. Most of these themes address both the long-term impact of constant, recurring violence, as well as the kind of exclusion faced in the aftermath of a major event, of which the BTAD has seen several in the last two decades. The last three years have also seen several major instances of violence, beginning with the riots between the Bodo and Bengali Muslims in July and August 2012, which caused displacement on an unprecedented scale in the region. A total of 485,921 persons were displaced across four districts, according to official estimates from district administrations.[33] Not even two years later, May 2014 brought another violent massacre of Bengali Muslims in Baksa district, while in December that year Adivasis in Sonitpur[34] and Kokrajhar districts were attacked and displaced by the insurgent outfit NDFB(S), along with retaliatory violence against the Bodo. Recent incidents help us understand how violence can shape and sometimes permanently affect social, economic, and political relations.[35]

2.1 Exclusion from security

The idea of security as a right, or as a public good that should be available to all, is not explicitly articulated in the Constitution of India, but has been interpreted from Article 21, pertaining to the protection of life and personal liberty. In *S. S. Ahluwalia vs. Union of India and others*, the Supreme Court held that

> in the expanded meaning attributed to Article 21 of the Constitution, it is the duty of the State to create a climate where members of the society belonging to different faiths, caste and creed live together and, therefore, the State has a duty to protect their life, liberty, dignity and worth of an individual which should not be jeopardised or endangered. If in any circumstances the State is not able to do so, then it cannot escape the liability to pay compensation to the family of the person killed during riots as his or her life has been extinguished in clear violation of Article 21 of the Constitution.[36]

This judgement built on a previous judgement of the Delhi High Court in a case pertaining to the Sikh riots of 1984, in which the court noted that

> It is the duty and responsibility of the State to secure and safeguard life and liberty of an individual from mob violence. It is not open to the State to say that the violations are being committed by private persons for which it cannot be held accountable.[37]

In addition to this, India is also party to UN

conventions like the United Nations Declaration of Human Rights and the International Covenant on Civil and Political Rights, both of which clearly spell out the right of a person to life, liberty and security. While the essence of these judgements and conventions is not articulated in legislation, the draft Communal Violence Bill proposed by the National Advisory Council in 2011 clearly articulated the duty of the state to protect its citizens from targeted and communal violence.[38] While we argue that conflict in the BTAD must be understood in its own context, and not in the framework of communal violence, we use this bill here as an illustration of the need to spell out the right of a citizen to feel safe and secure, and the duty of the state to provide this security.

Conversely, 'security' as interpreted by the state in the context of the BTAD, as in other parts of the Northeast, is understood within the narrow parameters of militarisation. The relationship with military and paramilitary forces is complex in the region. People have testified to a lack of confidence in the police force, placing more faith in paramilitary forces like the Central Reserve Police Force (CRPF) or the Sashastra Seema Bal (SSB), particularly during tense periods following a riot or targeted killings. Augmenting the military presence has been the government's response each time major violence has occurred in Chirang or Kokrajhar, and the presence of military and paramilitary forces is standard in BTAD. Post-conflict, this militarisation has led to villagers in sensitive areas—particularly areas where one community is in a minority—feeling safer, leading them to demand that the presence of the forces be extended, or made permanent. As most security pickets, even in the more sensitive villages, began to withdraw in October 2013, people began to express apprehension about what would follow, and what would now serve as a deterrent if things flared up again.

In November 2014, the Armed Forces (Special Powers) Act (AFSPA) was extended in Assam for another year, with Assam's definition as a 'disturbed area' being renewed once again after the original declaration in 1990.[39] The origins of AFSPA are in a colonial law known as the Armed Forces Special Powers Ordinance of 1942, which authorised 'competent officers' in the military with special powers to help contain the Quit India Movement.[40] Prolonged use of AFSPA, however, has led to various detrimental effects in other areas of the Northeast. The Justice Jeevan Reddy Committee, set up by the Ministry of Home Affairs, noted that the Naga Hills, a region experiencing AFSPA since 1958, demonstrates a record of particular controversy—including complaints of rape, torture, arbitrary killings and fake encounters.[41] The increasing presence of the military in the BTAD has ostensibly been to deal with insurgency; various insurgent groups have been present since the late 1980s, were at their peak in the 1990s, and continue to carry out violent attacks even today. Overall, however, the constant presence of the military has also led to great distrust between the military and ordinary people, with expressions of resentment following 'fake encounters' during counter-insurgency operations and the roughing up of young Bodo men constantly suspected as militants.[42] In December 2013, for instance, two Bodo school students were killed and one seriously injured in an 'encounter'; the police and army insisted afterwards that the children had links with the extremist outfit NDFB(S).[43] The incident led to days of protest against the army and district administration, and reinforced once more the alienation of army personnel from the locals they are supposed to protect. The trust deficit between people and the police means that even when people want to report militant activity, they are reluctant to do so, fearing retribution from the militants before they are afforded protection by the police.

Perceptions of local law enforcement agents like the police are no better. There is a severe shortage of police in the districts, and where they are present, people are unlikely to place much faith in them.[44] The bifurcation of power between the BTC and the state government means that law and order is the primary duty of the district administration (under the Assam government), and is done largely without any consultation with the BTC. At the village level, people would rather solve disputes internally, through village leaders, than involve the police. Even in extreme cases, such as those involving murder or sexual violence, going to the police may spell more harassment for all concerned, involving bribes and inefficiency. It is widely accepted that during riots the police are absent and unresponsive, rarely arriving in time to provide protection. Fact-finding reports from 2012 have confirmed the inability and reluctance of the local police force to step in during the riots.[45] In the village of Choraikola, five kilometres from Kokrajhar town and across the road from the 7th Battalion headquarters of the state police force, Muslim residents claim that during the riots, the police did not come to their aid despite repeated pleas from villagers. In their eyes, the police are either too scared to confront armed militants or, worse, in league with the Bodo and the BPF in particular.

Other agents of local government, for instance forest guards, can also be seen as aggressors. In May 2014, for instance, after the targeted killing of Bengali Muslims in Narayanguri village in Baksa district, villagers blamed forest guards in the area, whom they also alleged were ex-BLT members, for killing them as 'punishment' for the ruling party's loss in the Lok Sabha election of 2014.[46] Despite a lack of official verification for this claim (although the guards were arrested),[47] the perception of the guards as aggressors is firmly implanted in the minds of the victims. In stark contrast to the idea of the right to security and safety therefore, government law enforcement services like the police, army and paramilitary forces, and sometimes even officials from the BTC (although they have no jurisdiction over law enforcement), are in direct contradiction of this ideal.

The consequences of the constant sense of insecurity vis-à-vis state actors as well as other communities are evident. Although people of different communities and ethnicities have co-existed in BTAD for several centuries, the effects of a perpetual state of violence has meant that communities become increasingly polarised geographically, socially, and in extreme instances, also economically. In most villages of Kokrajhar and Chirang, it is common for villages to contain within them hamlets or *bastis* of particular communities, which may either be in close proximity, or in other instances, quite separate. Some villages may have inhabitants entirely of a single community, while 'mixed' villages may be mixed in degrees. Remote villages, particularly those surrounded by forests, also deal with the additional insecurity caused by insurgent outfits like the NDFB, and army and paramilitary camps set up to protect against them. Insurgents create their own sense of terror, sometimes killing people suspected of being informants, levying annual 'taxes' on villages and businesses, and kidnapping to extort money. Calling of strikes or bandhs by various groups and outfits is a routine occurrence, often making daily life come to a standstill.[48] Travelling or operating a business during a bandh can be risky, and people are unlikely to take the risk, especially when called by influential or powerful outfits like the NDFB.

The ever-present sense of insecurity is further exacerbated when an incident takes place between two groups, whether killings by insurgents, a fight that escalates in a particular village or region, or, as in 2012, full-blown riots that suspend normal living for months at a time. Despite the fact that 170 persons were arrested in connection with the violence, and a CBI investigation conducted, the sense of insecurity persisted.[49] Social relations between Bengali Muslims and the Bodo suffered tremendously after the riots, and were only aggravated by the ongoing economic boycott of the Bengali Muslims. The boycott also became a way of expressing the anger and resentment that many survivors of the riots felt. Even two years after the riots, there were villages where people of one community would refuse to enter the neighbourhood of another. Parents

Box 1. The Case of the Never-ending Camp

Joyma Camp is in Kathalguri village of Kokrajhar, just off Highway 31, which connects Guwahati with Barhi in Jharkhand. 163 families, originally from Rampurbhil village 30 kilometres away, have been settled here since July 2012, when Bodo-Muslim violence engulfed the BTAD for months together. The camp's residents still live in makeshift structures of plastic sheets, struggling with two barely functional temporary toilets and a few hand pumps donated by charities. While Joyma was set up as an 'official' camp during the violence, today it exists on no government record. Residents have been struggling to find land to settle on near the camp, being too afraid to return to their villages where their homes and shops no longer exist, and where they are in too small a minority to feel safe. Government efforts at rehabilitation are all but dead, and talks with the Jamaat-e-Ulema Hind, a charity that promised to buy them land, fell through in 2014. Currently, they stay on the agricultural land of a landowner in Kathalguri village, to whom they pay a small rent each month, to compensate for his loss in cropping. As the years have passed, residents have become increasingly bitter, no longer making trips to the Deputy Commissioner's office to check on progress. Jamaat-e-Ulema Hind's promises to build houses for people able to buy land on their own is materialising too slowly for complete rehabilitation to be anywhere in sight. As Imrad Hussain, a representative of the camp's population says, 'It's been three years, but feels like ninety.'

Joyma is not the only remnant of ethnic violence in the BTAD. Camp-like structures still exist across the BTAD districts of Kokrajhar and Chirang, although they do not exist on the official radar of the government. In such camps, there has been no state intervention after the distribution of the compensation amount. Any interventions on water, sanitation, health, education, food or livelihood are through civil society organisations like NGOs or religious charities. The phenomenon of camps that don't shut down is not new in the BTAD. In 1996, clashes between the Bodo and Santhals left more than 2.6 lakh persons displaced, while further violence in 1998 took the figure over 3 lakh persons. 1.26 lakh of these were still living in state-sponsored relief camps nearly a decade later, in 2005.[a] Even as late as November 2011, estimates put the number of persons still living in relief camps from both rounds of violence at approximately 36,000.[b] As the number of incidents increase with the years, so do the total number of permanently displaced persons in the BTAD. In many instances, camps become regularised as villages, as has happened for instance with Bengtol Camp in Chirang, formerly a relief camp from the 1996 violence, and now a recognised village. However, even this transition is neither swift nor easy, as is evident by the efforts of Joyma camp residents to resettle in Kathalguri village.

a Monirul Hussain and Pradip Phanjoubam (2007), *A Status Report on Displacement in Assam and Manipur*, Kolkata: MCRG, p. 7.

b Internal Displacement Monitoring Centre figures cited in Tiwari, Shishir and Gitanjali Ghosh (2014), 'From Conflict to Accord and a Decade Henceforth: The Plight of Internally Displaced Persons in Bodoland and the Law', *Elixir International Law*, no. 70.

became anxious about sending their children to ICDS centres in the *bastis* of other communities, and in other places, the Bodo or Bengali Muslims present in small numbers left their villages altogether, out of fear. The district administrations in Kokrajhar and Chirang attempted to create inter-village 'peace committees' after the riots with the purpose of providing a platform for dialogue to members of all the diverse communities in the village. Unfortunately, like many initiatives of the administration, these were half-hearted attempts with no follow-through after the initial, token meetings. Moreover, instead of fostering dialogue, they ended up creating a space for district officials to lecture publicly about the need for peace, with no clear plan as to how it could be achieved, or how such dialogue could be begun, let alone sustained.

2.2 Exclusions in relief and rehabilitation

One of the government's primary roles in the event of a major attack or violent incident is to address relief and rehabilitation needs. Typically, after a major occurrence, like riots, people flee their homes, seeking shelter in nearby schools or other buildings which may later go on to become relief camps. After the 2012 riots, the Bodo and Muslims reported staying in relief camps for anything between three and eight months, with the average being close to six months. As several newspapers, fact-finding teams and civil society members noted at the time, camps were overcrowded and often lacking in basic facilities, including sanitation, drinking water, bedding, utensils and so on. Where food rations, clothes or other necessary items fell short, NGOs were filling in for the state.[50] Particularly in areas such as health, education and sanitation, NGOs were responsible for fulfilling a role that the state either could not or would not fulfil.

Destruction of property, more than loss of lives, became the central theme of post-violence recovery during the 2012 riots. In some areas, Muslims alleged that this was deliberate, and that this was a ploy to drive them out of the BTAD by rendering them without property or assets.[51] While the burning down of houses and businesses was the most visible impact, much of the destruction of livelihoods also came from the looting of household property, cattle, stocks of grains, and so forth. While burnt-down houses were compensated for, stolen property was not. To avail of compensation, it was imperative to produce proof of ownership of one's land. Those who could received a total of Rs 52,700 in two instalments, the first of which was generally received in the camp itself. Nearly everyone interviewed affirmed that they used the compensation for day-to-day expenses, or to build a *kuccha* house from bamboo. Even so, rebuilding generally required further investment on the part of homeowners, significant amounts if they were rebuilding a *pucca* house. In other instances of targeted attacks, for instance being shot at by militants, people may never receive compensation at all, doing the rounds of offices even two years later and each time being turned away with the excuse of bureaucratic hurdles.

Many Bengali Muslims live on government land or *khasmati*, including many who have lived there since as early as the 1930s, and were thus unable to avail of compensation. In October 2013, the Assam government released, for persons without a title to their homes, Rs 50,000 as compensation 'on humanitarian grounds'. Attached to the compensation was the caveat that persons accepting this compensation must sign an affidavit affirming that they would not return to the previously 'encroached' land, and would not seek further compensation from the government. This caused a furore among Bengali Muslims, who saw this as a ploy to drive them out of the BTAD. Many in the villages refused to take the compensation, fearing that it might be used to drive them out in the future. By January 2014, the affidavit clause had been withdrawn, and the compensation was being awarded unconditionally. Although most of those who did not have *pattas* were Bengali Muslims, some in this category were Bodo, especially those who were less well off.[52] Local politics and land rules meant that the Bodo were more willing than Bengali Muslims to claim this compensation and try and buy land elsewhere, a prospect that is more difficult for Bengali Muslims, since non-tribals are only allowed to purchase land in a few areas of the BTAD that are not designated tribal belts or blocks.

Many local as well as international humanitarian organisations set up rehabilitation projects in Chirang and Kokrajhar, ranging from a few months to two years long. They provided rehabilitation materials, livelihood opportunities through cash-for-work schemes, implements to restart farming or other kinds of occupations, and one-off grants to set up small businesses or shops. These projects were the mainstay of rehabilitation efforts across the two districts with some humanitarian organisation covering each village. Government assistance stopped at relief materials, and did not extend to long-term rehabilitation measures. Rehabilitation in different areas thus followed different patterns, depending on the kind of assistance available. In some cases, assistance in rebuilding houses, procuring agricultural equipment, one-time cash transfers and long-term support for employment guaranteed some degree of stability, making recovery easier. In other instances, where support was patchy, or limited in terms of resources, villages tended to fall behind in terms of their overall development, or secured help in specific areas, such as drinking water and sanitation, but remained stranded with respect to other rehabilitation measures.

Camps began shutting down from September 2012 and rehabilitation continued into the early months of 2013.[53] In many cases, where people were too afraid to go back and re-occupy their homes, they set up camp-like structures on the outskirts of their villages, where they lived in harsh conditions under plastic sheets. There were no official or even other estimates for these, but extensive discussion and fieldwork with other organisations pointed to at least four informal settlements in Chirang, and two such settlements in Kokrajhar as of May 2014 (one with 160 households). These numbers do not account for those who refused to return to their villages at all, choosing instead to settle in other villages that had larger populations of their own communities, and where they felt safer. These villages are the most vulnerable in terms of rehabilitation—even three years after the occurrence of the riot, many are struggling for basic facilities like water and housing. A major critique of the state's rehabilitation efforts is also the lack of meaningful discussions on peace-building and long-term solutions. This concern is echoed across students' unions and their leaders, village leaders, civil society actors and ordinary people most affected by the violence. References to peace are mostly tokenistic, and do not address the difficult questions of politics and resources that underlie the tensions.

2.3 Exclusions in land and livelihood

A struggle for land and resources is, to a large extent, at the heart of conflict between different groups in the BTAD. Chapter X of the 1886 Assam Land and Revenue Regulation guides land police in the BTAD, aimed at the protection of land for SCs and STs.[54] For non-ST groups to purchase land, they must show proof that they were resident in the area since before the creation of the BTC in 2003, either through land documents or documents like voter identity cards. Such persons may purchase land only in those parts of the BTAD that are not notified as tribal belts or blocks, where STs have exclusive right to ownership of land.[55] Non-STs who do not have proof of ownership of the land they reside on are considered encroachers by the BTC administration. As repeated discussions with the BTC administration have revealed, particularly in the case of Bengali Muslims, 'encroacher' is considered nearly synonymous with 'illegal migrant', a term that is highly charged and divisive in the politics of both BTC and Assam, and is responsible for many of the negative perceptions about the community.

Land in the region is largely owned by the Bodo, while Bengali Muslims provide relatively cheap agricultural labour, and also run small businesses. This relationship can both take the form of sharecropping or agricultural labour on Bodo fields. In Kokrajhar, Dhubri, Chirang and Bongaigaon districts, which were particularly affected by the 2012 violence, Muslims fare the worst in terms of economic indicators compared to other non-ST and ST groups.[56] An economic boycott of the Bengali Muslims by the Bodo caused a breakdown in economic relations, with many Bodo refusing to allow Bengali Muslims to work on their lands, while Muslim outfits and student groups also urged Bengali Muslims not to work. In many villages, such as in Tulsibhil near Gossaigaon, this has led to the Bodo employing labourers from other communities, such as the Adivasi communities, or far less well-off members of their own community to provide labour instead, albeit at higher rates. As things returned to normal in some villages after a year, Bodo landowners in the more divided villages were still reluctant to resume economic relations with Bengali Muslims, although they admitted that they would have to eventually. Land thus was, and continues to remain, a highly contested resource around which conflict is constructed time and again. Studies from previous conflicts between the Bodo and Adivasis also point to the territorial nature of the conflict, with spaces like forest land and tea estates becoming contested sites around which violence occurred.[57]

More Bengali Muslim men in the post-conflict period migrated to other parts of India, even crossing borders into Bhutan and Myanmar in search of work, as agricultural production stalled in many villages in the first year following the conflict and did not recover completely even in the second year. In some major markets, such as the Koila Moila market in Chirang district, which has always been a mixed environment, Muslims were still barred from participating even two years after the riots. This exclusion has meant that many businesses that were traditionally owned and run by Muslims are now being taken over by Bodo traders, creating a shift in the longer-term economic structure of these markets. This phenomenon was seen in other markets of Chirang district as well, especially in areas where the Bodo were in a majority as compared to the Bengali Muslim population. Bengali Muslim traders in the Bengtol area, another popular market hub in Chirang district, say that their shops were closed for a year after the violence, and not even the district administration could get them re-opened. The long-term impacts of these changes remain to be seen; whether they will significantly affect the economic and social character of these areas is not yet clear.

2.4 Specific exclusions faced by children

Literacy levels in the four BTAD districts, on average, are 66.5 per cent, several points below the state average of 73.18 per cent.[58] While schools here face problems which are faced by other schools nationwide—teaching quality, absenteeism and educational attainment, these are also exacerbated by conflict. Frequent bandhs and bouts of violence mean greater disruption of schooling, both because of children being afraid to go to school, and classes taking place erratically. After the 2012 riots, young people from several communities, whether directly affected or not, reported feeling fearful and afraid to move about as before, even to go to school.[59] Boys were part of village patrols during the most tense months, armed with sticks as weapons. As seen in examples in this chapter, children can also become targets of violence, both by security forces and insurgents. During the May 2014 killings in Baksa, 22 of the 46 killed were children, while in the attacks on Adivasis in December 2014, 18 of the 62 killed were children.[60] A recent report from Kokrajhar also highlights that children in the BTAD are joining insurgent groups as child soldiers, often due to economic hardship and the lack of other viable employment alternatives.[61] The same report also cites evidence from Kokrajhar district, according to which more than 19,000 children have been living in relief camps for 15 years after internal displacement in 1996 and 1998.[62] Additionally, according to the Assam Police, 259 children have been orphaned due to insurgency in Kokrajhar district between 1994 and 2010.[63]

The divide between young people and children of different communities is striking in the BTAD, and although this has been exacerbated by the violence, its roots are much deeper. ICDS centres, as noted above, are divided, with children of different communities attending different centres. In some villages, a single *anganwadi* is present in the settlement of a particular community, thus discouraging members of the other communities from sending their children to ICDS centres at all. Such exclusionary dynamics prevail despite official figures indicating that 36 per cent of Assam's children are underweight and in great need of nutritional support.[64] Bodo children attend Bodo-medium schools while children of other communities, whether Rajbongshi, Muslim, Santhali, etc., attend Assamese-medium schools. Typically, each village or cluster of two or three small villages will have at least one of each at the primary level. As a result, it is rare to see even casual friendships between Bodo children and those from other groups. Schools very rarely get together to do joint activities between children studying in the two languages, and understanding between children of the two groups is extremely limited, except perhaps where they live in close proximity to one another (which after the violence has already become less common).

A telling example of this was a football tournament organised by a humanitarian organisation in Chirang district. As part of their efforts towards peace-building and rehabilitation, the requirement was for teams to be of mixed ethnicity to be eligible for participation. Many teams ended up with a token member from another community, but otherwise remained ethnically homogenous. Teams that were genuinely mixed suffered on the field as miscommunication between members ensued, resulting in an often comic lack of coordination. The final two teams were entirely Bodo, with the one or two members from other communities having been substituted on-field by Bodo teammates. And thus, through no malice on anyone's part, the 'mixed' football tournament lost its heterogenous character. Similar instances are noted when mixed-community events are organised in other schools or villages, where children were likely to stay with their own groups when left to themselves. This, of course, is no fault of the children, who cannot be expected to embrace diversity in one or two meetings, but of a system that in the process of acknowledging difference, provides little space for a common meeting ground.

3. Coping and Resistance

Over the last few decades, the BTAD has led to new social, political and militant formations, many of which are formed in response to recurring violence and a sense of insecurity and historical oppression. In the late 1980s, as the Assam movement grew in strength and the Bodo found themselves increasingly alienated from Assamese identity, resistance grew in the form of the demand for a separate Bodoland, led by the ABSU which continues to have major influence even today. A militant group associated with the ABSU, the Bodo Volunteer Force, also undertook violent activities like bomb blasts, killings, and so on. In 1993, after the failure of the interim Bodoland Autonomous Council Accord, militant activity increased, with groups like the Bodoland Liberation Tiger Force and the National Democratic Front for Bodoland (which demanded a sovereign nation) carrying out violent activities. Targeted killings of Bengali Muslims and Adivasis took place in 1993, 1996 and 1998, and armed conflict raged on during this decade. In 2003, the government signed an agreement with the BLTF, bringing into force the BTC which continues to exist today.[65] The NDFB still continues with its separatist demands, splitting into several factions, some surrendering, and the most powerful today being NDFB (Songbijit), which was also responsible for the December 2014 attacks on Adivasis in Sonitpur. How much popular support they enjoy among the Bodo is difficult to assess, although other Bodo organisations come out in public protest after any act of violence by the NDFB. The Bodo themselves are often victims of militant violence.[66]

In response to the growing insecurity felt by non-Bodo groups in the BTAD, many of them have their own militant outfits—the Rajbongshis have the Kamatapur Liberation Organisation, and the Adivasis have numerous outfits like the Santhal Tiger Force, Adivasi Cobra Military of Assam, and others. While there are no known Bengali Muslim militant outfits, recent times, particularly after 2012, have seen an increasing push towards fundamentalism. Groups like the Jamaat-e-Islami Hind or the Jamiat-e-Ulema Hind, both of which have also made contributions to reconstruction post-violence, mostly in Muslim villages, are increasingly making their presence felt. For the first time in many villages, girls and women may be seen in burqas and veils, and in reconstruction efforts, madrasas and masjids are often the sturdiest structures. Each group, whether Bengali Hindu, Nepali, Rajbongshi, Muslim or Adivasi, is also represented by its own students union, which declares strikes and bandhs, carries out protests and recruits cadres at the village and regional levels. The year 2013 also saw a renewed agitation for Bodoland, soon after the creation of Telangana in August. Many more dharnas, strikes, and agitations were called by the ABSU and by many other organisations opposed to the formation of a separate state. The timing, however, forced ABSU to deal with the question of how other groups, whether Muslim or Adivasi, would be protected under the framework of Bodoland, a problem its president acknowledges.[67] The Rajbongshi community, in addition to lobbying for ST status, is also lobbying for a separate state of Kamatapur for Rajbongshis, adding further to the level of unrest.

Mobilisation along community lines has been growing, and has recently made its presence felt in politics as well. After the BTC accord of 2003, ex-BLT leaders formed the Bodoland Political Front, a political party that won the first two elections of the Council in 2005 and 2010 with a comfortable majority, and also won the Lok Sabha seat of Kokrajhar. During the 2014 Lok Sabha elections, however, 18 non-Bodo groups, ostensibly against what they see as Bodo hegemony, came together to nominate a 'non-Bodo' candidate, an ex-ULFA cadre called Naba Kumar Saraniya. Within the Bodo community, a split appeared between the BPF and ABSU, who backed their own independent Bodo candidates. A decade of corruption and mismanaged governance at the hands of BPF left BTC residents jaded, while further insecurity among the non-Bodo finally led to the win of Naba Kumar Saraniya, the region's first non-Bodo MP since the signing of the accord. Non-Bodo groups and the ABSU once again drummed up political candidates for the BTC elections in April 2015, which the BPF won with an extremely narrow margin, barely passing the halfway mark. The ABSU-backed PCDR won seven seats, while AIUDF, a party that caters traditionally to the Muslim base in Assam, won four seats. The rest of the seats were won by independent candidates, some of whom belonged to the non-Bodo political front that emerged during the Lok Sabha election.[68] These new political formations indicate growing mistrust between the ruling BPF and the people they govern, but also of non-Bodo groups towards the BTC as an administrative structure and their apprehensions about their rights as citizens within it.

4. Recommendations

4.1 Military and paramilitary forces, and the police

In its report, the Justice Jeevan Reddy Committee has unequivocally recommended that AFSPA must be repealed and replaced with something more humane. The Committee has also noted that all problems of 'public order' cannot amount to 'internal disturbance' needing the intervention of the army, the latter term referring to large-scale and sustained disturbance on a serious level. Maintenance of public order is the duty of police forces at the state level.[69] Over-reliance on the military for all law and order solutions is neither practical nor desirable. As with other parts of the country, but perhaps desperately so here, there is a serious need for police reform. Some police stations in BTAD cover remote villages as far as 50 or 60 kilometres away, hardly a conducive or confidence-inspiring situation. Many plans to open new police stations or pickets remain in the pipeline for years, and staff shortages and vacancies make effective policing almost impossible at present. Police penetration in areas of militant presence is almost nil, and informing the police of militant activity is a dangerous prospect. If law enforcement cannot be local, it cannot remain credible or enjoy long-term support.

4.2 Relief and rehabilitation

After a major incident of violence, relief and rehabilitation efforts are majorly routed through the Deputy Commissioner's office, which functions under the State Government. Persons displaced are identified in relief camps through head counts, after which relief materials and compensation are distributed to affected persons. Compensation is awarded once damages have been assessed, and soon after this the government begins to encourage those in relief camps to return to their villages. However, the government is no longer involved in how day-to-day life functions are normalised. Nor does the state step in to assess where and whether people return to their homes. This glaring indifference perhaps undermines the true cost of long-term, persistent violence in the BTAD, and to some extent may also explain government apathy towards finding more creative solutions. For long-term solutions to become a reality, and also to truly compensate for the inability to provide security, it is imperative that the state provides comprehensive rehabilitation support to those affected. Related to relief and rehabilitation efforts are the concerns of people displaced by conflict, a number that seems to grow exponentially as the years pass. One suggestion is that a national policy on internally displaced persons should be formed, whether as a result of conflict, disaster, land acquisition, etc.[70]

During the 2012 riots, compensation was only awarded to those whose homes were completely burnt, while those with partial damage or those who reported theft or damage to shops, household assets and cattle went uncompensated. After the violence in December 2014, the government also awarded a small amount of compensation to those whose homes were partially damaged. However, the failure to compensate for losses of essential assets such as cattle severely affected economic opportunities. While these losses are on the government's radar,[71] they remain unaddressed during the award of compensation, as the first priority is to compensate for completely damaged homes. Such damage to economic assets must also be compensated, along with compensation for damage of homes.

4.3 Children

Apart from failing to protect children from violence at the hands of the state, insurgents, and in riots and attacks, there is also very little assistance available to children and young people to help them cope with the trauma of being witness to violence, or experiencing and surviving it. In relief camps, and sometimes after a major incident, temporary measures are undertaken by NGOs and volunteers but hardly any sustained help through experts or communities is available. Post-trauma counselling is an under-studied and under-utilised resource in a country and region that sees so much conflict. The need is perhaps not so much for medical help, but to develop ways to talk to children about violence, and to understand and mitigate the lasting impact such violence can have.

In addition, the practice of segregating *anganwadis* according to *bastis* should be actively reversed, and there should be a greater push towards organising joint activities for children from different neighbourhoods, schools, linguistic backgrounds and communities. Field experience makes evident a paucity of public spaces for children and young people of different communities to interact, so such measures are integral to achieving sustainable peace between communities.

4.4 Data gaps

After a major incident of ethnic violence, people are often driven to relief camps either due to loss of property or fear. When the government sets up a relief camp, it does a head count of the inhabitants as well as an assessment of the damage. Later, it keeps track of when compensation is collected and by whom. However, by its own admission, at this point the government considers that its work is done and stops assisting in rehabilitation or tracking what happens to people when they leave camps.[72] Effectively, this means that the government assumes that the affected people have returned home, and that normal life is resumed for them. In reality, however, people are often afraid to or unable to return to their homes, and either continue to live unofficially in camps (which are not recognised), or in camp-like situations on the edges of their own or another village (see the case study on camps). Thus, whether rehabilitation is accomplished in the true sense—i.e., regaining one's livelihood, a sense of security, and being able to move about freely—goes unrecorded. The long-term losses of violence are not known, and thus even harder to identify and correct.

Similarly, no studies are conducted by the government, even at a micro-level, on the effect of chronic, low-intensity violence on the educational attainment of children, food security, agricultural practices, or on public welfare schemes like ICDS, MDM, NREGA, and so on. Anecdotally, for instance, field research has shown that economic boycott led to lower agricultural production for not one, but at least two consecutive years in many villages. However, no studies have been conducted to examine the impact of this shortage, whether it was severe, and whether it could have a lasting impact on food security. Similarly, anecdotal evidence from field research shows that children may stop attending ICDS centres after a major incident of violence, but there is no official data to confirm or deny this. Measuring the long-term impact of violence, therefore, must be a priority of the government if a concrete plan is to be made not just to mitigate the effects of conflict, but also prevent further violence from taking place.

Endnotes

1. Jayeeta Sharma (2011), *Empire's Garden: Assam and the Making of India*, Durham: Duke University Press, pp. 147–176.
2. Sanjeeb Kakoty (2006), 'Agrarian Dynamics and Technology in the Ahom State', Fuzail Ahmad Qādrī (ed), *Society and Economy in North-East India*, Vol. 2, New Delhi: Regency Publications.
3. Makiko Kimura (2013), *The Nellie Massacre of 1983: Agency of Rioters*, New Delhi: SAGE India.
4. See: Sajal Nag, (1990), *Roots of ethnic conflict: Nationality question in North-East India*, New Delhi: Manohar Publishers.
5. Sajal Nag (2002), *Contesting Marginality: Ethnicity, Insurgence and Subnationalism in North-East India*, New Delhi: Manohar Publishers.
6. Mahmood Mamdani (2009), *Saviors and Survivors: Darfur, Politics, and the War on Terror*' New York: Pantheon, pp. 145–230.

7. Eric Hobsbawm (1995), *The Age of Empire: 1848-1875* (reprint), New Delhi: Viking/ Penguin, pp. 202–207.
8. Thomas Pulloppillil (1997), 'The Bodos: An Introduction', Thomas Pulloppillil and Jacob Aluckal (eds.), *The Bodos: Children of the Bhullumbhutte*, Guwahati: Spectrum Publishers, pp.1–3.
9. Sidney Endle (1883), *Report on the Census of Assam for 1881,* City Press: Calcutta.
10. D. Nath (1986), 'Early Hinduisation of the Ruling Tribes of North-East India', *Proceedings of North East India History Association,* p. 256.
11. Swidden agriculture or shifting cultivation refers to a technique of rotational farming where land is cleared for cultivation, usually using fire, and left to regenerate after a few years.
12. Hence one sees the dominant Bodo students' organisation, the All Bodo Students Union (ABSU), demarcate those whom it considers to be of the same racial stock yet not among the ethnic claimants of a Bodo territory because they 'have completely forgotten the language'. ABSU is referring to the Rajbongshi ethnic group who inhabit parts of North Bengal and western Assam. The Rajbongshi say that they belong to the Hindu fold, whereas the Bodo cannot make such an unambiguous claim.
13. Ajay Roy (1995), *The Boro Imbroglio,* Guwahati: Spectrum Publications, p. 2.
14. Noas Swargiary (1997), 'The Bodo Mass Movements Since Independence', in Pulloppillil and Aluckal (Eds), *The Bodos: Children of Bhullumbutter,* pp. 78–98.
15. Sayeeda Yasmin Saikia (1997), *In the Meadows of Gold: Telling Tales of the Swargadeos at the Crossroads of Assam,* Guwahati: Spectrum Publishers.
16. A.J. Moffatt Mills (1984), *Report on the Province of Assam* (reprint), Guwahati: Publication Board Assam, p. 171.
17. Roy, *The Boro Imbroglio,* pp. 27–28.
18. N. Vandekerckhove and B. Suykens (2008), 'The Liberation of Bodoland: Tea, Forestry and Tribal Entrapment in Western Assam', *South Asia: Journal of South Asian Studies,* 31(3), pp. 450–471.
19. The term indigenous is a contentious one when used in contemporary political discourse. The government of India avowedly rejects the definition provided by international bodies such as the International Labour Organisation (ILO). Instead, the government relies on the architecture of the colonial census to denote communities under the Scheduled Tribe category. The government's criteria for including groups within the Schedule are based on a predominantly 19th-century notion of primitiveness introduced by colonial anthropologists to classify non-caste societies in the Indian subcontinent. Many activists use both categories —tribe and indigenous–interchangeably. Despite my misgivings about the colonial roots of the category 'tribe', I shall use it here to denote communities that are part of the Scheduled Tribes category in the Census with a caveat on its usage. Most government officials and policy makers use the term without any concern about its pejorative roots and assumptions. Indeed, many might even believe that tribal communities are simply backward and be surprised and confused by their sophistication. Most activists, on the other hand, are wont to use the term 'tribal' to denote their difference from caste-Hindu and Muslim communities, many of whom might have shared the territory with them for an equal duration of time.
20. Bhupen Sarmah (2002), 'The Question of Autonomy for the Plains Tribes of Assam' in *Social Change and Development* (October), pp. 86–103. Sarmah's assessment of the constitutional safeguards and the context in which they evolved are comprehensive but do not deal with the dynamics of social movements within such regimes.
21. Bodo-speaking peoples are dispersed all over the region. The Dimasa speak a variant of Bodo as do the indigenous peoples of Twipra (Tripura). Rather than suggest a pan-Bodo identity, the BSS, move seems to suggest that Bodo-speaking people traversed the course of the region at different points in time. There is an implicit agreement that the geographical and political boundaries of a Bodo homeland are limited to western Assam.
22. The Plains Tribal Council of Assam was formed to articulate the demands of the tribal people living in 'tribal belts and blocks' in the Luit valley. This memorandum was addressed to the then President of India, Dr Zakir Hussain, on 20 May 1967. Biruchan Doley, Samar Brahma Choudhury, Charan Narzary, Praful Bhabara and Ajit Basumatary were the office bearers of the organisation and signed the said memorandum in Kokrajhar in Assam.
23. Swargiary in Pulloppillil and Aluckal, p. 80.
24. Karbi Anglong District Council Notification of 2 July 1979; No. KAC/XVII/1/63.
25. The Bodoland Autonomous Council Act. 1993 (http://www.neportal.org Accessed 30 March 2005).
26. Roy, *The Boro Imbroglio,* p. 80
27. Prasenjit Biswas and Sukalpa Bhattacharjee (1994), 'The Outsider, The State and Nations from Below: North East India as a Subject of Exclusion', in Ali Ashraf (Ed), *Ethnic Identity and National Integration,* New Delhi: Concept Publishing, pp. 232-259.

28. Michael E. Brown and Sumit Ganguly (1997), 'Introduction' in Michael E. Brown and Sumit Ganguly (Eds), *Government Policies and Ethnic Relations in Asia and the Pacific,* Massachusetts: Centre for the Study of International Affairs, pp.1–30.
29. This view is often reinforced by the support that settlers receive in areas where the potential and reality of ethnic conflict are common occurrences. For many indigenous rights activists in the Northeast, the Sixth Schedule seems like a trojan horse for greater centralisation that would allow the state to fill up the lands (belonging to indigenous persons) with ethnically acceptable groups (MASS, ASMS, NPMHR 2002).
30. G.B. Pant, cited in the *Constituent Assembly Debates, Vol. VII,* p. 865.
31. Stuart Murray (Ed) (1997), *Not On Any Map: Essays on Postcoloniality and Cultural Nationalism,* Exeter: University of Exeter Press, p. 11.
32. S.N.M Abdi writing for *Outlook* states that ethnic violence claims a disproportionate number of non-Bodo lives (http://www.outlookindia.com/article/the-5050-shot/282078) Accessed on 25 April 2015.
33. Nani Gopal Mahanta (2013), 'Politics of Space and Violence in Bodoland', *Economic and Political Weekly*, vol. XLVIII, No. 23, p. 52.
34. Bordering the BTAD.
35. Some findings in this chapter reference primary fieldwork that was conducted over a year between May 2013 and June 2014 in Kokrajhar and Chirang districts by the Centre for Equity Studies, as well as both authors' impressions from repeated visits to the BTAD.
36. S.S. Ahluwalia vs Union Of India & Ors on 16 March 2001, Writ Petition (civil) 232 of 1997.
37. Bhajan Kaur vs Delhi administration, 1996 III AD *Delhi* 333. In this judgement, the Supreme Court also cited several judgements that showed the range of applicability of Article 21, particularly those that justified adequate compensation for those whose Right to Life could not be guaranteed by the state.
38. Draft Communal Violence Bill, 2011.
39. See Notification no. S. O. 2818(E), Ministry of Home Affairs, Government of India, (http://mha.nic.in/notification).
40. Pushpita Das (2013), 'The History of the Armed Forces Special Powers Act', in Vivek Chadha, *Armed Forces Special Powers Act: The Debate*, New Delhi: Institute for Defence Studies and Analyses.
41. *Report of the Committee to Review the Armed Forces (Special Powers) Act, 1958* (2005), Government of India, Ministry of Home Affairs, p. 54.
42. A National Human Rights Commission report states that out of 555 fake encounter cases countrywide between 2009 and 2013, 52 have occurred in Assam, the third highest after Uttar Pradesh and Manipur. See '555 Fake Encounter Cases Registered in India over the Last Four Years', *The Hindu*, 15 July 2013.
43. The Telegraph (13 December 2013), 'Forces: "Killer" and Victim in Chirang: Gogoi Orders Probe', (http://www.telegraphindia.com/1131213/jsp/northeast/story_17675117.jsp#.VTngnYX3Xbk (Accessed 24 April 2015).
44. In Chirang district, for instance, as of December 2013, 35 of the 53 available vacant posts in the police service went unfilled. Source: Superintendent of Police's office, Chirang, December 2013.
45. Asian Centre for Human Rights (2012), *Assam Riots: Preventable but not Prevented*, New Delhi: ACHR, p. 6.
46. The Telegraph 'Camp inmates offer proof', (8 May 2014), The Forest Department falls under the ambit of the Bodoland Territorial Council.
47. Hindustan Times (5 May 2014), 'Police kill three Assam sectarian violence suspects', (http://www.hindustantimes.com/india/police-kill-3-assam-sectarian-violence-suspects/story-I1YdlnX1FE6B6fguB7LFdN.html)
48. To illustrate, *The Telegraph* has reported that two months into 2014, of a total of 63 days, on as many as 26 bandhs or strikes were declared in Lower Assam Districts. See 'Lower Assam districts worst sufferers of blockades', *The Telegraph*, 5 March 2014.
49. Lok Sabha Starred Question no. 63, answered on 14 August 2012, (http://164.100.47.132/LssNew/psearch/QResult15.aspx?qref=125663 Accessed 24 June 2015).
50. See Asian Centre for Human Rights (2012).
51. This assertion has also been noted in Sripad Motiram and Nayantara Sarma (2014), 'The Tragedy of Identity: Reflections on Violent Social Conflict in Assam', *Economic and Political Weekly*, vol. XLIX, no. 11, p. 50.
52. Interview with Deputy Commissioner Nitin Khade in Kokrajhar town, 27 November 2013.
53. An official release in February 2013 said that 20 relief camps still housed over 12,000 persons. See 'Over 12,000 people still in BTAD relief camps', *Assam Tribune*, 26 February 2013. (http://www.assamtribune.com/scripts/detailsnew.asp?id=feb2713/at08 Accessed 24 June 2015). As of 23 April 2013, the official claim was that all relief camps had been shut down. See Rajya Sabha Unstarred Question Number 4640, (http://164.100.47.132/LssNew/psearch/QResult15.aspx?qref=139170 Accessed 24 June 2015).

54. In the BTAD, provisions that apply to STs largely benefit the Bodo, who are the largest tribal group in the region. Other tribal groups like the Rabha and Garo are also present, but in far fewer numbers.

55. Approximately 40% of the total land in the BTC is demarcated as a tribal block or belt. Source: Former Circle Officer of Sidli circle in Chirang district, interviewed on 4 April 2015.

56. Monthly Per Capita Expenditure calculated using NSS level unit data in Motiram and Sarma (2014), 'The Tragedy of Identity', pp. 47–49.

57. Nel Vandekerckhove and Bert Suykens (2008), Bert Suykens (2006), 'Internal Borders and Conflict: Lessons from Bodoland, Assam (India)', *Working Paper no. 5*, Conflict Research Group.

58. Census 2011.

59. Group discussions with young people of six communities from Chirang, at Rowmari during 16–21 December 2013.

60. 'Massacre Mayhem: Bloodshed all year round', *The Telegraph*, 24 December 2014, (http://www.telegraphindia.com/1141225/jsp/northeast/story_5238.jsp); 'Assam Bodo Attack: Death toll reaches 70; Adivasis retaliate; kill 5 bodo militants', *The Indian Express*, 25 December 2014, (http://indianexpress.com/article/india/india-others/toll-rises-to-40-in-bodo-militants-attack-on-adivasi-settlers-in-assam/).

61. Raju Narzary (2014), 'Impact of Conflict on Children in Assam and Manipur States of India', NERSWN and Terre Des Hommes, (http://www.tdh.de/fileadmin/user_upload/inhalte/04_Was_wir_tun/Themen/Krieg_und_Flucht/Study_Impact_of_Conflict_on_Children_in_Assam_and_Manipur_States_of_India.pdf).

62. Ibid., p. 27. Another report puts more than 43,000 minors living in relief camps as of 2005 (according to official figures), as a result of the 1996–97 violence between the Bodo and Santhals. See Monirul Hussain and Pradip Phanjoubam (2007), *A Status Report on Displacement in Assam and Manipur*, Kolkata: MCRG, p. 8.

63. Ibid.

64. International Institute for Population Sciences (IIPS) and Macro International (2008), *National Family Health Survey (NFHS-3), India, 2005-06: Assam*, Mumbai: IIPS, p. 19.

65. See Sanjib Baruah (1999), *India Against Itself: Assam and the Politics of Nationality*, New Delhi: Oxford University Press, pp. 183–208; and Uddipanna Goswami (2014), *Conflict and Reconciliation: The Politics of Ethnicity in Assam*, New Delhi: Routledge.

66. A particularly gruesome incident involving the murder of a young Bodo girl on suspicion of being a police informer made national news in 2014. See 'Killing of Priya Basumatary by NDFB(S) condemned', *The Assam Tribune*, 23 August 2014, (http://www.assamtribune.com/scripts/detailsnew.asp?id=aug2414/state051).

67. Interview with Pramod Boro at Rowmari, Chirang on 10 February 2014.

68. 'Assam's Bodoland Elections: Gains for Perfume Barons while Congress draws a blank', *NDTV*, 12 April 2015, (http://www.ndtv.com/india-news/assams-bodoland-elections-gains-for-perfume-baron-while-congress-draws-a-blank-754237); 'Assam's Bodoland elections and after: The fall of BPF and the rise of AIUDF', *TwoCircles.net*, 13 April 2015, (http://twocircles.net/2015apr13/1428912434.html#.)

69. *Report of The Committee to Review the Armed Forces Special Powers Act, 1958*, pp. 25–27.

70. Shishir Tiwari and Gitanjali Ghosh (2014), From Conflict to Accord and a Decade Thenceforth- The Plight of Internally Displaced Persons in Bodoland and the Law', Elixir International Law Journal 70 (2014), p. 24516.

71. Interview with Deputy Commissioner Nitin Khade in Kokrajhar town on 27 November 2013.

72. Interview with Branch Officer, Relief Branch, Deputy Commissioner's Office, Kokrajhar on 1 April 2015.

Devadasis

Cultural Practice or Unacceptable Form of Work?*

*Smita Premchander, V. Prameela, Shikha Sethia and Coen Kompier***

1. Introduction

1.1 Historical context of Devadasi practice

The term 'Devadasi' is of Sanskrit origin. The women dedicated to temples and men's entertainment were called *Devadasis* in Karnataka, *Joginis* or *Mathammas* in Andhra Pradesh, *Mathangi/Murali* in Maharashtra, *Devaradiar* or *Dasis* in Tamil Nadu and *Kudikkars* in the Travancore region (Kerala).

The majority of Devadasis are dedicated to Goddess Yellamma whose other names are Renuka, Jogamma and Holiyamma.[1] The Yellamma cult is popular in Karnataka,[2] Andhra Pradesh and Maharashtra. A famous Yellamma temple was built in 1514 in Saundatti hills of North Karnataka, which illustrates the significance of the cult and by extension, Devadasis at that time. The temple continues to be a major site of dedication even today.[4] Devotees of Yellamma who dedicate young girls are mostly Dalits and Bahujans from the Madiga and Valmiki castes, and sometimes from other Scheduled Castes as well. The Devadasis are married to the god and hence are not allowed to marry mortal men. These girls are substitutes for human sacrifices for the deities in the temples and it is believed that Devadasis bring blessings to the entire community. As *Nityasumangalis,* meaning women who can never be widowed and are ever auspicious, Devadasis were at one time welcome guests at weddings and other auspicious functions but did not participate in funerals or other mourning rituals.[5]

In the Medieval period from 8th to 18th century AD, the Devadasis became more and more attached to the temples and some researchers report that they enjoyed a respectable status in society, next only to the priests, and that their families were inclined to matrilineal traditions and females had significant power within the household[6, 7].

This view is challenged by other research, which finds that while girl children were made Devadasis to consolidate family wealth and to make sure that daughters stayed within their families, the women had neither agency nor

---

* This paper is based on a study conducted by Sampark, Bangalore and International Labour Organisation, South Asia office, in Karnataka, Maharashtra and Andhra Pradesh on the present context of the Devadasi practice and the circumstances of Devadasis in these three states.

** Lead authors

*** Contributors: Sameer Taware, Swapna Easwar and Saumya Premchander
Reviewers and Advisors: Mrinal Satish, Rhea John and Anamika Lahiri

control. Srinivasan[8] states that women were made to be the 'economic backbone'[9] of the family, as 'earned and ancestral wealth was acquired through them'.[10] The temple allotted land to families who dedicated girls, to be kept within the family over generations, as long as someone was employed with the temple. Women were also not free to move to other professions, unlike men, keeping their ties with the temple property secure. This land however was owned by the temple rather than the household, and the money, jewellery or goods that the women earned through patrons was what really constituted household wealth. The senior-most female, usually a retired dancer, managed the wealth and its disbursement.

During British rule, the Devadasis began to lose their wealth and after independence this trend continued. By the late 1990s when Sampark started its research, hardly any rich Devadasi households could be found in the villages. We shall explore the present-day context to examine whether the practice is now more, less or differently exploitative than it was historically.

1.2 Current context of Devadasi practice

Many researchers have commented on the practice as a glorious one that makes women *Nityasumangalis,* taking cues from temple inscriptions and scriptures.[11] They tend to concentrate on the sacred and auspicious aspects of Devadasi duties and how the practice has helped in propagating temple culture and the associated wealth and traditions.[12] The present-day Devadasi and her glorious ancestors seen in temple scriptures and literature are two radically different people.

The term Devadasi, meaning 'servant of God', reflects the caste relations at play as it seeks to cover up the abhorrent elements of the practice. Other local terms such as 'Jogini' or 'Basavi', also obfuscate the nature of the practice, i.e. sexual exploitation of Dalit women. The real nature of the practice is reflected in the derogatory terms used for the institution at the local level, which are equivalent to 'free to fuck'.

In the 19th century, with the advance of British imperialism in India, native traditions, customs and practices like Sati, Child Marriage and the practice of Devadasi were under threat. Temples lost royal patronage and their wealth diminished. Devadasis had to resort to sex work for their livelihood. By the late 1800s, reformists who were heavily influenced by their colonial rulers had begun to criticise the Devadasi practice and they insisted on legally banning it.[13] The Madras Devadasi Act of 1947[14] was an outcome of such efforts. Further, The Karnataka Devadasis Act of 1982 (Prohibition of Dedication),[15] Andhra Pradesh Devadasi Act of 1989 (Prohibition of Dedication)[16] and Goa Children's Act (2003)[17] were implemented to abolish the practice in India.

Despite the Prohibition Acts being hailed as a positive step towards curbing the perpetuation of the practice, their enactment has been criticised because it criminalises the actions of Devadasis but not those of their patrons.

The practice of offering girls as Devadasis is followed by Scheduled Castes and Other Backward Communities.[18, 19] A majority of the households with Devadasi members at present do not have a history of dedication in the family indicating the fact that they were first-generation followers of the practice.[20.]

The study carried out by Sampark found that 84.57 per cent of the Devadasi women belonged to the Scheduled Castes, followed by 5.14 per cent Other Backward Castes (OBC), 4.57 per cent Scheduled Tribes, 4 per cent General and with 1.71 per cent belonging to other categories.

All the Devadasi women in Belagavi district belong to the Scheduled Castes and 14.55 per cent of Devadasis in Sholapur district are Scheduled Tribe women.

The other castes mentioned are Brahmin, Chamar, Dhobi, Gosavi, Hindu Marathas, Koli, Lingayath, Lingayath Wani, Maratha, Maratha Shinde, Matangi, and Vaddar. Among the Scheduled Castes, Devadasis belong to the Madar, Madiga and Valmiki communities. While the practice is caste-based, in some cases OBCs and upper caste families dedicate girls due to superstitions, for instance, like dedicating a daughter may be followed by the birth of a son, or that some illness in the family may be cured. The cultural construction of the Devadasi system as an SC practice has also contributed to non-Dalits starting to withdraw a little bit from it.

Earlier the partners of Devadasis were invariably from the landed castes, but now their profile too has changed. The women have found that SC people are kinder to them and generally become long-term partners. Often the women look for relationships which are more akin to marriage than sex work.

The traditional practice involves girls being dedicated at any age before puberty and forced into sex from the time they start menstruating. [21] Devadasis are therefore victims of the worst forms of child labour.[22] These women are trafficked into the practice and subjected to forced sex, rape and other violent atrocities (bodily disfigurement from biting, beating, torture etc.) from early adolescence. The Devadasi practice is much more abhorrent than sex work; it is a form of caste-sanctioned rape, made socially acceptable by giving it the status of local culture.

Devadasis are invariably asset-less, with little or no farmland, education or skills, and very low incomes (which is the case for a large majority of Dalits). In addition, traditionally, when families are superstitious, or consist of several daughters, or ill persons, there is a high likelihood that one or more daughters get dedicated as Devadasis. This reality contrasts with the literary narrative of the Devadasi wielding significant power and influence through her patrons. While this may have been the case for some Devadasis, the current reality is that behind the ritual dedication lies extreme poverty, vulnerability and sexual exploitation of young Dalit girls. In the case of the Bedia community, who follow a similar practice, the whole community is rendered helpless and confined to the sex industry, the women being socially assigned to sex work and the men becoming pimps or turning to alcohol-related businesses. The case then, is one of economic and social subjugation, resulting in extreme forms of sexual exploitation that have become a normalized part of the social structure. Men from castes in which the Devadasi practice is common are often not able to earn sufficient incomes for the family, which pressures them into again dedicating their young women to the Devadasi practice. This fact underscores the extreme need for creation of assets as a way out of the practice.

Devadasis are tied to one or more men during the dedication period but are never married to them. Marriage after becoming a Devadasi is virtually impossible, leading to depression, trauma and a sense of abandonment and isolation, as marriage in India is considered to be of key importance to the status of a woman.

Devadasis are sometimes barred from taking up other employment as well.[23] Devadasis have an economic arrangement with their partners by which they are supposed to get maintenance, but this is not enforced and the women don't have recourse to any mediating agency. Their earnings are low, haphazard and completely dependent on the 'generosity' of their partners. Once Devadasis lose their value as an object of lust, they end up in bonded labour, agricultural daily wage labour, begging or living by their participation in ritual functions surrounding festivals, births, cremations, and so on.

When patrons stop paying them any money, Devadasis are hard put to earn to sustain their families, which usually consist of one or two aged parents and two or three children. In order to earn more than what meagre agricultural wages offer them, Devadasis move to semi-urban and urban areas, taking up jobs in the construction industry, *beedi*[24] making, domestic work or sex work. In many cases, Devadasis begin to do both casual labour and sex work. In the construction industry, for example, chances are higher that these women will be subjected to sexual exploitation and begin practising sex work on a full-time basis. In Mehboobnagar in erstwhile Andhra Pradesh, the research showed Devadasi women to be living in abject poverty, while in Karnataka, where the community remained rural in nature and an NGO had supported the formation of groups, they improved their economic condition and got social support as well.

Another aspect of the practice is the caste glorification of the Devadasi, implying that Devadasis have a higher status than ordinary sex workers. Since the perception exists that Devadasi women have some social 'status', sex workers have been known to label themselves as Devadasis in an attempt to get some social acceptance for their work. This has particularly been observed in Maharashtra, where many sex workers claimed to be Devadasis, whether or not they had been dedicated at a young age.

While the practice has been legally banned, clandestine dedications continue even as recently as January 2015. The practice has mutated in different ways in each state. Saundatti in Karnataka continues to be a location for dedication. Sholapur in Maharashtra, on the other hand, is a site of more commercial sex work, whereby many sex workers claim to be Devadasis. The practice has also transformed, with caste oppression becoming less visible and market forces coming into play.

1.2.1 Size and geography of the group

The number of Devadasis in India is highly contested.[25] The most ironic fact about this highly vulnerable group is that official agencies do not acknowledge its existence. Many officials, especially in the state of Maharashtra, claim that as the practice is outlawed, Devadasis do not exist—almost by definition.

Sadly, this solace is not available to us. Although dedications are on a decline, there are thousands of Devadasis spread over the three research states. Estimates of the number of Devadasis are available to us from various sources for the three states in India where the practice is highly prevalent: Karnataka, Andhra Pradesh and Maharashtra.

The Karnataka government conducted two surveys, first in 1993–94 and the second in 2007–08. The first survey found 22,873[26] Devadasis and the second enumerated 23,787.[27] In undivided Andhra Pradesh, a survey in 1987–88 found 24,273[28] Devadasis. However, the one-man commission appointed by the government to examine the status of Devadasis estimated the number to be about 80,000 (across Andhra Pradesh and Telangana).[29] The State government of Maharashtra, reported the existence of about 3,900 Devadasis during a survey carried out by the National Commission for Women.[30] These figures are highly underestimated and, according to the one-man Commission report, the estimate is about 4,50,000[31] Devadasis spread across many states in India.

1.3 Classification of the practice

Activists and scholars have struggled to conclusively define the Devadasi practice in a way that captures its characteristics in relation to caste, culture, poverty, and labour. Devadasis have themselves embraced several identities in order to negotiate with the state and society for better living conditions. The practice has been alternately referred to as child labour, child marriage, child sexual abuse, sex work, caste-sanctioned rape, or, at the other extreme, a religious/cultural/traditional practice.

A singular classification is not sufficient, as the practice lies at the intersection of all these categories. For this reason it is valuable to look

I don't know my age. My eldest daughter has 4 children, so you can guess it.

'I make a living by doing agricultural labour. My youngest daughter, who is about 15 years old, also works as a labourer. She goes to school only when there is no work. I have no option but to make my daughter work. I sold the two acres of land I inherited from my grandparents to get my three elder daughters married but I have two more children to take care of. What's more, the mud house I inherited from my parents fell down and I had to take a loan from my relatives to build a concrete house. I am yet to repay this loan.

I am illiterate and all my children are illiterate. I begged, shouted and frequently beat my son to go to school but he didn't go. I did not want him to roam around the village like a vagabond, so I got him the job of a sheep/goat herder. He is now 12 years old and gets about Rs 15,000 per year. He goes in the morning and comes home in the evening. I have no cattle of my own even though I am from the Kurva community. I still have Rs 1 lakh as debt and all our earnings go in day-to-day living, I have no money to buy sheep or goats!

Except for the house I have nothing. I used to have silver bangles that Basavinis wear traditionally. But once in my village a caste panchayat was held, locally called "Gounithanam". In the Kurva community, when this panchayat is held, money is collected from the caste members. Rs 500 was levied on each person and I did not have the money. So a woman related to me paid on my behalf to save me from disgrace. But I didn't have any money to repay her, so I sold my bangles. I could not repurchase them because I had too many responsibilities. I had to perform one marriage after the other and take care of one delivery after the other. Even now I still have two children who are yet to be married.

My mother did not have any children except me and made me a Basavini so I could keep the lamp of the house lit and take care of my parents. The hell with the house lamp, my life is messed up. My parents died, what do they know what I am going through! My aunt's son, whom I call "Mama" tied the sacred thread at the temple and I became a Basavini at a very young age. I do not know the age when I reached puberty but after that my Mama started coming to me frequently. After one year of association with him, I gave birth to a daughter. My Mama did not pay a single paisa. In fact, in a few days after my delivery he left me and went away and later got married. He is not my husband so I can't demand anything at all. What can a Basavini say? After my Mama left, I met another man when I was working in the fields. We fell in love. He visited my house for 2 months. But he used to drink a lot and one day he drank some illicit toddy and died.

In a few months I fell in love again with someone who is distantly related to me. He's from the same village and community, but he's married and has children. He used to come home once in fifteen days. I had four children with him. He gave me saris and small amounts of money for vegetables and groceries. But he did not give me any gold or silver, forget about property! My children never asked me about why I had multiple partners. My partner did not bother about my children and my children did not bother about my partner. But after ten to fifteen years of living with him, when my two older daughters got married, I feared that my sons-in-law would look down upon me and my daughters. So I asked my partner not to come home anymore. He agreed without any fight. I told him that the children should be our joint responsibility. I asked him to help me take care of them. He said that he wasn't bothered and only came to me because I asked him to. I did not know what to say to that.

Luckily, I did not face any abuse from my partners. In fact my third partner's wife knew about me and was not angry that her husband was visiting me because I'm a Basavini and not a married woman. I am still on talking terms with her. My children were never discriminated against when it came to their marriage since they were born to a Basavini. When any marriage alliance came for them, my caste people would stand by me and say that I was made a Basavini because there were no sons in the family. They supported me, saying that I had not roamed with men irresponsibly.

Since I left my third partner I have not seen anyone. My health is okay. I never used a condom nor saw one, but when I had my third partner, I clearly told him that he cannot go out with other women. I know about AIDS and I know about people who got diseases because they had associations with many men. Knowing all this, I was careful not to do such stupid things.

People in the village are still making their daughters Joginis. They believe that it's easy to make money as a Jogini. I have not made any of my daughters a Basavini because it spoiled my life to have no husband, no stability. Why will I repeat that for my daughters? My relatives pressurised me to make my elder daughter a Basavini, but I vehemently disagreed. Being a Basavini, I have to do everything on my own—I have to take care of the house needs, run to hospitals when the children fall sick, if my son-in-law is sick I have to rush there! If I had a husband he would have accompanied me.

I've never tried to migrate. I just worked in the village itself. When MGNREGA works happen, I go there. We get anywhere between Rs 60 to Rs 100, but there is no consistency in the payment. I used to get pension when it was Rs 200, but since they enhanced it to Rs 1000 I haven't got any. It's been four months now since I got pension. I haven't been going to work for a few days now. My second daughter just had a caesarean while giving birth to her third child. Her mother-in-law was not taking care of her, so I brought her home.

Today I have no steady means of earning money, no asset and no husband. I drink a bottle of toddy every evening because of all my tensions. But I never go to the toddy shop. I send my son.'

—Narasamma, age 45 to 50, from Mahabubnar district in Telangana.

differently at the different stages in the life of a Devadasi. For clarity and guidance, we will look at many of the arguments made around the Trokosi tradition in Ghana that bears striking similarities to the Devadasi practice in India–although the push factors may be quite different.[32]

1.3.1 Cultural practice or forced labour?

Much of the literature on Devadasis speaks of it as a cultural practice and although the caste embeddedness of the practice is highlighted, the facets of forced labour are not.[33] These scholars have looked at the practice only through the cultural lens, valourising the ritual/aesthetic aspects of the practice, while ignoring the women and other actors involved.[34]

Devadasi practice falls within the definition of forced labour which includes 'all work or service which is exacted from any person under the menace

> *Saraswathi, a Devadasi from Belagavi says, 'When I was 8 years of age, my mother and her relatives took me to Saundatti Yellamma temple and made me wear a new sari, green bangles, lots of flowers in my hair. They sat me down on a blanket and the women sat around me and sang bhajans and then offered pooja to the Goddess. The poojari of the temple tied a pearl necklace around my neck. I enjoyed all the attention given to me on that day. I was happy as I got to wear new clothes and bangles on the day.' The true import of the dedication dawned on Saraswathi only when she attained puberty and her mother forced her to take a partner. She has taken another partner since her dedication and continues to live with him. She rues the day she was dedicated as a Devadasi. She has borne the brunt of stigmatisation of this cruel system and thus, has ensured that both her daughters are married.*

of any penalty and for which the said person has not offered himself voluntarily'.[35] Dedicating oneself to a lifetime of religious service is not forced labour, however, as for instance in the case of nuns in a religious order. Involuntary induction, the excision of control over her body and labour, and her inability to escape the Devadasi identity are what make this practice degrading and exploitative, and consequently, unacceptable.

Many ILO documents already recognise the Trokosi tradition as forced child labour and this is also a useful way of looking at the Devadasi practice. In both the Trokosi and the Devadasi practices, the child's labour is offered in exchange for relief for the family—whether it is economic or religious. The offering of a minor to the temple for a lifetime of servitude puts it firmly within the boundaries of the Worst Forms of Child Labour Convention of the ILO (no. 182) which bans 'all forms of slavery or practices similar to slavery, such as the sale and trafficking of children, debt bondage and serfdom, and forced or compulsory labour, including forced or compulsory recruitment of children for use in armed conflict', which has also been extended to include traditional forms of exploitation.[36]

Most Devadasis come from Dalit families that are asset-less and live in abject poverty, dedicating girls as a result of their economic vulnerability. Research findings showed that the majority of respondents, 79 per cent, were dedicated as Devadasi through close family members (father, mother or grandmother), in Belagavi 93 per cent and in Mehboobnagar 91 per cent. In Sholapur district, 31 per cent of the respondents said that temple priests and self-styled godmen (locally known as Gurus) were also involved in the induction.

An adult Devadasi seldom finds non-ritualised paid-work opportunities other than casual labour or sex work. Often, in order to survive, she must provide sexual services to all that demand it from her or face punitive action and starvation. One report even refers to Devadasis as the collective 'property of the village'.[37]

> *Even Families are Exploitative Swarnalatha, from Sholapur who is involved in sex work says, 'All relations depend on money. Till the time I was giving money to my family, they were supportive to me but after my daughter's birth when I stopped giving them money, they stopped all relations with me. My mother and sister always demanded money and other things from me but now, when I stopped helping them they don't take care of me and my daughter. If my own family does this to me, then how can I trust my partner? I know that he will also look after me only till I give him money. Here I am happy with my peer group in the brothel house as they help.' me, so now this is my family'.*

1.3.2 Child labour and child marriage

Research findings showed that as many as 70 per cent of the Devadasis were dedicated before they attained the age of 15 years and 37 per cent of the girls were dedicated between 6 and 10 years of age. At such young ages, Dalit girls are not aware of the implications of turning into a Devadasi and later, once they attain puberty, they are forced to enter sex work.

Children who are dedicated at a young age face extreme risks to their health due to early sexual encounters and routine sexual abuse with multiple partners. Many are raped as soon as they reach puberty and some even earlier. While there are child protection laws under which offenders can be prosecuted for child rape, and the Protection of Children from Sexual Offences Act can be invoked, these laws are never used to book the criminals, including parents. The normalisation and social sanction of this practice provides a cover for this heinous crime. The fact that there are multiple partners also provides anonymity to the offenders. Instances of these offences being reported are almost unheard of. These children are denied their fundamental right to education and spend crucial years in conditions of slavery. The cumulative impact of this situation on their psychosocial development is immense and the damage is irreparable.

1.3.3 Sex work or slavery?

Some scholars maintain that this ritualised sexual activity must be viewed as prostitution, as the Devadasis receive compensation in return for sexual services. Others argue that it is similar to marital support and therefore not exploitative.[38] However, neither is a fair assessment as the Devadasis do not

'When I was a child, we had our own land where I worked. My father told me that they had given me to Goddess Yellamma and he planned to sell the land for my future. My father then sold the land after 10 years for the Devadasi ceremony. They performed the ceremony like a marriage. They did Abhishek with curd, banana, sugar, lemon, bhandara mixture, I had a new saree and they put moti mala on me. The priest was my own aunt. At that time, I didn't realise what they were doing. It was only after two years that I realised that as a Devadasi I cannot get married to anyone. I remember that as a child my parents had given me an idea that they might make me a Devadasi, but they didn't until my sister started to face problems in her marriage. This usually happens with people in the Below Poverty Line bracket, they are the ones who decide to give their girls up to the Devadasi system.

I used to have a sexual association with my neighbour when I was very young. He promised to marry me and spoke to my parents about it but they opposed it. He was 16 years old and in the 9th grade. They told him that if he was willing to stay in our house without marriage they were fine with it. But he was not ready. So after 10 years, he left me. I engaged with him sexually during this period. I was very young and knew nothing about sex till I had sex with him. In his house no one knew about our relationship. We met at parks and hotels. Once even the police caught us but the police officer left us as he was a nice man. After that incident he ran away and I realised he was not good for me. I told him that I didn't want to continue our relationship. After some time he got married, and now has two children. I got to know from others and I felt very bad. He tried to speak with me but I didn't respond.

After some time, I got involved with another partner. He was a Muslim and worked as a construction worker. He also worked in a hotel so I shared with him the fact that I was a Devadasi. He was ready to stay with me. We began to interact and also engaged in a sexual relationship. I spoke about him to my parents and begged them to give me one chance to live a good life. I assured them that he would take good care of me. So they allowed me and we left. We stayed together happily but after seven months my parents asked us to return as both of them were alone.'

'My partner gave me money for expenses but after sometime he got married to another girl and he didn't tell me. He shared with me after three years that he has three daughters. I felt very bad when he came to meet me with his wife, but I asked him not to leave his wife and children. He told me that he got married because of his parents, and his wife was very jealous of me. When we were staying together, I used to work as a construction worker and he used to help me. He used to give me Rs 200 everyday. I had two children with him, a boy and a girl. It was our decision to have children and my family also knew. I also lost one baby due to a miscarriage. I was always happy with him even as a sexual partner. He never forced me to have sex nor did he ever harass me. But, I left him after two years. I didn't know about the use of condoms at that time. I got the knowledge about condoms much later from an NGO.

I met my next partner through a friend. He was 33 years old. He knew everything about me. We slowly got acquainted and we are staying together for the past four years. He always helps me and asks me not to have relations with other men. I have asked him to marry me but he says he is not ready. Marriages are not allowed in the Devadasi system, but living with multiple partners is! I was not pleased about this when my parents told me.

Society looks down upon us. Many times people have created problems for my partner and me, but my partner has always helped me. I know that people talk badly about me behind my back. And I know I am doing wrong things according to the societal norms by being a Devadasi. I feel that women who are married have a better life as they can enjoy familial activities. They also have respect in society and can mix in society openly. I feel sad since I have missed these things. All my 5 sisters are married and live in Sholapur. They know I am a Devadasi and feel bad for me, but they don't help me.

I have had three regular partners till date but no one has abused me physically.

Finally, I have found a good partner and I hope for a better future. My partner looks after me well. He respects me. He always thinks about my future. I am happy.'

–Shavithri, from Sholapur, Maharashtra

determine what they receive for their services—the men do. Whatever the Devadasi receives in the form of money for basic expenditures, land or assets is not compensation but should be recognised for what it is—an exercise in patronage. The slave must remain alive for her to be available for exploitation. For a Devadasi to be said to have undertaken sex work, she must be in a position to demand payment and to refuse to provide sexual services if the conditions of the transaction are not acceptable to her.

Unlike Trokosi slavery, sexual slavery is not traditionally integral to the Devadasi practice but a consequence of her inability to marry, her caste status and her poverty. The vulnerability of young girls to sexual abuse is heightened through the absence of the security usually offered by families.

The conditions under which Devadasis agree to have sexual intercourse with men, therefore also meets many of the conditions of 'Unacceptable forms of work', defined as those that 'deny fundamental principles and rights at work, put at risk the lives, health, freedom, human dignity and security of workers or keep households in conditions of poverty'. This also allows us to conceptualise the Devadasi system as a highly hazardous form of work, which increases workers' vulnerability to being sexually exploited. However, the normalisation of the practice as well as the gender, caste and economic status of the victim do not allow this exploitation to easily come to light. Incidents of non-consensual sex are not reported or taken seriously by government authorities as the rape of Devadasis is both socially acceptable and expected.

While all sexual interactions with Devadasis in return for money may not be termed as sex work, it is an inescapable fact that Devadasis are highly likely to take up sex work as an occupation. Being uneducated, female and Dalit, most jobs, except for the most physically strenuous or humiliating, are out of their reach. Most Devadasi women interviewed in the study reported taking up sex work voluntarily, although there are clear links to trafficking that have been noted in other reports.

'I belong to the SC-harijana community. My father died when I was very young and my mother and brothers tried to educate me, but I didn't like studying. So, remaining illiterate, I started working in the agricultural fields along with my mother where we earned Rs 40 to Rs 50 per day. When I turned 14, my family started looking for a groom for me. A number of suitors visited our house but nothing materialised. I got fed up and told my family I was not interested in getting married.

When I was 17, I liked a man who worked in the same field. He was the first man I had sex with and our relationship was secret for a long time, until one day my mother found out. My brothers beat me and threw me out. My mother couldn't bear it and came with me. We hired a small place in the same village and struggled to earn a living as nobody gave us work. My mother was too weak to work. That's when I heard about the brothel and considered visiting it. One day the brothel contacted the women in the street and they took me there. I used to get 2 to 3 clients a day at the rate of Rs 100—Rs 150 client, but for every Rs 100, I had to give Rs 20 to the brothel. I worked there for nearly one and a half years but wasn't happy. The Devadasis who lived in our street couldn't bear my struggle and persuaded me to become a Devadasi. They arranged the ceremony and took me to the temple, where I became a Devadasi.

I took to one partner and stayed with him for about 15 years. He had come to Athani to work in a hotel. He was not married and used to visit me once in 4 days or so. He took me to his village and introduced me as his colleague. He supplied a monthly ration and gave me Rs 100 or more for vegetables.

I was 20 when my son was born. When he came of age, my partner started drinking a lot and stopped supporting us. He used to fight with me often and finally left when my son got married. I haven't known about his whereabouts since. As time passed, I went back to the brothel to earn a living—my son wasn't supporting me. I used to go to the brothel in secret as I didn't want my son and his wife to know.

I was adamant to become a member of the SHG for Devadasis' promoted by MASS NGO and did so with my weekly savings of Rs 20. I now have a total of Rs 5000 in savings at the SHG. I even availed of a loan once for my son's wedding and paid it back. Today I live with my son and his family in the pukka house that I got from the Government under the Devadasi scheme and get the Devadasi pension of Rs 500. MASS organization helped me to get treated as I am suffering from tuberculosis and am in the primary stages of HIV.

I wish I had agreed to get married when I was younger and had settled down so I didn't have as many regrets as I do today. As for my brothers, I am going to fight them to get a share of my family property.'

–Khushboo, age 45, from Belgaum district in North Karnataka.

Devadasis who have not been trafficked are much more likely to be able to demand payment as sex workers, set the terms of the exchange, and be in a position to refuse the exchange if they are unhappy with the terms. This is a significant step up from coercion and exploitation under the guise of a 'traditional practice'. Moving to an urban environment also brings anonymity and an escape from the area they associate with their ritualised exploitation. Sex workers are better organised in terms of claiming their civil and political rights and this identity could potentially aid Devadasis in claiming their own rights.

1.3.4 Gender norms as basis for the practice

The Devadasi practice is deeply rooted in gender stereotypes and pre-defined gender roles—all Devadasis are women (both cis and trans) and are 'married to serve' God. Article 5 of CEDAW draws attention to the discrimination inherent in 'the social and cultural patterns of conduct of men and women… and customary, and all other practices which are based on the idea of the inferiority or the superiority of either of the sexes or on stereotyped roles for men and women'.[39]

While the conceptualisation of this practice as a 'forced marriage' to God may seem absurd, scholars have drawn attention to the fact that the violation in forced marriages occurs when 'one or more parties lose their right to choose their partner',[40] which is certainly the case here. This is mentioned explicitly in Article 16 of CEDAW, which protects a woman's 'right to freely choose a spouse'.[41]

Even when in long-term relationships with a single partner, Devadasis have no legal right over the assets or incomes of their partners. However, gender discrimination is nowhere more explicit than in the highly sexualised form of exploitation suffered by Devadasi girls and women. The preference for young, pre-pubescent girls also indicates the preference for 'virgins' as dedicated slaves, which is further evidence of patriarchal ideas of pleasure and control.

1.3.5 Caste-based discrimination

As noted previously, most Devadasis are Dalit women and there is a distinct caste character to this practice. The priest and members of the highest castes are actively involved in the dedication—the priest sometimes actively recruits the girls, performs the dedication ceremony and is also often involved in their sexual exploitation post-dedication.

While in traditional slavery, economic benefit was also crucial, the situation is slightly different in the case of Devadasis. Here, the priests and elders maintain the socio-religious order through the continuation of the practice, as the post holds a religious significance. It also maintains the gender and caste order through the exercise of power by men of higher status (most notably the priest) over the bodies and labour of the Devadasi.

The importance given to caste oppression with regard to organizing and rehabilitation is, however, currently contested. While some activist organisations (for instance, Navsarjan[42]) highlight caste oppression as the key problem to be addressed, locating the problem as one of caste oppression will not serve the needs of Devadasi women today. Ending the Devadasi/Jogini system requires focus on issues specific to Devadasis, which would be lost if attention is directed to caste oppression more generally.[43] Further, if rehabilitation programmes of Devadasis are placed under SC welfare programmes, the special focus on Devadasis may be lost, and Devadasis would find it difficult to gain access to official benefits.

Civil Society Organisations engaged in working with Devadasis hold that caste oppression lies at the foundation of the system and unless eradicated firmly, the oppression of Dalit women will emerge in new forms. They also caution that without addressing caste-based discrimination and stigma, rehabilitation programmes for Devadasis would not yield the desired results.

Others further point out that caste indoctrination is also achieved by using women as the gateway of the caste system. In contrast to Dalit women, women from dominant castes are kept out of public view by 'purdah', meaning they stay at home to the maximum extent or appear veiled in public. These patriarchal tactics also prevent a degree of solidarity between women from different castes. Women from non-Dalit castes do not oppose the oppression of Dalit women through the Devadasi system. This reinforces the role of caste in oppressive practices, showing that the women's movement in India has failed to create solidarity of women across castes and class.[44]

1.3.6 Unacceptable form of work

A key question that arises after a comprehensive discussion of Devadasi lives and livelihoods relates to whether it can be classified as an unacceptable form of work (UFW). Three key considerations of such classification are relevant:

1.3.6.1 Lack of basic rights at work

The situation of Devadasis in relation to their work can be evidenced by the following facts:

- **They are socially excluded:** They have no political recognition as a group, with inadequate estimates of their numbers and the mandatory committees for the elimination of the practice being non-operational and ineffective. They also face discrimination in temples, at social functions, etc., with most customs associated with them being insulting and degrading, such as dancing, begging, etc.
- **Child labour:** Girl children are dedicated at a very young age, when they are not in a position to comprehend the violence that would be inflicted on them. Their social fate as sex workers is already decided at this time.
- **Forced labour:** Once dedicated, Devadasi girl children are forced into sex work on attaining puberty, without their consent. They have no scope for escape, as they are not able to marry and any attempt to escape this work is seen as a violation of their promise to God. Once dedicated, the Devadasi girl is doomed to a future of sexual slavery to men, sex work or other unskilled, manually strenuous work if she has the possibility to do so.
- **Low collectivisation:** Devadasi women are not organised, except in very few cases where NGOs have facilitated such organisation. As unorganised workers, they lack voice and recognition, and as their work does not have the legal status of being 'work', there is total absence of legal protection. Social norms also militate against them, as there are no social means or fora whereby they can demand payment or maintenance from their patrons/partners.

1.3.6.2 Risk to lives, health and security

The risk to the lives, health and security of Devadasi girls arises from:

- **Risk to health:** The practice amounts to human trafficking, with girls being forced into the sex trade, and physical abuse in occupation, even if the site of such forced sexual activity is the homes of their parents, and at social functions. They experience pregnancy at a young age, causing poor health and anemia. They are at the risk of sexually transmitted diseases (STD), isolation, alcoholism, depression and psychological disorders.

Sold for Rs 25

Lakshmi, a Devadasi from Utkur, Mehboobnagar recounts her tale of dedication and how her father identified her first partner thus: 'My parents decorated me by wrapping flowers around my wrist in clockwise direction and they also decorated a sacred mound in the temple with lot of flowers, garlands, bead chains, etc. They got two pendants (locally called Basingam) and tied one to me and one to the mound. The most important part of the ritual is when the Dasari (priest at Temple) unties the flowers around my wrist in an anticlockwise direction. This signifies that I am married to the Dasari who is representing God. My father gave the Dasari a new pair of clothes. Soon after this ritual, there came along another man who gave Rs 25 as dowry to the Dasari and took possession of me. I was literally purchased from the Dasari by this man for Rs 25! According to the ritual I can never reveal the name of my partner to the society even if I bear children with him.'

- **Denial of right to freedom:** Once dedicated, the Devadasis cannot get out of the socially sanctioned sex work, nor can they demand payment for their services or a sharein the property of their partners. They also lack access to education, skill development and livelihood opportunities.Dedication at this young age also implies being denied their right to education and a gainful employment leading to stable livelihood. The very aspect of right to life is at stake here. They cannot marry or introduce their partner as their husband or the father of their children. Due to this they also face discrimination at the workplace, temples, functions and other social occasions. Devadasis do not have social right to their partner's property. As mentioned earlier, this chain of discrimination gets transferred to their children's lives in various significant ways as well.

The Lack of Social Security

Narsamma from Utkur Mandal, Mehboobnagar, does not know her age, she thinks she is between 45 to 50 years. She belongs to the backward community of Kuruva, who traditionally rear goats. She sold her ancestral property of 2 acres to get her three elder children married. Now she struggles to eke out a living, in which the labour of two of her children also plays a vital role. Her youngest son, aged 12 years works as goat herder and earns about Rs 15,000 per annum. Her daughter, aged 15 years, works as an agricultural labourer. Narsamma has little or no access to state-run schemes. She says: 'I have no land today. I lost both my parents. I have 2 children to take care of. Who in these days will give me anything at all! They will say we gave you children and that is it.' I have never tried to migrate. I just worked in the village itself. In summer when there is no work I take loans and repay them when working season comes. When Mahatma Gandhi National Rural Employment Guarantee Scheme (MGNREGA) works are implemented I go to those works. The works have not yet started this year. We get anywhere between Rs 60 to Rs 100 per day as wages. There is no consistency even in MGNREGA payment. They pay whatever. I have no sheep or goats though I belong to Kuruva community. I still have a debt of Rs 1 lakh to repay. All our earnings go in day-to-day living and repaying the loan. Where will I have additional money to buy sheep or goat? I used to get pension when it was Rs 200. I stopped getting any pension from the time they enhanced it to Rs 1000. It has been 4 months now since I got pension.'

- **Lack of security for workers:** The Devadasi practice being a social practice, its nature as sex work is undermined; with informal arrangements being made for sexual partnerships and meagre, uncertain or no financial contributions being made available by the partners. Rejecting sex work is often not an option, with the only alternative for sufficient earning being through migration to semi-urban and urban areas for work.

- **Denial of human dignity:** Devadasi girls are denied the status of married women, and their children are not legitimate children of their partners, with no social acknowledgement of the paternal descent of the children. The children are also put at risk, with their sense of belonging and dignity being denied, as their identities are not socially acknowledged as respectable. Devadasis are also at risk of abuse not only by their partners, but also the general public, through social practices such as dancing in *Jathres*, where they are sexually abused by women.

1.3.6.3 Extreme Poverty

The life of a Devadasi is characterised by extreme poverty. This arises due to:

- **Lack of livelihood opportunities:** Devadasis come from the poorer Dalit households and typically have low literacy levels, with few skills other than in manual agricultural work. They therefore do not have access to gainful employment. Given their low incomes, they are also unable to educate and provide skills to their children, thus becoming caught in a vicious and perpetual cycle of poverty. They are tied to sex work in rural areas, and even when they migrate for construction or other work, their identities as Devadasis and single women put them at high risk of entering sex work.
- **Lack of social protection:** Presumably, Devadasis who are poor should have access to official social welfare schemes or those which are specifically targeted at them. However, most Devadasis are either unaware of, or unable to access these schemes for various reasons. Support to help them educate their children is also lacking, thereby perpetuating inter-generational poverty.
- **Ineffective legal provisions:** The lacunae in the implementation of Devadasi Abolition Acts has led to the continuation of the practice, albeit at a low-intensity level and having undergone mutation due to the market and other factors. Due to the lack of prosecutions, Devadasis do not have access to the compensation and rehabilitation they can claim by statute. The provisions themselves lie unused, with government officers claiming that the practice has been eradicated. Devadasis do not have legal rights to the property of their partners. Therefore, legal provisions do not provide significant support for Devadasi women's livelihoods, recommendations for which are discussed later.

These facts show that on all counts, Devadasis are in an unacceptable form of work, which needs political, administrative and social attention.

2. Processes of Exclusion

2.1 Access to public goods and rights?

Devadasi households face several consequences as a result of following the practice. The current research on the lives and livelihoods of Devadasis finds the following evidence:

2.1.1 Literacy

Of the 175 respondents in the three study states, around 77.71 per cent of women were illiterate. Only 6.29 per cent of them were able to complete high school, and the remaining 16 per cent had to drop out after their primary education. Mehboobnagar has the largest proportion of illiterate Devadasi women at 83.33 per cent, followed by Belagavi at 75 per cent and Sholapur at 74.55 per cent.

I do not know my surname because my mother was a jogini too. My grandmother converted my mother into a jogini because she didn't have any male children. My siblings and I are all born of different men. I was made a jogini because I was born weak and fell ill frequently. My brothers didn't look after me and this made my mother feel very concerned. She decided to make me a jogini, so that I would have partners and bear children. But things did not work out quite that way!

While we were growing up, my mother moved to Hyderabad to make a better living and support us. Soon my elder brother got married and moved out with his family. My second brother started doing some painting work and my younger brother worked at a hotel. I was only eight when I started working as a domestic servant and was happy enough doing this till I was 14.

A year later my mother was in a road accident and died.

I was distraught. At this time, I started working in the fields and met Venu. Venu promised to marry me. I believed all his talk. In the two years I was with him, I got pregnant twice. He got me medicines to terminate both pregnancies. After terminating my first pregnancy I kept asking him to get married to me. He said he would once he got a good job in the municipality (he is educated). Venu was raised by his aunt who was not happy with our relationship. When I got pregnant for the second time, she found out and shouted at me, using foul language. There was a big fight. I got very scared and when Venu asked me to terminate my second pregnancy I accepted immediately. After that Venu never came back to me.

Venu never hit me but used very abusive language. He used to doubt my loyalty and accused me whenever I spoke to anyone. But I really loved him. He would get me food from the kirana shop that he was running and even got me a few dresses. If not for his aunt, I believe he would have married me. But it has been 3 years now and Venu is married to someone else.

My brother, who lives with me, gradually lost his health. Due to muscle deterioration he could hardly do anything. During that time a lady that I know introduced me to Balappa, who owned a gold shop. She told me that though Balappa was 50 years old, he would take care of me. His family stayed in a big house and he let me live in his second, vacant house where he would visit me. We had a good relationship in the beginning and he'd come to me at least every other day. He showed me places, got me clothes often and even gifted me gold earrings and silver anklets.

However, Balappa started verbally abusing me when he came to know of Venu. I had stopped working and would make do with the money he gave me, which was only Rs 100 for the entire week. I didn't have enough food to eat. While I was with him I got pregnant again—twice. He got my pregnancies terminated. I agreed because I was angry that he was not taking care of me. After a few months of being with Balappa, a neighbour advised me to go to Mumbai for household work and I did. I borrowed money from here and there and gave it to my brother for his welfare. In Mumbai, I stayed with the family of my employer and the men in the house treated me with respect. I used to earn Rs 5000 at that time.

Soon Balappa came to Mumbai and convinced me to return. After I came back, he took care of me for two to three days. He even promised that he would not see any woman other than his wife and me. But within a few days, I saw a woman coming out of his room and questioned him. He got defensive and shouted at me. He said he would sleep with as many women as he liked and it was none of my business. From that day he stopped visiting me and we haven't spoken since.

He never beat me, but if I denied him sex he would come home drunk and shout at me. He would threaten to beat and rape me. I was scared that neighbours could hear and would quietly give in. I wasn't close enough to anyone to share my feelings. But I met Eswaramma who works in the anti-Jogini campaign. I told her my story. I wanted to punish Balappa. He taunted me that I couldn't live without him. I want to show him that I can live, and that too much better without him.

I went to Hyderabad for a couple of months to work in a hostel. They were paying me Rs 3000, but my brother's health deteriorated and I had to return. I didn't have money to get my brother treated. He is now 30 and cannot even get up and cook for himself. I have to stay with him. I have a ration card; we get 20 kilos of rice from PDS. When I have money I get vegetables and pulses else we just eat rice and chilli powder. My other two brothers do not acknowledge our existence. My second brother's is a love marriage and they stay nearby but they never come home. All my brothers are doing well except the second one. So I felt bad and decided to take care of him.

I now work in a house where they pay me Rs 1000 to do all their work. I go at 8 in the morning and come back at 12. I don't have energy to work in the evening. I get fever and become bedridden for 15 days at a stretch. The doctors suggest that I should eat good food and rest. But how can I? What option do I have? I attended school till the 5th standard but I don't know how to read or write.

I used to go for construction work earlier and they paid me Rs 80 per day. Now the wages have increased to Rs 120, but I hardly get work and they don't pay on time. I'm afraid to migrate as a construction labourer because I have heard stories of people falling off buildings and dying. More importantly, when I had gone to Mumbai and Hyderabad, some relatives snatched a piece of empty land in front of my house and built their house. I am still fighting to get it back, so l have to stay here. People suggest that I should run a kirana shop. I'm told that the road will get widened soon and my house will come onto the main road. Even now if I had seed capital I would run a kirana shop. I have the courage and interest as well. I want to stand on my own feet rather than do this domestic work.

I do not face ridicule in the society. No men tease or solicit me. But what good is a jogini life? There's no stability. We have to go to various men. I've heard of diseases that are caused by not using condoms, though I've never seen a condom nor have my partners volunteered to wear them. If someone is being converted into a jogini I inform the madams. I know that laws exist. People call me infertile and say I have no children. What do they know of the pregnancies I've lost? I feel like having a partner but I do not trust anyone. I have already been cheated twice. Now I am not interested in men. I want to show my partners that I do not need them and am capable of living on my own with dignity. It should be a slap on their faces.

–Gauri, age 20, from Mahabubnagar, Telangana.

2.1.2 Health

Devadasis are highly vulnerable to Sexually Transmitted Diseases (STDs) including HIV/AIDS from a young age, due to multiple sexual partners. More importantly, the study showed that although most women knew about the importance of using condoms, they were unable to influence partners and clients to use them. As many as 69 per cent of Devadasis are sexually active and they may start bearing children at the early age of between 12 and 16 years. There is a lot of pressure from partners to get pregnancies terminated at that early age and whether they give birth or terminate the pregnancies, they suffer poor health due to undernourishment and anaemia. Most Devadasis, especially the younger women, have taken to drinking alcohol. They drink toddy, beer and other types of liquor and are also addicted to tobacco, which causes a huge drain on their finances besides harming their health.

2.1.3 Denial of sexual and reproductive rights

Research by Sampark shows that Devadasis are being dedicated at ages much younger than 21 years. In fact more than 70 per cent of the respondents were dedicated at less than 15 years of age. 69 per cent of Devadasi women were made sexually active at the age of less than 16 years. In spirit, the Prohibition of Child Marriage Act, 2006 is clearly being violated. However, since the Devadasi is not married, no action can be initiated under this Act. Statutory Rape as per section 375 in the Indian Penal Code states that having sexual intercourse with a woman of age below 16 years is legally considered rape. As Devadasis are involved in work by the age of 16, it is also a violation of The Child Labour Prohibition and Regulation Act, 1986. Most Devadasis are from the SC caste, so dedications and sexual offences against them are also a violation of the SC and ST (Prevention of Atrocity) Act, 1989.

A Devadasi loses the freedom to get married after being dedicated and is also not free to announce her partner as the father of her children. Due to this, children of Devadasis face social discrimination and are also denied admission to schools. This amounts to a violation of human rights.

Vulnerability can be heightened in certain situations, as illustrated in the case studies. When Devadasi women have regular partners who give them sufficient maintenance for themselves and their families, they can lead reasonably comfortable lives. However, such cases are rare.

Devadasis do often select partners from among the Dalit communities, with whom they may share short-term or long-term relationships[45]. Short-term relationships stem largely from the Devadasis' need for financial support. In shorter-term relationships, male partners are seen to reduce their association with Devadasis after they get married. Generally, within their own community, Devadasis share good relationships with other members and with Self Help Group members, with whose help they access credit and other facilities.[46,47] Community members usually help Devadasis in childbirth and serious illnesses. The reasons for termination of relationships with partners from their own community are economic pressure and lack of support from the partner, the partner's inability to take care of their households, failure to meet the cost of religious rituals (e.g., gold ceremony) and domestic violence.

Most Devadasis are involved in manual labour like agricultural work. All Devadasis are also sex workers. Many Devadasis have relationships with a patron and a few of them are married. As many as 95 per cent of the women were not able to register their patrons as parents in the admission records of schools for their children. This indicates that the children of Devadasis are not able to prove connections to a father and are therefore unable to claim any inheritance rights.[48]

In addition to the above, Devadasis may face discrimination from their own children, who question the mother about her practices. The situation gets worse when the children marry. In many cases, particularly among earlier-generation Devadasis, they were compelled to give up their relationships with their partners completely after the children had grown up. There are also instances where the spouses of the children have abused the Devadasi mother both verbally and physically. The Devadasi woman often becomes very lonely at this point in her life. Her parents have died by then, her siblings are busy with their own lives and she is discriminated against and punished by her grown-up children for a situation which she had little control over.

NGOs working with issues of Devadasis and sex workers found that most Devadasis stop getting any maintenance from their partners very soon, and are forced to move to the city for better incomes. Typically, they enter construction and other sectors requiring unskilled work. From these occupations, they frequently slip into sex work again, as they are also marked as single or Devadasi women and approached for sex work.

As a result of the various laws prohibiting it, the practice now unfolds in secrecy and in some cases it has been converted into trafficking[49]. Dedications in the state of Karnataka and parts of Andhra Pradesh are no longer cause for a public celebration out of the fear of fines or imprisonment.

2.2 Laws and their violations

The Devadasi practice violates laws that have been specifically enacted to prevent the practice. In the three study states, these are as follows:

- **The Bombay Devadasi Protection Act** was promulgated in 1934, and later amended in 2005. The amendment was intended to strengthen the Act and offences under this act are cognisable and non-bailable. The amendment sought to address the problems with the procedure, the appointment of officers, and the authority to take action against those dedicating Devadasis. In order to address these gaps in the previous law, the amendment provided for:
  - Rescue, care and protection, and welfare and rehabilitation of women in the units of the government,
  - Appointment of a Devadasi dedication prohibition officer with powers to prevent dedication, and
  - Authority given to the police department/magistrate to arrest those dedicating Devadasis.
- **The Andhra Pradesh Devadasi (Prevention of Dedication) Act,** first promulgated in 1947, was amended in 1988. However, the rules under the Act have not yet been formed and adopted. The rules outline the procedures for action in case of violation of the law and the authorities responsible for examining the case and pronouncing judgements. In the absence of rules, therefore, implementation of the law has not been possible.
- **The Karnataka State (Prevention of Dedication) Act** was enacted in 1982, and amended in 2010. Although the amendment was not significant, it brought attention to the law and provided the impetus for the government to identify and support Devadasis.

While the Devadasi practice spreads over many other states, only three states have enacted legislations to prohibit and outlaw the system, and identify and rehabilitate Devadasis. However, there are very few cases registered or filed by the district collectors and superintendents of police, who are the officials responsible for implementation of the Act. Further there are no prosecutions and penalties imposed on perpetrators under the Acts in Andhra Pradesh and very few in Karnataka and Maharashtra[50].

Given our understanding of the Devadasi practice and its implementation, described in the previous section, there are several laws that are violated by Devadasi practice. In spirit, the Prohibition of Child Marriage Act, 2006 is clearly being violated.[51] However, since the Devadasi is not married, no action can be initiated under this Act. Statutory Rape as per section 375 in the Indian Penal Code states that having sexual intercourse with a woman of age below 16 years is legally considered rape.[52] Section 370A is also applicable, which addresses the offence of human trafficking,[53] as does the Immoral Trafficking Act, 1956.[54] As Devadasis are involved in sex work by the age of 16, it is also a violation of The Child Labour Prohibition and Regulation Act, 1986 and the Protection of Children from Sexual Offences Act, 2012,[55] as well as the UN Convention on the Rights of the Child, 1989. Most Devadasis are from the SC caste, so dedications and sexual offences against them are also a violation of the SC and ST (Prevention of Atrocity) Act, 1989.[56] Most Devadasis are from the SC caste, so dedications and sexual offences against them are also a violation of the SC and ST (Prevention of Atrocity) Act, 1989.[57]

Many Devadasis are also subject to intimate partner violence that could be addressed by the Protection of Women from Domestic Violence Act 2005[58].

The promulgation of laws for protecting a special group has both advantages and disadvantages. The advantage is that it outlaws unacceptable and exploitative practices, as is the case of Devadasis, manual scavengers and bonded labour. The disadvantage, however, is that once these laws are promulgated, they draw attention away from the root cause of the practice. The duty bearers for implementation of these laws (the police, district officials, judicial officers, even NGOs) do not take cognisance of the underlying phenomenon as one rooted in caste, gender and structural inequalities, and simply limit it to the realm of traditional practice. This is why one finds hardly any prosecutions not only under the Devadasi Acts, but also under the other Acts, e.g., SC/ST Prevention of Atrocities Act.

2.3 Government schemes for Devadasis

When Devadasis were recognised as a vulnerable group, the government made schemes to provide them with rehabilitation assistance. The programmes and schemes for Devadasis may be summarised in the following table:

To begin with, some of the schemes suffered from faulty design. Further, implementation has created problems as well. For instance, the state of Karnataka perceived that the Devadasis need marriage to improve their condition, hence it provided a financial incentive for the marriage of Devadasis. Some men came forward to marry the Devadasis and got the incentive of Rs 10,000 from the government. In most of these cases, the men left the women soon after and the women were further ostracised socially for having broken their contract to God! After the first round of such marriages, the Devadasi women stopped availing of this scheme and the government stopped implementing the scheme as well.

These schemes have been implemented with varying effectiveness over time and across the states, and some issues that have plagued the implementation of these schemes are as follows:.

2.3.1 Lack of information/ demand-side issues

Devadasis did not know about the schemes and did not know how to access them, so the demand for these schemes has remained low.

Table 1: Government Schemes for Devadasis

	Karnataka	Maharashtra	Telangana
IGA support	Rs 20,000/- with 50% subsidy	None	Rs 20,000/- with 50% subsidy
Devadasi pension	Rs 500 per month, for Devadasis, as per Devadasi card Demanding for Rs 1,000/- month	Rs 500 per month for *Joginis*	Rs 1,000 per month, some disqualified in new survey because this was a widow pension
Land distribution	After the first survey, 2 acres of land was given to some Devadasis	Land distribution was not considered	3 acres of land per SC/ST landless household, by the SC/ST corporation
Housing scheme	Rs 75,000 to 1,20,000/- under called Indira AwasYojana/Rajiv Gandhi Grameen Housing scheme	Not offered	Rs 75,000/- to Rs 1,00,000/- from The Scheduled Caste Corporation[59]
Marriage grant	Rs 10,000/- (earlier provision, not provided any more)	Rs 10,000/- (earlier provision, not provided any more)	
Create Awareness to eradicate the practise		Rs 10,000/- per year programme to the NGOs	

2.3.2 Departmental variation in success when implementing schemes

Government officials reported that when the scheme is with the women and child department, many programmes got implemented: mass awareness, campaigns, to stop dedication, etc. are conducted. However, when the scheme is implemented by the SC/ST department, the Devadasi issue competes with other caste-related schemes and does not get sufficient attention or funds.

2.3.3 Livelihood financing schemes

Among the official livelihoods promotion support, two major types of financing schemes have been initiated in Telangana:

- Housing scheme of the corporation (IAY)
- Income generating activity

The SC/ST cooperation has a provision to extend loans and subsidies; usually they give a proportion of the total funding needed (60:40), with the latter coming from the bank. The amount available ranges from Rs 75,000 to Rs 1 lakh. However, as there have been earlier defaults on loan repayments by their family members, most Devadasis are not considered creditworthy by bank standards and are unable to use the provision.

Consequently, even when subsidies and loans are available, Devadasis are unable to use these to build homes or their businesses.

2.3.4 Non-accessibility of government welfare schemes

Many government schemes require that the beneficiary provide the husband's name, an income certificate, or a marriage certificate. Many Devadasi women are not able to produce this evidence and hence are unable to access these welfare schemes, especially the ones emerging from the Women and Child and SC/ST departments. Lack of these certificates also prevents Devadasis and their children from getting passports, depriving them of income-earning opportunities outside India.[60]

2.3.5 Landless Devadasis and key challenge of land possession

The Andhra government had announced a scheme for allotting land to Devadasis during the land reform programme, however very few Devadasi families were allotted land and received legal deeds. Some received the deeds but do not have possession over their land. Consequently, many Devadasis are landless and sometimes do not even have a roof over their heads.[61]

2.3.6 Stigma and Discrimination in Labour market

Most Devadasi women who have not entered commercial sex work are daily wage labourers or work in unorganised sectors like agriculture and construction. Devadasi women in Karim Nagar district of Andhra Pradesh are working in the *beedi* industry, mainly rolling *beedis*. These women do not get equal wages for equal work compared to other labourers, and are also deprived of the provident fund scheme. These facts were noted by the one-man Commission on Devadasis in Andhra Pradesh. The discrimination, social exclusion, the stigma related to being temple prostitutes and the attitude of the general community have prevented Devadasis from engaging in alternate professions.

2.3.7 Lack of psycho-social counselling support service and health security

Devadasis are dedicated during early childhood or at puberty, at 6 to 12 years of age and are later sexually exploited by patrons and also by upper caste men of the village. They are subjected to forced sex, abuse and exploitation at an early age, causing emotional trauma and psychological disorders, as well as sexually transmitted diseases. They also suffer problems arising from isolation, social exclusion, and stigmatisation, leading many Devadasi girls and women to become depressive, which may manifest in abnormal changes in their behavioral pattern, including psychosomatic disorders.

2.3.8 Pension scheme

Devadasi women are unable to avail benefits of any pension schemes such as widow pension, single women, etc., due to their nomenclature. They are neither widows as they are married to a deity, nor single women because of their association with their patrons. The government has not been able to consider the case of Devadasis as single women, as this is open to abuse by non-Devadasi single women who claimed to be Devadasis, thus depriving the actual beneficiaries.

2.3.9 Lack of funds with the government

Although the government has announced

schemes for the rehabilitation of Devadasis, the implementation has been wanting for lack of funds as well. In Karnataka, an NGO working with Dalits reported that Devadasi women had not received their pensions for the past 19 months, as they had not received funds from the central government. Hence, non-disbursements of funds, lack of appropriate allocations and allotment of funds are key challenges in the implementation of state rehabilitation schemes.

2.3.10 No property rights for Devadasis and their children

Typically, Devadasis and their children are given no share in the property of their partners (fathers of their children). Recent judgements by the Supreme Court have granted these rights to partners, and children from live-in relationships.[62] While the provision has not yet been used, Devadasi and Dalit associations have cited the judgements in a few disputes to get Devadasis their due maintenance from partners. On the basis of these experiences, the associations believe that in cases where Devadasis have relatively long-term relationships with their patrons, an effort should be made by them to claim maintenance for themselves and a share in the property of the partner for their children. NGOs need to support them in these efforts and provide legal assistance to claim these property rights.

Such measures have not been initiated so far under any government programme for rehabilitation of Devadasi women.

The Judiciary's presumption of marriage in live-in relationships is valid only among partners who are both unmarried at the time of co-habitation. Hence, the Devadasis suffer a further disadvantage as their partners are often married men engaging in extra marital affair/intercourse'. Though the above interpretation is limited in its application, the benefits of property rights and child legitimacy could be availed of by the Devadasi if the partner is unmarried and all conditions provided in the 2010 judgement are fulfilled.

2.4 Deliberate invisibilisation

Discussions that revolve around numbers of Devadasi women and their identification process are similar to those around other highly exploited and extremely vulnerable groups such as manual scavengers, bonded and forced labourers, child workers, etc. These practices are outlawed, and duty-bearers such as the police and local government officials are charged with preventing these practices and prosecuting those found practising them. The fallouts are many.

The first is that there is an underestimation of numbers of people in these groups. In the case of Devadasis, all CSOs and even the commission representatives admitted that the government data of Devadasi women is highly underestimated and unreliable. The report submitted by the one-man commission estimates the number of Devadasis in Andhra Pradesh to be about 80,000—much higher than the figure of 24,273, provided by the AP social welfare commission. Importantly, the Commission report was submitted to the (undivided) Andhra Pradesh Government two years ago and has still not been made public. Furthermore, Ms. Subhadraa, a leading Hyderabad-based activist mentioned that more than 100,000 Devadasi women gathered last year for Yellamma deity's annual festival, indicating that the number of Devadasis in the country is much higher than what the government estimates.[63]

Another reason for the underestimation of the number of Devadasis is the lack of official funds for rehabilitation. While welfare schemes for Devadasis exist in some states, the government has been resistant to identifying their numbers correctly through a comprehensive survey for fear that the number of beneficiaries may increase dramatically, putting a strain on the meagre resources available.

Identification of Devadasis would also increase the pressure on the government to take action to prevent this practice, which is another deterrent to the survey that has often been demanded by many civil society groups. The experience with governments across states has been variable. In Karnataka, there is a separate cell working for the welfare of Devadasis, which is active in the eradication of the practice. In Telangana, neither the social welfare department nor the women and child department has taken responsibility in the identification of Devadasis. The police too are either unaware of the law or not being proactive; they prevent dedications only when complaints are made. Without proper identification, it is difficult to stop this practice or to provide welfare benefits to existing Devadasis.

Superstition, blind faith and financial vulnerability are the reasons that made Prabhavathi, from Sholapur, a Devadasi: Her father was a scrap dealer and her mother worked in cotton fields. When she was 7 years old her father left them and went away to Pandharpur. He gambled and lost everything they had. They were left without a house and started living near a bus station. Every year her family visited the Saundati temple in Karnataka during Jathre. Once during Jathre, her mother noticed that Prabhavati's hair was completely entangled and had formed a 'jat', considered a symbol of God's will and calling. 'Her mother took her to the temple town, worshipped their deity and when Prabhavati was given a bath, a garland fell around her neck. This was again taken as a sign she was needed for the God. Also, a lady who was possessed by a Goddess (Devi) came to their house and said, 'I want this girl to be initiated into a Devadasi.' Initially her mother refused, but obstacles and financial problems made her mother relent. Prabhavati was immediately taken to a guru called 'Majukh' who performed various poojas, tied a moti mal around Prabhavati's neck and took her under his care. Ceremonies were conducted, gifts were given to guests and the ritual of going to the jathre every year began. She was also taught music, singing and dancing and was made to perform at the jathre each time in the festive season.

The illegalisation and criminalisation of Devadasis and their families is another feature that creates problems. When people are caught dedicating, it is the Devadasi's parents who are punished. Thus public policy blames the group that is victimised to begin with, i.e., the Dalits. The fact of non-Dalit oppression over the years that has sanctioned the exploitation of Dalit girl children is overlooked.

3. Good Practices and Suggested Interventions

Some good practice examples of interventions and support to Devadasis, for partial or complete 'inclusion' for this excluded group are detailed below:

One key change that has made a significant difference is a change in the norm and practices relating to school admissions. Earlier, children of Devadasis had to fill in the name of their fathers, and found this difficult. More recently, Devadasis have been permitted to admit their children to schools with only the mother's name being filled in the admission forms. With the enactment of the Right to Education Act, it has become compulsory to admit children regardless of parents' names being available, making it much easier for children of Devadasis to gain admission to schools.

Another good example is in the field of livelihoods support. Sampark, an NGO with field projects in Koppal district, mobilised women into Self Help Groups (SHGs) in about 100 villages.

While paying special attention to the poorer women, Sampark realised that the Devadasis were some of the poorest and most marginalised people in the society. They brought Devadasi women into these groups and to reduce their marginalisation, included many Devadasi women in SHGs formed by other Dalit or non-Dalit women. This reduced the stigma that Devadasi women face and also enabled them to benefit from the higher savings, loan taking and loan repayment capacities of non-Dalit women and women who are less poor. Over time, the Devadasi women transited from taking consumption loans to taking loans for income generation and asset building, and many have built assets and overcome poverty. In addition, the Devadasis also gained voice and social empowerment, as SHGs have reduced caste-based inequalities in the SHGs, cooperatives and villages. The example shows the value of investing in organisation-building, voice, and livelihoods enhancement of excluded groups such as Devadasis.

The research in Belagavi and Mehboobnagar offers similar lessons. In both locations, 70 per cent of the Devadasis are members of Self Help groups, or collectives of sex workers, and such membership provides them the opportunity to access credit, discuss their problems, collectively increase their awareness of and access to government schemes. By contrast, in the third research location, Sholapur, more than half the respondents were not part of any collective, because most of the women are geographically scattered and cannot attend the meetings of collectives. Consequently, they had lower access to government schemes and financial cooperatives.

These collectives do not yet, however, work as forums to stop the Devadasi system, which has to happen within households, i.e., women deciding within their families that they will not dedicate their children and in caste associations, which are mostly led by men.

4. Recommendations

The recommendations follow the Gender Equality and Social Inclusion (GESI) framework which outlines three domains of change for inclusion and empowerment: provision of assets and resources, organisation-building for creating voice, influence and agency and changing norms and institutions that create exclusionary processes, and bringing in policies, norms and institutions that encourage inclusionary systems and processes. The recommendations for action by state and NGOs, as well as Dalits and Devadasi households themselves are presented in four categories: those relating to data and monitoring systems, those relating to providing assets and services for rehabilitation of Devadasis, especially through livelihoods promotion; those relating to organisation-building to aid agency and voice of the Devadasi women, and effective prevention and rehabilitation through changing norms and institutions at the policy level and in society.

4.1 Information and monitoring

Critical to designing schemes for the rehabilitation of Devadasis as well as strategising prevention is a measure of the extent of the problem. Devadasi practices should be recognised and repeated surveys should be conducted to find out where Devadasis are locatedand what is happening to them. Caste-based organisations, such as Dalit Sanghas,[65] can be used to keep track of Devadasis and assist the government in discovering dedications. More data is also needed on the reproductive health problems and psychological disorders faced by Devadasis, and the legalities of property rights to Devadasis.

As the practice exists in different forms in many states other than the three states where research was carried out (such as Madhya Pradesh, West Bengal, Odisha, Kerala), a comprehensive study needs to be undertaken across the country. The study would need to be conducted under the aegis of the Ministry of Women and Children at the national level, with the participation of state departments of Women and Child Development, National and State commissions of Women, and NGOs in each state. The participation of the Ministry and Corporations looking after Scheduled Castes and Scheduled Tribes will ensure that they engage with the identification of Devadasis and with increasing the outreach of departmental schemes to Devadasis.

The state also needs to form Committees at the national level and in each state for effective monitoring of spots where Devadasis are dedicated, making prevention more effective. The committee can also monitor the effective implementation of the schemes for Devadasi households. The membership of the committee needs to draw from the Department of Women and Children, SC/ST and national and state Rural Livelihoods Systems, NGOs, Dalit associations and community-based collectives and cooperatives of Devadasis and sex workers.

The National Commission for Women (NCW) has commissioned a research study to develop a database and profile of Devadasi women in the states. Hence it would be worthwhile to advocate learnings and best practices in the identification of Devadasis with the Commission as well as with academic institutions, e.g., Chennai University.

The government needs to provide budgetary support for the monitoring, prevention as well as the implementation of state schemes.

4.2 Providing more assets and resources to the excluded group: Devadasis

Ensuring rehabilitation of Devadasi women is a crucial challenge; although there are initiatives undertaken by the government as well as civil society organisations, a comprehensive rehabilitation (socio-economic and political) policy and programme for Devadasi women is still lacking. Some key suggestions for effective rehabilitation programmes are detailed below:

- **Compulsory free, quality and discrimination-free education** to children up to graduation level ensuring that all girls from the community and Devadasi girl children get priority education, admission, and scholarship.
- **Hostels for girls**: Given that parents are culpable in the dedication of Devadasis, there is a need to ensure that girl children at the risk of dedication are removed from such an environment and given the opportunity for safe stay in residential homes, where they can have access to education as well.
- **Skill development programme:** Children above 14 years of age should be imparted training on life skills and vocational skills for increasing their employment opportunities once they are out of school.
- **Livelihood support**: For Devadasis with no land or unproductive land, the government could provide fertile land with irrigation facility, easy access to credit along with backward and forward linkages. In addition to land, the government needs to provide grants for income-generating activities, and enterprise-promotion support. As with groups such as bonded labourers and manual scavengers, Devadasis could also be classified as a special group eligible for 100 per cent subsidies for income generating assets. This provision has been drafted in Telangana but is yet to be approved.
- **Marriage and financial assistance:** The government should promote Devadasi marriages and provide monetary assistance as reward.
- **Financial inclusion and services:** Bank accounts should be opened for Devadasis so they are financially included and can claim

official rights and entitlements easily and without any leakages.

- **Pension for Devadasis:** Given the problem of identification of Devadasi women under the widow or single women's schemes, a separate pension scheme should be formulated and targeted at such caste communities from which girls are dedicated as Devadasis.
- **Universal old age pension for poor families:** As mentioned earlier, one of the main reasons for dedicating girls as Devadasis is that the parents do not have social security schemes in their old age. There is a need to design effective universal old age pension scheme and ensure that the amount is sufficient to meet their food and health care needs.

In addition to economic support, Devadasis require social, legal and psychological support. These include social security schemes, counselling and mental health support, legal aid services, pension schemes, etc. These measures would rehabilitate Devadasis who have been identified by the government, and will ameliorate the extreme poverty and vulnerability that they have faced till now.

4.3 Organisation building

Lessons from working with excluded, exploited and vulnerable groups clearly show the advantage of organising, which provides safe forums for sharing common issues and collaborationin order to have a stronger voice. The agency and voice of Devadasi women would be significantly strengthened by helping them to organise themselves into collectives such as Self Help Groups (SHGs), federations, unions, and cooperatives through which they can claim their rights and resources, as well as derivemutual support. The collectives will also provide the women with safe spaces where they can discuss mutual needs and organise themselves to communicate these needs to the government and other organisations.

4.4 Changing norms and institutions

A comprehensive policy should address the stigma and discrimination faced by Devadasis and their children. There is also need to address labour market discrimination which is often neglected in rehabilitation policies. Norms, laws and policies need to allow for the following:

- **Law for providing property rights to Devadasis:** This provision will seriously deter exploitative partnerships by landed and rich villagers with Devadasis. The provisions of 'live-in relationships' may be used to get Devadasis and their children their due maintenance and property rights from the partners, as detailed earlier in the chapter.
- **Engaging males of Devadasi families and communities:** The male members of the relevant communities and families there in are substantially under-employed and often suffering from excessive alcohol consumption. They therefore make no conscious efforts to stop this dedication or retaliate against the practice. Caste norms are ingrained and deeply rooted in the psyche of the community, hence raising critical awareness and conscientization are crucial to turning community members into social advocates who could help end the practice. Proactive action by a sensitised male population will result in a reduction in the family pressure faced by Devadasi women at the family level.
- **Education to children of Devdasis:** It is important to ensure discrimination-free education and respectful socialisation in family and schools for the children of Devadasis in order to bring about social

change. In addition, children as change agents could be instrumental in sensitising parents against the Devadasi system.

- **Prevention of dedications:** Prevention strategies are crucial to uproot any social evil, and this is also true for the Devadasi system. These strategies include conscientization and raising awareness of the ill effects of the Devadasi system. In addition members of these vulnerable communities should be made aware of their rights so they can challenge cultural norms, and demand accountability from the State and society. The parents, priests, implementing government officers, NGO staff and police need to know the laws and the procedures by which they can prevent the practice.
- **Using laws as deterrents:** For effective prevention of the Devadasi practice the government, police and civil society organisations need to invoke not only the Devadasi law, but also other legislations such as the relevant sections under the Criminal Penal Code (CrPC) and the Indian Penal Code (IPC), the child marriage act, atrocities against SC/ST and other relevant acts. For effective enforcement of the laws it is required that the Acts have teeth; rules for acts need to framed and adopted, responsibilities and time frames for this need to be fixed, and the parents of the girl should not be criminalised, as they are not the perpetrators, but also victims of a practice that involves caste-based oppression. The real perpetrators who may be parents, but also the pimps, self-styled gurus and other brokers of the system need to be penalized. The partners should be punished too, and the provisions for those 'living in partnership' be applied to Devadasi children, conferring on them the right to inherit the property of their fathers. The application of these laws will have a strong deterrent effect on dedications and the sexual exploitation of Devadasis by non-Dalit and Dalit men.
- **Attending to the larger needs of the SC/ST groups:** As most Devadasis are from the SC/ST groups, it is important to organise and create awareness among this community, enlisting the support of Dalit groups in preventing the practice. Further, socio-economic and political concerns of these communities such as education, health security, livelihood, shelter need to be addressed in order to ensure that their fundamental rights are protected.

In conclusion, Devadasis represent a highly exploited group, whereby exploitation is on the grounds of caste, gender and poverty. Despite laws to the contrary, the practice has continued to exist, and even though new entrants to the traditional system have reduced significantly, the market for commercial sex has led to the mutation of the practice whereby many sex workers have adopted the label of Devadasi. Furthermore, the marginal economic security available to Devadasi women, has led many of them to move into sex work. The eradication of the practice will require a concentrated effort by government and civil society organisations, and will need close monitoring till the system is fully eradicated from the country.

Endnotes

1. Maria Costanza Torri (2009). 'Abuse of Lower Castes in South India: The Institution of Devadasi'. *Journal of International Women's Studies*. 11(2). 31-48. Available at: http://vc.bridgew.edu/jiws/vol11/iss2/3
2. Treena Rae Orchard (2007). 'Girl, Woman, Lover, Mother: Towards a new understanding of child prostitution among young Devadasis in rural Karnataka.' *India*. Social Science & Medicine. 64(12) pp 2379-2390.
3. The numbers cannot be estimated, however, as dedications are illegal, and most of the dedications are done secretly. Devadasis report that the villagers find out about Devadasis sometimes one or two years after the dedications.
4. Jogan Shankar (1994). *Devadasi Cult: A Sociological Analysis*. New Delhi: Ashish Publishing House.
5. William M Reddy, (2012).*The Making of Romantic Love: Longing and Sexuality in Europe, South Asia and Japan, 900-1200 CE*, Chicago: University of Chicago Press.
6. Anil Chawla (2002), *Sinners or Sinned Against: An Attempt to Look at the Myth and Reality of History and Presence Status of Devadasis*. Accessed at www.samarthbharat.com on 2 August, 2014.
7. Karuna Sharma (2007), 'The Social World of Prostitutes and Devadasis: A Study of the Social Structure and Its Politics in Early Modern India', Journal of International Women's Studies, 9(1), 297-310. Available at: http://vc.bridgew.edu/jiws/vol9/iss1/17
8. Amrit Srinivasan (1985), 'Reform and Revival: The Devadasi and her Dance', Economic and Political Weekly, (20:44), pp 1869-1876. Available at: http://www.jstor.org/stable/4375001
9. Ibid, p. 1872.
10. Ibid.
11. Frederique Apffel Marglin, (1985), '*Wives of the God-King, The Rituals of Devadasis of Puri', New Delhi:* Oxford University Press.
12. Saskia C. Kersenboom (1987), '*Nityasumangali, Devadasi Tradition of South India' New* Delhi :Motilal Banarsidass Publication.
13. Allen Matthew Harp (1997), '*Rewriting the Script for South Indian Dance'*, The Drama Review 41, (T155), New York:New York University.
14. For details, see: http://Devadasi.in/docs/Madras_Devadasi_Act_1947.pdf
15. For details, see: http://dpal.kar.nic.in/1%20of%201984%20(E).pdf
16. For details, see: http://www.tgnns.com/andhra-pradesh-2/the-andhra-pradesh-Devadasis-prohibition-of-dedication-rules-2015/2015/12/09/
17. For details, see: https://www.nls.ac.in/ccl/Acts%20to%20be%20loaded/Goa%20Childrens%20Act%202003.pdf
18. See for instance: Chawla, *Sinners or Sinned Against: An Attempt to Look at the Myth and Reality of History and Presence Status of Devadasis* and
19. See for instance: Ekaterina K Nikolova (2009), 'Understanding Obstacles and Stimuli to Exit from Ritual Prostitution', University of Amsterdam.
20. See, for instance: Marglin, 'Wives of the God-King, The Rituals of Devadasis of Puri' and Nikolova, 'Understanding Obstacles and Stimuli to Exit from Ritual Prostitution'.
21. Sampark (2015),'Gender based Violence on Scheduled Caste Girls: A Rapid Assessment of the Devadasi Practice in India', Bangalore: Sampark
22. As defined by Articles 3a, b and c of ILO The Worst Forms of Child Labour Convention No. 182.
23. T N Sathyanarayana and G.R. Babu (2012), Targeted sexual exploitation of children and women in India: Policy perspectives on Devadasi system, Ann Trop Med Public Health 2012 5, pp 157-62
24. Local cigarettes rolled in a dry leaf.
25. This section draws on minutes of a Regional Consultation organized by State Women's Commission, Andhra Pradesh, Hyderabad, 23, February 2015 on 'Conditions of Devadasi's in India', provided by Sameer Taware.
26. *Indian Express*. 13 February 2014. *'SC Tells Karnataka to Check Devadasi Practice.' Available at: http://www.newindianexpress.com/states/karnataka/SC-Tells-Karnataka-to-Check-Devadasi-Practice/2014/02/13/article2054851.ece*
27. Ashwini, Y.S. '*Schemes Fail to Curb Devadasi Practice.' Deccan Herald*. 21 August 2011. Available at: http://www.deccanherald.com/content/185378/schemes-fail-curb-Devadasi-practice.html
28. Srilaba Vadlapatla, '*Devadasi System Still Exists in Telangana, AP, says Report'*, *Times of India*, 23 February 2015. Available at: http://timesofindia.indiatimes.com/india/Devadasi-system-still-exists-in-Telangana-AP-says-report/articleshow/46337859.cms
29. Government of Andhra Pradesh. (2013), 'Report Submitted by Sri V. Raghunath Rao One-man Commission in Respect of Problems Faced by

Joginies, Basavis, Mathammas and Devadasis and their Children.' Hyderabad: Government of Andhra Pradesh, pp 4.

30. Rekha Pande (2008), 'Ritualized Prostitution' in Rohini Sahni, V. Kalyan Shankar and Hemant Apte (eds). *Prostitution and Beyond: An Analysis of Sex Work in India,* New Delhi: Sage Publications, pp 107.
31. Government of Andhra Pradesh, 'Report Submitted by Sri V. Raghunath Rao', pp 24.
32. In the case of Trokosi slavery, parents offer their girl children to the priests as penance for sins and transgressions. In the Devadasi practice, girls are dedicated due to social and economic vulnerabilities of the household. See, for instance, D.I. Dyansi and P. Biga (2014), ' *Trokosi* - Slave of a Fetish: An Empirical Study. Stud Tribes Tribals, 12(1): 1-8 (2014). Available at: http://www.krepublishers.com/02-Journals/T%20&%20T/T%20&%20T-12-0-000-14-Web/T%20&%20T-12-1-000-14-ABST-PDF/S-T&T-12-1-001-14-336-Dzansi-D-Y/S-T&T-12-1-001-336-Dzansi-D-Y-Tx[1].pdf
33. Torri, Abuse of Lower Castes in South India: The Institution of Devadasi.
34. See for instance, Kersenboom, 'Nityasumangali, Devadasi Tradition of South India' and Orchard, 'Girl, Woman, Lover, Mother: Towards a new understanding of child prostitution among young Devadasis in rural Karnataka.'
35. For details, see: International Labour Organization (ILO) (1930).The Forced Labour Convention No. 29. http://www.unrol.org/files/ILO_Convention_29.pdf
36. For details, see: International Labour Organization (ILO) (1999). Worst Forms of Child Labour Convention No. 182.
37. For details see: http://www.dfn.org.uk/info/slavery/42-information/slavery/94-ritual-sex-slavery
38. Andrea Parrot and Nina Cummings(2008), '*Sexual Enslavement of Girls and Women Worldwide*'Connecticut: Greenwood Publishing Group, , pp 49
39. The Convention for Elimination of all Forms of Discrimination (CEDAW), 1979. Available at: http://www.un.org/womenwatch/daw/cedaw/text/econvention.htm
40. Cheryl Thomas (2009),'Forced and Early Marriage: A Focus on Central and Eastern Europe and Former Soviet Union Countries with Selected Laws from Other Countries', Expert Group Meeting on Good Practices in Legislation to Address Harmful Practices Against Women. 25-28 May 2009, Addis Ababa, Ethiopia. available at (http://www.un.org/womenwatch/daw/egm/vaw_legislation_2009/Expert%20Paper%20EGMGPLHP%20_Cheryl%20Thomas%20revised_.pdf)
41. CEDAW, 1979.
42. Navsarjan is a Gujarat-based grassroots Dalit organization that works on human rights and the elimination of discrimination.
43. Expert Group Meeting on good practices in legislation to address harmful practices against women.
44. As stated by Ms. Ruth Manorama, at the Hyderabad conference, February, 2015.
45. Sampark (2002). 'Devadasis and their Livelihoods, An Exploratory Study for Developing Intervention Strategies: A Study Conducted for National Institute for Mental Health and Neuro Science', Bangalore: NIMHANS.
46. Ibid.
47. Sampark engages itself with women's thrift and credit cooperatives in Koppal district of North Karnataka. Out of 11,000 women members associated with more than 600 Self Help Groups, 400 members are Devadasis.
48. Sampark, Devadasis and their Livelihoods.
49. Nikolova, 'Understanding Obstacles and Stimuli to Exit from Ritual Prostitution'.
50. N.D. Shiva Kumar,, 'Finally, an End to the Devadasi System', *The Times of India*, January 23, 2009. Available at: http://timesofindia.indiatimes.com/city/hubballi/Finally-an-end-to-Devadasi-system/articleshow/4023672.cms
51. The Act prohibits the solemnization of marriages where either of the parties is a 'child' i.e. below 18 years if female or 21 years if male, providing for the penalisation of individuals who abet, direct, conduct or perform these marriages, including guardians and the men above the age of 18 years who marry a child.
52. Section 371 applies to habitual dealing in slave, section 372 to selling minors for purposes of prostitution, etc., Section 374 to unlawful compulsory labour, and Sections 375 and 376 to rape and punishment of rape.
53. This defines human trafficking and 'provides stringent punishment for human trafficking; trafficking of children for exploitation in any form including physical exploitation; or any form of sexual exploitation, slavery, servitude or the forced removal of organs'.
54. Enacted in pursuance of an International Convention signed in May, 1950 to combat trafficking of women and children; the Act defines prostitution as, 'the sexual exploitation or abuse of persons for commercial

purposes or forconsideration in money or in any other kind' and clearly penalises trafficking (recruitment, transport, transfer or harbouring) or abetment of trafficking of individuals, for prostitution as well as those who live knowingly on earnings from the prostitution of others.

55. The Act penalizes sexual offences (encompasses touching children with sexual intent and penetrative sexual acts, including the performance of oral sex) committed against any person below 18 years of age as well as abetment/aiding of sexual offences against children.

56. Signatories to the Convention are required to enact necessary legal measures to prevent inducement or coercion of a child to engage in 'unlawful sexual activity' and to prevent the exploitative use of children in prostitution.

57. The preamble of the Act is 'to prevent the commission of offences of atrocities against the members of Scheduled Castes and Tribes, to provide for Special Courts for the trial of such offences and for the relief and rehabilitation of the victims of such offenses and for matters connected therewith or incidental thereto'. The sexual exploitation of a woman belonging to a Scheduled Caste or a Scheduled Tribe, where the offender (not being SC/ST)uses their position to dominate and sexually exploit the woman, is punishable under the Act.

58. The Act provides protection to females who have shared a household with the abuser and are related through marriage or a marriage-like relationship and consanguinity. In addition to covering live-in relationships, the Act broadens the definition of domestic violence to include verbal, emotional, mental and economic abuse and threat of abuse, in addition to physical violence. As it is a civil law, only monetary sanctions are applicable on the accused.

59. Telangana Schedule Castes Cooperative Finance Corporation

60. Justice Raghunath Rao, the One-man commission on Devadasis.

61. This was reported by Devadasis in a workshop in Hyderabad in February 2015. The findings of the survey in the study show that 75% of the Devadasis have a home, which could be due to the fact that the sample was largely drawn from among NGO-assisted Devadasis.

62. In the case of Lata Singh v. State of U.P. AIR 2006 SC 2522, the Supreme Court observed that a 'live-in relationship between two consenting adults of heterosexual sex does not amount to any offence even though it may be perceived as immoral'. In the case of Indra Sarma V.K.V. Sarma 2014-1-L.W(Crl.) 129, it was held that in-equities exist within 'live-in' relationships and when they break down, the woman is invariably the sufferer. Besides, she also suffers from social disadvantages and prejudices and has been regarded less worthy historically. The SC also empathised that it is unfortunate that there is no express statute or legislation governing termination and disruption of live-in relationships in India.

- In this context, the nature of relationship existing between the Devadasi and her partner is said to fall within the parameters of a 'live-in' relationship, thus protecting her right of inheritance of the partner's property. The Bench of M Y Eqbal and Amitava Roy cited in their judgement, 'Where a man and woman are proved to have lived together as husband and wife, the law will presume, unless contrary is clearly proved, that they were living together in consequence of a valid marriage, and not in a state of concubinage.'
- Another progressive judgement by the Supreme Court is the affirmation of the legitimacy of a child born out of live-in relationships in Bharata Matha & Ors v. R. Vijaya Renganathan & Ors.
- Justice Markandey Katju laid down the following criteria for live-in relationships in the D. Velusamy V. D. Patchiammal Case.
- (a) The couple must hold themselves out to society as being akin to spouses; (b) They must have attained the legal age of marriage; (c) They must be qualified to enter into a legal marriage, including being unmarried; (d) They must have voluntarily cohabited for a significant period of time.

63. Taware, Conditions of Devadasis in India.

64. See: Sampark, Devadasis and their Livelihoods *and* Marglin, Wives of the God-King, The Rituals of Devadasis of Puri.

65. Sanghas are associations of different types of groups; here the reference is to Dalit Sanghas, associations of scheduled caste persons.

The Jarawa of the Andamans

*Rhea John and Harsh Mander**

India's Andaman Islands are home to some of the most ancient, and until recently the most isolated, peoples in the world. Today barely a few hundred of these peoples survive. This report is about one of these ancient communities of the Andaman Islands, the Jarawa, or as they describe themselves, the Ang.

Until the 1970s, and even to a degree until the 1990s, the Jarawa people fiercely and often violently defended their forest homelands, fighting off a diverse range of incursions and offers of 'friendly' contact—by other tribes-people, colonial rulers, convicts brought in from mainland India by the colonisers, the Japanese occupiers, independent India's administration, and mainland communities settled on the islands by the Indian government. Since the 1990s, two of the three main Ang communities have altered their relationship with the outsider of many hues, accepting their 'friendship' and all that came with it, including health care support, clothes, foods like rice and bananas that were never part of their hunting-gathering existence, trinkets, roads, a range of intoxicants, tourists, and sexual and economic exploitation.

The conundrum of reporting in an Exclusion Report about a community like the Jarawa is that, in many ways, what we conventionally describe as 'inclusion' is actually exclusion—or what some scholars describe appropriately as 'adverse inclusion'.[1] The experience of other Andaman tribes like the Great Andamanese and the Onge highlight poignantly and sombrely the many harmful consequences of such inclusion.[2] The continued dogged resistance of the Sentinelese to any contact with outsiders makes them perhaps the most isolated people in the world. On the other hand, the early adverse consequences of exposure of the Jarawa people to diseases and sexual exploitation by outsiders, suggest that safeguarding many forms of 'exclusion' may paradoxically constitute the best chance for the just and humane 'inclusion' of these highly vulnerable communities.

However, the optimal balance between isolation and contact with the outside world of such indigenous communities is something that no government in the modern world has yet succeeded in establishing. Perspectives about what indeed is in the best interest of hitherto isolated hunting-gathering communities continue to vary hugely.

Methodological Note

Before we proceed further, another caveat is in order. Writing about people who do not participate in the discourse to which the text seeks to contribute

* Rhea John and Harsh Mander are the lead author and contributing author, respectively.

** Advisors for this chapter were Samir Acharya, Shekhar Singh and Alia Allana.

*** This chapter has been reviewed by Sophie Grig

necessarily runs the risk of misrepresentation. With the indigenous peoples lumped into the evolutionary-anthropological classification of 'tribes', taking their views into account has itself only recently become part of the approach adopted by academic and policy establishments. The discourse continues, for instance, to refer to the people studied in this chapter as the 'Jarawa' ignoring the name they use themselves—'Ang'—and their right to decide what they are to be called. In the present chapter we have used the two names interchangeably, in an effort to acknowledge the history of this contact.

Despite the objective of this chapter being to represent the Jarawa as fairly as possible, its methodology is constrained not just by difficulties in understanding those whose language and culture are profoundly different from our own, but by the policies in place. To protect what is still officially a relatively uncontacted tribe, the administration proscribes interactions with the Jarawa except with a permit, or for members of the welfare society that forms the interface between the state and the tribe, the Andaman Adim Janjati Vikas Samiti (AAJVS). Given the problematic outcomes of their interactions with the 'outsider', including health problems, the restrictions on our meeting Jarawa people was not unreasonable, but became a major challenge to writing the chapter.

As a result, this account relies on secondary literature, interviews with those who interact with the Jarawa or have authority over them, as well as on some limited primary observation.

The administration was willing to discuss their work with the Jarawa, their policy and its outcomes. Even if speaking to the Jarawas directly had been officially permitted, there would still be many challenges, both practical and ethical. The translation—of not only language, but also cultural context—was impossible within the time and resource limitations of the study. We wished to accomplish the objective of the chapter—to describe the situation of the Jarawa specifically in relation to their rights and the policies enacted by the state—without the disruptive interaction that such a study might impose on the tribe. It is hoped that this limited methodology would not be construed as ignoring the voice of the Jarawa. Our object has not been to cast an anthropological spotlight on a relatively isolated tribe[3] but to critically evaluate state and society in the Andamans, in relation to a specific population with different rights and vulnerabilities from most of the rest.

Historical background

The Jarawa tribe, along with the Great Andamanese, Onge and Sentinelese, constitute the four major tribes of the Andaman Islands. Of these, the longest and most extensive colonial interaction was with the Great Andamanese, initially through violence and repression, and thereafter active assimilation, from the side of the colonialists. The Great Andamanese were resettled on Strait Island, but by then they had been exposed to diseases to which they had no prior exposure, and consciously to tobacco, alcohol and drugs to foster submissiveness, as a cumulative result of which they have seen a rapid decline in numbers. The Onge have lost most of their former territory to logging interests, and have been made dependent on regular handouts from the state administration for all their needs.[4] The Sentinelese have persistently and fiercely rejected contact with the rest of the world till date.

The Ang or Jarawa occupy large forested tracts of Middle and South Andaman Islands, which are being reduced by both official and encroached settlements of outsiders. There are three main groups of Jarawas, each referred to by the name of the town closest to their location: Kadamtala Jarawas in the North, Middle Strait Jarawas close to Baratang, and Tirur Jarawas in the South of the reserve area. The groups visit and maintain relations with each other, but each defines itself as distinct from the others.

The reserve area was first created in 1956, but its size has changed multiple times over the years in the absence of clear demarcations on both maps and the ground. Today the reserve consists of 1,024 square km of forests, creeks and coastal waters (out of the A&N Islands' 8,073 square km). In 2007, a buffer zone of 5-kilometre radius was added, within which no large-scale commercial activity is permitted. Under the tribe's protection, the Jarawa reserve area remains the best-preserved ecosystem of the islands.

The Jarawa were considered a 'hostile' tribe by the British from the time of the initial settlement at Port Blair, as they were at war with the 'friendly' Great Andamanese tribes who occupied the same territory, and resisted all attempts by outsiders to enter their area. The Jarawa were also subjected to extreme violence during the Japanese occupation of the Islands during World War II, which further alienated them from outsiders.[5] The Indian government, in an attempt to gain fuller control over this outlying territory, began to send 'friendly contact' expeditions to the western coast of the Jarawa territory with gifts of food, cloth and iron from the 1950s. In the meantime, thousands of people arriving in India as refugees after Partition were resettled by the Government along the uncertain borders of the Jarawa reserve. This settlement by the Indian government on territories adjacent to the Jarawa territory paved the way for their increasing interaction with outsiders, which has especially grown during the last three decades.

'First voluntary contact' by the Jarawa with outsiders was made in 1974, when some Jarawa emerged from their forest unarmed and met the expedition's boats to collect the gifts themselves. However, they continued to be suspicious of outsiders, and violent towards those entering the forest to use its resources. They also long opposed, with violent attacks and ambushes, the construction of the Andaman Trunk Road (hereafter ATR) through the reserve, which only accelerated the highly unequal interaction with the outside world. If the Indian state had not taken the two crucial measures of resettlement and constructing the ATR, the current situation of the Jarawa—fraught in certain ways that we will observe—could have been avoided or at least minimised.

The construction of the highway was accompanied by temporary settlements of workers along it that became permanent villages over time, encroaching on the reserve territory. The Jarawa undertook punitive expeditions to surrounding settlements to protest the invasion of their space, even taking lives in the process. The Bush Police was formed before Independence, first to protect British interests, and then to protect settlers from the Jarawa. Today the Bush Police has been reaggregated as the Jarawa Protection Force to protect the Jarawa from outsiders. In 1975, the Andaman Adim Janjati Vikas Samiti (AAJVS) [The Andaman Primitive Tribes Development Society] was created under the aegis of the government to work directly with tribal groups for their welfare.

In 1998, for the first time, small groups of Jarawa began to initiate friendly contact with the outside world. They began to engage with the local administration and with travellers along the Andaman Trunk Road, asking for bananas and coconuts—familiar gifts from the contact missions—and later demanding rides on vehicles. The popular story used to explain this shift is of a Jarawa boy named Enmei who, having been treated for a broken leg in Port Blair for three months, returned to the reserve with positive news about the outsiders. He led the exuberant 'contact party' of the Jarawa who arrived at Uttara jetty unarmed, causing shock and panic among those present, and demanded coconuts from the policemen who were rushed there to handle the situation.[6,7] However, at the time a vast majority of Jarawa remained in the forest and did not participate in these excursions.

Whatever the cause of the shift, its effects in terms of increased poaching and entry into the reserve were unmistakable. The administration fulfilled the

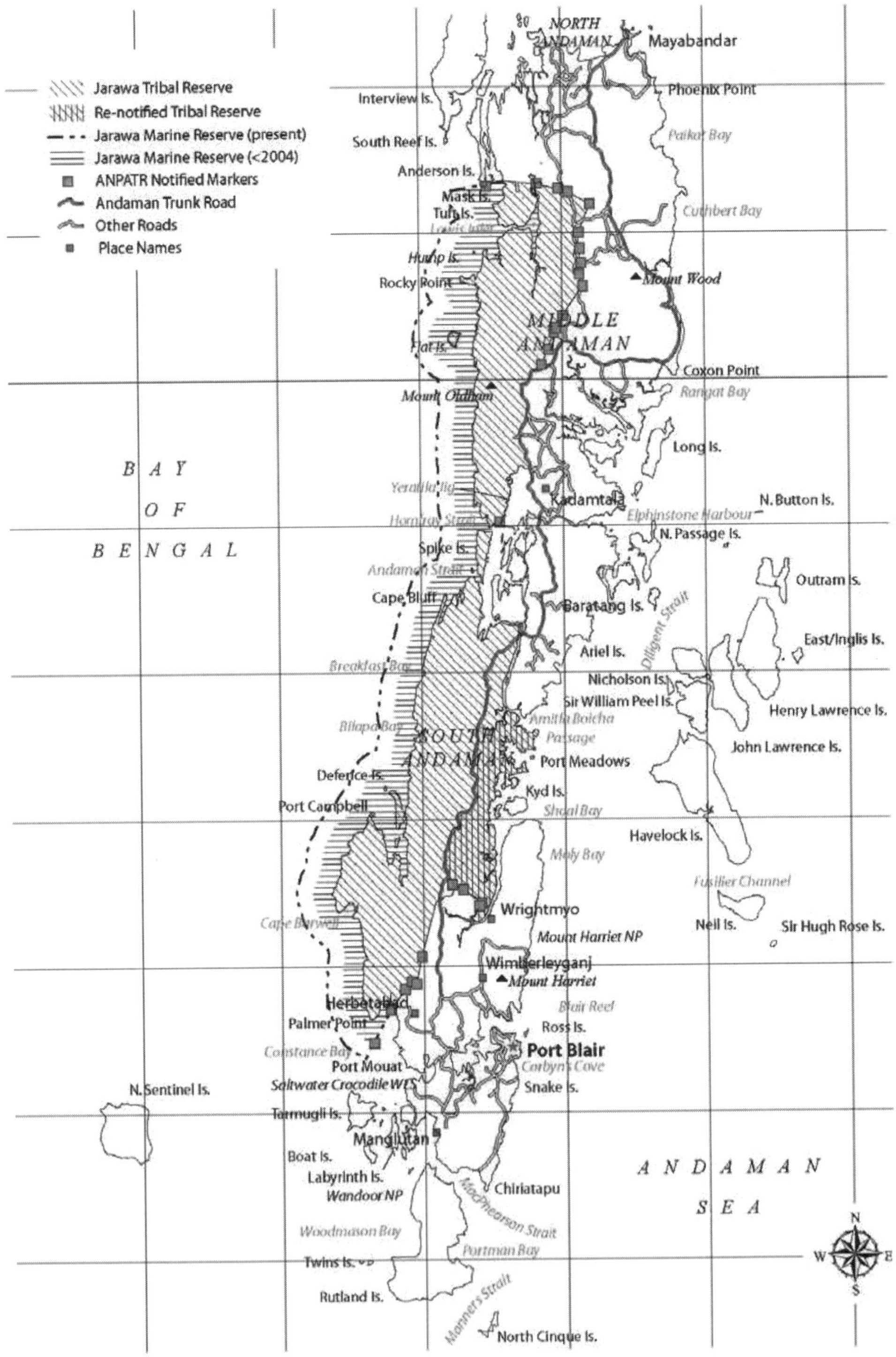

MAP II: THE JARAWA TRIBAL RESERVE
Notified Boundary
Source: Andaman and Nicobar Protection of Aboriginal Tribes Regulation (ANPATR) - 1956

NOT TO SCALE

Fig.1: Map of the notified boundary of the Jarawa Reserve Area, showing changes over time (Source: *The Jarawa Tribal Reserve Dossier*, 2011:UNESCO)

Jarawas' demands, trying on the one hand to prevent or minimise contact with outsiders, while on the other, considering demands to integrate the tribe into the mainstream. At the local level meanwhile, the newly sociable Jarawa had become a sensation among the local settlers, who had been brought up in fear of Jarawa arrows and with stories that they 'used blood to play *Holi*'.[8]

In 1999, Shyamali Ganguly, a lawyer from Port Blair, noticed the Jarawa 'begging', or accepting food from travellers, along the ATR and filed a Public Interest Litigation in the Calcutta High Court—in her view, to protect the tribe's interests. In the case, she pleaded that the administration cease its neglect of the Jarawa and begin providing them access to welfare provisions considered essential in mainstream society, such as food rations, education and health care,[9] as well as clothes and modern amenities.[10] Subsequent interventions in the case by Kalpavriksh and the Society for Andaman and Nicobar Ecology challenged two assumptions—of the administration not having played a part in bringing about the present situation, as well as of 'mainstreaming' being the most desirable outcome for the Jarawa people. The Court-commissioned report by the Anthropological Survey of India argued that the ATR had disrupted the Jarawa's lives, livelihoods and rights over their territory like a 'public thoroughfare through one's private courtyard'. Based on this, the Supreme Court ordered the closure of the Andaman Trunk Road in 2002.

This order, however, was never implemented, and remains breached even up to the time of writing this chapter, 13 years later. A new 'Jarawa policy' was introduced by the A&N administration in 2004 that advocated a stated policy of 'maximum autonomy to the Jarawas with minimum and regulated intervention', by which they would be left at liberty to develop 'according to their genius and at their own pace'. The stated intention was to protect the tribe from the 'harmful effects of exposure'.

However, the policy did not provide for the closure of the ATR, and instead prescribed only 'regulated' movement along it—allowing travellers to use the road only via a convoy system. Ironically, the Jarawa were to be protected from them by the same method which had previously been deployed to protect travellers from the Jarawa—while the road remained in use.

The justification offered by the administration for continuing movement on the ATR was that the settlers required the trunk road, and claimed that it was administratively unfeasible to separate the local settlers from the tourists. The latter used the bus convoy hoping to spot the Jarawa in the way tourists in tiger safaris scour the landscape for sightings of the tiger in the wild. Starting in the 2000s, Andaman tour operators began to promote what Survival International terms 'human safaris': travel along the Andaman Trunk Road with the specific intent of seeing and interacting with 'uncivilised tribes', or '*junglees*'.[11] Bribes to policemen could also purchase contact, dances by Jarawa women and photographs with them.[12]

Based on a case filed by an irate tourist resort, in 2012 the Supreme Court upheld a ban on all large-scale tourist and commercial activities within a 5-kilometre radius of the reserve, upholding the 2007 A&N administration notification creating a buffer zone in that area. The road, however, is still in use and there are continuing signs of other violations of the reserve such as encroachments, poaching, sexual exploitation, encouraging the use of intoxicants, and facilitating encounters with tourists through bribery.[13] While the Andaman administration had given an assurance of developing an alternative sea-route to Middle and North Andaman by March 2015, the completion of this project is nowhere in sight.[14]

In 2012, a media storm broke out over videos made public by the *Guardian*, a UK-based newspaper, of Jarawa girls being made to dance by men in uniform—either police or armed forces.[15]

Investigation revealed that the video was actually shot in 2008, by a group of armed forces personnel who had been exempted from the convoy system.[16] Locals were quick to point out that such exemptions are also regularly made for 'VIP' guests of the administration visiting the Islands.[17] In 2014, a member of the tribe gave a controversial interview to the *Andaman Chronicle* describing frequent sexual exploitation by outsiders under the influence of intoxicants.[18]

At present, the actual level of interaction between the Jarawa and outsiders is unknown due to the government's nominal—and imperfectly enforced—adherence to the policy of isolation. In November 2014, the administration issued a notification announcing a new 'protocol of surveillance' of the borders of the (JRA), based on 'many instances of unauthorized contact by outsiders with the Jarawas' having been brought to the notice of the administration.[19] This policy has not yet become operational.

Context

1. The Policy Debate

Until recently, the Jarawa were part of an official category problematically titled 'Primitive Tribal Groups' (PTGs). These communities were only recently re-titled a more dignified Particularly Vulnerable Tribal Groups or PVTGs in official documents. With tribes that have been mostly isolated till date, like the Jarawa, the policy debate in India has largely oscillated between positions of 'isolation' and 'integration', with implicit and sometimes explicit calls for 'assimilation', while assuming the right to decide on behalf of the tribes in question.

The 'isolation' position argues that these tribes carry a unique ancient cultural heritage, one that needs to be preserved from the influence of the vastly more powerful mainstream society. Jawaharlal Nehru and his advisor on this issue, the anthropologist Verrier Elwin, were of this persuasion, which consequently underlay independent India's initial tribal policy, although Elwin did temper his views somewhat over time.[20]

The 'integration' or assimilation side of the policy debate was represented, for instance, by the Indian anthropologist G S Ghurye. Ghurye argued that the stage of civilisational backwardness that these tribes' lifestyles indicated should not be allowed to continue, as it amounted to depriving them of rights due to them as citizens. They deserved the benefits of modern technology, education and healthcare, and to allow them to continue without these was a denial of their humanity.[21]

Subsequent experience has moderated these positions, initially articulated in the 1950s and 1960s. It was realised that the integration of uncontacted tribes exposed them to diseases to which they had neither exposure nor resistance, leading to vast casualties—or as Meenakshi Mukherjee starkly put it, 'assimilation is ethnocide'.[22] Moreover, the attempt to subsequently absorb them into the mainstream economy, whether through cultivation or reservation in government services, left them at the very margins of the economy—as was the case with the Great Andamanese and Onge. These tribes were highly vulnerable to diseases, dependent on food items like rice, coconut and bananas which can only be grown, not hunted or gathered and, more harmfully, dependent on outside intoxicants. This left them culturally uprooted and alienated, sometimes in anomie and without the joy, self-confidence or hope that cultural mooring gave them in the past.

Being uprooted from their traditional lands and livelihoods left them culturally and economically adrift, eventually leading to a drastic fall in birth rates and the decimation of various tribes.[23] Nathan and Xaxa call this process 'adverse inclusion'.[24] Of the Great Andamanese tribes, once the majority residents of the Andaman islands, only 44 individuals remain, and they remember little of their original culture and language. At the same time, the increasing value of the scarce natural resources now found almost solely in the well-preserved tribal reserve ecosystem has ensured that total isolation is no longer an option. Moreover, tribes like the Jarawas, who chose to end their self-imposed isolation and actively maintain links with settler individuals, have to be respected as agents in their own futures.

Survival International, the international organisation working for tribal rights, has been long advocating the closure of the Andaman Trunk Road, alongside many activists and researchers who have worked in the islands. They argue that their opposition to the ATR is not founded on an ideology of isolationism, but because the road forces the Jarawas into a degree and kind of unequal interaction with the outside world that they never agreed to and find difficult to cope with. The road opens up possibilities for incursions into the reserve all along its length, particularly from the numerous small settlements —mostly illegal—that have come up there. Apart from the fact that the Jarawas never agreed to outsiders entering their reserve at all, the road opened up a new frontier that was extremely difficult to police. The road enhanced the settler communities' familiarity with the reserve, which enables and incentivises them to find ways around the convoy system and the 'three-tier' patrolling of the coastal borders of the reserve by the AAJVS, Police and Coast Guard.

The famous quote by the anthropologist R. K. Bhattacharya on the ATR being 'like a public thoroughfare through one's private courtyard' highlights the question of ownership.[25] One of the ways in which Jarawa difference is most frequently illustrated is to assert that they have no conception of private property. This example is used to explain (almost to excuse) their tendency to raid villages for food and other items. The other implication of this assertion, however, is that Jarawas have no sense of ownership whatsoever.[26] This in turn feeds into a view of the reserve area as government land on which the Jarawa are allowed to live based on the status quo in 1956 (when the A&N Protection of Aboriginal Tribes Regulation was enacted), rather than as land collectively owned by the tribe. This allows the government to redraw the boundaries of the reserve without consulting the Jarawa.[27] In the case of the Onge, Sekhsaria shows that the resettlements and deforestation in Little Andaman were recommended and carried out by the administration after the entire island had been declared a tribal reserve, actively violating the rights of the tribe.[28] While it is possible to argue that the Jarawa, being hostile at the time, could not be consulted about their opinion on the ATR, the latter case seems adequate proof that the administration at the time did not value the ownership rights of tribes over their reserves in any case. Moreover, the Jarawa demonstrated their opposition to the road by their violent ambushes, but the state chose to ignore their opposition. The ATR today is kept open despite there being research to show that it is mostly used by tourists and supply trucks (which could both be diverted to sea routes) rather than by the settlers along the road for their livelihood, whose rights the A&N Administration claims to be defending.[29] The Forest Rights Act (2006), a law that operationalises the rights of forest-dwellers over the territory they occupy, is yet to be notified in the Islands. On the ground, the AAJVS fieldworkers' efforts to 'persuade' Jarawas to stay away from the ATR, rather than limiting or stopping its use, shows consistent indifference to Jarawa rights of ownership over their territory.

We believe, with Survival International, that the Jarawa must have the right to decide on their futures, and on the degree and nature of their interaction with mainstream society. The freedom of their choice, in Survival's view, depends heavily on the security of their position: on the protection of their right to livelihood, and consequently, to the Jarawa Reserve Area itself. If the availability of these resources were to decline such that the Jarawa were no longer able to sustain themselves by hunting and foraging, they would be forced into an unequal exchange with the outside world to ensure their own survival.

Samir Acharya, of the Society for Andaman and Nicobar Ecology, who has long battled for the rights of the Jarawa and the Islands' environment, worries about the situation today, in which curiosity has led at least some Jarawas to experiment with, and develop a taste for, outsider food, clothing and commodities. If the Jarawa were to start valuing these over their traditional resources, they would barter away priceless forest produce to gain access to these, particularly if they were not being allowed to purchase them openly (having no official access to money, ways of earning it or places to spend it). This practice is now widely observed: the exchange of, for instance, highly priced crabs caught by Jarawa women for plastic bottles filled with rice. While Dr Pandya of the Andaman and Nicobar Tribal Research Institute (ANTRI) considers barter one of the methods by which the Jarawa creatively negotiate with the pressures of mainstream society (and so need to be empowered to negotiate it better), Acharya considers it tentative proof of the final surrender of Jarawa culture: its devaluation by Jarawas themselves.[30] Survival counters this contention with the evidence of the Jarawas' refusal so far to give up their traditional livelihoods for the sake of passive consumerism, suggesting that an active choice is being made. But they simultaneously point out the urgency of communicating to the Ang the potential consequences of pursuing these disparate acts of consumption for the long-term sustenance of their livelihood and culture.

2. Policies on the Jarawas

As a signatory to the United Nations Declaration on the Rights of Indigenous Peoples (UNDRIP), India has formally recognised the rights of groups such as the Jarawa to 'self-determination', meaning the right to pursue their economic, social and cultural development without outside interference.[31] Domestic laws and policies in letter conform in part to the UN Declaration, but the practice falls short in significant ways.

2.1 Andaman and Nicobar Islands (Protection of Aboriginal Tribes) Regulation, 1956

Under this Regulation, the administration is authorised to reserve any area 'predominantly inhabited by' a Particularly Vulnerable Tribal Group (PVTG) for their use exclusively, and to demarcate boundaries within which ownership of land, conduct of trade or business in the products of the area, as well as entry into the area, are reserved for members of the tribe. After its amendment in 2012, the maximum punishment under ANPATR is imprisonment up to 7 years, and fine up to Rs 10,000.[32] However, according to news reports, habitual offenders under this Act are regularly let off on bail extremely quickly, even with multiple cases pending, and even video testimonies by Jarawas have not been sufficient to ensure prosecution.[33]

An especially instructive case was that of the French filmmakers of the documentary 'Organic Jarawa', who entered the reserve without permission and filmed Jarawa people multiple times over a period of three years. None of the agencies tasked with patrolling the reserve or maintaining contact with the tribe were aware of their existence. The Jarawas themselves, having been given food and other objects, did not mention it to officials. Embarrassed by the incident, the administration filed a case against the filmmakers, and international pressure from Survival International and others helped prevent the release of the film in October 2014. In November, the administration also issued a notification on joint patrolling of the borders of the reserve area by AAJVS, Police and Forest departments, which had not been implemented till July 2015. No steps

Fig.2: The boundary between the Onge Reserve forest and the settled areas on Little Andaman Island, 2015

to prevent infiltration from the porous 'hotspots' of settlements bordering the reserve, such as Tirur and Kadamtala, have been announced.

2.2 Jarawa Policy, 2004

Drafted in the aftermath of the Supreme Court ruling of 2002 ordering the closure of the Andaman Trunk Road, the Jarawa Policy emphasised allowing the Jarawa to 'develop according to their own genius and at their own pace'[34]. It explicitly eschewed any further attempts at mainstreaming, rehabilitation or relocation, as well as interventions in their cultural life. The A&N Administration also undertook to prevent any exploitation of natural resources by non-tribals in the reserve, including government agencies. Based apparently on the 'Master Plan 1991–2021' drawn up for the tribes, yet overturning many of its key suggestions, the policy places an indefinite moratorium on any attempts to encourage the tribe to join the mainstream, while implicitly suggesting that they will inevitably do so at a time of their choosing.

Simultaneously, the refusal of the administration to close the ATR, failures to prevent tourist traffic as well as poaching in the Jarawa reserve, and the creation of dependence on agriculturally raised products like rice, bananas and coconut, undermines the realistic space for the Jarawa people to preserve genuine autonomy even if they so choose.

2.3 Buffer zone notification, 2007

The ANPATR prevents outsiders from entering the reserve, but cannot prevent Jarawas from leaving it.

As a result of both this and the frequent poaching, the demarcation of the territory remains largely on paper, marked at some points by Bush Police camps and with little monitoring of the rest. The Jarawa being a semi-nomadic tribe do not have a fixed notion of boundaries, which in any case have undergone various changes over time without their consent or even knowledge. Whereas virtually the whole area north of Tirur on the South Andaman Island was considered Jarawa reserve area in 1957, the 1979 notification excluded the area east of the ATR, and permitted its use for settlement, logging and replanting for commercial forestry.[35]

To reduce incursions, a Buffer Zone of 5km around the existing boundary (and 1 km of coastal area) was notified in 2007. Commercial activities employing more than 20 persons or with a turnover of more than 1 crore (as defined by ANPATR) were forbidden in the zone. Residents of the 31 affected villages, supported by political leaders, opposed the buffer zone, and a resort forced to close under the notification challenged it in the Supreme Court, based both on the lack of a previous recommendation to this effect, and on inconsistency of implementation. The Court-appointed Commissioner suggested that the rather arbitrary criteria of turnover and employment be replaced by impact assessments and other relevant criteria. Moreover, he recommended that the boundary of the reserve be properly demarcated on the ground and at sea before mandating a blanket 5 km buffer, the borders of which would be equally uncertain. These recommendations did not find a place in the final ruling.[36]

2.4 Scheduled Castes and Scheduled Tribes (Prevention of Atrocities) Act, 1989

The Scheduled Castes and Scheduled Tribes (Prevention of Atrocities) Act, seeks to punish a wide range of actions which enact discrimination against these historically marginalised groups, irrespective of whether the actions are punishable under other laws. The failures of implementation of this Act are mostly due to the reluctance to charge offenders under this law, and the use of milder laws instead. In the case of the Jarawa, this Act has been used to charge offenders for violations of the reserve, provision of intoxicants and sexual offences. In the case of reserve violations, it is used in the place of the more relevant legislation, the Forest Rights Act of 2006, which according to a forest official has yet to be notified in the Islands. Difficulty in getting Jarawa witnesses who are articulate and unfazed by the unfamiliar courtroom situation, poor evidence, and difficulty in apprehending and maintaining custody of repeat offenders have led to poor disposal rates.[37] This is despite special hearings conducted within the reserve area for these cases. Also the failure of Jarawa people to report poacher incursions suggests that they perhaps have more faith in the poachers than the welfare and police officials they are in contact with.[38]

2.5 Forest Rights Act, 2006

An Act that could perhaps have helped prosecute those violating the reserve—but is not in use in the Andamans—is the Forest Rights Act (known in full as the Scheduled Tribes and other Traditional Forest Dwellers (Recognition of Forest Rights) Act, 2006). According to the Union Ministry of Tribal Affairs' Report on FRA Implementation for August 2015,

> The Andaman & Nicobar Administration has informed that there are no non-tribal forest dwellers as defined in the Act in A&N Islands. The Act, therefore, is applicable only to the Forest Dwelling Scheduled Tribes of these islands. The area inhabited by the Scheduled Tribes of A&N Islands has been declared as reserved area under the A&N Islands Protection of Aboriginal Tribes (Regulation), 1956. The interest of the tribals in the land situated in the reserved areas is fully protected under the provision of the regulation.

> The tribal reserves have been notified as reserved or protected forest reserve.[39]

The existence of the ANPATR is no reason for the FRA not to apply to the tribes. In particular, some of the rights granted under FRA would supplement those assured by the ANPATR—legally ensuring that the forest is owned by the community, and not subject to the discretion of political authorities.

Apart from the lack of specific application of existing laws, the lack of transparency also inhibits public scrutiny of relevant policies, especially due to a heavy reliance on government data. NCRB data for 2013 on cases involving Scheduled Tribes in the Andamans, for instance, characterises most cases as 'Miscellaneous' and further disaggregated data is not available.

3. Special Vulnerabilities

3.1 Increased contact

While, according to locals, the AAJVS field workers have had some success in 'managing Jarawas' and keeping them away from the ATR through persuasion and patrolling, interactions of the Jarawa with outsiders are still frequent, even commonplace. It is agreed by all sources that Jarawas often exchange highly valuable forest produce, like crabs and venison, for far less valuable objects, such as small quantities of rice packed in plastic bottles to enable storage. They have been observed to use these objects, procured both from exchanges as well as from their raids on villages, as gifts while visiting other Jarawa groups.

Raids and exchanges are frequent forms of interaction between Jarawas and border villages. Metal cooking vessels, one of the objects frequently given by contact missions, are often taken, and villagers who admit to having entered the reserve report that Jarawa hospitality now includes rice and meat cooked with salt and masalas.[40]

Objects like soap, mirrors and talcum powder are other frequent takes; they may aid the tribe's enduring interest in body ornamentation. Jarawa women working along the ATR were observed to be wearing kurtis and leggings, much in line with the fashions of Port Blair. The objects perhaps most useful for the Jarawas' way of life, however, are plastic containers: members of the tribe have long been using plastic bags and buckets to carry their possessions during their constant movements around the reserve. The traditional weaving of baskets and carving of honey-buckets have correspondingly been affected.[41]

Speaking Hindi and interacting with outsiders have become status symbols among the younger Jarawa, and young Jarawa males are so habituated to wearing clothes that they have now developed a fashion-sense and the ability to make a statement with the clothing they wear[42]. Alcohol, tobacco and marijuana have long been used by outsiders to ensure Jarawas' cooperation.[43] Some Jarawa are now often found actively in conflict with the law, ironically assisting in the poaching of the resources the administration tries to protect for their use[44]—while the rest suffer the consequences of decreasing forest resources.

While ANTRI and the A&N Administration pursue a research-driven policy with the objective of setting the terms for cultural exchange between the Jarawa and the outside world, such a high degree of existing interaction would render the objective irrelevant.

3.2 Conditions for the settlers

When refugees from Bengal arrived in the Andamans, they were allotted five-acre parcels of land, promised to them by the government if they left their homeland behind. Radhaji told the story of how her father received a parcel of land out at Wandoor, then thick jungle, and was told to go ahead and cultivate it.[45] Working hard to clear the area, constantly fearing attacks by the Jarawa of whom they had heard terrible stories, they began to grow crops there. Now her brothers find it difficult to survive on the produce of the same small piece of land (now divided between them), and she cannot therefore ask them to help support her own family. Married to a man who owns land near what is now Wandoor beach, the news about its development for tourism had made them believe that their struggles would soon be over. But as of now they live off a small tea stall that caters to tourists, waiting for the job promised to her son in compensation after their land was acquired by the government.

Unlike the Nicobars, where five perennial rivers ensure water for agriculture, the Andamans are not good cropland.[46] High salinity, poor access to water, and the rugged terrain are especially unsuitable for the crops that mainlanders—particularly those from Bengal, Tamil Nadu and Kerala—are accustomed to growing for subsistence, such as rice. In consequence, the islanders subsist on food items brought from the mainland, from vegetables to milk powder.

In terms of livelihoods, opportunities are few and far between, and a government job seems the best option to many. Fishing, which the government is trying to promote as a local industry, contributes little to development, especially in the absence of processing infrastructure. While some contend that the 'fish in Andaman die of old age',[47] political leaders contend that competition from the large boats of the international fishermen have left little for local fishermen to survive on. Opinions vary on whether the poachers in the Jarawa reserve are Burmese, Bangladeshi, or poachers from Port Blair and Mayabunder with virtual legal immunity.[48]

This insecurity lies at the heart of the strong protests among settlers against the five-kilometre-wide buffer zone proposed by the administration. The borders of the reserve were effectively drawn to exclude the people already officially settled there, and it is precisely those communities which are now seeing, in their view, an infringement of their right to a decent livelihood through business—especially that of tourism. 'The government put us here', many say, 'Why are they now saying we shouldn't be here?'[49]

3.3 Environmental concerns

The conflict over resources with settlers, particularly food resources like pig and deer meat, ambergris, water, and non-timber forest produce, is compounded by the scarcity experienced by those living outside the reserve. Wild pig, for instance, is a resource that is now rarely found outside the reserve.[50] After the early practice of taking timber from the reserve for the maintenance of the ATR, the forests within are now officially protected. Although no recent survey of the quality of the reserve could be found, the forests are yet better preserved than any other on the islands, and are the last remnants of the original tropical rainforest vegetation of the Andaman Islands, besides including various other ecosystems such as the semi-evergreen, the littoral forests, and others.[51]

According to the August 2003 report of the Indian Institute of Remote Sensing and the A&N Department of Environment and Forests, satellite maps and GIS have clearly shown the qualitative difference between the forests within the JRA and those outside. The latter have lost their original canopy, been converted to deciduous forests after logging operations, or have given way to cropland and settlements.[52]

The commercial value of this vast stretch of land in the centre of South Andaman Island, as well as that of the forest and natural resources within it, are all sources of vulnerability for the Jarawa. Conversely, the protection of the tribe and their right to pursue their traditional hunter-gatherer livelihood helps to ensure the protection of the territory over which the resources on which they depend are dispersed.

3.4 Role of state actors

The State buffer that is supposed to protect the Jarawa has itself often been a source of exploitation. Bush Police and even early recruits to the AAJVS were known themselves to engage in sexual exploitation, introduction of intoxicants and poaching of pork and venison. (Halder contends that this is still the case.) The Jarawa often responded violently in the past, particularly to sexual violence, but after they abjured violence the situation worsened significantly. The videos released in the *Guardian* exposé as recently as 2012 also recorded a policeman in complicity with tourists who were filming nude Jarawa women dancing.[53]

Currently it is maintained by the administration, settlers and local observers that the reduced Bush Police presence and their replacement with trained AAJVS staff has reduced the exploitation and violence that the Jarawa are exposed to. ANTRI has also conducted sensitisation workshops for AAJVS workers over the past year on gender, health, settler-Jarawa relations, and the politics and ethics of photography. AAJVS officials also point out that all new recruits receive sensitisation and training before entering the field. Since we could not visit the Jarawa area, we cannot verify whether the welfare staff are indeed respectful, non-intrusive, supportive and non-exploitative.

4. Outcomes

'Hunger may induce them to put themselves in the power of strangers; but the moment that want is satisfied, nothing short of coercion can prevent them from returning to a way of life, more congenial to their savage nature.' —Lt.Col. Albert Fytche, 1861[54]

The health and survival outcomes of the Jarawa people are still far better than most PVTG groups at the time of writing. In terms of health, measured by conventional indicators such as nutrition, disease prevalence, maternal and infant mortality, the Jarawas' situation is good by most accounts, although complete data is not available.[55]

The Andaman and Nicobar Tribal Research Institute has attempted, through its various projects to develop policies in consultation with the Jarawa, to address the concern that the Jarawa are being denied the fruits of modern society. Working through the AAJVS, they address Jarawas' stated interest in clothing, in education, and in pursuing nomadism—in the way that the Jarawas see most culturally relevant.

The problem that might emerge in this process is an institutional one: even in seeking 'consultation' with the Jarawas (as emphasised in ANTRI reports) they end up 'prioritising' some of their expressed desires over others (as one AAJVS staff member explained is frequently required of them). They negotiate based on needs they consider important and in the best interest of tribal people, what they can deliver, and what they can justify both to the A&N government as well as the academic establishment. Their reports then tend to reveal, unsurprisingly, a remarkably harmonious view of the situation and action taken.[56]

4.1. Health

The most positive outcome of increased interaction, arguably, is the Jarawas' acceptance of allopathic medicine for certain illnesses. This treatment is made available to them at outposts within the reserve by a 'field pharmacist', while more serious complaints may be addressed subsequently at the PHCs in Kadamtala and Tirur, at GB Pant hospital in Port Blair, or at hospitals on the mainland. Each PHC has a separate 'Jarawa Hut', and hospitals a 'Jarawa ward', which is legally part of the reserve territory and therefore bears the same restrictions on the entry of outsiders, protecting Jarawa patients from contact with unfamiliar diseases. This also enables their treatment and interactions to be monitored by AAJVS workers, and for both patients and their families to be provided the kind of food they are accustomed to. These provisions, combined with a strict disease surveillance regime implemented by the AAJVS, have ensured no further epidemic outbreaks since the outbreak of measles in 2005. The medical officer at Kadamtala PHC states that tuberculosis and conjunctivitis too have not been reported at all in the last three years, due to the efforts of the AAJVS in preventing interactions with outsiders.

At the same time, according to the AAJVS, Jarawas are encouraged to use their traditional medicines for diseases that they are familiar with, and minimise both intake of strong allopathic medicines and stay at medical centres.[57] Information on hygiene is also shared through *Ang Katha* sessions (discussed below).

The other side of the health story is encapsulated in the deaths of four Ang children in three months in late 2014.[58] Two deaths were believed to be due to the children having been given expired allopathic medicines and the others were due to a lack of proper post-natal care. Investigation revealed expired medicines in the possession of Ang people, indicating a lack of follow-up by the AAJVS staff to ensure completion of prescribed courses of medicines.[59] While the Director of the AAJVS, as well as a doctor who has worked in the Reserve for many years, commended practices around childbirth that Jarawas use, such as the squatting posture, an AAJVS worker mentioned a high maternal mortality rate and the need to train mothers for safer practices in childcare[60]. This suggests significant variations in the attitude to the Jarawas' traditional practices within the administration itself.

Recently there have also been concerns raised about instances of 'DNA mining' of the Ang, after publication of various papers, including one by the Centre for Cellular and Molecular Biology (CCMB) Hyderabad and Regional Medical Research Centre, Port Blair, studying the genetic variation of the Jarawa as a part of 'evolutionary studies'.[61] The Jarawa, along with the Onge, are believed to evidence a unique haplotype, showing that they were early participants in the migration to Asia and have been almost entirely isolated since. Their DNA, therefore, might hold the key to a better understanding of auto-immune diseases, genetic variation and other issues. What is more disturbing, however, is that the Director of CCMB has publicly spoken of the importance of his being allowed to take gene samples from the Jarawa 'so that we could do something to preserve the tribe', which the papers refer to as 'nearly extinct'. Such attitudes echo the views of British anthropologists such as Radcliffe-Brown, whose interest was to preserve the tribe in their publications as they retained no hope for their survival in person.[62]

The Jarawa Policy 2004, taking into account this special form of vulnerability of the tribe, states that, 'it shall be ensured strictly that the confidentiality of genetic resources on the Jarawas will be maintained and not used for commercial exploitation by any agency or organization which is not directly concerned with the welfare and protection of the Jarawas.' But it is also important that if such samples are required for any reason, they should be taken with the informed consent of the Jarawas, and not of the administration.

4.2 Education

Recognising that mainstream education can at best train those brought up outside its language and culture to be its marginal labour force, Jarawas and the administration have agreed that it will not be implemented in the Jarawa reserve. At the same time, the difficulty of mutually translating Jarawa and *ennen* (outsider) experiences in the absence of a common language has historically led to misunderstanding, 'hostility', and exploitation. Instead, in accordance with a survey of a cross-section of the community, the AAJVS now provides a location for the experiment they call 'Ang Katha', which they describe as 'bilingual, bicultural education'.

Held at 'hotspots' within the Jarawa reserve (chosen based on convenience of access for the constantly moving Jarawa), the gatherings of adult and young Jarawas involve elders teaching the younger generation about the tribe's myths, rituals, environment and medicines. The curriculum and lesson plans are synthesised with the seasonal calendar of activities, including hunting and foraging, performance and aesthetics. AAJVS staff also teach the tribe Hindi and numerical literacy, as well as provide basic information about hygiene. The Jarawa are also advised on how to assist the administration in protecting the reserve—especially by reporting incursions. Interestingly, a project of genealogical mapping carried out by AAJVS staff allows them to help Jarawas trace their ancestry and relationships, assisting collective memory.

The purpose of the project, according to Pandya et al., authors of the report *Ang Katha*, is to help Angs develop and better communicate a sense of their collective identity, indigenous knowledge systems and aspirations. To further these ends, the sessions use or at least include Hindi in order not to alienate the younger generation who speak the language. Political literacy is also recommended for the curriculum, to enable the Angs to assert their rights. Jarawas have also reportedly asked to be trained to use *dinghies* (motorised boats), but that is likely a more long-term prospect.

The latter reflects one important problem with ANTRI's initiatives. Jarawas express desire for all sorts of 'outsider things', which the AAJVS ignores in the effort to prioritise health and education. If the urgency of these demands were to surface, or the AAJVS' screening of them were to cease, a very different, far less 'isolated' picture of the Jarawas might emerge. It is important to note that the desire for mainstream technology or commodities, does not necessarily connote 'mainstreaming' as long as its full implications are understood and willingly accepted by them. The explanations for these—that dinghies require fuel, maintenance and money—remain the task of the welfare agency to deliver, along with a system enabling fair interaction and exchange.

4.3 Clothing

Under the Kangapo project ('Kangapo' meaning clothes in Ang), ANTRI determined (through open-ended discussions with a representative cross-section, it emphasises) that Jarawa women wanted clothes to wear while travelling on the ATR. The women got the idea from the free maxis distributed to them when visiting the PHCs, but found those to be constraining free movement in the forest. After considering various possibilities, the Jarawa women and AAJVS staff decided on a kurta-pajama arrangement, of which one set is provided to women in exchange for a basket woven by them. Men were not prioritised in Kangapo as they have more access to clothes (as to the outside world generally), and because Jarawa women are more prone to exoticisation and exploitation by virtue of lack of access to clothes. This argument of the report is contentious because, as in the case of the ATR, outsiders create exploitative conditions that force the Jarawas to adapt to the negative consequences. In this case, apart from sexual exploitation itself (the connection of which to clothes is problematic even in mainstream society), gender differences and a construction of the female as more vulnerable are promoted by this interpretation, which may not be part of Jarawa social norms. Jarawa women themselves have also begun to manifest 'shame', according to the report, although they maintain that their markings, waistbands and headbands have symbolic meaning and definitely do not equate these with nakedness, or with shame.

The exchange framework under Kangapo is meant to create a sustainable arrangement that emphasises the concepts of private property and exchange rather than creating (further) dependencies. The baskets are to be marketed by the government as 'genuine Jarawa handicrafts' to fund the creation of more clothes. The state thus remains a buffer between Jarawa traditional activities and the market economy, and there is currently no plan to remove that buffer. In creating this plan, however, ANTRI is either denying or ignoring the existence of such transactions in status quo, and their inevitability in the future. According to the AAJVS, the purpose of providing literacy and numerical literacy to the Jarawas seemed precisely to be to enable more empowered participation in such economic exchange.[63]

4.4 Access to food and water

It is important to recognise that for the Jarawa, these basic goods are sufficiently provided by the reserve ecosystem itself—if the forest is required to provide only for the tribe. The traditional system of food use, in the absence of storage methods, allows the various species to regenerate while providing sufficient nutrition to the Jarawa in each season. Particularly valued foods such as wild pig and honey are however used by settlers as well, and this creates competition and scarcity. Fishermen straying into the reserve also collect crabs, shells and sea cucumbers, the latter attracting poachers from as far away as Myanmar due to its high value in South East Asian markets. Venison is another important resource hunted by poachers, and now by some accounts by Jarawa themselves, who do not consume it but hunt it for exchange.

The question of whether the reserve can currently, and will continue to be able to, sustain the Jarawas in terms of food resources is a fundamental question—one, according to the TW Director, that is under consideration by the administration at present. This is particularly pertinent considering the growing Jarawa population (240 in Census 2001 and 380 in 2011).

Mohan Halder, Pradhan of Tushnabad panchayat in South Andaman, is the best known dissident to sufficiency: he says that need is driving the (Tirur) Jarawas out of the reserve and that hunger and malnutrition are rife. According to Halder, this forms the basis for both conflict and collaboration with outsiders, and is a violation of Jarawas' human rights as well. AAJVS maintains that the reserve is currently sufficient—and that the Jarawas' health and nutrition status is, as always, good. They do, however, express uncertainty about the future, between the competing pressures of poaching and population growth. One plan is to augment food resources through plantation within the reserve of plants Angs use—and to involve them in the cultivation process. However, negative consequences could well result from interfering with the ecological balance, as well as from allowing the forest department such leeway in the reserve. After all, in the recent past, the forest department chose to plant coconuts and bananas in the reserve in their attempt to encourage Jarawas to cultivate—ignoring the well-established ways of both tribe and forest.

The complementary question is whether the Jarawa are acquiring a taste for outsider foods and practices, to the eventual exclusion of their own. There is sufficient evidence of their use of outsider food and intoxicants, as well as cooking practices. ANTRI's response is that outsider food like rice is merely a stopgap measure for Jarawas: it can be easily stored uncooked, but once cooked cannot be stored, is heavy in the stomach, and makes one 'hungry again and again.'[64] Their study finds pork and honey as still the most valued foods, both in taste as well as in ritual significance as items of tribe commensality. However, at least in the case of the Tirur Jarawa a more pessimistic evaluation seems reasonable. If not preference for outside food, addiction—including to Corex cough syrup—is making Jarawas enter into exploitative arrangements with outsiders.[65]

The recommendations of an ANTRI report voice the uncertainty that then develops: should the administration declare the ongoing economic exchanges illegal due to their exploitative nature? Or should they be made transparent and regulated?[66] In either case, the logistical difficulties of oversight might throw a further spanner in the works. Records of past cases of poaching show very low rates of conviction, due in large part to lack of cooperation by Jarawa witnesses.[67] While the police express frustration at Jarawa 'stupidity',[68] a study by ANTRI concludes that the refusal to recognise the accused as poachers is the outcome of a consensus among the tribe in favour of collaboration[69]—losing sight of the fact that the responsibility of policing the reserve belongs to the administration.

4.5 Intersectionality

As mentioned above, incidents of sexual exploitation of Jarawa women are reported from time to time in the news, suggesting that the practice is ongoing. Editor of the Andaman Chronicle, Denis Giles, says that even 10 years ago when he entered the reserve as an investigative reporter, there were *chaddas* at the border of the reserve where only young, vulnerable women stayed—all orphans, perhaps 14–17 years old— and the huts held evidence of alcohol and tobacco having been frequently used there, suggesting that outsiders frequented the place. One girl was also pregnant—he had reason to suspect the child was part *ennen* or outsider.[70] Giles was forced to conclude that orphan girls and half-blood children were not taken care of by the community, at best; at worst, the community might be abetting their exploitation.

A group that is particularly vulnerable is that of children of Jarawa women with outsiders. According to one account, elders of the tribe when asked how they deal with this situation, replied that the women are welcome to come back and settle down with Jarawa men.[71] The children, however, were not extended this invitation. According to Moidu's paper, the Jarawa do not accept children out of wedlock, especially children of *ennen*—and do not expect the children to survive that rejection. This starkly contrasts with the observation of many anthropologists that the Jarawa are among the most tender carers of young children, whom they adore.

4.6 Special Category in Discourse

Particularly Vulnerable Tribal Groups, of which classification the Jarawa are officially a part, are defined as groups with 'pre-agricultural level of technology, stagnant or declining population, particularly low levels of literacy, subsistence-based economy and forest-dependent livelihoods'.[72]

The Jarawa population has finally shown a rise in the 2011 Census (380 individuals, compared to approximately 240 in 2001), demonstrating that low literacy (unrelated to linguistic ability or practice), subsistence-based economy, pre-agricultural technology and forest-based livelihoods may coexist with health and well-being. Unlike the situation of the Great Andamanese or the Onge, described previously, the case of the Jarawa in PVTG policy is unusual—in which their right to their alternative lifestyle is not only acknowledged but actively protected in principle by policy and administration—suggesting that a different view can be taken of PVTG policy as a whole. At the same time, although the Ang are placed in a situation of high level of exposure to mainstream society, this is not a barrier to their continuing (and desiring to continue) their 'forest-dependent livelihoods', suggesting an alternative possibility for those PVTGs being forcibly 'integrated' on the mainland. At the very least, it contains a clear message about the crucial importance of protecting indigenous communities' rights to land and to pursue their traditional livelihoods.

The case of the Jarawa also contains learnings for the way the administration should choose to deal with communities at the other end of the spectrum, who have been totally isolated from the mainstream—such as the Sentinelese. The A&N administration now clearly states that it will not make any attempts at 'friendly contact' with the tribe. One official described this as the 'Hands off, Eyes on' approach: that aerial and naval surveillance of the island would continue, as the administration could not 'abandon' the tribe, but there was to be no attempt at interaction or interference.

Recommendations

There are very few examples of isolated indigenous communities with rich self-contained cultures, living through non-agricultural hunting and gathering livelihood patterns, being integrated with outside economies and cultures in ways that are genuinely voluntary, humane, just, non-exploitative and egalitarian. On the contrary, most such contacts have typically been of 'adverse inclusion'. In most parts of the world these have resulted in intense dispossession, sexual and economic exploitation, alarming health and nutrition declines as well as profoundly endangered and precarious survival. There is also pervasive anomie, the collapse of cultural self-confidence, self-reliance and pride, and the extinguishing of both their cultures as well as their collective hope for the future.

India's first Prime Minister Nehru demonstrated, in our opinion, a rare sensitivity to the formidable challenges of crafting just and egalitarian public policy and legal regimes for indigenous communities, enabling the community to access development while protecting their rights to pursue development on their own terms. Through the Jarawa policy of 2004, a renewed commitment to this vision forms the basis of independent India's official approach to the indigenous communities of the Andaman Islands. This contrasts with the colonial policy of violent suppression and cultural submergence of what they saw to be 'savage' ways of life.

However, the actual practice has been fraught and flawed in many ways. The Great Andamanese were reduced by their colonial encounter to somewhat abject subordination, and the Onge to excessive dependence on the Indian administration for everyday survival. The violent suppression of their histories combined with epidemics, exploitation, and exposure to intoxicants to drastically reduce the numbers of both these peoples. Even today their populations remain stubbornly stagnant despite the numerous health and educational inputs of the A&N administration—perhaps because of the persisting association of stigma with their cultural identities.

The Ang avoided several of these consequences until recently, because of their long hostility to outsiders and to their penetration into the Ang traditional forest habitats. The administration however forcefully reversed their isolation by the construction of the Andaman Trunk Road. Mukerjee speaks of the patterns of roads, innocuous to start with, all over the world: '(T)hey take people into the forest, who chop the trees and settle in. Many of the outsiders living in the Jarawa reserve were first brought by the public works department to help build the road; after it was finished, they just didn't move'.[73] The road brought in the government officials, the settlers, the traders, the poachers, and the tourists, who forced on the Ang people exploitative relationships and unequal dependence. Despite clear directives of the Supreme Court to close this highway as far back as 2002, it remains open, with the administration pitting the interests of settlers against those of the indigenous community to defend their position.

The government policy of 'gifts', beginning in colonial times, also created dependencies that ultimately threatened the dignified and self-reliant survival of these relatively isolated peoples. Colonial administrators actively encouraged first the Great Andamanese and then the Onge to depend on nicotine to build submission. This was not the approach of the Indian administration, although contact inevitably brought alcohol, drugs and tobacco into tribal reserves. The Indian government did, however, pursue the policy of 'contact visits' that disbursed food items like rice, bananas and coconuts, dependence on which would transform the diets and render unsustainable the livelihoods of the Jarawa people.

The impact of both these official measures are to some extent irreversible. But there are also positive aspects to the Indian state's approach to the Jarawa. The administration has reserved more than 1600 square km for Jarawa and other PVTG reserves, constituting as much as 25 percent of the total area of the islands.[74] These communities, if left to themselves, are best equipped to conserve these rich biodiversity treasures.

Despite the availability of rice, bananas and coconuts, the Jarawa people still demonstrate an adherence to their hunting and gathering way of life. They show a general appreciation of the state's health services, including allopathic medicine— the health support to the Jarawa people (when requested by them) has helped save lives, and the Jarawa are the only PVTGs in the Islands to have shown an increase in numbers during the last census. The administration is also attempting to engage with the Ang on their own terms and in accordance with their expressed will, as evidenced in the Ang Katha and Kangapo initiatives.

However, the response to the efforts for education are more complex and ambivalent. The presence of welfare personnel working and living in close proximity to the Jarawa always carries the danger that they may not be adequately trained, guided and supervised, and may therefore act in ways that might be overbearing, patronising and even exploitative.

We believe the future of the Jarawa people remains strongly tied to the early closure of the highway, along with far more effective policing of the reserve to prevent penetration of outsiders, poachers and tourists. The legitimate interests of settlers can be met through the strengthening and popularising of sea transport services, originally planned to have been completed by March 2015, and perhaps also by constructing an alternative highway along the Eastern sea coast. Ferries from Port Blair to Baratang, Rangat, Mayabunder, Diglipur, etc. would take on the burden of passenger, freight and tourist traffic, minimising the use of the ATR to just emergencies, or for settlements unreachable in other ways, simultaneously disincentivising further encroachments into the reserve.

Policing of the reserve must improve on a priority basis. In order to more effectively prevent sexual exploitation, entry into the reserve, sale of poached materials, and purveying intoxicants, it is imperative that those found poaching there be punished promptly and with the full force of the law. Simultaneously, the administration must economically assist and support the settlers so that they do not need to resort to poaching. Settlements within the reserve boundaries will need to be negotiated with more actively—otherwise they only grow, and use the reserve for what their fields cannot provide.

Additionally, a complete mapping (preferably using satellite technology) of settlements, both legitimate and encroachments, would give a more realistic picture of the condition and prospects of the reserve, and additionally help evaluate claims of timber poaching within it. Besides, the borders of the reserve need to be made visible on the ground, to concretise what so far is still an 'imaginary line on a government map'.

Along with the immediate closure of the ATR and more effective protection of the Jarawa reserve, with no further reductions in their territory, our most important recommendation is that all those who interact with the Ang need to treat the tribe as equals, possessing the agency and wisdom to decide their best interests. The Jarawa must be effectively in charge of their own futures and as such only changes or projects that are initiated by the tribe themselves should be implemented. It is vital that no 'development' or 'welfare' programmes are devised by outsiders and then handed down to the Jarawa to 'participate' in. The Jarawa must choose and control any projects that concern them, at all stages of the process.

The inalienable community rights of the PVTG

to the forests that they have inhabited for millennia must be legally notified through the application of the Forest Rights Act in the Islands. The position held by the administration, that the A&N Islands (Protection of Aboriginal Tribes) Regulation, 1956, protects their rights adequately is not legally tenable. The state has exercised unilateral rights to alter and reduce the Jarawa reserve. The further affirmation of their legal community rights to forests they inhabit would also give them greater legal protection in future from incursions like the ATR.

The Great Andamanese, and to a lesser extent the Onge, demonstrate the consequences of adverse inclusion. The experience of 'friendly contact' of the Jarawa is much shorter: a little over two decades at the time of writing. The story is mixed so far. While there are unmistakable signs of adverse inclusion setting in quite early in this contact with the outside world, the Ang are still exercising agency and choice, and the administration must enable them to do so, not only in letter but also in spirit. As far as the Sentinelese are concerned, we take the opportunity to recommend continuing to respect their decision to refuse contact by not attempting to make any contact with them, and only properly policing the waters around their island. There are some unconfirmed suggestions that the administration is contemplating a slightly more proactive approach —one that helps the Sentinelese distinguish between 'friendly' administration and 'harmful' outsiders like poachers. This would be a disastrous strategy as it would encourage contact, which even with the administration could be extremely dangerous for the Sentinelese. The experience with the Jarawa demonstrates that even 'friendly' interactions with the outsider can quickly propel grave adverse consequences.

Fig.3: Vehicles queued at Jirkatang checkpost to enter the Jarawa reserve (Copyright G. Chamberlain/Survival International)

Endnotes

1. Dev Nathan and Virginius Xaxa (2012), 'Introduction and Overview' in Dev Nathan and Virginius Xaxa (eds), *Social Exclusion and Adverse Inclusion: Development and Deprivation of Adivasis in India*. New York: Oxford University Press, pp 1–19.
2. Both the Andamanese as well as the Onge have been recipients of the Administration's efforts at 'mainstreaming' since the 1800s—through both violence and welfare. The measures, aimed at giving them access to mainstream education, healthcare, housing, livelihoods and nutritional support, have not however led to any improvement in their populations or well-being, as recorded by the 2011 Census. Those (mostly Andamanese) who succeed in leaving their settlements and traversing the education system find themselves in marginal government jobs, increasingly marry outsiders and have forgotten much of their language and traditions (See: Madhusree Mukerjee (2003), *The Land of Naked People: Encounters with Stone Age Islanders*. New York: Houghton Mifflin.)
3. This essay also reluctantly makes use of the term 'tribe' because of its broad recognition, while acknowledging the urgent and complex debates that must underlie the usage. (See, for example, Virginius Xaxa (2008), *State, Society and Tribes: Issues in Post-Colonial India*, Delhi: Dorling Kindersley.)
4. D. Venkatesan (1990), 'Ecocide or Genocide: Onge in the Andaman Islands. *Cultural Survival Quarterly*, Vol 14.4 (Winter 1990): Land and Resources. [http://www.culturalsurvival.org/ourpublications/csq/article/ecocide-or-genocide-the-onge-andaman-islands. Accessed 14 August 2015]
5. Census of India (2011), 'Enumeration of Primitive Tribes in A&N Islands: A Challenge.' [http://censusindia.gov.in/Ad_Campaign/drop_in_articles/06-Enumeration_of_Primitive_Tribes_in_A&N_Islands.pdf Accessed 11 September 2015]
6. Pankaj Sekhsaria (2014), 'Jarawas at the Jetty' in *The Last Wave*, Noida: Harper Collins.
7. Interview with Samir Acharya (29.06.15)
8. Interviews with Samir Acharya (01.07.15) and AAJVS official (04.07.15).
9. Pankaj Sekhsaria (2001), 'Delivering the Jarawas'. *Frontline* 18(17). [http://www.frontline.in/static/html/fl1817/18170650.htm] Accessed 10 September 2015.
10. Mukerjee ,*The Land of Naked People: Encounters with Stone Age Islanders*, pp 205–10
11. Sophie Grig (2014), Working Paper. Presented at '*Thinking Futures: The PVTGs of Andaman and Nicobar Islands*' conference, 4–5 December 2014.

    Manish Chandi (2010), 'Colonisation and conflict resolution in the Andaman islands'. In Pankaj Sekhsaria and Vishvajit Pandya (eds) *The Jarawa Tribal Reserve Dossier.* Paris: UNESCO, p. 15.
12. Zubair Ahmed (16 January 2012) 'Jarawa Dance Video: Army Personnel Involved'. *The Light of Andamans.* [http://lightofandamans.blogspot.in/2012/01/cover-story-jarawa-dance-video-army.html Accessed 5 August 2015]

    The Light of Andamans (08 February 2012), 'Jarawa Video Safari Continues'. [http://lightofandamans.blogspot.in/2012/02/editorial-jarawa-video-safari-continues.html Accessed 5 August 2015]
13. Alia Allana (2015), 'Loot in the Andamans'. *Fountain Ink*. March 2015. [*http://fountainink.in/?p=6772* Accessed 15 August 2015]
14. Survival International (2015), 'India misses deadline to end Andaman 'Human safaris'. [http://www.survivalinternational.org/news/10735 Accessed 15 August 2015]
15. Gethin Chamberlain (07 December 2012), 'Andaman Islanders 'forced to dance' for tourists'. *The Guardian.* [http://www.theguardian.com/world/video/2012/jan/07/andaman-islanders *The Land of Naked People: Encounters with Stone Age Islanders* -human-safari-video Accessed 14 August 2015]
16. Zubair Ahmed (16 January 2012), 'Jarawa Dance Video: Army Personnel Involved'. *The Light of Andamans.* [http://lightofandamans.blogspot.in/2012/01/cover-story-jarawa-dance-video-army.html Accessed 8 May 2015]
17. *The Light of Andamans* (16 January 2012), 'Why MoRD Team Visited Jarawa Tribe at Tirur?' [http://lightofandamans.blogspot.in/2012/01/why-mord-team-visited-jarawa-tribes-at.html Accessed 8 May 2015]
18. *Andaman Chronicle* (1 February 2014), 'Poachers Sexually Exploit Jarawa Girls under Influence of Alcohol and Ganja' [http://www.andamanchronicle.net/index.php?option=com_content&view=article&id=4298:exclusive-jarawa-man-speaks-out&catid=49:highlight&Itemid=200 Accessed 15 August 2015]
19. Andaman and Nicobar Administration Order no. 405. (28 November 2014) p.1.
20. Virginius Xaxa (2008), '*State, Society and Tribes: Issues in Post-Colonial India.*' Delhi: Dorling Kindersley, pp 6.
21. Ibid.
22. Pankaj Sekhsaria (2001), 'Deforestation in the Andamans: Effects on the Onge'. *Economic and Political Weekly* Vol. 36, No. 38 (Sep. 22–28, 2001), pp. 3643–48

Madhusree Mukerjee (2014) 'Why the Andaman Islands are Headed for Disaster' [https://in.news.yahoo.com/why-the-andaman-islands-are-headed-for-disaster-045113050.html]

23. A. R. Radcliffe-Brown (1964), *The Andaman Islanders.* Cambridge: Cambridge University Press, pp. 22–26

24. Nathan and Xaxa (eds.), *Social Exclusion and Adverse Inclusion: Development and Deprivation of Adivasis in India.*

25. K. Mukhopadhyay (2010), 'The ATR is like a public thoroughfare through one's private courtyard', in Pankaj Sekhsaria and Vishvajit Pandya (eds), *The Jarawa Tribal Reserve Dossier: Cultural and Biological Diversities in the Andaman Islands.* Paris: UNESCO.

26. A question may be raised about the legibility of concepts between cultures. Pandya argues that, in the question of ownership at least, illegibility is the excuse used to ignore the tribe's rights—which they categorically defend. To quote him, 'Some settlers seem completely oblivious of the fact that what belongs to the Jarawa is not just the forest territory but also the right to own certain material possessions.... on 16 April 2005, settlers destroyed honey stored by Jarawa at Philip Nallah within their reserve territory. In retaliation Jarawa entered Forest valley and "looted gold ornaments, cash, watches, clothes, and utensils from 17 houses"... The police recovered some material from the Jarawa,... but no action is on record for loss caused to the Jarawa by the settlers.' Vishvajit Pandya (2010) 'From Dangerous to Endangered: Jarawa "primitives" and welfare politics in the Andaman Islands.' [http://meenamahi.blogspot.in/2010/12/from-dangerous-to-endangered_14.html Accessed 15 August 2015]

27. Zubair Ahmed (21 July 2012) 'Why Jarawas don't have a say?', *AniNews.in* [http://www.andamansheekha.com/2012/07/21/why-jarawas-dont-have-a-say/ Accessed 15 August 2015]

28. Sekhsaria (2001), 'Deforestation in the Andamans: Effects on the Onge.' pp. 3643–48.

29. Richa Dhanchu (2003), 'Traffic on the Andaman Trunk Road.' In Annexures, *The Jarawa Tribal Reserve Dossier.* Paris: UNESCO.

30. Correspondence with Dr Vishvajit Pandya (7 July 2015) and interview with Mr Samir Acharya (30 June 2015)

31. Article 3, *United Nations Declaration on Rights of Indigenous Peoples* (2008), New York: United Nations.

32. Amendment to A&N Protection of Aboriginal Tribes Regulation (9 July 2012) [http://tribal.nic.in/WriteReadData/userfiles/file/AN4(9_7_2012).pdf] Accessed 10 September 2015.

33. Zubair Ahmed (21 October 2014), 'Jarawa Tribal Reserve: A Potemkin Village', *The Light of Andamans.* [http://lightofandamans.blogspot.in/2014/10/jarawa-tribal-reserve-potemkin-village.html]

34. *Policy on Jarawa tribe of Andaman Islands.* December 2004. Andaman and Nicobar Administration. p.3.

35. Sanjay Upadhyay (4 April 2012), 'The Buffer Zone around Jarawa Reserve and Andaman Trunk Road: To be or not to be.' *Report of the Supreme Court-appointed Commissioner in Lt. Gov. versus Barefoot India ((SLP (C) 12125 of 2010).*

36. Ibid.

37. Interview with Superintendent of Police, South Andaman district, on 8 July 2015.

38. Ahmed. 'Jarawa Tribal Reserve: A Potemkin Village.'

39. Ministry of Tribal Affairs, Government of India (August 2015), 'Status Report on Implementation of the Scheduled Tribes and other Traditional forest dwellers (Recognition of Forest Rights) Act, 2006 [for the period ending 31 August 2015]' [http://tribal.nic.in/WriteReadData/CMS/Documents/201510281110537367495MPRAugust2015.pdf Accessed 29 October 2015]

40. Interview with Mohan Halder, Pradhan, Tushnabad Gram Panchayat (5 July 2015).

41. Vishvajit Pandya et al. (2013), *Jarawa Movements in Relation to Time and Space.* Port Blair: Andaman and Nicobar Tribal Research Institute

42. Vishvajit Pandya et al. (2014) *Ang Katha.* Port Blair: Andaman and Nicobar Tribal Research Institute.

Vishvajit Pandya (2013), *Kangapo.* Port Blair: Andaman and Nicobar Tribal Research Institute.

43. Alia Allana (31 March 2015).

44. Shabana Moidu (2014) 'Notion of Jurisprudence: In the context of Jarawa tribe and Non Tribes of Andaman Islands.' Presented at *Thinking Futures.* Andaman and Nicobar Tribal Research Institute, December 2014.

45. Interview with Radhaji Wandoor, 5 July 2015.

46. Alia Allana (2 April 2015), 'Stringing the Pearls.' *Fountain Ink.* [http://fountainink.in/?p=6798&all=1 Accessed 24 August 2015]

47. Ibid.

48. Ibid. and Interview with Mohan Halder, 5 July 2015.

49. Interviews with Radhaji (5 July 2015) and Mohan Halder, Tushnabad (5 July 2015).

50. Manish Chandi. 'Colonisation and conflict resolution in the Andaman islands' . p. 35.

51. Manish Chandi and Harry Andrews (2010), 'The Jarawa Tribal Reserve: the "Last" Andaman Forest.' In Pankaj Sekhsaria and Vishvajit Pandya (eds), *The Jarawa Tribal Reserve Dossier.* Paris: UNESCO, pp. 42–53.

52. Ibid., Box-II, p. 46.
53. 'Andaman islanders 'forced to dance' for tourists.' *The Guardian* (7 January 2012). [http://www.theguardian.com/world/video/2012/jan/07/andaman-islanders-human-safari-video Accessed 10 September 2015]
54. Lt. Col. Albert Fytche (1861), 'A Note on Certain Aborigines of the Andaman Islands'. *Journal of Asiatic Society,* Vol 30, pp. 263–7.
55. B.N. Sarkar and R. Sahani (2002). 'A Demographic and Health Profile of the Jarawas of Andaman Islands.' In *Jarawa Contact: Ours with Them, Theirs with Us.* Kolkata: Anthropological Survey of India.
56. See, for instance, 'Conclusion' from Vishvajit Pandya et al. (2013) *Jarawa Movements in Relation to Time and Space.* Port Blair: Andaman and Nicobar Tribal Research Institute.
57. Interview with Arun Gupta, Director, Tribal Welfare. (5 July 2015).
58. 'Investigation Still on?' *The Light of Andamans* (22 October 2014). [http://lightofandamans.blogspot.in/2014/10/jarawa-tragedy-four-deaths-reported-in.html Accessed 12 September 2015]
59. Ibid.
60. Interview with Arun Gupta (5 July 2015); Interview with AAJVS official (4 July 2015)
61. Sunita Singh et al. (2004), 'Single nucleotide polymorphisms in two genes among the Jarawa, a primitive tribe of the Andaman and Nicobar Islands'. *Current Science.* Vol.86, No.2.

    K. Thangaraj et al. (2003), 'Genetic affinities of the Andaman Islanders, a vanishing human population'. *Current Biology.* Vol.13, pp. 86–93.
62. A. R. Radcliffe-Brown (1964), pp.19
63. Vishvajit Pandya et al. (2014) *Ang Katha.* Port Blair: Andaman and Nicobar Tribal Research Institute.
64. Vishvajit Pandya et al. (2013), *Jarawa Movements in Relation to Time and Space.* Port Blair: Andaman and Nicobar Tribal Research Institute.
65. Alia Allana (31 March 2015)
66. Vishvajit Pandya et al. (2013), pp.78
67. Moidu. 'Notion of Jurisprudence: In the context of Jarawa tribe and Non Tribes of Andaman Islands.'
68. Interview with police representative, South Andaman district (8 July 2015)
69. Shabana Moidu. 'Notion of Jurisprudence: In the context of Jarawa tribe and Non Tribes of Andaman Islands.'
70. Interview with Denis Giles (6 July 2015).
71. Shabana Moidu. 'Notion of Jurisprudence: In the context of Jarawa tribe and Non Tribes of Andaman Islands.'
72. Government of India. (2014) '*Report of the High Level Committee on Socio-economic, Health and Educational Status of Tribal Communities of India*' (May 2014). Ministry of Tribal Affairs, Government of India, pp. 59.
73. Madhusree Mukerjee. *The Land of Naked People: Encounters with Stone Age Islanders*, pp.139.
74. Manish Chandi and Harry Andrews in P. Sekhsaria and V. Pandya, pp. 46-47 [box].

About the Authors and Contributors

1. Aditi Rao is currently a Research Consultant at PHFI, working on projects of Urban Healthcare, Knowledge Translation Initiatives and Post-2015 Sustainable Development Goals. Email: aditi.rao93@hotmail.com

2. Agrima Bhasin is an independent researcher based in Delhi and was formerly a Researcher at the Centre for Equity Studies.

3. Anamika Lahiri is a Researcher at the Centre for Equity Studies, New Delhi. Email: anamika.lahiri27@gmail.com

4. Anushree Deb is a Research Associate at the Indian Institute for Human Settlements (IIHS), Bangalore.

5. Chaitanya Mallapur is a policy analyst and research writer working with IndiaSpend, a data journalism initiative based in Mumbai. Email: chaitanya@indiaspend.org

6. Coen Kompier is a Specialist on International Labour Standards with the International Labour Organization. Email: kompier@ilo.org

7. Devaki Nambiar is a Research Scientist at the Public Health Foundation of India (PHFI), New Delhi, working on health equity and the Social Determinants of Health. Email: devaki.nambiar@gmail.com

8. Geetika Anand, is a Senior Associate at the Indian Institute for Human Settlements (IIHS), Bangalore. Email: ganand@iihs.co.in

9. Harsh Mander is the founder and Director of the Centre for Equity Studies, New Delhi. Email: manderharsh@gmail.com

10. Kanchan Gandhi is a visiting faculty member at the School of Planning and Architecture, New Delhi. Email: kanchanisthere@yahoo.com

11. Kavita Wankhade is a Project Manager and Consultant at the Indian Institute for Human Settlements (IIHS), Bangalore. Email: kwankhade@iihs.co.in

12. Kinjal Sampat is a Researcher at the Centre for Equity Studies, New Delhi. Email: kinjalsampat@gmail.com

13. Prachi Salve is a policy analyst and writer working with IndiaSpend, a data journalism initiative based in Mumbai. Email: prachi@indiaspend.org

14. Prathibha Ganesan is an independent researcher and was formerly a Research Associate at the Public Health Foundation of India (PHFI), New Delhi, working on health equity and the Social Determinants of Health. Email: prathibha.ganesan@gmail.com

15. Radhika Jha is a Researcher at the Centre for Equity Studies, New Delhi. Email: radhika.n.jha@gmail.com

16. Rajanya Bose is a Researcher at the Centre for Equity Studies, New Delhi. Email: 89.rajanya@gmail.com

17. Rajeev Malhotra is a development economist and Professor at the School of Government and Public Policy at the O.P. Jindal Global University, Sonepat (Delhi NCR).
E-mail: rmalh1@hotmail.com

18. Rajiv K. Raman is an independent consultant based in Bangalore and is a Senior Advisor on water and sanitation, at the Indian Institute for Human Settlements (IIHS), Bangalore.

19. Rhea John is a Researcher at the Centre for Equity Studies, New Delhi.
Email: rheasjohn@gmail.com

20. Saba Sharma is a Doctoral student at Cambridge University, UK.
Email: sabasharma4@gmail.com

21. Sajjad Hassan is the Founder of MISAAL and a research fellow at the Centre for Equity Studies, New Delhi. Email: iamsajjadhassan@gmail.com

22. Sanjay (Xonzoi) Barbora is an Associate Professor at the Tata Institute of Social Science (TISS), Guwahati.
Email: xonzoi.barbora@gmail.com

23. Saumya Tewari is a policy analyst and writer with IndiaSpend, Mumbai.
Email: saumya@indiaspend.org

24. Sejal Dand is a founding member of Area Networking and Development Initiatives (ANANDI), Gujarat

25. Shikha Sethia is a Masters student at the International Institute of Social Studies, the Hague. Email: s.sethia@gmail.com

26. Sita Mamidipudi is a Researcher at Area Networking and Development Initiatives (ANANDI), Gujarat.

27. Smita Premchander is the founder and secretary of Sampark, Bangalore.
Email: smitapremchander@gmail.com

28. Sridhar Kundu is an economist working at the Centre for Budget and Governance Accountability (CBGA), New Delhi.
Email: sridhar@cbgaindia.org

29. V. Prameela is a Programme Director at Sampark, Bangalore.
Email: prameela@sampark.org

30. Vishnu MJ is an Associate in the Practice Division at the Indian Institute for Human Settlements (IIHS), Bangalore

PHOTO COURTESY

p. i: Amin Reza Khan

p. x: Sonal Matharu

p. 26: Still from the documentary created by volunteers for HAUSLA—The National Resource Team for the Urban Homeless

p. 28: Atish Patel

p. 162: Amin Reza Khan

p. 164: Anjuman Ara Begum